Pioneers of Industrial Organization

Pioneers of Industrial Organization

How the Economics of Competition and Monopoly Took Shape

Edited by

Henry W. de Jong

Emeritus Professor of Economics, University of Amsterdam, The Netherlands

William G. Shepherd

Professor of Economics Emeritus, University of Massachusetts, Amherst, USA

Edward Elgar

Cheltenham, UK • Northampton, MA, USA

Published by
Edward Elgar Publishing Limited
Glensanda House
Montpellier Parade
Cheltenham
Glos GL50 1UA
UK

Edward Elgar Publishing, Inc.
William Pratt House
9 Dewey Court
Northampton
Massachusetts 01060
USA

A catalogue record for this book
is available from the British Library

Library of Congress Cataloging-in-Publication-Data
Pioneers of industrial organization : how the economics of competition and monopoly took shape / edited by Henry de Jong and William G. Shepherd.
p. cm.
Includes bibliographical references and index.
1. Industrial organization (Economic theory) 2. Economists—Biography.
I. Jong, H. W. de. II. Shepherd, William G.
HD2326.P5 2007
338.6'048—dc22

2006021904

ISBN 978 1 84376 434 2

Printed and bound in Great Britain by MPG Books Ltd, Bodmin, Cornwall

Contents

Contributors

EUROPEAN

Patrizio Bianchi Professor of Economics, University of Ferrara, Italy. He previously taught and studied at the University of Bologna where from the early 1970s Romano Prodi developed the field of industrial economics. Bianchi has long been the Director and Chief Editor of *l'Industria – Rivista di Economia e Politica Industriale*, a Review that has united Italian researchers in the field since 1978. He has published several books and scores of articles. Currently he is the Rector of the University of Ferrara.

Jacques De Bandt Director of the French National Research Institute at Sophia Antipolis and also President of the *Revue d'Économie Industrielle*, the professional publication of French industrial economists. He has published extensively on theoretical topics such as scale and optimum output, on French industrial policy and on the worldwide dimensions of particular sectors of industry such as textiles.

Nicolai J. Foss Professor of Strategic Management and Organization and Director of the Center for Strategic Management and Globalization at the Copenhagen Business School. His principal area of research concerns how organizations contribute to competitive advantage. He also maintains an interest in process approaches to industrial economics, such as evolutionary and Austrian economics.

Peter Møllgaard Professor of Law and Economics and head of the Department of Economics at the Copenhagen Business School. His principal area of research is the application of industrial organization to competition policy. He has done work on market dominance, market power, horizontal and vertical coordination, innovation and technology transfer. His empirical studies deal with industries such as automobiles, cement, concrete and electricity.

Peter Oberender Professor of Economic Theory at the University of Bayreuth. Thomas Rudolf is his assistant. Oberender is the Chairman of the Competition Policy Section of the German Association of Economists, the Verein für Sozialpolitik founded in 1890. He has edited several volumes on market structures in German industry and for many years has specialized in health economics.

Michael A. Utton Professor of Economics (Emeritus), University of Reading. His main interests have been in antitrust economics and policy. He has published on concentration, diversification and competition; a major book was *The Political Economy of Big Business* (Martin Robertson, 1982) which discussed the ambiguities of business size from both a thematic and a policy point of view. His latest books are *Market Dominance and Antitrust Policy* (second edition, Edward Elgar, 2003) and *International Competition Policy* (Edward Elgar, 2006). He is currently working on a book concerned with the growth and prosecution of international cartels.

NORTH AMERICAN

(Those authors who are themselves covered elsewhere as pioneers are merely mentioned here.)

William L. Baldwin Professor of Economics, Dartmouth College, Hanover, New Hampshire, 1956–98, now Emeritus. He has written many research papers since the 1950s, and is also the author of numerous books, such as *Antitrust and the Changing Corporation* (Duke University Press, 1961), and *The Structure of the Defense Market* (Duke University Press, 1967).

James A. Brock Professor of Economics, School of Business, Miami University, Miami, Ohio. BS, MS University of Wyoming, 1973, 1975, PhD Michigan State University, 1981. He has been the author of many books, articles and chapters on monopoly power and antitrust issues.

John Howard Brown Professor of Finance and Economics, Georgia Southern University, Hattiesburg, Georgia. BA, MA University of Akron, 1977, 1982, PhD Michigan State University, 1989. He is writing an extensive history of the field of industrial organization.

Richard E. Caves Professor of Economics Emeritus, Harvard University (see the profile of him as a pioneer).

William S. Comanor Professor of Economics, University of California at Santa Barbara, and Professor of Health Economics, University of California at Los Angeles (see the profile of him as a pioneer).

John E. Kwoka Professor of Economics, Northeastern University, Boston, Massachusetts. (see the profile of him in the Introduction to Part II).

Bruce Marion Professor of Economics, University of Wisconsin, Madison, Wisconsin, now Emeritus. BS, MS Cornell University, 1954, 1955, PhD Ohio State University, 1963. He is the author of numerous books and many articles.

Stephen Martin Professor of Economics, Krannert School of Business, Purdue University, Lafayette, Indiana (see the profile of him in the Introduction to Part II).

Willard F. Mueller Professor of Economics, Agricultural Economics and Law, Emeritus, University of Wisconsin, Madison, Wisconsin (see the profile of him as a pioneer).

Sam Peltzman Professor of Economics, Graduate School of Business, University of Chicago, Chicago, Illinois (see the profile of him as a pioneer).

F.M. Scherer Professor of Economics Emeritus, Kennedy School of Government, Harvard University, Cambridge, Massachusetts (see the profile of him as a pioneer).

John C. Spychalski Professor of Economics and Business Logistics, Smeal College of Business, Pennsylvania State University, College Station, Pennsylvania. BS St. Joseph's College, DBA, MBA Indiana University. He has written extensively on the transport sector.

Harry M. Trebing Professor of Economics Emeritus, Michigan State University, East Lansing, Michigan (see the profile of him as a pioneer).

About the editors

Henry W. de Jong was born in Rotterdam in 1925 where both parents were teachers. Because of the war, the start of his studies in economics at the Rotterdam School of Economics (as from 1969: Erasmus University) was delayed until September 1945. But the guidance of prominent teachers such as François de Vries, Jan Tinbergen and Henk Lambers more than compensated for the lost years. They inspired a lifelong interest in the theory and practice of economics. A decade of international economic advisory work, practised in a Dutch multinational firm, producing steel, paper and plastic containers in the five continents of the world focused de Jong's thinking on markets, industries and firms. With H.W. Lambers, he wrote a PhD dissertation on market theory (1972) at Erasmus University. This was preceded by a book on industrial concentration, dealing with postwar developments in Europe, the United States and Japan (1970) and by several papers on similar topics in Dutch, German and French publications (1965–70). In 1968, de Jong took part in the Hearings on Economic Concentration, held by the US Senate Committee on Antitrust and Monopoly with a paper titled, 'Concentration in the Common Market'.

There followed a nomination as reader in market theory at the Faculty of Economics of the University of Amsterdam in 1969, a professorship in 1977 and a professorate at the Nyenrode School of Business in 1973. Between 1972 and 1986, de Jong also served as a member of the Dutch Competition Commission. After doing research work on behalf of the European Commission (DG 4) during the 1970s and 1980s he was appointed a member of the Commission's Advisory Group to the Merger Task Force. Jointly with Professor A. Jacquemin, the introductory lectures were given on the occasion of the Inauguration of the European Merger Control Law in September 1990. From 1992 to 1993, de Jong was President of EARIE, the European Association for Research in Industrial Economists.

In 1991 de Jong retired from the University of Amsterdam and was knighted in the Order of the Dutch Lion by the Queen. He has been a long-term member of the F. de Vries Foundation's Board, an institution to promote the study of theoretical economics in the Netherlands.

MOST RELEVANT PUBLICATIONS

(1970), *Enterprise Concentration*, Leiden: H.E. Stenfert Kroese N.V. (in Dutch).
(1972), *Dynamic Market Theory*, Leiden: H.E. Stenfert Kroese N.V. (in Dutch, with editions in 1981, 1985, 1989 and reprints in the 1990s).
(1977), *European Industrial Organization*, London: Macmillan Press (with A. Jacquemin).
(1981), *The Structure of European Industry*, The Hague/Dordrecht/Boston: Kluwer Academic Publishers, 1988 and 1993.

(1976–2004), Editor of the series: Studies in Industrial Organization (with A. Jacquemin and W.G. Shepherd).
(1997), *Monopoliseren of rivaliseren*, Weteringbrug: Edclusa (in Dutch).

William G. Shepherd is Professor Emeritus, Department of Economics, University of Massachusetts at Amherst. From 1963 to 1986 he was on the faculty of the Department of Economics, University of Michigan, in Ann Arbor.

He was educated at Amherst College, BA 1957, and Yale University, MA 1958 and PhD 1963. His research has explored most of the technical areas within industrial organization, and his policy research has dealt with all relevant branches: antitrust, regulation, deregulation and public enterprise.

From 1990 to 2001 he was the General Editor of the *Review of Industrial Organization*, a research journal that fits the technical and policy coverage of this book, including international research. He expanded the *Review* from three to eight issues per year.

From 1989 to 1990 he was President of the Industrial Organization Society, which sponsors the *Review of Industrial Organization*. From 1990 to 2001 he also managed the Society's activities and policies. In 2002 the Society designated him as its fourth Distinguished Fellow.

He has published over 13 monographs, textbooks and joint volumes, and over 90 articles in professional journals and chapters in books. His textbooks include *The Economics of Industrial Organization* (5th edn, Prentice Hall, 2003), and *Public Policies Toward Business* (8th edn, Richard L. Irwin, 1991).

From 1967 to 1968 he served as Special Economic Assistant to the head of the Antitrust Division, Donald F. Turner, in the US Department of Justice. This involved him in many leading cases and policy decisions dealing with the automobile, computer, petroleum and other industries, as well as mergers.

In 1976 he was President of the Transport and Public Utilities Group of the American Economic Association, a professional society focused on regulation and deregulation. In 1996 he was given that group's Distinguished Member award.

He considers himself fortunate to have been acquainted with nearly all of the pioneers alive in the years since 1955. Some of them, both in North America and in Britain and Europe, have been close colleagues. Of all the 90 pioneers detailed in this book, he has known about 80, of all schools and technical skills. He has also known many excellent scholars who are not included here. To them he apologizes if he has misjudged their contributions.

MOST RELEVANT PUBLICATIONS

(1965), *Economic Performance under Public Ownership*, Yale University Press, New Haven, CT: Yale University Press.
(1970), *Market Power and Economic Welfare*, New York: Random House.
(1975), *The Treatment of Market Power*, New York: Columbia University Press.
(1975), *Public Policies Toward Business*, 5th and 6th edn (1975, 1980) with Clair Wilcox, 7th and 8th edn (1985, 1990), Homewood, IL: Richard D. Irwin.
(1982), *Microeconomics*, Englewood Cliffs, NJ: Prentice-Hall.

(2005), *The Economics of Industrial Organization*, (1st–4th edn, 1980, 1985, 1990, 1995, Prospect Heights, IL: Waveland Press), 5th edn, Englewood Cliffs, NJ: Prentice-Hall.

Edited books:

(1965), *Utility Regulation: New Directions in Theory and Policy*, New York: Random House.

(1976), *Public Enterprise: Economic Analysis of Theory and Practice*, Lexington, MA: Lexington Books.

(1986), *Mainstreams in Industrial Organization* (with H.W. de Jong), Boston: Kluwer.

Acknowledgements

This history of scholarly pioneers is itself a pioneering venture, involving us in a complicated process during the several years it took to design and finish the book. When Edward Elgar Publishing approached Shepherd in 2002 to do a 'pioneers in industrial organization' book, they set no rules, format or boundaries to follow. When the need to cover European and British pioneers became obvious, it was a blessing that Henry W. de Jong – long a close colleague and friend – agreed to take over that part.

Although de Jong judged that Europe required separate chapters for each language area, Shepherd decided to retain the array of individual profiles that he had planned from the start. Hence the book itself relies on two different literary approaches. We think that this dual approach nicely fits the distinctive realities on the two sides of the Atlantic Ocean.

Quite a few gifted colleagues have generously helped us through the process, and it is a particular pleasure to thank them here.

We sought their advice on the whole design of our coverage, including the right time periods, the range of innovations that should be included, and our choices between country chapters and the more detailed write-ups of individual pioneers. We also asked their advice about the specific people to include and their relative importance.

Henry W. de Jong designed the six-chapter coverage (Chapters 2–8) of European and British pioneers; invited colleagues to write the chapters; and guided the process, with close attention to quality, accuracy and details. William G. Shepherd chose instead to rely on a unified Introduction to the North American pioneers; invited a wide range of colleagues to write major profiles on the pioneers; wrote the Introductory chapter; guided the writing of the individual profiles; and wrote the remaining profiles that complete the coverage. Actually, he found that the authors needed little guidance beyond the general format and type of information required. The authors were remarkably effective in writing fine contributions that needed little editing.

Naturally, our greatest thanks go to those authors of whole European–British chapters and of the individual North American entries.

For the North American section, a large number of colleagues gave thoughtful advice about coverage and individual pioneers. They included Richard E. Caves, F.M. Scherer, Leonard G. Schifrin, the late Donald J. Dewey, John Howard Brown, Willard F. Mueller, William S. Comanor, Harry M. Trebing, John E. Kwoka, William L. Baldwin, Stephen Martin, Sam Peltzman, James W. Brock and Bruce Marion.

Notably, several colleagues also went well beyond the task of writing one profile. In particular, F.M. Scherer drew on his encyclopedic knowledge of the field, not only advising us on the dimensions of our coverage but also identifying some unusual people. And several times he agreed to write additional profiles, ending with a total of six: Charles

Ellet Jr., Joseph A. Schumpeter, Leonard W. Weiss, Jacob Schmookler, A. Michael Spence and Joseph E. Stiglitz.

John Howard Brown also drew on his deep knowledge of the field, from his current writing of a masterful new history of the field. Generously, he wrote important profiles on five innovators: John Bates Clark, Jeremiah Whipple Jenks, Gardiner C. Means, Harold Hotelling and William G. Shepherd.

Richard E. Caves gave us our first individual write-up, of Joe S. Bain, done in splendid style and with lucidity. This provided us with instant momentum and high standards of quality. Harry M. Trebing wrote on three pioneers specializing in regulation: Henry Carter Adams, Martin G. Glaeser and James C. Bonbright. William L. Baldwin wrote the two important profiles on John Maurice Clark and Edward Hastings Chamberlin.

Stephen Martin wrote about two pioneers: William Jack Baumol and Dennis Cary Mueller. Willard F. Mueller presented George Ward Stocking. William S. Comanor wrote about Richard E. Caves, the major pioneer since 1960. John E. Kwoka covered the prolific Frederic M. Scherer, while James A. Brock presented Walter Adams.

Sam Peltzman summarized George Joseph Stigler, the pivotal figure between the old and new Chicago schools. Bruce Marion wrote on Willard Fritz Mueller, while John Spychalski presented John R. Meyer.

All other individual write-ups were done by Shepherd, both in the introductory essay about North Americans and in the set of profiles about individuals. He wishes to thank the fates that allowed him to know personally nearly all of the pioneers in this book who were alive after 1955.

From the start, Alexandra O'Connell provided the finest level of advice and steadfast help in arranging the progress of the entire project, from start to finish of our work and assembling of the book's content. David Vince then supervised the book's process of editing and production with exceptional skill and patience. The copyediting by Margaret Pugh was as thorough and perceptive as possible, with a complex manuscript like this one.

The two editor-authors of this book have worked together on various books, conferences and research projects since 1976. This new project has been even more enjoyable than the others. They wish to thank Els de Jong and Theodora B. Shepherd for the finest intellectual and practical support, advice and encouragement.

Every effort has been made to trace the copyright holders, but if any have been inadvertently overlooked the necessary acknowledgement will be made at the first opportunity.

Henry W. de Jong
Hoorn, The Netherlands

William G. Shepherd
Washington, DC, USA

Introduction to the pioneers and the issues

William G. Shepherd and Henry W. de Jong

INTRODUCTION

This book is about pioneers, the scholars who have created the economics field known as 'industrial organization' (it has also been called 'industrial economics' in Britain and Europe). The field's core is about: (i) *competition*, the driving force of most modern markets, and (ii) *monopoly power*, which interferes with competition's good results.

The field also has a *public-policy* side. The pioneers have analyzed the policies which try to prevent monopoly, or to cure or restrain monopoly once it exists. The policies have mainly included: *antitrust*, to prevent or reduce monopoly power; *regulation* to restrain 'natural monopolies'; *deregulation*, which removes restraints, in the hope that competition will take over; and *public enterprise*, which aims to provide various public interests when competition will not work.

The field dates from the 1870s, and it has been worldwide in scope. Its best-known pioneers since the 1870s have worked in Europe, Britain, the United States and Canada. Americans have developed much of the field's technical content since about 1900. But some early British and European innovations began before that, and many others continued during the twentieth century. They too are presented here.

Although the subject has ancient roots, the modern research innovations began primarily in the 1880s and 1890s, when basic concepts were invented as the new 'neo-classical' microeconomic theory rapidly emerged. The pioneering was also driven by turbulence in many real industries, where mergers, anti-competitive actions, and new technology were creating industrial monopolies.

In response to that, American antitrust and regulation policies were also being created, as ways for the public to prevent or to control the rising monopoly problems. These anti-monopoly efforts created spectacular dramas in the US during 1900 to 1920. Antitrust officials hit most of the very biggest companies with lawsuits, and new regulatory commissions began to set limits on powerful new electric and telephone monopolies. In contrast, European and British governments in the 1920s encouraged a massive spread of cartels, which fixed prices and rigged markets in most industries.

In the 1930s the field began a more 'modern' phase, with new technical ideas, and there have been many more changes in the decades since then. Some of the new ideas have led to great progress, while others have ranged down to modest value or little at all, or even backward steps and detours. All of the innovations have stirred sharp debate, and most of the new ideas have aimed to increase competition.

As we have developed this book, we have had to create our own format and methods, and we have tried two different approaches to the British–European and North American parts. We hope that the whole book conveys the excitement of the field, as well as its unusually broad and diverse content.

Brilliant Writing about Brilliant Pioneers

We present those pioneers here, explaining and assessing their innovations. The main share of the writing has been done by a group of fine writers in Europe and North America, drawing on their deep scholarship and familiarity with the field's modern growth.

In the introductory section that follows in this chapter, we review the main lines and periods of innovation in the entire global field. Then in the Part I, we turn to Britain and Europe. First there is an introduction, and then a review of the earlier, larger trends during 1200–1800. Next come six chapters on major countries: German-language areas, the Low Countries, France, Italy, Britain and Scandinavia. There are also nine individual profiles on important pioneers.

Then comes Part II, which covers North America. First there is an introduction to the field's development in the United States and Canada. It mentions the 43 leading pioneers, and it also briefly summarizes some 51 other innovators. Then follows the individual profiles on those 43 prominent North American pioneers.

Our coverage is meant to be concise and readable, perhaps even enjoyable, and not overly detailed. We focus on the main innovations, rather than on the entire lives and careers of the innovators.

Controversy is Pervasive

Have no illusions: this field is both important and quite contentious. Capitalism's main driving force – the competitive process – attracts intense emotions and arguments about what is fair, who is really the most creative or efficient, which players should get rich (or shouldn't), and how society itself is shaped. Large blocs of corporate power and momentous industrial policies have taken form in Europe, Britain, the US and around the globe. Many blocs have had sharp effects, often for many decades.

The field's findings about such deep and spectacular events are often controversial. The conflicting points of view can create high tensions, and the evidence about the blocs and their impacts is rarely conclusive. Further, the cleft between pure theory and applied real-world research has deepened since about 1970. Theories are often disputed sharply, on both small and large points, and the scholars' debates often shift directions quickly.

Moreover, the companies involved in the issues have often worked ruthlessly to win the debates and their own legal cases, and to bend national policies their own way. They have often tried to marshall scholars as their friendly spokesmen and favorable expert witnesses.

We try to show how – even amid these pressures – the scholarly innovators have used new concepts and methods to study competition and monopoly, both in the many real markets 'out there' and also in purer realms of lonely thought and collegial seminars. Also, the pioneering scholars have often helped to develop and weigh the policies (antitrust and regulation, as well as *laissez-faire*) that might get the best market results.

The pioneers shown in this book are actually few, compared to the many thousands of scholars who have tilled the field since the 1870s. Many of those others have labored productively, but with less impact on the field's ideas.

For each North American pioneer, we aim to focus on the original contributions, with just enough personal details to set the context and give life to the person. Each write-up is therefore much more concise than would be a rounded biographical review of the scholar's whole life and works. For example, none of the North American pioneers is given as much as 10 printed pages, even though some major innovators would merit a book of their own.

Our task here requires care, long experience in the field, technical skill, and a sense of caution, not to mention humility. We have consulted widely among colleagues about which pioneers have been important and why. We have sought consensus, but ultimately this book reflects our best judgments about people, issues and the evolving shape of the industrial organization field. Each of us brings a half-century of scholarly experience to this book, and we have actually known most of the pioneers personally.

The next part of this chapter gives a road-map to the changing ideas and debates. We note the field's very early history, and we explain and interpret the shape of the more modern field as it grew after the 1870s and again after 1930. We note that some supposedly 'new' ideas have actually been introduced long before, as often happens in many scholarly fields. We place the pioneers in context, and we discuss the importance of the innovations within the whole field.

WHO IS INCLUDED, AND WHY

But first, we explain here this book's criteria and methods; why the various pioneers were included, and how the book is designed.

Criteria for Including Pioneers

In 2002, Mark Blaug invited Shepherd to prepare a comprehensive book on 'pioneers in industrial organization', to be issued by Edward Elgar Publishing. Shepherd accepted with enthusiasm, but also with a sense of great caution. Enthusiasm, because the field is exciting, important, and packed with fateful issues. Caution, because any presentation of pioneers is bound to touch on touchy debates and contrasting views.

Shepherd has frequently asked Blaug and Elgar's editors for guidance in designing the book, especially: what whole period to cover, what methods are best for choosing pioneers, whether to write individual profiles or national chapters, and many other matters of form and method. No such guidance was given. All dimensions of the book were left entirely to the author.

Shepherd soon realized he would need to find a co-author to cover the Europe-and-Britain side, and he was exceedingly fortunate to secure Henry W. de Jong for that task. The choice was obvious. An erudite scholar who also sets high and precise standards, de Jong has long been a prolific and reigning research expert in the Netherlands and Europe – as well as Shepherd's close friend and colleague.

With a free hand from Edward Elgar Publishing, we have taken great care in defining what 'pioneers' should mean, setting the time coverage, designing the book's format, deciding which types of details to include, and every other dimension. So we have had to develop our own definitions and designs, while seeking much advice from our colleagues.

The pioneering in this field has involved research both into the nature and facts of markets, and into the public policies that might be best. The *research* pioneering may enlarge the specific concepts, the underlying research methods, or the information about real conditions in real markets. Each of those categories has involved a large variety, with important changes as the decades have passed. An innovation may also involve the content, specific choices, or methodology of *policies*, such as antitrust or regulation. Each of those policies, too, has contained much variety and change over the decades; think of strict versus lenient periods of antitrust, and of regulation (1920s–1960s) versus deregulation (from 1975 on).

A pioneer does not just explore, but rather – in the ideal case – creates order, a new system, and new research capacity. To use homely metaphors, a pioneer does not just explore a wilderness, but mainly clears the underbrush, sets boundaries, makes fields to plow, and builds roads, houses and whole farms. That is, pioneers add new research ways to define reality, to measure its conditions, and to interpret the issues.

The new capacity can be new concepts which come from pure deductions using abstract theory, or instead come from more practical ideas based on inductive thinking and experience. Pioneering can involve doing the first work on a new or neglected topic, on a new set of information, on a little-known sector of the economy, or on a novel idea for policy devices or methods. The pioneers' new research capacity can also create new evidence, by adding facts or by showing how to process data – and interpret the results – in more effective ways.

A few truly protean pioneers have gone on and on, providing decades of substantial innovations which have lasted well. The other innovators have scaled down by gradations of importance, and some have made just one or two brief additions to narrow points. Some have stayed in this field, while others have moved on to other subjects.

'New' Ideas Can Have Great Value, or Merely Modest Worth, or Even Reduce Understanding

As in every field, mere novelty in itself is not enough. Some 'innovations' are actually dead ends, which inject 'new' ideas and methods that unfortunately turn out to be neither fruitful nor lasting. The resulting detours and false leads can displace good ideas, rather than genuinely improve the field's content.

A common reason for dubious innovations is the universal dynamic of 'the career'. Young scholars often advance their careers by publishing whatever 'new' and 'seminal' ideas they can think up, while disparaging the existing ideas as 'obsolete' or 'not rigorous'. This activity may often yield real progress, but it may instead replace sound knowledge and research methods with false leads.

Genuine pioneers are those who really enhance the field, adding superior ideas and evidence without crowding out effective and important ideas. The judgments about these true innovations can be debatable. Robust debate and sifting out the superior competing ideas is what 'the literature' is supposed to achieve. But the literature's debating process can be distorted or confused or led astray, at least for a while. Sometimes, many years or even decades of debate are needed to evaluate 'new' ideas and methods properly.

Time Coverage: Mainly from the 1870s to the Mid-1980s

We could have begun with the 1930s, when the 'modern' twentieth-century analysis of oligopoly began in a blaze of excited theorizing. To some colleagues, those 1930s seem ancient, at 70 years ago. A number of young scholars since the 1970s are even more sure that 'new is best'. They have scorned all pre-1970s ideas, brushing off the 1930s–1960s as dim and shallow. As for the pre-1930s period, that is a hopeless Stone Age. Only the 'new IO theory' since 1970 is true pioneering.

But that view is, to put it mildly, ignorant and wrong. There was major pioneering from the 1870s on. The European field has deep roots in even earlier centuries, as de Jong and his authors explain in Part I. And on both sides of the Atlantic Ocean, major innovations were made in the 1880s and 1890s, when this field was being formed. Many of the supposedly 'new' ideas in the post-1950s literature were actually debated brilliantly and extensively well before 1910. In the US, the post-Civil War booms and rising market warfare involved massive new problems: competition of many kinds, monopoly and dominance, scale economies, mergers, collusion, tactical price discrimination, 'predatory pricing', the blocking of entry, utility pricing, and other classic market actions. All these had already put the most important market concepts into dramatic industrial practice. And that sparked intensive discussion, often with great analytical clarity, practical knowledge and wisdom.[1]

'Newness' has often been over-claimed by scholars, especially since the 1950s. A review of 'modern pioneers' requires us to recognize the earlier true pioneers. Some scholars since the 1920s have said they were 'pioneering', but they were in faux jungles that had been explored, clarified and tamed long before. Later scholars have often added refinements and nuances, but the really large innovations since the 1930s have been much less than their advocates have claimed.

So the beginnings of pioneering go back at least to the 1870s; what is the suitable end-point for our coverage in this book? Today, yesterday, the year 2000, the 1980s? After debating the choices and consulting with many others, we have ended the main coverage in the mid-1980s, at about 1985.[2] That makes sense, because the ideas and trends since 1985 are still too new, open to question, and ripe for revision. Trying to include all the recent new research thoughts and claims would be premature. There will be time enough later to recognize the best ones, perhaps in a new pioneers book.

How Many Pioneers?

Pioneers might seem to be a very few protean giants. But this field has had many important innovators; over 40 from North America are given individual profiles here, and over 50 more less-prominent innovators are noted. There is also a wide range of European and British pioneers. Perhaps these numbers may seem high to some of our readers, but there are many causes at work.

The field is uncommonly wide and inclusive, and it is unusually diverse and rich in its differing research methods. Those methods range from pure theory (including mathematical modeling) and applied theory, all the way over to factual studies of many kinds on many topics and scores of major industries. There is also a wide array of public-policy instruments (antitrust, regulation, deregulation and public enterprise), all subject to hot debates and big changes since the 1880s. Shepherd's 'Introduction' below (to the North American pioneers), lists no fewer than 16 important topic areas in this field, and each of them contains further specialized subjects.

Moreover, the research and real-world conditions have stretched over many countries, including the US, Britain, those in Europe, Japan, Australia and others. The time period extends well over 100 years, and it contains several distinct eras. The innovations have been quite numerous, and there have been rapid changes in topics, styles, methods, fact sources and economic sectors. The sectors alone show dramatic shifts. They began with industrial metals and railroads and the telephone and electric utilities during 1860–1900, to automobiles, chemicals, plastics and medicines during 1900–1950, then to computers, communications and space technology during 1950–1970, and now to internet-related markets, genetic manipulation and nanotechnology. There have been many contending ideas, and the research field has not moved smoothly toward concise, universally-accepted truths. Progress has often been choppy, even chaotic, and given to hot debates.

Economists Only

This book is about economists, creating economic ideas. It is true that some other types, including lawyers, have sometimes influenced economists and the field.[3] But the correct professional focus is on genuine economic pioneers who were professionally trained in economics, engaged in the methods and the refereed research literature of economics, and were under the sustained discipline of professional economic criticism.

The Sequence

This field is very wide-ranging, and moreover the timing of ideas sometimes is complicated. Some pioneers contributed numerous ideas over several decades, not just once or twice. Many pioneers cannot be neatly assigned to a short time-period or even to a specific decade. So a coherent account of those pioneers needs to extend over their pioneering activities, to reach a rounded assessment of everything they did.

Most North American pioneers are placed at the time when their innovations began taking hold. That involves some judgment on our part. The North American pioneers are grouped into a single broad category, which embraces research into markets and theory, as well as policies including antitrust, regulation and deregulation.

Varying Lengths of Profiles for Varying Pioneering Contributions

A few pioneers have had fundamental effects, or have worked on a variety of topic areas over several decades, while others have ranged down to creative but highly specialized work during a brief period. Relying on much consultation and advice from colleagues, we have tried to fit the write-ups to the pioneers' roles and importance. The main method is to vary the number of pages: more for big innovations, fewer for the lesser ones. A uniform length would not fit the true range of pioneering.

In Britain and Europe, some leading pioneers are given specific coverage in 'profiles'. In the North American coverage, the pioneers' relative importance is suggested partly by the length of the profile. Our authors did not stick rigidly to the suggested page lengths we gave them. Some came in a little short, or a little long, as economists often do. But the lengths here do suggest the relative importance. Colleagues and other readers will, of course, reach their own judgments about these matters of relative importance.

As for the book's whole length and the depth of detail, our estimable publisher was willing to provide up to 500 printed pages for the book's length. But we and our authors have worked to make it more concise and clear, with brevity to appeal to a wider readership.

Disagreements and Schools, Amid Corporate Pressures

The field has always been tumultuous. New methods and data have frequently come in abrupt shifts, or irregular waves, some with wide agreement but others with acerbic debates. And mathematics and pure theory versus applied research have bred fractious debates for over a century. Even personality can matter; some facile scholars with outsized personalities have often rattled the field – at least for a while – more than their cautious and understated colleagues.

Some of the pioneers have written mainly about their own contributions, but some other scholars have rebuked others' research and methods for being 'obsolete', while praising their own for 'rigor' and power. When ideas and scholars have been mobilized directly on opposite sides of important policy cases, the arguments can grow rough.[4] The field's literature is itself supposed to function as a high-class debating society, to thrash out correct judgments among such claims, some of them quiet, others loud. But a successful sifting is not guaranteed. We have sought a fair balance among these diverse contending views, amid the frequent overstatements.

Available Authors

The coverage here has also been affected by our access to first-rate colleagues who were both interested and available to write these contributions when we invited them. Securing the authors has been a challenge, as they say, amid the high pressures of modern research and the attractions of expert-witness work. Both de Jong and Shepherd have chosen to write some of the profiles, but they have also filled in by writing others when authors were scarce.

What's in the Write-ups

For Europe, one scholar deals with each country. Although standard formats were suggested, the authors have followed their own judgments in dealing with matters of content.

For the North American innovators, the authors were asked to provide the standard personal basic facts about the pioneers: birth and death dates and places, their educational degrees, their main professional positions, and other details where relevant. On the main innovations themselves, the authors were asked to describe them and their importance, their effects on the field, any debates about their nature, and a summary of where the contributions stand now. At the end of each profile, we asked for a listing of the main publications where the innovations were presented.

HOW THE FIELD'S MAIN TOPICS HAVE EVOLVED

Now we turn from this book's design to matters of intellectual history. We present a review of the field's main issues. We review briefly the background and emergence of the whole field, and then its main shifts from the 1870s to 1985.

Background

The most basic and ancient questions in this field have been: what moves the market to its actual prices, and are those prices acceptable to the market's participants and to society? These questions go back at least to the century beginning in 1200, far before the modern era. A brief summary of those early issues will give depth to this book.

Scholastic price theory developed in Europe after 1200 to assess whether prices are acceptable or too high, and if government-set prices would be better for the public good. These questions are still central: how can we explain the prices in the market, and how are the outcomes valued (value being the balance of advantages and disadvantages to all the parties)? In those early times, the goods were basic foodstuffs, land and natural resources, labor, money and other liquid capital. Now of course they also include a vast array of advanced products and services.

But the issues are still much the same. Monopoly pricing could come in many ways; by individuals who raised prices by the famous engrossing, forestalling and regrating, or by using still other illicit agreements, secret pacts or conspiracies. Or various actions by guilds or other groupings could also fix prices or set minimum prices. Against that, the free-market process (then often called 'common estimation'; the term competition did not yet exist) might give the benefits of moving prices down toward costs, or at least mediating between surpluses and deficits.

In those early times, schools developed. An example is the Parisian school (1200–1350), which was almost unanimously in favor of free-market pricing and opposed to monopoly. The majority in this school favored competition (or 'common estimation'). But a few, for example, Henri van Ghent (writing about 1280), would allow entrepreneurs some influence, in an embryonic Schumpeterian idea. Even so, all in the Parisian school would accept government pricing or related constraints, if the common good required it.

By the 1700s, Adam Smith and Anne Robert Jacques Turgot were seeing competition as the basis for achieving the public good. They opposed all forms of monopolizing control and did not mention any entrepreneurial contribution. By contrast, Richard Cantillon held that entrepreneurs set markets in motion. On the whole, continental theory followed Cantillon, while the Anglo-Saxon British view fitted Smith (though with exceptions).

Smith's 'invisible hand' did not make valuations, which instead are done by persons or institutions. If the market's outcome is valued as negative on balance, then its rules or structures can be changed. This continental view is seen in the nineteenth century and later, with Friedrich von Wieser and Robert Liefmann, who were German-area economists in the 1920s and 1930s. It accorded with the closed markets of the time. Since the Second World War, world markets have opened and integrated across borders, and the strong rise of competition rules in the European Union have applied pressure on the individual governments.

Many 'new' ideas are actually familiar and 'old'

By the 1870s, evidently, some basic ideas had already been debated and clarified down the centuries. As debate continued further, many more basic issues were illuminated by the 1920s. Some later 'new' ideas were actually superfluous. Some pioneers merely selected among the various known ideas, to refine and rename one or two of them.

At each moment, the field is not a sum of all previous innovative ideas. Many 'new' ideas have little merit and usually they do not get accepted at all. Others have some play but are soon whittled down to a modest role, or they may be displaced entirely. Sometimes a new idea will replace one or several of the 'established' concepts. So the pioneers' contributions have had a variety of fates; some still retain importance now; many others have faded, and some are entirely gone; others have faded and then regained importance. So you should bear in mind that ideas come and go as debates proceed.

The early concepts were pretty simple, as seen from today's technical varieties, but they were basic and powerful. Later innovations had varied importance. Fundamental ideas were installed rapidly during 1870–1910, even though the mail was slow by today's internet standards. Ideas might take years to emerge among the few scholars in the elite academic campuses (as with Augustin Cournot in Europe and Charles Ellet in the US). Some early ideas seemed just to materialize, rather than to appear from one scholar's paper at one precise moment.

Computers and the internet have sped things greatly, but the human brain is still the source where new ideas emerge and are judged, and it remains both fertile and fallible, and judgments often take a long time to gel. The best thinkers in this field still take care and time to assess innovations, and debates can proceed for many years.

The field's main ideas, and the problem of causation

As we noted at the start, the core of the field has been about competition and monopoly, and how they affect markets and the whole economy. The modern field has divided into several main subtopics:

1. *Degrees of competition and monopoly* How much competition or monopoly power is there in a given market? Market structure is often important in this.
2. *Determinants of competition or monopoly* What determines the degree of competition? Technology, and the economies and diseconomies of scale, are important in this.
3. *Behavior* How do competition and monopoly affect firms' behavior? Pricing and other strategies are important, by one dominant firm or by several oligopolists.
4. *Performance* How are profits, prices, efficiency, innovation and other elements of performance affected by the degree of competition and monopoly power?

Underlying these subtopics is the fundamental question of causation: which way does causation run, from competitive structure forward to behavior and performance? Or is it the reverse: from a firm's performance back to shape its market position? Mainstream scholars have urged the first view. Competition (or monopoly power) in a market shapes the behavior and performance of firms in that market; usually, competition yields excellence, while monopoly harms performance (raising prices and reducing innovation). When markets have imperfections, firms can capture monopoly power and exert it harmfully.

An opposite view urged by free-market advocates is that firms can gain market power only if they truly earn it, by being genuinely more efficient and innovative. For that to be so, markets would need to be essentially perfect. Free-market advocates do assume that markets are perfect, and so they argue for the reverse causation: performance shapes structure and behavior. Strong monopoly occurs rarely, they say. When monopoly does occur, it is actually good rather than harmful. And it will not last unless government interferes to protect it.

This question of cause and effect may seem arcane and dry, but it is quite fundamental. The debate has been intense and divisive from the start – and particularly since the 1960s. Your belief about causation affects whether you believe that monopoly usually causes trouble (the mainstream view) or usually is beneficial and welcome (by free-market doctrine). Our pioneers have recognized these opposed possibilities. Some have had neutral attitudes toward the answers, while others have lined up firmly on one side or the other.

These four subtopics further divide into many specific topics, involving concepts and measurement. Those detailed points are presented in Chapter 9, introducing the North American pioneers.

The Beginnings

The basic ideas have been familiar since earliest civilized times, and we have noted how the 1200s brought scholastic analysis. Competition induces extra efforts and, sometimes, creativity. Firms that can exert control over markets will raise their prices and restrain output, aiming to gain riches. They will also take anti-competitive actions to entrench their power. Richard Cantillon and Adam Smith noted both these points, and installed the consumers' choices in the market, among many or even a few competing suppliers, as the anchor of efficient economic systems.

During the next 100 years, from the 1770s to the 1870s, a few further concepts were added. Johann Heinrich von Thünen united thoughts deriving from Smith's dynamic equilibrium economics with Continental emphasis on entrepreneurial moves. However, his message, which stressed the productivity growth as the main solution to the 'social problem', got lost in the move towards neo-classical static analysis. Some politicians used crude Manchester school 'competitive markets' ideas to excuse the widespread social harms of the new industrial capitalism. But a specialized research field did not develop. Cournot wrote about duopoly in the 1830s, but his work was noted only decades later. Ellet in the US also developed sophisticated early ideas abut pricing, but he too gained little notice at the time.

But when neo-classical theory burst forth in the 1870s, perfect competition – and its practical variations – began to be analyzed in detail.[5] Competitive outcomes became defined as a set of precise technical conditions of equilibrium costs and prices. Monopoly's conditions and impacts were also studied, in theory and fact.

Real industrial events reinforced the urgency of research during these formative 1880–1900 decades. The spokesmen for big business claimed that new economies of scale made necessary a rising flood of mergers and dominant firms, which threatened to eliminate competition in hundreds of markets. That pressured the handful of rising scholars to think and write in detail about the field's central topics. They also were driven to debate the need for policies like antitrust and the regulation of utilities.

By 1900 most of the big, permanent topics – market imperfections, anti-competitive abuses that created dominant firms, the harms of monopolies as well as their possible benefits, economies of scale and 'natural monopolies', price collusion and discrimination, innovation – all of these had been faced and debated, often clearly and wisely. Monopoly's damages were known, but neo-liberal free-market advocates had also arisen to defend monopoly, both in Europe and Britain and in the US.

Looked at broadly, by 1900 the field ranged from pure theory to highly-applied research, along with an intense exposure to many important real industries. Applied research was the field's mainstream activity.

Leading Innovations During the Twentieth Century

It is helpful now to survey briefly the main series of topics that arose during the whole twentieth century. Next, the European chapters, and then the North American coverage, will fill in the details about the pioneers and their specific innovations.

1900–1920

Research activity was moderately active in Europe, as some scholars moved beyond neo-classical theory to study practical features of competition. But there was little research on policies against monopoly, either in industry or utilities.

In contrast, US research was deeply involved in antitrust policies and new regulation of the nascent utility monopolies.[6] Decisive rulings were made against price fixing (the 1899 *Addyston Pipe* case) and single-firm dominance (the Standard Oil, American Tobacco and AT&T cases, among others). But actual 'trust-busting' was moderate, and early regulation fitted careful and sound economics.

The 1920s

The 1920s brought forth fewer new ideas in both Europe and the US. Amid depression in Europe, policies there retreated into a widespread encouragement of cartels in thousands of industries. In the US, both antitrust and regulation receded.[7]

The 1930s

European thinking still focused on cartels, but in the US this decade erupted with major innovations, amid the stresses of the Great Depression. The control within large US corporations was rethought, and oligopoly theory rapidly emerged in 1932–33, displacing single-firm dominance as the leading topic. Other pioneering included an index of monopoly, kinked demand curves, the nature of the firm, and the studies of major new datasets on industrial concentration, costs and revenues. Other innovations involved vertical integration and controls, natural monopolies, economies of scale, and the structure–behavior–performance triad.

The 1940s

The US debates intensified further, and they brought in new concepts. Joseph Schumpeter defended large firms for being engines of innovation, yet the antitrust attacks on major firms actually increased. Game theory was created, and the mathematizing of theory took hold. Yet a wave of industry studies also brought new practical research into oligopolies.

The 1950s

Now began a rich era for research and policy, in both North America and Europe. In Europe the 1950s began with French innovations of marginal-cost pricing for electric utilities, soon joined by British economists and policies. By 1956 there were also strong new research and policy moves against the thousands of entrenched cartels, toward installing pro-competitive laws and agencies to reduce monopoly in the new European Union as well as in individual countries.

US scholars developed new methods for defining markets, and these were soon used in leading antitrust cases. New concepts included 'countervailing power', the possible benefits of price discrimination, barriers against new competition, and 'engineering estimates' and the 'survivor technique' for measuring the economies of scale. Meanwhile free-market defenses of market power were increasingly asserted. And though this was a golden era for regulation, early critiques of it were emerging.[8]

The 1960s

This decade was also highly innovative, and methods grew even more diverse and the debates grew even more active. In Europe and Britain, research deepened into competitive conditions and the economies of scale. Also, the antitrust policies toward dominance, mergers and price fixing were strengthened and refined. Public enterprises in coal, electricity and telephones improved their pricing and efficiency, especially in France and the UK.

In the US, new computers enabled large-scale econometric research, covering many conditions: industrial concentration, entry barriers, prices and profit rates, advertising, innovation, discrimination in employment, and wages. The concepts and facts of innovation were studied in unusual depth. There was both much variety and a broad balance among many research methods.

The economic rigor of US antitrust policies was raised, while the Supreme Court applied tight criteria to mergers and pricing. New critiques alleged that utility regulation caused inefficiency and excess investment. There were rising calls for deregulation, especially in financial markets, the transportation industries (airlines, railroads and trucking), and telephone service.

In parallel with neo-liberal critics in the UK and Europe, free-market critics at Chicago, Los Angeles and Rochester increasingly attacked all public policies. They asserted that markets were virtually perfect, so that public actions could only distort economic efficiency.

The 1970s

European and UK research developed further, especially on the economies of scale and on mergers. In 1979, Britain began to privatize nearly all public enterprises and to remove public regulations to constrain monopoly power. This created many unregulated private monopolies, but new competition often failed to develop.

In the US, research proliferated and diverged even more into real-world and pure-theory styles. The decade began with two landmark monograph-textbooks: by F.M. Scherer on mainstream research, and by A.E. Kahn on utility regulation and possible competition. The 1970s also brought more econometric analysis of monopoly and performance, individual dominant firms, profitability, innovation, mergers, wages, and discrimination by race and gender. Mergers and economies of scale also both received intensive study, as also did transactions costs. Areeda and Turner in 1975 urged testing for 'predatory pricing' by using marginal costs, and this was quickly accepted by many colleagues and the courts.

In parallel, pure theory also spread rapidly. Called 'new IO theory' by its advocates, abstract modeling became popular, especially using game theory. Free-market theorists asserted an 'efficient-structure' hypothesis, though with little research basis. Major US antitrust cases challenged AT&T's telephone monopoly and IBM's dominance of computers. Deregulation spread to many sectors in the US, especially financial markets, airlines and railroads.

The early 1980s

European research advanced on many levels in the early 1980s, and pro-competitive policies in the UK and Europe became comparable or even stronger than US policies. Europeans joined cautiously in the rising US focus on game theory and mathematical models.

In the US, game theory's popularity rose to a peak, and a theory of 'contestable markets' was announced. After 1980, the Reagan Administration cut US antitrust policies deeply and inserted 'new IO theory' to replace the evidence about market definition and concentration. They also pressed deregulation into more sectors.

* * * *

These summary points are a framework for the individual innovators and details that follow. First come the Europeans and British pioneers, and then the North Americans. We do not imply relative importance or leadership by this sequence. Various Europeans and British pioneers contributed before 1900, but the North American scholars soon made large innovations in both research and policies. European governments eased back, treating monopoly and collusion much more tolerantly until the 1950s, and they quietly relegated much of the utility-monopoly problems (pricing, efficiency and innovation) to public firms.

The most important European pioneering came later, beginning in the 1950s. And as US policies came to be dominated by free-market advocates and theorists after 1970, European policies to promote and protect competition actually became stronger and more consistent with the mainstream.

NOTES

1. Examples include: 'predatory pricing' by Standard Oil in the 1870s, the 'survivor technique' idea by John Stuart Mill before 1860, Alfred Marshall and the 'evolution' of firms in 1890, and John Bates Clark's discussion of entry barriers in 1887.
2. It is true that a few of our writers have taken the liberty to discuss a few of their pioneers' post-1980s developments. Some of those later works often relate closely to their pre-1985 innovations.
3. Active lawyers have included Thurman Arnold, A.A. Berle and Walton Hamilton in the 1930s and 1940s, Aaron Director in the 1950s, and Robert H. Bork and Richard A. Posner from the 1960s on. The legal scholar Donald F. Turner may seem to be an exception from the 1950s–1970s, but he held an economics PhD from Harvard and much of his work met strict refereed-journal standards.

   In some degree of contrast, the Chicago school led by George Stigler and its journals (especially the *Journal of Political Economy* and the *Journal of Law and Economics*) often gave easy acceptance to papers from its like-minded group of legal writers, including Bork and Posner.
4. For example, many leading scholars were drawn into the huge US antitrust cases toward IBM and AT&T in the 1970s, and the Microsoft cases in the 1990s and early 2000s.
5. See Almarin Phillips and Rodney E. Stevenson, 'The historical development of industrial organization', *History of Political Economy*, Fall 1974, pp. 324–42.
6. William Letwin, *Law and Economic Policy in America* (Random House, New York, 1965); Hans B. Thorelli, *The Federal Antitrust Policy* (University of Chicago Press, Chicago, 1954); Walton Hamilton and Irene Till, *Antitrust in Action*, vol. 16, Temporary National Economic Committee, Washington, DC, US, Government Printing Office, 1940; Philip Areeda and Donald F. Turner, *Antitrust Law*, 7 vols (Little, Brown, Boston, MA 1978).
7. Though an exception was John M. Clark's *Studies in the Economics of Overhead Costs* in 1923.
8. Including Walter Adams and Horace Gray's *Monopoly in America: The Government as Promoter* (Macmillan, London, 1955, and the 1959 attack on railroad regulation by John Meyer, Merton Peck, John Stenason and Charles Zwick, *Competition and the Transportation Industries of the United States* (Harvard University Press, Cambridge, MA).

PART I

Market theory and its pioneers in Europe

1. Introduction to market theory and its European pioneers

Henry W. de Jong

This part of the book on pioneers in the theory of industries and markets needs an introduction to explain the editorial choices and decisions. What did we consider to be the subject and its boundaries from a European perspective? The subject is competition and monopoly (or dominance of the market) in real-life markets, the organization of industries related to both and the application of the acquired knowledge to policy questions. Obviously, the construction and use of models or theories, abstracting from concrete details in order to concentrate on essential factors and relationships, is not shunned. On the contrary, they are indispensable to guide our thinking and to understand the problem. But a *l'Art pour l'Art* approach, whatever its merits elsewhere, is rejected here:

> It is in any case not superfluous to remind ourselves that scientific theories aim at stating something that is true of the world, whatever profitable actions they might enable us to take. This point is at times forgotten by those who see in theories no more than abstract formal systems, just as they forget that numbers are used for counting. (Bertrand Russell, *Wisdom of the West*, 1959, p. 311)

With respect to the question posed in the first paragraph, the old continent, with its long and divided history, diverging nationalities and different languages presented a particularly difficult nut to crack. Where to start the story, what to include, how to deal with the various topics, how many and what type of authors to include?

After consulting a number of colleagues we decided to take the inevitable decision to ask one from every major language area in Western Europe to contribute his selection of pioneers. This choice of between five and ten scientific writers on industrial economics should be related to the period between the early nineteenth century and 1980. The latter date was agreed with Professor W.G. Shepherd, the editor of the American section.

In a heartening response, Professors Bianchi, De Bandt, Foss, Møllgaard, Oberender and his assistant Thomas Rudolf, as well as Professor Utton agreed to write a survey of pioneers in their own language area or to contribute profiles. The editor is most grateful for their efforts which required an investigation beyond the scenery of persons and ideas in which they grew up. One will recognize from their contributions how different the developments in thinking between the various countries were. And, notwithstanding the tendency for English to prevail, knowledge of the separate languages remains indispensable: anyone who wants to be accurately informed about the decisions coming from the European Commission and the Court of Justice should know that only the text of the language of the addressee is binding in competition policy matters.

But why has a long, general chapter been added? It exposes the fundamentals of market theory as it developed between 1200 and 1800. Investigations unearthed several pioneering authors and even schools of economic thinking in those ages, which surpassed by far what the ancient Greeks and Romans had to say. The reasons are given in the beginning of the chapter. It became obvious that thinking about the market economy had not started with the writings of Adam Smith or Jean-Baptiste Say; on the contrary, those economists were rather the terminal point of a long line of authors who analysed the working of markets in two, principally different, ways. The one was a disequilibrium economics in which the entrepreneurial function figured prominently. Within this approach several versions came forward, only two of which are mentioned here: either the entrepreneur created the uncertainties of the market's proceedings, for example through innovations. Or he reacted and adapted to its fundamental presence as a result of external disturbances.

The other was an equilibrium solution. It was postulated that disequilibria would, rapidly or slowly, but unavoidably revert to a position of natural equilibrium of demand and supply. The various approaches generated a pattern of different pricing methods, actors and institutions.

After Adam Smith a cleavage manifested itself increasingly between the two types of thinking about markets. In Anglo-Saxon writings, the equilibrium theory came to dominate, issuing into Alfred Marshall's neo-classical and partial analysis. Continental economists strove to reconcile both approaches while retaining the entrepreneurial emphasis, as is clearly visible with Johann von Thünen, Say or Jacob Leonard de Bruyn Kops. Or, if they were of a more active mind, such as Friedrich List or the historical economists, defended policy-oriented interference by the state. Economists from the Austrian school conceived the disequilibria to be the result of external disturbances: coming from outside of the market (technological shocks, discoveries, natural disasters, wars, government measures and so on) they stirred up the actions of entrepreneurs which brought about a tendency towards equilibrium of prices, costs and quantities without ever reaching it.

As the chapters on the several language areas show, these lines of thinking about markets and industries continued as the twentieth century arrived and progressed. Neo-classical theory was further refined and formalized; and when industrial organization appeared as an application of that theory, numerous efforts were undertaken to fill the theory of market structures with empirical contents. But not in Europe. Nor were leading British economists enticed to make much of such an approach. As Mike Utton shows, Mary and Alfred Marshall's *Industry and Trade* (1919, as a sequel to the *Economics of Industry*, 1879) provided the guide together with the latter's *Principles*. The principal task of the economist is to study the behaviour of men and firms within the framework of the institutions; these change and the behaviour which is largely determined by them, does so too. Two prominent economists in the field, Sargant Florence and E.A.G. Robinson, devoted much attention to those institutions, the division of labour and economies of scale, thereby pursuing the Smith–Marshall tradition in their own peculiar ways.

The other countries did not basically differ from this pattern, although national factors and traditions coloured thinking. In Germany and the Low Countries, size and scale had not been much of a problem, being located in the heart of the continental market. Only protectionism was a hindrance to growth. Industrial economists, both in the 1920s and after the Second World War, focused their attention on the conditions and patterns of firm and industry growth, and subsequently on dynamic analysis. French and Italian thinking reflected the particular circumstances of those countries: a relatively large agricultural sector, retarded industrialization, many small firms and fragmented industries, and extended state interference in the economy. Competition and regulatory policies were not much in demand. Things changed only with the advent of the Common Market and then rather gradually. That eminent economist and teacher Jacques Houssiaux, was one of the first to draw attention to the changes in the industrial structures which economic integration would bring about and the challenges posed thereby (Houssiaux, 1958 and 1960). As a special adviser to the EEC Commission, Houssiaux was closely connected with policy making in the field until his untimely death in the early 1970s. He was succeeded by Alex Jacquemin and, later on, by others who devoted much time and effort to serve as policy advisers to European or national governments, or exceptionally, to play a role as decision makers like Romano Prodi and Mario Monti.

Equally, the industrial economist as an educator was important and continues to be so. Those who wrote handbooks which gained a wide acceptance have contributed exceptionably to the development, or dissemination, of the science. Some prominent examples are listed below but these should not make us forget several others. Indeed, the concept of the pioneer is multifarious and, most probably, those are right who maintain that the growth of knowledge is the result of our common adventure.

LITERATURE

George, K.D. and C. Joll (1971 and subsequent editions), *Industrial Organization: Competition, Growth and Structural Change*, London: Allen & Unwin.

Houssiaux, J. (1958), *Le Pouvoir de monopole*, Paris: Sirey.

Houssiaux, J. (1960), *Concurrence et marché commun*, Paris: Genin.

Jacquemin, A.P. and H.W. de Jong (1977), *European Industrial Organization*, London and Basingstoke: Macmillan.

Kaufer, E. (1980), *Industrieökonomik. Eine Einführung in die Wettbewerbstheorie*, Munich: Vahlen.

McLachlan, D.L. and D. Swann (1967), *Competition Policy in the European Community: The Rules in Theory and Practice*, Oxford: Oxford University Press.

Schmidt, I. (1981 and subsequent editions), *Wettbewerbspolitik und Kartellrecht*, Stuttgart: Lucius & Lucius.

Zwan, A. van der and J. Verhulp (1980), *Grondslagen en techniek van de marktanalyse*, Leiden: Stenfert Kroese.

2. Market theory in Europe

Henry W. de Jong

INTRODUCTION: THE MEDIEVAL BACKGROUND

Industrial economics or market theory has developed simultaneously with the market economy in Europe. The latter arose from the beginnings of the twelfth century and went through a prosperous period until about 1316. However, population growth outran food production and a collapse had to follow; in 1316 there was the first general famine and this catastrophe was succeeded by recurrent epidemics of the black death and the devastating wars – of which the Hundred Years War between France and England (1337–1453) was the worst. It was only after 1450 that a renewed expansion took place, based on the upcoming, substitutive maritime trade, which lit the torch of growth for the following centuries. Initially, the rise of commercial capitalism was linked with the trade fairs of which those in the Champagne were the most developed. Throughout the year, in market cycles of six weeks, there was an exchange of Flemish cloth for a large variety of goods from Italy and southern Europe, furs from Scandinavia and silver from Bohemia, feeding the coinage. The markets were wholesale markets, new in human history; the contrast with the local markets of the cities 'was not simply a difference in size, but a difference in kind' (Pirenne, 1953, pp. 97–103). The merchants were exempted from lawsuits, executions and usury prohibition, that is, of loans at interest and at maximum rates. The Champagne fairs also became the money market of Europe and from the thirteenth century onwards, debts were settled there by compensation, that is, clearing arrangements. The drawbacks of the system, especially the underdeveloped road network, were partially made good by an absence of political interventions and protectionism. For about two centuries Europe had a free, internal market in goods, money and credit.[1]

Naturally, economic thinking was concentrated upon markets, value, pricing, profits and money; macroeconomic theory made its appearance only with the rise of nation states, the so-called mercantilism. Market theory flourished particularly in the University of Paris, located like the fairs between the urbanized centres in north and south. This university drew scholars, permanently or temporarily, such as Albert Magnus, Thomas Aquinas, Henry of Ghent, Giles of Lessines, Richard of Middleton, John Duns Scotus, Gilbert Olivi, Jean Buridan and Gerald Odonis to mention the most important from the economic viewpoint. Being near contemporaries, knowing each other personally or through their works, these men developed what is known as scholastic economics.[2]

As a fortunate prelude, in 1202, Leonardo Fibonacci of Pisa published a work called the *Liber Abaci*. It taught merchants and bankers the principles of computing prices and profits by introducing oriental algebra; in addition, Fibonacci is said to have invented double bookkeeping. His work may have laid the foundations of the advanced Italian thinking and practice in money and banking, improving the tools for economic acquisition, one of the strongest of human motives (Langholm, 1992, pp. 17–18; Goetzmann, 2005). In due time (fourteenth and fifteenth centuries) economic calculation made possible the growth of companies with a sizeable, multi-market, multi-period organization, led and managed by the remote control of the owners. 'The example of the powerful Italian companies in the thirteenth century had now found followers north of the Alps' (Pirenne, 1953, p. 215; see also de Jong, 1997, esp. pp. 58–69).

SCHOLASTIC ECONOMICS: THE PARISIAN SCHOLARS

The concepts and economic arguments introduced by the Parisian scholars were innovative and, moreover, part and parcel of a system of thinking which covered both positive and normative aspects. The latter developed out of the confrontation between analysis and the moral and political views dominant at the time. Henry of Ghent (?–1293), an author who evidently took a personal interest in economic subjects, deserves to be seen as a central figure. He drew copiously on various elements originating in Greek philosophy, Roman law and Christian moral theology and united these in a whole close to a scholastic economic synthesis (Langholm, 1992, pp. 249–65). Throughout his Parisian career (1273–93) a number of quodlibet questions were disputed in semi-annual sessions relating to property, exchange, value, prices, money and so on. His views earned him the reputation as the most liberal writer, defending both goods and money exchange, provided that the terms are just. For a just price to emerge, parties should move their terms 'like the arms of the scales until justice is attained and the tongue of the scales rests in a perpendicular position between arms carrying equal weights' (pp. 255–6). This is most likely the first statement of the principle of equilibrium in the history of economics. Such a price was called the 'common estimate of value' (that is, the competitive price) and it is based on the actions of free and understanding sellers and buyers who negotiate to reach agreement. It presumes freedom of decision, consent and absence of 'fraud'. 'Fraud' covers not only deceit, but also monopolistic practices, such as price discrimination.

A second contribution is the added-value principle. 'Something new and different' is added by the artisan who buys materials for making saleable goods which pay for his labour and skill; likewise, the merchant produces utilities of location, storage, labour and assumes risk. And he may act on goods which abound at some time whereas they are rare and valuable at other times.

Third, Henry distinguishes between pricing by means of supply and demand, generating a fluctuating price and valuation by means of price fixing. Using a secular favourite of economists – the horse market – he posits the case of a fleet of ships bringing horses to a seaport market; suddenly, all head for another town. If then, a horse which was bought for a low price becomes expensive due to scarcity is this to be considered 'fraud' or monopoly pricing? Not at all: whether or not the shift was foreseen or due to additional cost, the just price may be a function of supply and demand. In contrast, suppose a man with exceptional knowledge about horses and their market. Such a trader will be observed by others, less knowledgeable, but knowing that he knows better. When he buys and sells they may profitably imitate him. Thus he sets the price and leads the market, earning something extra: 'the work of his industry which he has exercised with regard to those horses by buying them'. The word '*industria*', used in scholastic economics in connection with the use of borrowed money expresses not merely diligence but especially business acumen. Thus Henry recognizes the entrepreneurial function, linking value creation, imitation, credit giving and price fixing: an embryonic Schumpeterian theory. His economics, including the advanced views on money, shows all the marks of his descent from the largest city in the most urbanized region; in 1290, Ghent had some 60,000 inhabitants and nearby Bruges 40,000.

Somewhat later, Jean Buridan put forward a surprisingly modern demand theory. Langholm (1355 [1979], p. 139), makes the link between Buridan, Ferdinando Galiani and Carl Menger through Buridan's concept of *indigentia*, interpreted as effective demand. However we may think about such a claim, Buridan (1300–58), a logician and philosopher of Flemish origin and twice rector of Paris University, had the main contents of demand theory. He states preference scales (on which trade is also based, he says), discusses the surplus which the consumer derives from purchases at the going market price, sees the alternatives which may be considered because of relative scarcities, and disposes of the notion of an inherent and different usefulness of goods. This comes down to recognizing their potential economic character. (On Buridan's economics, see especially Krop (1988, pp. 48–76) who provides a translation in Dutch of the text with notes on economic sources.)

There were several other Flemish writers of which Giles of Lessines (1230–1304) may have been the first to author a treatise on economics, written between 1276 and 1293. Its name, *De Usuris in communi et de usurarum contractibus*, suggests less than it contains for it discusses not only usury but also value, price, exchange, labour, risk and profits. In total the book has 20,000 words, packed in 21 chapters and is divided in three equal parts containing general principles, cases and policy precepts. So, was not the lay-out a direction indicator?

Not long ago the book of Giles was ascribed to Thomas Aquinas but this has been corrected (Langholm, 1992, p. 299). It states the central dictum of scholastic economics: 'A thing is justly estimated according to the utility which it brings to its possessor, and it is justly worth as much as it can be sold for without fraud' (Giles, as cited by Langholm, p. 306). Fraud offended the common good.

SCHOLASTIC TERMS: COMPETITION

Scholastic theory had the just price as its main concept. It was derived from Roman law practice and, moreover, in substance agreed with Aristotle's idea of virtuous, good or just conduct which is the mean or intermediate between excess and deficiency. With respect to the just price the scholastics were challenged by Aristotle himself for he said: 'We must, however, not only make this general statement, but also apply it to the individual facts. … Our statements must harmonize with the facts in these cases' (*Nicomachean Ethics*, Book 2, translation W.D. Ross, Oxford, 1925 and reprints). What more could be said about the just price?

According to de Roover 'A bewildering variety of answers have been given to this question, but it seems clear to me that the just price was nothing more mysterious than the competitive price, with this important qualification: the Doctors never questioned the right of the public authorities to set and regulate prices' (de Roover, in Kirshner 1974, p. 277). Likewise, Schumpeter states that neither Aristotle nor Thomas Aquinas should be interpreted as clinging to some 'objective value' when they discuss the just price: 'His [St Thomas's] *quantitas valoris* is not something different from price but is simply normal competitive price' (ibid., p. 93).

The problem we encounter when explaining the just price in this way is that scholastic writers rarely mention the word 'competition'. This is not insignificant in view of the fact that as from Aristotle onwards, they knew the word and substance of what we consider the contrary, namely monopoly.

The first author to use the word competition in the sense of rivalry was Luis Molina (1535–1601). Molina belonged to the Spanish–Portuguese school of Salamanca, famous for its monetary analysis, and was a professor at the University of Evora in Portugal. In his published lectures of the years 1568–83, entitled *De Justitia et Jure* (1593 and following years published in instalments) he gives an account of his method of investigating a conflict between Spanish wool growers and Venetian merchants.

The complaint was that the merchants conspired to bring down the purchase price, but Molina found out that the Spanish king had raised the tax rate on wool sales, increased the export levy and that only a few percent of the price reduction was due to the Venetian action. Moreover, he had good reason, he says, for they had advanced money to the farmers on the next year's wool clip. So the just price was not contravened even though the buying number of merchants was small and they had coordinated the purchases. But Molina remained an exception for neither the other scholastic authors nor their Protestant counterparts in the northern European countries such as Hugo Grotius, Johannes Althaus, Pieter de la Court or Edward Misselden availed themselves of the opportunity to use the term. In the eighteenth century Montesquieu (1689–1755) wrote in his *Défense de l'Esprit des Lois* (Defence of the Spirit of the Laws) published in 1748, the sentence 'C'est la concurrence qui met un prix juste aux marchandises et qui établit les vrais rapports entre elles' (Book 20, ch. 9). The sentence summarizes the theory by stating that it is competition which achieves a just and socially acceptable price and also establishes the true price differences between the several goods.

However, Molina and Montesquieu were the black swans and all the other writers based themselves upon the 'free market' or 'free trading' when they opposed monopoly or exclusive dealing.

MONOPOLY

In contrast, 'monopoly' as a term has found an entrance in the literature since Aristotle exposed its doings in his *Politics* (1943, pp. 63–74). His tales about the Sicilian who bought up all the iron ore on the island and the philosopher Thales of Milete who acquired the olive presses of his native city are well known; both sold at very high prices and Aristotle recommended the monopoly principle to rulers as a device of 'universal application' to amass riches. Of course, such a precept did not fall on the deaf ears of practitioners. However, the scholastic academics and their successors rejected the advice almost unanimously and turned the argument full circle: society should be on guard against the exploitation of power by the rulers who would indeed use every opportunity to enlarge or replenish their treasure. Also, they were generally opposed to the monopolizing leanings of guilds or corporations of merchants, and price and other restrictive agreements did not find favour, either. Consequently, they required interventions by state and city governments to prevent and correct monopolies, agreements and conspiracies, exclusive dealings and so on. Price discrimination was rejected from the point of view of reasonable or just prices which had to be equal for all buyers or sellers unless justified by objective circumstances. Because of these broad descriptions and policy requirements, the scholastic economists and their successors were the first to argue in favour of an active antitrust policy. De Roover wrote: 'To my mind there is no doubt that the conspiracy idea of the anti-trust laws goes back to scholastic precedents and is rooted in the medieval concept of the just price' (de Roover, 1958, pp. 426–8). Grotius extended the argument towards the international field and spoke of 'the unimpeachable axiom of the Law of Nations, called a primary rule or first principle, the spirit of which is self-evident and immutable, to wit: Every nation is free to travel to every other nation, and to trade with it' (*Mare Liberum*, 1609, Introduction).

Adam Smith, who clearly saw the great gap which separates the two prices – for did he not write in *The Wealth of Nations* (1776 [1976] pp. 78–9): 'The price of monopoly is upon every occasion the highest which can be got. The natural price or the price of free competition, on the contrary, is the lowest which can be taken, not upon every occasion, indeed, but for any considerable time together'? – was more reticent. He underlined the drawbacks of the restrictions to and the regulations of free trade (ibid. pp. 140ff.) and, as clearly as his scholastic predecessors pointed out the reason for these impediments, but he did not share their advocacy of authoritative interference in the market's proceedings. The reason for the impediments, he remarked, was price: 'It is to prevent this reduction of price, and consequently of wages and profit, by restraining that free competition which would most certainly occasion it, that all corporations, and the greater part of corporation laws, have been established'. And on top of the restrictions to national trade and manufacturing he seemed not to see merit in the high duties upon foreign goods imported by alien merchants (ibid. p. 144).

But why did Smith show so much equanimity, not to say indifference, to the inflictions of economic damage which he recognized as being of nationwide importance? The famous sentence about the 'People of the same trade, [who] seldom meet together, even for merriment and diversion, but the conversation ends in a conspiracy against the publick, or in some contrivance to raise prices' appears in the middle of an extended discussion of this phenomenon. He remarks that charters to found a corporation that restricts competition 'have been readily granted … upon paying a fine to the king' (ibid., pp. 140–41); from continental countries it was known that the licences to guilds or corporations were given in exchange for annual taxes (Pirenne, 1953, pp. 183–84). Thus the 'defence of the common liberty against such oppressive monopolies' (*The Wealth of Nations*, p. 170) came to nothing.

THE JUST PRICE

However, let us return to the Schumpeter–de Roover interpretation of the just price as the normal competitive price. Not only was the word 'competition' hardly mentioned by nearly all authors up to and including Adam Smith (who, as de Roover reminds us, prefixed it by the article and did not use it as an abstract term). More important are the substantial arguments which should pass for review. In discussing this issue it may be helpful to consult the schematic presentation of scholastic price theory and to remind ourselves constantly of the overriding importance of the concept of the common good, the compass of scholastic thinking as was mentioned earlier (Table 2.1). The general term 'scholastic theory' covers the market and price theories developed between 1200 and 1800 (as the rough bounds of the period) and which shared almost unanimously the scheme of a basic, relatively constant price encircled by a more or less fluctuating price. In this respect the theories of Cantillon and Smith in the eighteenth century were not different from those of Molina in the sixteenth century or from those of Henry of Ghent or Giles of Lessines in the thirteenth century. Terms changed nevertheless, from 'common estimation' or 'just price' in the earlier times to 'natural price' or 'free-market price' later and even to 'normal price' in the late nineteenth century when Marshall used it.

Table 2.1 Scholastic price theory: actors, methods and themes

Authoritative pricing	Market pricing	
	Monopoly pricing	Free-market pricing
By governmental decision (state, crown, city & town)*	By individual persons or groups of persons* Engrossing** Forestalling** Regrating** Illicit agreements, secret pacts, conspiracies, bidders' rings**	Common estimation*
By an appointed mediator*	By associations: guild regulations on fixed or minimum prices*	Entrepreneurial estimation* Cost–plus pricing** Effective demand pricing** Market mediation between surpluses and deficits** Target pricing**
Supervised and/or controlled regulation by an organization or association*	By corporations with an exclusive charter*	By one-to-one negotiation, including 'in country buying'**
		Auctions and other public sales* Bidding-up** 'Dutch' auction (lowering the price until a bid is made)**

Notes:
* Who or what institution determines the price?
** Method of price determination. Fix-price and flexible-price methods were used in several categories.
Subjects priced: Goods, especially basic foodstuffs; land and natural resources; labour services; legal rights; money, both domestic and foreign (exchange); bills of exchange, loans and other liquid capital.

A second aspect which was shared by the authors of the period was their common aversion to monopoly and monopolistic pricing, though in varying degrees. For, naturally, a price deviating to some extent from the 'common' or 'natural' or 'normal' price which was supposed to reflect the common good had to be investigated and explained. If then (see Table 2.1) a wide variety of methods of price formation were found, the question naturally arose whether the results thereof could all be considered acceptable or just. Opinions soon differed substantially, and they also underwent important changes in the course of time. If we phrase the question not as 'What is the just price?' but 'What person or institution determines the price that best serves the common good and how should this be done?', we may gain another perspective and have a useful taxonomy for ordering and comparing the answers.

In the views of the Parisian school, a just price could be fixed by some authority (such as emperor or king or town rulers), by guild associations, if – as was mostly the case – under the control and having a retractable permission of the community, or by licensed corporations. The literature also admitted as just the pricing by means of free-market estimations and negotiations. Included in the latter category were the price-fixing actions by entrepreneurs of the type described by Henry of Ghent, even if done by only a few.

The range of options to arrive at a just price was therefore rather wide. The main choice was between authoritative or legal pricing and free-market pricing as private monopolistic price setting was practically unanimously rejected: only a few writers approved of guild regulations and they said so during the first part of the period covered when these organizations were not yet strong enough to leave their mark. It is true that some corporations with an exclusive charter had monopolistic prerogatives (for example, the Indian companies of the various nations) but their real powers were limited as international rivalry continued unabated. Also, protectionism against outsiders was motivated with non-economic and predominantly military arguments. Examples were the Portuguese Carreira da India in the sixteenth century, the Dutch and English East India Companies in the seventeenth and eighteenth centuries and the British Act of Navigation (1651), rejected by Grotius and defended by Adam Smith. These creatures of authoritative interference made their appearance only after the Parisian school had ceased to exist. The strongest opponent to an authoritative monopoly was probably Nicolas Oresmius (c. 1330–82) who not only denounced debasement of the currency by the prince as a tyrannical abuse but extended this condemnation to commodities like salt, grain and other necessities. It was in the name and on behalf of the newly arisen class of free burghers that Oresmius protested against these misuses of royal powers which he compared to the princely 'authority to misuse the wives of any of its citizens' (Oresmius, ca. 1360 [1956], p. 40). The argument backing up these condemnations was that the coins, made of precious metals, belonged to the people like other goods and that the princely stamps on the coins were only a nominal imprint.

Gradually the balance shifted against authoritative pricing, whether inspired by monopoly considerations or not. The Spanish Salamanca school which embraced a group of influential theologians and lawyers during the sixteenth century (they taught at southern European universities and were advisers to Charles V, Philip II and several popes) was critical of any governmental price decisions. Some prominent authors like Martin de Azpilcueta (1492/3–1580, often called Navarro in the literature) rejected legally fixed prices. The arguments were much more economic than the politically inspired reasoning of Oresmius. Navarro said that a '*tasa*' (a price legally fixed) allows traders to sell goods of inferior quality at a price defended as rightful in a legal sense. Moreover, a *tasa* price was not appropriate; for in times of great urgency and need no supplier would respect it, whereas in times of plenty the fixed price would be undercut and consequently be superfluous. Being well versed in market tactics, Navarro also mentioned that a legally fixed price invited merchants to tie sales of a free good, for example wine, at a high price to a transaction of a good like wheat which was subject to a legal price that was lower than the natural price.

Molina, who studied at Salamanca but lectured at the Portuguese universities of Evora and Coimbra between 1561 and 1591, also expressed an aversion to the *tasa*, though he left some room for it by stipulating that a fixed legal price had to follow the natural price – and, in a sense assumes it – if the latter moves within some customary band. The natural price, which is identified with the just price, is so-called 'because it follows from the things themselves, without any human law or decree, yet dependent on many circumstances through which it is changed' (*De Justitia et Jure*, as cited by Höffner, 1941, p. 113). A further distinction, within the natural price, brings Molina on the trail of Henry of Ghent; he distinguished between the current market price (if free from fraud) for long-existing goods such as wheat, wines, cloth and shoes, and the new goods coming from overseas such as Brazilian wood, Indian spices and so on. While the former rest on common estimation the latter can be set unilaterally or be negotiated bilaterally. Molina even defends the colonial trade monopoly of the Portuguese Crown with a reference to the pioneering activities of King Henry the Navigator (who died in 1460) because he financed the overseas travel at his own expense. Therefore he was entitled to monopolistic revenues, either directly or by means of licensing, which moreover saved the country extra taxes. Molina conceals that 'In order to help finance the cost of the initial voyages, the Infante Dom Henrique had received from the Crown a wide variety of commercial monopolies', not only overseas but domestic too, and: 'His activities as a monopolist and engrosser provoked reiterated protests from various sectors of Portuguese society' (Boxer, 1969, p. 322).

Authoritative pricing could also be effectuated using mediators, according to scholastic theory and practice. Already in the thirteenth century brokers had appeared throughout Europe, and in Venice even earlier. With the rise of cities and detailed regulation of economic life, one big gap in the system which was left concerned the continued imports of necessary and worthwhile goods. The traders in such goods escaped the city rules and about the only measure the town government could take was to appoint a mediator. In this way the city could use the size of its market to put pressure on the alien merchants and internalize part of the benefits (if there was sufficient competition among the suppliers). If successful: 'the merchant found himself compelled to make all his contracts with the burgesses through the intermediary of an official broker' (Pirenne, 1953, pp. 177–8). Names testify to the widespread occurrence: *sensales* in Venice, *Unterkäufer* in Germany, *makelaeren* in the Low Countries and broker in England. These persons, legally appointed after the practice had become established, usually earned a high income and often rose to social prominence. Another type of mediator often mentioned in the scholastic texts was the 'good man', incidentally called in to make estimates of risk, cost or loss and in particular when just or future prices were involved. Price fixing when a credit sale at future prices under uncertain conditions is at stake was one of those cases where an agreed or appointed mediator (being knowledgeable and impartial) could be helpful in oiling the wheels of commerce.

Recently, Henry W. Spiegel (1991, p. 629), notable historian of economic thought, has voiced the view that: 'The just price was the market price prevailing at a certain place at a certain time, as estimated by a fair-minded person. The estimate might be expressed in the form of a range of prices rather than as a fixed amount'. We cannot agree with such an appreciation: the mediator was only one of the possibilities to determine the just price and it was not he who fixed the range; in fact there were two ranges. First, the definite range of the *laesio enormis*, derived from Roman law, which stipulated that a seller who overcharged by more than 50 per cent (over the just price) could be taken to court and if so, was liable to indemnification; likewise, a buyer who had pushed down the price to a seller by more than 50 per cent. The second range, within the previous one, had recourse to what was the deviation from the normal or common competitive price. Langholm (1992, pp. 580–81) has pointed out that the common or normal competitive price may cover two diverse things: a price which usually obtains in the market and a price which expresses a joint estimate or a sort of community consensus. The latter price may be out of reach of poor people but that is a matter of charity not of justice. If common means usual, it is a matter of market actualities: the price of wheat fluctuated much more than the prices of oxen or of cheese.[3] If common means consensus, it pertains to political or moral standards which may likewise change or diverge but surely because of other determining factors. A mediator operating in such a tangle of rules, customs and circumstances might try to find some range(s) but his task was to fix a price binding on the parties.

MOVABLE AND FIXED PRICES

Among the scholastic authors Henry of Ghent was the first to draw attention to this distinction in the context of free-market transactions. Roman law in the *Digest* (the systematic collection of Roman non-statute law, made by Justinian in 533) formulated the first principle quite clearly: 'the prices of things do not work on the basis of the affection or utility of single persons but commonly', which implied that such a price, movable because of the many buyers and sellers, could also be a just price alongside a price fixed by some authority. At the end of the twelfth century, Bolognese lawyers began to restate the maxim and shifted the emphasis towards the justness of a price reached by the estimations of all parties in an open market: 'A thing is worth as much as it can be sold for – commonly' (*communiter*) (Langholm, 1992, pp. 260–62; Gordon, 1975, pp. 128–31). But Henry also justified a price fixed by a man with expert knowledge even if such a price was above the common estimation and if it was imitated by others. That opened the way for an individual to know better than the market or, by means of adding value, to improve upon the current price or even to mediate between the diverging relative scarcities of different markets – a practice which not a few earlier writers had frowned upon.

Moreover, wide areas of pricing were withdrawn from the discussion, either because they were hardly visible, such as was the case with negotiations on a personal basis: people often went out of town for 'country buying' with farmers. Or the business was probably too special and technical for the authors who were mostly generalists. Auctions, together with *pandingen* (pawnings) and other vendue-sales, are examples. Wagenaar, the Amsterdam city historian, remarks (1760, Vol. 3, pp. 24–31) that auctions and public sales covered a great variety of goods and he divides these into several categories: ships and parts, buildings, merchant goods, luxury goods like jewels, paintings, mirrors, wines and liquors, and so on, and he discusses the city bylaws and other regulations often made in medieval times. He also points out the techniques of auctions, bidding-up and bidding-down or Dutch auction together with the moves, undertaken by the players, to bend the market in their favour. In combined auctions, where the highest bidder-up received money (*plok-* or *plukpenningen*) even before the bidding-down had started or been ended, some people joined in the process without being able, as it turned out, to make the required deposit

– just to pocket the money and to speculate on a better selling price in case the bidding-down went to the level of the bid-up price. If caught, such persons, called 'sheep', could be imprisoned for several months or whipped.

Much bigger transactions, such as those involving Indian spices and peppers, were initially sold – like the Portuguese had done – in big lots and, after some preferential deals had become known, were sold at auction as from 1640. But combinations of brokers interfered with free pricing at some periods by limiting their jointly agreed bids. And the strategy of the big merchants *vis-à-vis* their international and national competitors, used targeted prices to hinder them or drive them out of the market. In sum, free-market pricing was not only of the impersonal, objective variety with fluctuations around a natural or equilibrium level. Fluctuations could be enormous and have devastating effects, as the section on the corn market, below, will show. Langholm therefore speaks of the 'fictive' or 'hypothetical' competitive market: 'In real life there are all kinds of markets, all degrees of competitiveness and irregularity' (Langholm, 1992, p. 231). To equate the common estimation with the just price and then with the competitive market price in a normal situation is a truism, and if it has to have any meaning serves as a standard or measuring rod. It is an 'as if' price, as we know from the discussions during the 1970s in Europe when, in order to determine whether a particular price or price level was adequate in a particular country, reference was made to another country considered to be 'more competitive' (for example, in pharmaceutical markets). The hypothetical character was recognized and underlined by various authors of the sixteenth-century Salamancan school. Höffner (1941, pp. 113–16) quotes five writers of that school who ask themselves whether in the price range usually assumed, there is not an exact price more adequate and just which is only known to God (for example, John de Lugo). To us, John says, this 'mathematically just price' is unknown because we do not know, like God, all the determining factors and their relative weights.

To avoid further digressions it would seem to be opportune to contrast the two main forms of price determination considered acceptable as a way of valuing transactions, both by scholastics as well as modern authors, in free markets (Table 2.2).

Table 2.2 Price determination

	Movable or mobile prices	Fixed and stable prices
Determined by	Demand and supply	Supply or demand
Submitted to	Fluctuations	Adjustments
Parties consider	Price as a datum	Price as a factum
Competition features & price formation	Anonymous, everybody is a price taker and nobody knows the price before market opens	Price makers & takers Personal and recognizable, institutional Price set before market opens
Prevailing market price is	Result of contest	Challenge to contest
Performance test	Price = marginal cost = minimum average cost	Level and growth of net added value per unit of measurement

One main reason for distinguishing the two versions of free-market pricing is their divergence in the course of time since Henry of Ghent presented them as in one breath. But before the Salamancan school subscribed to the equilibrium paradigm, Buridan laid the foundations for the entrepreneurial or disequilibrium alternative. This fourteenth century rector of the Parisian University followed the trail of the nominalists and was, it is said, responsible for 'the most interesting dynamical theorising before Galileo' (Gordon, 1975, p. 223).

ENTREPRENEURIAL THEORY FOUNDATIONS

As we have seen earlier, Buridan's economics was demand oriented: he introduced the idea (though not the name) of consumer surplus based on 'effective demand' (Langholm, 1979, pp. 123–45). In addition he also has the producer's surplus in view. If one focuses on the value which is added in economic activity both for the producer and the consumer and which is basically different for individual parties, an explanation is required which puts human decision making in the centre of things. Man is not intent on adapting to uncontrollable events whether stemming from natural or human forces. Human willpower drives his reason or at least acts in conjunction with it. Reason is nevertheless essential in spotting and distinguishing the options. Any man who works and lives through reason only – the perfectly rational man – will perish, Buridan maintains, when confronted with situations where he is unable to choose. In modern language this may be the case when the choice is between perfectly homogeneous goods or when there is a superfluity of heterogeneous goods: 'the embarrassment of choice' as the French say (*L'embarras du choix*).

Buridan's ass demonstrates the dilemma: the animal, located equi-distant from two heaps of hay is unable to make a rational choice between the two identities and perishes of hunger. In a comment, Murray Rothbard has argued that the ass was not perfectly rational because it neglected the third choice, namely starving to death (Rothbard, 1995, p. 74). Having chosen not to opt for that possibility, the animal could have chosen to eat one of the bundles at random, he says. This objection is unfounded. It ignores the fact that choosing to opt for not starving means to opt for living, and that choice was as impossible as the one between the heaps of hay. For death was an unknown. Thus, on the basis of the assumption of rationality as the exclusive guidance to human action, no choice can be made. More is necessary.[4]

Buridan opposes two concepts of freedom, namely the freedom to choose (*libertas oppositionis*) and the freedom to set a goal (*libertas finalis ordinationis*). He also confronts the latter with universal causality and they seem incompatible. But regressing on experience, he says there are actors with a will and actors without one. Unavoidable causality does indeed steer the latter but not the former. Their free will supersedes an impossible or absent choice. Only if willpower is absent does causality reign supreme; then the actor is out of control. Freedom to set a goal is rated higher by Buridan than the other freedom because, though free choice is indispensable and necessary to find the options, it is important to realize the potentials included in these. If one is prepared to admit that experience plays a role, Buridan's argument sweeps away the basis of the choice theory as it has come to dominate economic theory.

It hangs in the air as a hypothetical, unable to cope with uncertainty, many cases of unforeseen change or future development and so on. This means that it cannot see the function and role of the entrepreneur as the pivotal figure in economic activity. It legitimizes a view of economics in which, apart from the entrepreneur, the consumer is also reduced: to an undistinguished utility sucker. Status, identity and style, or the social influences on demand are eliminated as if the world needs only consistent 'rational fools' as Sen has called them (Sen, 1979, pp. 87–109). Fortunately, a study has recently appeared which shows that the incorporation of the wider aspects of consumer behaviour in valid theory is a distinct but neglected possibility (Mason, 1998).

Buridan's logic has cleared the way for the development of European market theory, but, obviously, the authors who devoted themselves to the study of the entrepreneurial factor may not have been directly influenced. On the other hand Buridan, who was very popular in the scientific community, wrote on logic, mathematics, physics and ethics and there are still known to exist 50 manuscripts and four early printings (in the Paris National Library) as well as a late printing from Oxford (1637) of his *Ethics*. The range of his topics is rather wide, though in this respect he does not deviate much from contemporaries who also wrote on economics.

CONFLICTS OF INTEREST

At all times there has been not only opposition between the interests of producers and consumers but also between various groups of producers. This manifested itself in particular during the fourteenth century when Buridan wrote. Two types of entrepreneurs began to make their appearance. The older established artisans and small merchants united, with the aid of some pressure from the town rulers, into guilds. These craftsmen-entrepreneurs lived by the local market, owned their tools, had limited personnel and had prices fixed by the associations or independently but under the control of the guilds. The aim was to regulate competition within the group and to protect against outsiders. However, it cannot be denied that as a rule those associations also secured high quality standards, which have remained throughout the ages, as was testified by *Time Magazine* in a special issue on European craftmanship.[5]

The other group were the export-entrepreneurs. They produced for international commerce or much beyond their home towns, purveying to the wholesale merchants who were involved in international trade. From these merchants they received the raw materials and to them they delivered the finished goods. Capital and labour were divided and the workers had no contact with the market. The cloth industry was the prototype *par excellence* and was represented in all European centres of importance: Florence, Ghent, Ypres, Leyden and so on. It was closely followed by the metalworking industry (Lucca, Dinant and so on) and other branches and all these export industries were growing strongly. Conflicts arose between those groups when the large traders started to interfere with the markets of the locals or when they complained about the high wage standards inside the manufacturing towns or the rigid trade regulations. In addition, in the sixteenth and seventeenth centuries there were conflicts between the large corporations, run by the elite of the merchant class and other merchants or newcomers who wanted access to the overseas trades secured by monopoly licences of the corporations.

These conflicts provide the background for the writings of the most important Dutch economist in industrial matters, Pieter de la Court (1618–85). His books are interesting to read for they paint a picture of the time and they provide a clear view on the role of the large merchant, such as he was himself, in the textile and cloth manufacturing industry of his native city, the largest manufacturing centre in the Netherlands. One of his books, *The Interest of Holland* (1662 with an extended edition of 1669) was translated into German (three times, in 1665 and 1668), into French (1709) and into English (in 1702). John de Witt, the most important politician of the 1660s in the Dutch republic, is given as the author, but this is an error for de Witt was murdered in 1672. The reason is not clear; did the publisher want to draw attention to the book or to hide the identity of the real author? Another book was *The Wealth of the City of Leyden*, 1659, which circulated initially in manuscript. These books do not stand out so much because of new concepts (which were not there) or because, as was to be expected, the author attacks the monopoly positions of the guilds, the weighing halls, and the East India Company, in the name of economic freedom. Rather it is the type of argument he uses. This gets a new twist as de la Court points out the static and dynamic inefficiencies of their construction. The guilds are reproached for not having regard for the different tastes of their customers but only to their own members' desires. Too high a quality and ditto prices eliminate too many customers, who defect to other towns and rural industry. Entrepreneurs miss profitable sales. If qualities are differentiated, for example, by means of labelling, the clients can weigh the costs against the utilities and production rigidities can be avoided. These also hamper initiative and prevent new things from making their appearance. In sum, 'it is clear that this country can only prosper with those who row best'. This translation hides a quibble, for the term '*welvaren*' which is given here as 'prosper' has a double meaning in Dutch. It may designate economic prosperity or 'to steer a ship well'. In this chapter (*Interest*, 1662, 15, p. 41) he argues against the Indian corporations; their exclusive licences foster the position of the managers, who, being secure, become negligent and exclude more capable people, and whose monopoly reduces general employment. More companies in this profitable trade would decrease the profits of the East India Company indeed, but not total profits and employment for the country as a whole. Smith discusses joint stock companies having a monopoly with similar arguments but grants them a 'monopoly of the trade for a certain number of years … like a monopoly of a new machine … and that of a new book to its author'. Having a monopoly on a book of his already for 28 years and hoping for another 14 years, how much is a reproach of a trading monopoly really worth? (See *The Wealth of Nations*, 1776 [1976], Vol. 2, p. 754 and note 69.)

Summing up, de la Court was neither a mercantilist nor a free trader; he advocated a society led by the great, independent entrepreneurs. He favoured a republic of the type he lived in but also voiced the well-known disdain that big businessmen have for universities and their research; stressing the demand side again he wryly remarks: 'if there are students, one can make as many professors as one wants to have' (*Wealth of the City of Leyden*, 1659 [1911], p. 31).

COMPETITION AND UNCERTAINTY

With Richard Cantillon (1696–1734) we arrive at the economist who drew together several of the distinctive lines of thinking from previous times in a view of the market process that was quite unique. It is not suggested that he knew the preceding literature, only that its main elements were recognized in contemporary society.

First, there was individual property of labour and resources and there were general as well as special needs among the members of the society. The latter were divided into landowners, entrepreneurs and those working for wages. The landowners possessed the land and other natural resources; they did no work and spent their income on the greatest variety of goods in conformity with their preferences.

Second, the entrepreneurs were the active economic agents, demonstrating the willpower described by Buridan, for they strive after profits from their operations. These profits flow from the discharge of their economic function which is to buy or rent at some fixed price from landowners and workers, land, produce and labour in order to sell the goods and services to consumers and other entrepreneurs at an uncertain, fluctuating price. The difference between those two prices is profit or loss. The class of entrepreneurs is the only one to run a risk in their activities and that risk is basically a profound uncertainty.

Third, the wage earners are hired to work for the other classes but mainly for the entrepreneur. They do not engage in active decision making, receiving their orders from the farmers, industrial producers, transporters, middlemen such as wholesale dealers and retailers and all others who buy 'fixed' and sell 'movable'. Service providers such as lawyers, doctors, painters, chimney sweepers and even beggars (!) also belong to the entrepreneurial group. They have certain costs such as expenditures and always have their time as an alternative cost.

Cantillon's entrepreneur therefore reacts to the shifts in demand in markets and the price differences that continuously widen and narrow. This occurs between city and countryside, between products and services, and between necessary, convenient and luxury products.

Cantillon's entrepreneur is the prime example of the mediating, arbitraging agent in our scheme. Essential in his operations is the forward-looking, discerning and anticipating ability of the central figure in this economist's view of the market economy. In this respect, Cantillon differs from his predecessor de la Court who stressed the productive, organizing function of entrepreneurs. Cantillon takes the analysis one important step further on the road of theorizing. He embeds the role of his hero within the system of interdependent markets. The economy is a unified whole; conflicts there are, certainly. But all groups and classes are submitted through the pricing system to a measure of coordination which limits their autonomy. The hinges in this 'apparatus' (which is not Cantillon's word, he does not cherish a mechanistic view of the world) are the profit and loss accounts. Through prices, profits and losses the enterprises are distributed over the branches of economic activity and regions. Some grow, others decline; prosperity will be unevenly divided.

Cantillon has an interesting example which shows that the number of competitors is not essential for rivalry to occur. Suppose a village has two tailors who serve the community. Their income will be different, for, he says, the one will have more clients than the other. He may be better in winning over the customers; or he works more aptly or durably or one of them spots the fashions in cutting clothes better than his competitor. Nevertheless, the prices they quote cannot diverge too much. Suddenly one of the tailors dies. The other will raise his prices to a monopoly level and there are no other ways to avoid these but to go to a tailor in a neighbouring village or city or to wait for another one to establish himself. The first option, costing time and money, has the advantage of limiting the level to which the monopolist can raise his prices. This duopoly case is interesting for a number of reasons.

First, it is a heterogeneous duopoly; as such it is much more of a reality than the homogeneous cases of the mineral water suppliers, who, having no production costs, disregard each other's pricing manoeuvres, or quantitative adaptations. Duopolies with a supply of varied goods in a particular market are frequent in the modern world too: Boeing versus Airbus; chipmachine maker ASML against two smaller Japanese producers; Unilever–Nestlé in packaged icecream; Microsoft versus Linux and so on.

Second, the case shows that there is a price band between the 'pure' monopoly price and the competitive price plus the cost which consumers have to incur by going to a distant supplier. The higher the latter price the smaller the price range will be, given that the 'pure' monopoly price is there. The latter may be very high if a monopolist has to serve a market which has the same dimension as previously without any supplies coming from an alternative producer, and, in addition, if the product is a necessary good.

Third, neither the pure monopoly price nor the competitive price plus cost can be considered a just or acceptable price if governmental policy measures are possible: one may think of recruiting another supplier from elsewhere, paying a newcomer for learning the trade (the case of Airbus), or obliging the monopolist to provide for a coercive licence (in the case of a technically advanced and essential product).

The conclusion would seem to be that it is not the duopoly which is problematic in a heterogeneous case but the level to which a quasi-monopoly price can be raised. Further, all customers benefit from the restoration or continuation of a duopoly, including those from the country where the monopolist is established, if the relevant market is wider than a purely national one.

BAUDEAU'S INNOVATIONS

If de la Court and Cantillon were the first to propose new and alternative interpretations of the entrepreneurial function, Nicolas Baudeau (1730–92) added the third one. He was a clergyman who was initially opposed to, but in 1766 joined, the group of 'economists' called the physiocrats. He did so by founding a weekly publication in 1765, to disseminate physiocratic ideas (Meek, 1962, p. 32). Thus, one may consider him together with François Quesnay and Comte de Mirabeau, as a leading expositor of the doctrines of this school. He was, however, no more than Anne Robert Jacques Turgot one decade later, a pure representative, for both contributed to the broadening of physiocratic concepts in important ways. In particular, they extended the entrepreneurial concept to manufacturing and commerce, making it a general one.

Still more important was Baudeau's incorporation of innovations and inventions in the entrepreneurial function. By means of new ideas or new techniques, an entrepreneur will be enabled to reduce the cost of output and to increase the revenues of sales. Through long-term leases the rents for farmers are fixed and wage levels are depressed to a fairly stable subsistence standard, Baudeau wrote in his main economic text (Baudeau, 1767 [1910], p. 47). Output, on the other hand, fluctuates as to prices and quantities, and so the entrepreneurial income is uncertain. It varies with the vagaries of the product markets. This resembles Cantillon's contribution, and, there is direct evidence that Cantillon's *Essai*, which was published in 1755, was known to Quesnay, Baudeau and other members of the school (Meek, 1962, pp. 267–8).

Baudeau takes Cantillon's position two steps beyond the coping and adaptation to uncertainty. First, like other members of the physiocratic school he was strongly in favour of better education and the dissemination of knowledge. That included technological and agricultural knowledge as well as general and practical education. The information thus gathered, they believed, would induce action by at least a number of people to undertake innovations and run their businesses in good order. The country schoolmaster, Quesnay says in his *Maxims*, is not to be disparaged by the haughty 'city men of elevated rank' (who in reality are 'nothing but hirelings paid by the wealth of the countryside'); he is the one qualified to teach the peasantry to read and write, to bring security and order into its business and to extend the farmers' knowledge of the different aspects of their calling (Meek, 1962, pp. 247 and 258).

Second, if obstacles to profitable enterprise could be removed and the right incentives were created, people would take up the opportunities and work towards the improvement of the results. The entrepreneur, who is an active agent, may apply his acquired knowledge to the reduction of costs, the improvement of produce, transport and trading arrangements and raise his income. After deduction of paid-out costs of cultivation or manufacture and an amount to compensate the advanced capital, a net income or profit would remain; this would be 'a just compensation' for the entrepreneurial efforts (Baudeau, 1767 [1910], p. 118). The removal of obstacles had regard to monopolies, regulations and protection such as had been brought into being by Colbert's mercantilistic policy, but was also related to the pricing system. In an early article, in which Quesnay had exposed his economic principles (*Hommes*, 1757, pp. 511–78 in INED ed. 1958; extracts in Meek, 1962, pp. 88–101) three price levels were distinguished. There could be '*cherté*' or an unnaturally high price as a result of monopoly or an artificial division of markets; or the price could be high due to good demand in the market ('*bon prix*') or it could be '*bon marché*', a vulgar description for a price which 'constantly failed to exceed the fundamental price'. The fundamental price of commodities 'is determined by the expenses or costs which have to be incurred in their production or preparation' (ibid., p. 93). A very low price would be ruinous for the country, its rulers, population and producers alike and could be prevented by international trade. If there is unobstructed trade within the nation, price becomes equal to the common prices which are current in other countries. Also, they will fluctuate much less than is the case within the internally broken up French market, where regional surpluses and deficits cannot be equalized.[6] And the 'large and frequent variations in prices are the deadly causes of poverty and depopulation' (ibid., pp. 94–5).

THE INTERNATIONAL MERCHANT AND TIME

Most probably, Quesnay or the other physiocrats will not have read him, but the principles of the international corn market had already been exposed more than a century before, and in some respects even more clearly. The Dutch economist Dirck Graswinckel showed in a book how the international markets in relatively homogeneous goods, especially corn, work and why government interference is, in all but the most dire circumstances, a common nuisance. Nevertheless, he also pointed to the conditions and the time element which have to be considered.

Graswinckel (1600–60) was sworn in as a lawyer and rose to the position of '*advocat-fiscaal*', managing extensive property of the states of Holland. He published a book in 1651 containing the Edicts, Decrees, Regulations and so on concerning the subject of wheat and corn. The book dealt with the possible consequences of food shortages and measures such as import and export regulations and the prohibition of advance purchases or price measures. Grains were very important in Dutch trade: they came from the countries around the Baltic sea, amounted to between 50 and 65 per cent of total imports from that area during the hundred years from the mid-sixteenth to the mid-seventeenth century, had to feed a fast-growing population and were an input to industries such as beer brewing and cattle-feeding.

But Graswinckel, in a lengthy commentary on the regulations (1651) showed nearly all of them to be harmful or superfluous. Describing Amsterdam's market as 'the warehouse of grains for the whole of Christendom' (pp. 124–5) because of the re-exports abroad, he argued that, in general, the prohibition of imports or exports would undermine the staple market and thereby Dutch food security. Domestic and foreign merchants would be loath to ship grains to this market and store it there if they could no longer be sure to benefit from the best prices to be had, either in foreign countries or in the home market. Analytically this seems obvious though politically it was far from generally accepted, even in his own country.

What made Graswinckel, at least from the point of view of market economics, an outstanding writer, was his 'keen sense of the price system' as Schumpeter remarked. Let me summarize the following points:

1. A society's wealth is, given the erratic fluctuations of resource prices, dependent on high prices and abundance of goods. Though the lower classes would be the beneficiaries of low prices, especially of foods, labour and its products will have a ready market in prosperous times. 'Nothing better than dearness in abundance', Graswinckel says (p. 122) because 'fertility' (he uses the word in the sense of productivity of land, labour and inventions) is at the basis of an abundance of goods, to be sold at high prices.
2. The grain and similar markets cannot be easily monopolized because trade in corn 'is in a thousand hands which are not dependent upon each other' (p. 146); 'monopoly is not to be feared when there are many, but few' (p. 158).
3. But suppose the merchants 'make a treaty among each other of a certain price not to sell below that price' (p. 115): they can be penalized under Article 1.6 D of the Law. However, he knows such regulations are of limited value; without such treaties they 'may preserve a silent intelligence' (that is: a tacit agreement) and be assured of each other's private interest to join in a common price rise. What should the rulers do?
4. Graswinckel says that a price control measure is useless, except in the case of the most dire circumstances (for example, war). He realizes that price increases are not brought about by treaties but are caused by scarcities and can only be made to hold by means of supply or transport restrictions. In the case of natural market developments: 'the one who stocks on the expectation of a price increase is not the cause of the rise, but the expected rise is the reason he keeps his stocks' (p. 117). And, if the market development is an artificial one, the high price will draw supplies from every corner of the world.

5. This is sustained by advance purchases and sales, which should not be opposed, as is often the case, for they span longer time periods and stimulate output with the producers by means of financing them. This will stabilize markets.
6. If governments are nevertheless apprehensive of scarcities and high prices they should, first, make an investigation of stocks in the warehouses and publish the statistics: one will invariably find that stocks are a multiple of annual consumption; second, government should buy in the market and sell at cost price to the bakers and other retailers, but intermittently and in a controlled fashion, otherwise there will be losses when the market turns. In other words: market transparency is of primary importance.

In sum, Graswinckel's theory of the grain market is imbued by considerations of time: the expectations of the market's actors, their behaviour over short and long periods and the intention to manipulate prices if they can, which, however, is not often the case. If it occurs at all, it will be short-lived.[7]

NOTES

1. For a very useful collection of documents relating to this period (texts, tables, charts, graphs, pictures and so on), see Aerts et al. (1985).
2. The new vision on scholastic economics, opened by Raymond de Roover (see Kirshner, 1974, Part 4) and Joseph Schumpeter (see Schumpeter, 1954, Part 2, Ch. 2, pp. 96–99) in the 1950s has found a confirmation and extension through the painstaking research of Odd Langholm's various publications. I refer to his monumental *Economics in the Medieval Schools* (1992) for chapters on most of the authors mentioned in the text. In addition, see his *Price and Value in the Aristotelian Tradition* (1979).
3. Postan (1972, p. 242) gives the seven-year moving average of the prices of wheat (per quarter), of cheese (per wey) and of oxen during the period 1208–1325 as based on Farmer (1956). Wheat prices fluctuated more than oxen prices which, in turn, moved more than cheese prices.
4. Rothbard seems to confuse omniscience with rationality. Apart from that, one is reminded of Pascal's wisdom: 'Le coeur a ses raisons que la raison ne connait pas'.
5. ('The quest for quality: a journey to the heart of craft', *Time*, vol. 158, no. 8, 2001, pp. 50–123).
6. There is no need to go into the debates concerning the French famines of 1764–70. Hutchison (1988, pp. 265–9, 292–4, 302–5, 345–6) reviews the contributions of the main economists in the eighteenth century to the debate about free corn markets. His assessment of the work of the physiocrats (pp. 295–7) has much to recommend. But it becomes insufficiently clear that Quesnay, like Graswinckel (1651) earlier, had stressed the need for free domestic trade alongside unrestricted international exchange. From this point of view Galiani's severe criticisms seem overrated and too late: he published the *Dialogues on the Corn Trade* only in 1770 when the famines had ended.
7. It is noteworthy that the British made the same mistake as the French policy makers when they refused to repeal the Corn Laws in 1845. A potato blight wrought a disaster in Ireland's food supply; behind the import tariff on corn, England appropriated Ireland's wheat output at rising prices. Notwithstanding David Ricardo's cogent proposals much earlier (1822) and Robert Peel's timely pleas in 1845 to lift the import restrictions, both men lost out against the great landowners in Parliament. The complicated disaster which followed is well described by Helen Litton in *The Irish Famine* (1994).

LITERATURE

Aerts, E., W. Dupon and H. van der Wee (1985), *De economische ontwikkeling van Europa*, Leuven: University of Leuven.
Aristotle (1943), *Politics*, translation B. Jowell, New York.
Aristotle (1972), *Nicomachean Ethics*, translation by W.D. Ross, London (World Classics).
Baudeau, N. ([1925] 1767), *Première introduction à la philosophie économique*, ed. A. Dubois, Paris 1910.
Boxer, C.R. (1969), *The Portuguese Seaborne Empire, 1415–1825*, Harmondsworth: Penguin Books.

Buridan, J. (1355), *Ethics*, Latin editions in Paris 1489, 1518 and in Oxford 1637.
Cantillon, R. (1952), *Essai sur la nature du commerce en général*, Text of the original 1755 edn, Paris: INED.
de la Court, P. (1659), *Het welvaren der stad Leyden*, Ed. F. Driessen, The Hague, 1911.
de la Court, P. (1662–69), *Het interest van Holland ofte gronden van Hollands welvaren*, Various editions.
de Jong, H.W. (1997), 'The European corporation', in P.H. Admiraal (ed.), *The Corporate Triangle: The Structure and Performance of Corporate Systems in a Global Economy*, De Vries Lectures on Economics, Oxford: Oxford University Press, pp. 58–69.
de Roover, R. (1958), 'The concept of the just price', *Journal of Economic History*, vol. XVIII, pp. 418–34.
Farmer, D.L. (1956), 'Price fluctuations in Angevin England', *Economic History Review*, ix.
Goetzmann, W.N. (2005), 'Fibonacci and the financial revolution', in W.N. Goetzmann and K.G. Rouwenhorst, *The Origins of Value*, Oxford: Oxford University Press, pp. 123–45.
Gordon, B. (1975), *Economic Analysis before Adam Smith*, London and Basingstoke: Macmillan.
Graswinckel, D. (1651), *Aenmerkingen en betrachtingen bij 't Placaetboek op 't Stuck van de Lyftocht* (Comments on the edicts concerning the trade in corn), Leyden.
Grotius, H. (1609), *Mare Liberum or Freedom of the Seas*, Introduction, various editions.
Höffner, J. (1941), *Wirtschaftsethik und Monopole im fünfzehnten und sechszehnten Jahrhundert*, Jena: Verlag Fischer.
Hutchison, T. (1988), *Before Adam Smith: The Emergence of Political Economy, 1662–1776*, Oxford: Oxford University Press.
Kirshner, J. (ed.) (1974), *Business, Banking and Economic Thought in Late Medieval and Early Modern Europe*, Selected studies of Raymond de Roover, Chicago and London: University of Chicago Press.
Krop, H. (1988), 'Johannes Buridan', in *De Ethiek*, Baarn: Ambo.
Langholm, O. (1992), *Economics in the Medieval Schools*, Leiden: Brill.
Langholm, O. (1979), *Price and Value in the Aristotelian Tradition*, Bergen: Universitetsforlaget.
Litton, H. (1994), *The Irish Famine: An Illustrated History*, Dublin: Wolfhound Press.
Mason, R. (1998), *The Economics of Conspicuous Consumption: Theory and Thought since 1700*, Cheltenham, UK and Lyme, USA: Edward Elgar.
Meek, R.L. (1962), *The Economics of Physiocracy*, London: Allen & Unwin.
Molina, L. (1593 and later), *De Justitia et Jure*, Discussion by Höffner, pp. 67–71 and 113–46. (Molina's life and views on prices, taxes, competition, monopoly, agreements and policies to be applied.)
Oresmius, N. (ca. 1360), *A Treatise on the Origin, Nature, Law and Alterations of Money*, Translated by C. Johnson, Camden, NJ, 1956.
Pirenne, H. (1953), *Economic and Social History of Medieval Europe*, London: Routledge.
Postan, M.M. (1972), *The Medieval Economy and Society*, London: Weidenfeld & Nicholson.
Quesnay, F. (1958), *François Quesnay et la Physiocratie*, Annotated text, Vols 1 and 2, Institut National d'Etudes Demographiques, Paris: INED.
Ricardo, D. (1822), *On Protection to Agriculture: The Works and Correspondence of David Ricardo*, Vol. 4, Pamphlets and Papers, 1815–1823, ed. P. Sraffa, Cambridge: Cambridge University Press, 1951.
Rothbard, M.N. (1995), *Economic Thought before Adam Smith*, Vol. I, Aldershot, UK and Brookfield, US: Edward Elgar.
Schumpeter, J.A. (1954), *History of Economic Analysis*, Oxford: Oxford University Press.
Sen, A. (1979), 'Rational fools. A critique of the behavioural foundations of economic theory', in F. Hahn and M. Mollis (eds), *Philosophy and Economic Theory*, Oxford: Oxford University Press, pp. 87–109.
Smith, A. (1776), *The Wealth of Nations*, 2 vols, ed. by 1976, Oxford.
Spiegel, H.W. (1991), 'Scholastic economic thought', in J. Eatwell, M. Milgate and P. Newman (eds), *The World of Economics. The New Palgrave: A Dictionary of Economics*, London and Basingstoke: Macmillan, pp. 627–33.
Wagenaar, J. (1760), *Amsterdam in zijne opkomst, aanwas, geschiedenissen*, 4 vols, Amsterdam: Isaac Tirion.

A. ADAM SMITH (1723–1790)

Henry W. de Jong

A Scotsman born in Kirkcaldy, Adam Smith spent most of his life in Glasgow and Edinburgh, where he died in 1790. He was one of the greatest polyhistors of the eighteenth century. He wrote extensively on astronomy, logic and metaphysics, language and the arts, law and government, moral theory and history as well as economics. It is opportune to point towards the Glasgow edition of the *Works and Correspondence* which covers all Smith's writings, so eminently readable in the elegant eighteenth-century style. This edition, commissioned by the University of Glasgow to celebrate the bicentenary of *The Wealth of Nations* in 1976, contains the best and most comprehensive text of the various works, complete with references, cross-references and elucidations.

Smith's market theory is exposed in Book 1 of *The Wealth of Nations* (WN). His views are of the scholastic equilibrium type, but the analysis is more encompassing and more elaborated than that of any of his predecessors. In two respects, Smith puts a different order and emphasis on his treatment of the market economy: first, he discusses a moving equilibrium. Although there is a 'natural' level of all prices, wages, interest rates, profits and rents (which are in fact 'ordinary or average rates'), these are regulated by the general circumstances of the society concerned, its riches or poverty, its advancing, stationary or declining condition, and partly by the particular nature of each employment. Market prices move above and below these natural levels in accordance with the forces of demand and supply and it is the competition between sellers and buyers which makes the prices of all commodities 'continually gravitate' towards the natural or central price. Richard Cantillon had called this the 'perpetual ebb and flow' of market prices around the 'intrinsic value' (that is, the quantity of land and labour which enter into the production of a commodity) Thus, prices move in a double sense, namely both with and within the system.

Second, Smith differs from most earlier scholastics in that he presumes that human beings display – in contrast to animals – 'the propensity to truck, barter and exchange one thing for another'. Human beings are seen by Smith in the WN primarily as commercial people; their inclinations occasion the division of labour which is the unintentional result of human endeavours but also the main lever of society's wealth.

Scholastic theory had departed from the idea of private property owned by people which requires them to specialize and exchange. The difference is that the earlier view accommodates production as antecedent to exchange whereas Smith has difficulty in explaining where the trucking propensity derives from if it is not an innate faculty. And this is debatable.

The double approach outlined ensures that the 'invisible hand' of the market brings about the best possible (or in modern terms the 'optimal') result of free human actions in terms of the common or 'publick good'. In WN, pp. 455–6, that result is related to the annual revenue of society. In *The Theory of Moral Sentiments* (TMS, pp. 184–5) Smith also makes the claim that:

> [People] are led by an invisible hand to make nearly the same distribution of the necessaries of life, which would have been made, had the earth been divided into equal portions among all its

> inhabitants, and thus without intending it, without knowing it, advance the interest of the society and afford means to the mutiplication of the species.

That obviously, is a big claim and when he says 'the beggar, who suns himself by the side of the highway, posesses that security which kings are fighting for' (TMS, p. 185), one is apt to ask whether Smith thinks this applies too when it rains cats and dogs or when the ice cracks.

The impartial spectator

The commercial orientation of people does not exclude their taking up a position with respect to the propriety of action. In the first part of TMS, Smith discusses extensively the passions, ambitions and corruptions of our moral sentiments but also the feelings of sympathy we have and how far they go in explaining our behaviour. Indeed, the opening paragraph in TMS reads:

> How selfish soever man may be supposed, there are evidently some principles in his nature, which interest him in the fortune of others, and render their happiness necessary to him, though he derives nothing from it except the pleasure of seeing it. Of this kind is pity or compassion, the emotion we feel for the misery of others ...

Smith is not an economist who defends or advocates people's behaviour on the basis of a presumed egoistic rationality. In TMS he makes the crucial distinction between self-interest (mostly called self-love in the book) and selfishness. The latter is spoken of in a pejorative sense when harm is done to others; the former is approved as 'natural'or 'harmonious' if it fits in with the views of the 'impartial spectator'. At the end of TMS he severely reproaches Dr Mandeville for not having seen the difference ('another system which seems to take away altogether the distinction between vice and virtue, and of which the tendency is, upon that account wholly pernicious', pp. 306–14). Who is this impartial spectator and what is his function or role? The concept runs through the whole of TMS.

It cannot be exposed here in its fullness, so a pertinent quotation from Immanuel Kant, the German philosopher who had read the translated version of 1770, must suffice: 'the man who goes to the root of things and who looks at every subject not just from his own point of view but from that of the community ...' (*der Unpartheyische Zuschauer*). (Cited by D.D. Raphael and A.L. Macfie in their *Introduction to the Theory of Moral Sentiments*, Oxford, 1976, p. 31. Apparently the quotation is taken from Kant's *Reflections in Anthropology*.) With this theory, which was developed in the course of the successive editions of TMS, Adam Smith not only had a view of human behaviour which distinguished him from his contemporaries David Hume and Francis Hutcheson. According to an expert in the field, '[Smith's] theory can certainly stand comparison with the best known of modern psychological explanations of conscience, Freud's account of the super-ego' (D.D. Raphael in his article 'The impartial spectator', in *Essays on Adam Smith*, edited by Andrew S. Skinner and Thomas Wilson, Oxford, 1975, p. 97).

3. Economists from the German language area (nineteenth and twentieth centuries)*

Henry W. de Jong

INTRODUCTION

At the end of the eighteenth century there occurred a double methodological shift in economics.

First, it went the way of abstraction and model building in the exposition of its doctrines. The physiocrats had already done this in an original way but had restricted their attention to macroeconomics as was also the case with David Ricardo.

In 1826, Johann Heinrich von Thünen (1783–1850) published a stylized version or model of a market economy complete with extensive numerical illustrations, even more than those of his French predecessors. Such endeavours had been outside the view of scholastic economics which is best typified as methodological realism.

Second, the earlier economists had neglected the distribution problem; what determines wages, interest, rents and profits? Von Thünen opened a new vista on this question which commanded the attention of the profession during the rest of the century and beyond.

Third, von Thünen encompassed the elements of the entrepreneurial function as they had been developed until the beginning of the nineteenth century in an integrative theory which also added the spatial dimension.

Von Thünen was therefore a pioneer in several respects though he was not raised in academic circles and did not spend his working life there. Born in northwestern Germany, he probably inherited his inquisitive, pragmatic attitude from his father who was a landowner in the neighbourhood of Jever in eastern Frisia. During the years when young von Thünen grew up, agricultural colleges were founded in northern Germany: near Rostock (1793), near Hamburg (1798) and in Celle (1802). Von Thünen went to Hamburg in 1802 and the next year to Celle where he found inspiring teachers and made connections with advanced agricultural owners. One of these, Baron von Voght, had laid out his estate in accordance with a quasi-industrial model practised in England. This was the Norfolk system standing as the prototype of the 'new husbandry', as it was called at the time. It was introduced by Sir Richard Weston in the late seventeenth century on the basis of intensive studies carried out in the Low Countries (*A discourse of husbandrie used in Brabant and Flanders, 1652*).[1] What astonished Weston was the high agricultural productivity achieved on rather meagre soils in those areas since medieval times. The solution seemed to reside in the high degree of manure applied. This was only feasible in densely populated areas, however. The English solution was to keep cattle in large stalls from which the manure could be spread efficiently.

Thus, agricultural methods were adapted to the ever-present problem of exhaustion of the soil in its varying degrees; basically there were three:

1. Letting land lie fallow every other year or with intervals of more years, thereby raising the intensity of cultivation. This might have damaging consequences if practised too far.
2. The coupling or exchange system which allowed for alternative cultivations of tillage and cattle breeding, practised in Flanders since the fourteenth century in rolling periods of six, but mostly of nine years. The emphasis was on the latter to get sufficient manure.
3. The products were alternated: mainly fodder plants serving animal production and commercial crops like hops, rapeseed, mustard seed, hemp, madder and so on. Various trades were thereby stimulated in their expansion, such as beer brewing, textile colouring and others.

Now, agronomists, including von Thünen's revered teacher A.D. Thaer, were devotees to one of the systems referred to, which allowed for variations, but which nevertheless differed substantially in their basic characteristics. The merits and demerits of the methods were, in other words, argued on the basis of technical qualifications.

Von Thünen rejected such an approach, having read Adam Smith's *Wealth of Nations*, which linked production systems with the extension of the market. In 1803, he published an embryonic version of his theory, later to be published in *The Isolated State* (1826). In the earlier version, entitled 'Description of agriculture in the village of Groszflottbeck near Hamburg', the young author wrote that if one assumes that in a country with a diameter of 40 miles there lies a city where this country can only sell its products and that its agriculture is on the highest levels of cultivation, then one can deduce that the production systems around this city will be divided into four classes. This introduces the relativity of systems of agricultural production, varying in intensity of output processes that change with the data and especially the size of the market. This the author expresses with the dictum: 'As the wealth and the population of a state increase, so a more intensive agricultural system of production will be of advantage' (cited after the second German edition of 1842, p. 262). He thinks of the successive intensities linked with the three-year fallow system, the coupling and the product-alternation systems, more finely differentiated into seven types. Not only transport costs and difficulties of movement of the produce towards the city are considered but also the costs of carrying manure in the other direction are acknowledged to be influential. Thus,

> [There] will develop pretty definite and distinct concentric circles around the town in which either this or that crop will be the main one. In so far as we consider the production of a particular crop the main goal of economic activities, we shall find in each of the different circles radically different economic arrangements since the whole character of economic life changes with the cultivation of a different crop. (Hall, 1966, p. 8)

THE PRODUCTION CIRCLES

We cannot survey the circles in detail so let us focus on some general characteristics. Perishable products and those having high transport costs will be produced, bought and sold in the first circle: garden products, fresh milk, clover to feed cattle in the barn, savings on labour cost, manure acquired from the city, hay and straw to be sold, whereas grains will play a subordinate role. In addition, potatoes, cabbage, turnips and so on will be cultivated also, being too voluminous for the wider circles. Rents in this circle will be high and no land will be left fallow; in addition, ample amounts of manure will be spread. There may be crop rotation, but here too, price–cost considerations are dominant and no generalizations as to systems of rotation are possible. This circle is called the 'free economy' because it provides so many options.

The second circle will begin where own production of manure is more advantageous than buying it in the city. In general, rents decline in the higher circles with the distance from the city until the margin of cultivation is reached which determines the boundaries of the isolated state. Rent there will be zero for the estate where production and shipping costs are just equal to the price of grains in the city: it is the marginal supplier. This position changes only when demand from the city increases or decreases. Von Thünen, like Ricardo, expressly acknowledges the influence of soil fertility (alongside distance and transport costs) on rents. In sum, the price based on market demand will determine the type of output, the area under cultivation and the surplus, if any, which is rent. The last is a differential advantage measuring location and the quality of the soil.

THE PRODUCTIVITY OF CAPITAL AND LABOUR

In the second volume (paragraph 8) of his *Isolated State*, published for the first time in 1850, von Thünen examines the manner in which capital comes into existence and the question whether an increase in output, resulting from the use of capital instruments, will be proportional to such use. The first is a matter of saving from current output and devoting the time gained from using up these savings in the construction of the instruments. The second is denied,

> for not every amount of capital in the form of tools, machines and buildings will make labour proportionally more effective … there is always a limit beyond which a further addition of the implement ceases to be useful and to yield a rent. Once this limit has been reached, labour devoted to the creation of capital has to be diverted to the production of other valuable commodities. (Dempsey, 1960)

Von Thünen realizes that capital deepening runs into limits; he figures out a series of a geometrical nature which declines progressively with a fraction of the base number of 9/10. The conclusion is that 'the rent which the total capital yields if it is lent is determined by the use of the last unit of capital still applied'. But capital widening opens only initially another track; so, the same process will make itself felt, to be sure with a fraction of another dimension.

In other words, von Thünen has discovered the marginal productivity principle which governs the application of increasing amounts of a production factor when other cooperating factors remain constant. And he recognized that it was competitively supplied demand that ruled the limiting price. Agricultural production evolved into an optimizing problem. For this insight he was rightly praised by John Bates Clark, Alfred Marshall, Joseph Schumpeter and others in later times. Moreover, his mid-nineteenth-century agricultural estate was ideally suited to test these principles as we shall also see in the last section.

ENTREPRENEURIAL ROLES

The German economist was deeply convinced that increasing applications of the production factors, and in particular land and capital, would yield increasing output only up to a maximum. After that, stagnation would occur and no further progress in income and wealth was to be expected: 'Capital will give results and is in the strict sense of the term capital only if used productively; on the degree of this usefulness depends the rate of interest at which we lend capital'. The hidden assumption underlying 'productive capital' is, naturally, that someone moves it and combines it with labour and land. Academic economists might slide-over such an assumption by looking at the economic process as something that proceeds by itself, but for an estate owner and practitioner like von Thünen the message was: 'Productive use presupposes an industrial enterprise and an entrepreneur. The enterprise gives the entrepreneur a net yield after compensating for all expenses and costs. This net yield has two parts, business profits and capital use'. Three pages earlier he had distinguished interest on capital invested, insurance against business losses, the wages of managing the enterprise and a residual called uninsurable risk. The last is the part of business risk which no insurance company will ever take on and which the entrepreneur will have to bear himself. The result of enterprise – that is, the probability of gain being greater than that of loss, a positive expectation of profit – cannot be insured, for it is primarily of a subjective nature and, in so far as objective circumstances are determinant, they are of a general nature. The distinction between the manager and the entrepreneur is relevant here: whereas the former fulfils an allotted task, the latter will have the persistent troubles of running the enterprise – the cares and sleepness nights, the doubts about investments, the measuring up of competitors, the loyalty of the workmen, and so forth. The manager can work according to a system; the entrepreneur's work cannot be systematized. But such uncertainties are far from being unproductive. They stimulate the entrepreneur to think of improvements and innovations:

> Necessity is the mother of invention; and so the entrepreneur through his troubles will become an inventor and explorer in his field ... what the entrepreneur brings about by greater mental effort in comparison with the paid manager is compensation for his industry, diligence and ingenuity. (Von Thünen, 1850, Dempsey's translation, pp. 245–50).

In this way the author links Richard Cantillon's uncertainty explanation of profits with Nicholas Baudeau's innovation theory and, moreover, also succeeds in distinguishing and linking the managerial and organizational elements, stressed by Jean-Baptiste Say in the early nineteenth century, with the previously discovered features. Von Thünen's explanation was a tremendous step forward in the foundation of a unified entrepreneurial theory. It only needed the addition of Jacob Leonard de Bruyn Kops's fundamental element, brought forward in the same year 1850 (see Chapter 4, 'Market theory in the Low Countries') that entrepreneurial cost reductions, based on innovations and improvements and also comprising quality improvements, or alternatively, new products, hit upon broadening income layers. Then the innovating entrepreneur will reap the profits, benefit consumers and extend the market at the same time. Imitators will ultimately destroy the advantage and generalize the gains. Here the origin of the economist's views becomes manifest: de Bruyn Kops's was an industrial one whereas von Thünen's agricultural background focused his attention not on such breakthroughs but on other issues, in particular on the uncertainties of an agricultural origin.

LABOUR AND WAGES

Finally, von Thünen's theory of labour and wages has raised eyebrows though it shows a similar originality as his other writings. It maintains that labour's compensation is not determined by supply and demand in the market – and comes down to the subsistence wage of the classical economists – but will also reflect the productivity (increases) of labour. Von Thünen thought up a formula to express his view and which so impressed him that he had it inscribed on his tombstone: the 'natural' or 'just' wage $W = \sqrt{a \cdot p}$; in this formula, a represents the necessary living standard of the labourer who is considered to be of a common homogeneous quality while p denotes the value of the products made by labour. Both could be expressed in money or produce (von Thünen, 1850, Vol. 2, para. 15, pp. 150–56).

How should the formula be interpreted? Is it an ideal or normative expression saying what a just wage should be? Or does it indicate a relationship to be found in reality, but of course, on the basis of the assumption that free land, as some critics said, or free access to new products or new markets should be available?

The first interpretation need not bother us even if it cannot be excluded that von Thünen, who was socially engaged with his workers, meant it that way. Economically, the validity of the formula hinges on the second interpretation, however. As it stands, the formula says that labour does not claim its full output but neither is it or need it be satisfied with a subsistence wage. Results achieved by economic progress must of necessity also be partially distributed to workers.

In this form the formula can be upheld in modern times, too, provided we drop von Thünen's assumption of homogeneous labour. In his own model this assumption was already difficult to accept. His model of progress departed from the assumed division of the labour force working on the marginal farms to be established on free land, in two sections: one cultivating the farm in a normal way as was done elsewhere, the other section of workers manufacturing the capital goods to be used on the production farm (let us call this the 'firm'). Von Thünen maintained that all workers would earn the same wage rate because any discrepancy between the farm's and the firm's rate would be equalized by labour moving to the location with the highest compensation.

But this is hardly convincing. The capital instruments made by the 'firm' need skilled, more qualified labour (engineers, designers, craftsmen and so on) especially if progress is to be continuous; the increased productivity benefits the farms but only on the condition that the firm's workers earn a rent rewarding their ingenuity and skills. Thus the workers on the farms and the firms are not homogeneous and there are wage differentials.

However, von Thünen's formula is valid if interpreted in the second way as stated above. It then means the following.

An economy needs a group of firms making capital instruments to be applied in other, more conventional businesses, if it is to make economic progress. The making of the instruments is an activity requiring special skills and ingenuity and is rewarded above average. As such it is an attraction for the workers who are able and willing to devote themselves to the acquisition of the required qualifications. Government policies with respect to education and training as well as the promotion of saving may strongly promote the growth. Then, even in a situation of classical unlimited labour supply, wages need not stay at a general subsistence level but can be raised above this in widening circles. Is not the fast expansion of the Chinese economy with its high investment share and ditto mass schooling of the population in both advanced and practical skills an illustration of this adapted von Thünen model?

PRACTICAL EXPERIMENTS

From 1 July 1847, von Thünen ordered the wages on his Tellow estate near Rostock in north Germany to be paid in accordance with his wage formula, and no longer follow the prevailing competitive standards. Profit participation was continued after his death in September 1850 until 1896. Every year, as per the end of June, total revenue of the estate was calculated, expenditure deducted and a fixed share was allotted to the owner. Initially 16,500 marks, later 18,000 marks. Of the remaining surplus all employees got a proportional share, amounting to 68.46 marks on average per family during those 49 years or 3354 marks in total. Looked at from another point of view, the average family earned an extra 15 to 20 per cent of its wage or salary, which was between 300 and 500 marks per annum (Damaschke, Vol. 1, pp. 381–6, 13th edn, 1922). The system was discontinued when the estate was sold in 1896. A well-known Dutch entrepreneur, J.C. van Marken, a 'social' industrialist, who, as his socialist opponents acknowledged, paid above-average wages and replenished several social funds with important contributions, also ran a profit-sharing system in his firm. In the quarter-century 1870–95, labour's share amounted to nearly 60 per cent; he himself retained some 40 per cent of the 5 million guilders made during the period, net of interest on loans, depreciation and reservations including bonuses (de Jong, 1988, p. 57).

Dobb (1946, pp. 82–5) recounts some early British instances of profit sharing; but mostly these schemes had conditions attached such as the abstinence of membership of a trade union, no participation in collective bargaining, the renunciation of strike action and so on. Moreover, the benefits were rather meagre: 'On the average the profit-bonus amounts to some 5–6% of the worker's wage, and seldom exceeds in all 10% of the total profits' (ibid., p. 84).

CARL MENGER (1840–1921): THE PRIMACY OF THE CONSUMER

This well-known economist and founder of the marginal utility school of value (together with William Stanley Jevons) was not a great contributor to market theory in the sense of Cantillon, Smith or von Thünen. These men had matched an explanatory scheme of the functioning of markets with many concrete and practical insights and deductions and thereby secured for themselves a wide public audience. Menger was the analytical, theoretical economist who brought original points of view into the discussion, though at the same time there were some curious lapses.

Within the row of nineteenth-century German economic thinkers, Menger was the one who emphasized most persistently the role of the final consumer in economic decision making; who also stressed the time element in the progress of society and who added to these elements, almost necessarily, the uncertainty prevailing in economic transactions. This may have a different impact on various economic activities, but will be almost universally increasing with the lapse of time. These elements found their place in Menger's theory, which emerged in 1871 when he published his *Grundsätze der Volkswirtschaftlehre*, or *Principles of Economics*. The book was meant to throw a new light on the market process, in particular to stress the character of the economic system as 'a system of dependent prices' (Schumpeter, 1952, pp. 84–5). Menger's aim is to discover the laws of price formation, starting from the recognition that people produce and exchange goods to satisfy their needs. The basic tool was the '*Grenznutzenlehre*' or the marginal utility principle as one of Menger's pupils, Friedrich von Wieser (1851–1926) later called it. Schumpeter stated (not without exaggeration) that once this solution to the pricing problem had been found: 'the whole complex mechanism of economic life suddenly appeared to be unexpectedly and transparently simple' (ibid., p. 84).

Menger himself, in the Preface to the *Principles* (Menger, 1968, edited by F.A. von Hayek) submitted a large claim when he took up the problem raised by Jean Buridan in the fourteenth century, namely the relationship between universal laws and the human freedom of will-power to realize set goals. It will suffice to give two citations from this Preface which make clear the principles upon which Menger's book is built:

> If and under what conditions something is useful to me, if and under what conditions it is a good, if and under what conditions this will have value to me and how large the measure of this value is to me, if and under what conditions an economic exchange of goods between two subjects will take place and within what limits, etc., all this is so independent from my will power as a law of chemistry is from the will and consent of a practical chemist. (*Principles*, 1968, Preface, p. 11)

On the same page Menger writes:

> [T]he reference to the freedom of human will power may indeed be understood as an objection against the full 'law-submitted' character of economic acts, but never as one against the 'law-submitted' events, which, being independent of human will power, condition the result of human economic activity. It is the latter which are the subject of our science, however. (Ibid.)

These passages were meant to sustain Menger's claim that economics is an exact science and that this cannot be denied by referring to the freedom of human beings to decide otherwise: 'because economics as an exact science is thereby neglected' (ibid.).

Alongside exact laws Menger distinguished empirical laws. These are the first type of laws mentioned above and they may be changed by human interference. Such laws are, in contrast to exact laws, not always true for all nations and all times which have a traffic in goods (Menger, 1985, p. 72). They allow for exceptions and are to be determined only by observation. Exceptions may be induced by impulses, other than the economic ones, by errors or ignorance and so on. The exact orientation of theoretical research will, on the other hand, reduce human phenomena to the most original ones and to the most general forces and impulses of human nature. This theory teaches us to follow and understand 'the efforts of humans aimed at the provision of their material needs' (ibid., pp. 86–7).

At this stage in the argument it seems opportune to draw the attention to some remarkable points:

1. Menger still clings to the material concept of economics: the provision of material goods, though he later on in his book dubs the efforts of middlemen in markets as productive. Post-Mengerian Austrians have corrected this, but the lapse throws a curious blot on the exact economics that would be valid for all times and places.
2. Methodologically Menger is an Aristotelian, that is, one who wishes to discover the essence of the phenomena he studies, or to expose their real nature. The discussion of this position is best left to writers who specialize(d) in this field (Hutchinson, 1981, ch. 6; White Introduction to the New York University Press edition of 1985; and W. Meyer, *Grundlagen*, 2002, ch. 9). But it seems relevant to point out that Menger argued causally, that is, from cause to effect, and neglected the aspect of interdependency. A review in 1872 had already remarked that the relevant economic relationship between goods and needs is one of means and goals, not of causes and effects (Hayek in the Introduction to the *Principles*, 1968, note 12).
3. From the point of view of market theory, the distinction between exact and empirical laws seems without merit: it may be considered superfluous or untrue or confusing. In market theory the institutional structure is necessarily linked up with the process in a mutually interdependent way.
4. It is Menger's radical consumer orientation which remains. Goods are classified by him according to their directness in satisfying human needs. This follows from the utility or usefulness which they have for the ultimate consumer. Higher-order goods have only an indirect importance, in contrast to the lower-order goods which have an immediate want-satisfying potential. Naturally, the transformation of goods from higher- into lower-order ones, which is what production is concerned with, is a time-consuming and uncertain process. Menger's entrepreneur is the one who copes with the problems arising from these uncertainties and, in particular, aligns the vertically disintegrated productive resources.

   Throughout this time-consuming transformation process the entrepreneurial function comprises: the procurement of all necessary information; the calculation of economic magnitudes; the will to organize and assign the economic goods to their most efficient places, and finally, to supervise the process and bring it to a successful close. Note that such an entrepreneur is, for all his activities, only one who executes the final consumer's desires by responding to his wishes and whims. For this, markets are all-important and constitute the core of economics.
5. His Chapter 16 (*Principles*, 1968, pp. 212–24) on the nature, relationships and the changes therein of use values and exchange values is an illustrating example. Use value is all but forgotten in modern economics. But Menger shows its importance if both kinds of valuation are relevant.[2] Then the highest of the two is decisive: 'to appreciate the economic value of goods … whether their use value or their exchange value is the

more economical, belongs to the most important tasks of economically active humans. This decision depends on the determination of economic advantage: what goods to keep and which to sell' (*Principles*, 1968, p. 219). He lists and discusses the changes in the nature of goods, of social relationships, of lifestyles and emotional involvements, but, above all, the effect that the quantities of goods and assets (including fixed property and businesses) have on the satisfaction of needs and the decisions to buy and sell goods. The growth of eBay-type firms amid the disasters of so many internet firms underlines this view in our times.

COMPETITION AND MONOPOLY: THE AUSTRIAN VIEWS

Austrian theory has inspired continental economists with the idea that markets evolve in time, and develop, as Menger maintained, from 'bilateral monopoly' to trade between more parties and ultimately to large-scale competitive markets. Monopoly comes first when a new market arises, and only with time does the growth of markets make competition possible (Menger, 1981, pp. 191–225). All markets start with monopoly and move towards becoming more and more competitive. If markets grow larger, monopoly is reduced and competition is broadened. Varying Adam Smith's famous dictum, one could say that competition is limited by the extent of the market. The 'economic progress of civilization' leads to competition (ibid., pp. 224–5), for market forces break down monopoly. If the monopolist behaves in the traditional way, by undersupplying the total market, potential buyers are not satisfied when demand increases and the market grows, and the monopolist will bring about his own demise. This is not because competition reverts to a state of perfection, which does not exist. Menger denies that a good in a state of competition has a unique price; instead, prices are varied and dispersed (ibid., pp. 191–3 and 236–85). Von Wieser extended this analysis to what he called the 'monopoloid constructions', such as public and private groupings like cartels and trusts, in which 'monopoly and competition do meet not only externally, but one and the same construction unites both, so that theory is posed with a new problem'. Here again, it is the consideration of time which colours the analysis and thereby supports the previous point, namely, that the market organization forms stand in a dynamic, even dialectical relationship (von Wieser, 1927, pp.158–62).

Schumpeter and Levy rounded off the analysis by arguing that the Mengerian view of declining prices if the number of competitors increases, implies that both the level of the extra profit rate and the duration of that rate diminish with market growth and make structural changes necessary (Schumpeter, 1926, pp. 99–103; Levy, 1936, pp. 61–5, 85, 156–7). Monopoly can only persist in exceptional circumstances, for monopoly is at once the first and the unique seller. The idea, entertained by Karl Marx, Marshall and later on Piero Sraffa and Joan Robinson that monopolists exist because of a continuously declining long-run average cost curve is not accepted by Austrian theory. When demand increases, new product varieties and new processes can be introduced in accordance with the Smithian principle, and the chances that a monopolist will be able to realize these better than competitors are extremely small. Figure 3.1 demonstrates the sequence. Revenue curves R_1, R_2 and R_3, both shift to the right and become more elastic. Cost curves C_1, C_2 and C_3 (representing improved and more varied products as well as lower cost processes) are pushed downward and the profit rate declines continually. In addition, Schumpeter solved the basic question implied in Figure 3.1: why do entrepreneurs come forward, either as initiating monopolists or as imitating competitors?

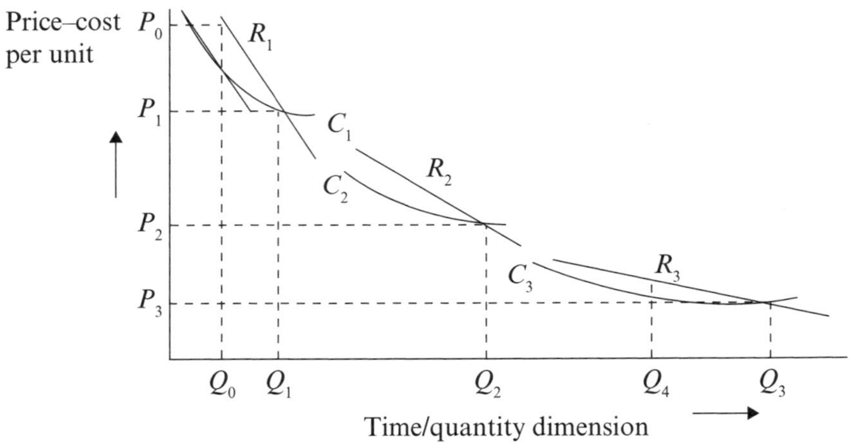

Figure 3.1 The Mengerian process

In the second edition of his *Theory of Economic Development*, Schumpeter clarified the points made by Menger and von Wieser by defining the entrepreneur as the economic agent who exerts leadership through setting different goals and behaving differently from the common run of economic decision makers. Such entrepreneurs are generated by an ethnically homogeneous population according to a frequency curve: entrepreneurial capacities are distributed like the capacities for singing, playing chequers, tennis and so on. This position explains at once:

1. why the number of competitors cannot explain competition;
2. why a developed society generates a continuous stream of entrepreneurs;
3. why there are small and big entrepreneurs;
4. why entrepreneurs are always a minority of the population; and
5. why entrepreneurs are different from 'normal' businessmen ('*Wirte schlechtweg und Unternehmer*').

To do different things in a different way, however, encounters three obstacles: it is objectively difficult, it requires subjective capacities for initiating change and it meets social resistance. Economic leadership ('innovation') overcomes these obstacles because it is motivated by the *plus ultra*: to found an empire, to battle and succeed and to create something new (Schumpeter, 1926, pp. 122–39). This view of the entrepreneur – perhaps somewhat exalted – is not debased when one includes material motives. The German definition: *Durchsetzung neuer Kombinationen* expresses it pointedly.

Levy[3] while being fundamentally in agreement with the above – carried the pre-war analysis an important step further by discussing concentration that takes the form both of trusts and cartels. In Figure 3.1, the initial monopolist would like to restrict supply to Q_0 and fetch the high price P_0. He cannot. Competition will force the price down to P_1, where no profit is left. New product varieties and processes have to come forward (C_2) and, again, after an interval, competition reduces the price to P_2. The process is repeated until P_3 is reached. No profits (apart from 'normal' profits required to attract able managers and risk capital) are made by the numerous competitiors in the larger-sized market.

This situation, according to Levy, may persist. But if some enabling conditions prevail, it may be changed towards concentration and even monopoly. In that case, output would have to be diminished to Q_4 (Figure 3.1) and that could be achieved by a cartel, buying out some competitors or a trust rationalizing production and/or sales.

Here, it is not simply a matter of reducing the number of competitors. For the suppression of competition depends not, as classical economists maintained, on the number of competitors, but on the relationship between number of suppliers and 'the anticipated monopoly advantages accruing from combination' (Levy, 1911, pp. 291–2). The greater the number of competitors, the higher must be the anticipated increase in extra profits and the longer their prospective duration (t) in order to make effective combination (cartel or trust) worthwhile. A combination among a small number of competitors can be achieved if the rewards are modest and/or limited in time whereas high extra profits on a long-term basis are required to unite numerous competitors.

What can be accomplished by means of concentration, depends, according to Levy, on five enabling conditions, and their degree of fulfilment:

1. Whether the national market is protected by import duties or not. Pre-1914, this was more applicable to many industries under British free-trade conditions than to US or German markets which were protected; similar considerations apply to other protective institutional arrangements.
2. Whether the scale of optimal plant or firm in relation to market demand is large or small. The higher the relative scale, the more the risk of excess capacity for an intruder is enhanced. Even with a higher anticipated profit level, he will not enter.
3. Inelastic supply of (essential) inputs is again a factor moving a rewarding combination to exploit the market situation.
4. Another factor is vertical integration, which can be achieved with reductions of average cost per unit.
5. 'Finally, the reputation of an established firm, with its own accustomed markets or regular clientele, or the inherited skill of a special class of operatives, forms in certain circumstances, an element in a monopoly which must not be undervalued' (ibid., pp. 303–4).

At first, the Mengerian competitive process exerts a pressure towards (but probably never arriving at) the state of equilibrium, both by increasing the number of competitors and by shifting market demand to the right. But because both factors interact, entrepreneurs can hardly determine at what location they are. Only if demand growth stabilizes, and the growth rate becomes predictable, can an entrepreneur spot an opportunity for combination, and see what form this combination should have and how stable it may be.

All this means that entrepreneurial action (the process) determines the market structure, and, vice versa, given structures may (provided the enabling factors prevail) prompt entrepreneurs to start a process of combination. Process and structure are seen as interdependent.

Thus, in Levy's model the formation of a combination and its possible and tenable profitability depends on:

- the supply–demand relationships during market development;
- the intensity of competition, only partially given by the number of competitors; and
- a set of objective, enabling factors, partly of technical and partly of an institutional/political nature.

However, the moving agent is always an entrepreneur, spotting the opportunities inherent in the situation.

The widely read German economist Robert Liefmann, for example, distinguishing between the absolute monopoly of a single seller (mostly based on legal privileges) and the relative monopoly (a dominant firm with a few, mostly smaller suppliers having some disadvantages) and introducing a new term, remarks that 'latent competition' is always in the background and will be activated by price increases.[4] In reverse, competition, which in the modern economy is fiercely stimulated by the progress of technology, by the extension of communications and the reduction of transport costs and by the growth of capital, so that new firms are founded, may become so intense that monopolistic combinations like cartels and trusts arise. Economic reality is therefore pictured as a dialectical process of competition moving towards loose and tight combinations of firms (including monopolies) and vice versa.[5] The background of this process is also the power of the other side of the market: the choosing consumer. The possibility of creating cartels and monopolies that work, depends on the relationships prevailing on the demand side; for, says Liefmann: production costs do not determine prices, but prices determine the upper level of costs. He goes on to list the alternatives which consumers can command (Liefmann, 1930, pp. 133–6). The picture drawn up is far removed from the static, neo-classical market forms. It explains rising concentration (in the sense of larger firms) as the result of market extension, and the accompanying mass production and mass distribution.[6]

The culmination of research into the concentration problem found expression in the publication of the two volumes of *Economic Concentration* in 1960 (2nd edn, 1971), edited by H. Arndt. Arndt said in the introduction that concentration had become an all-embracing phenomenon in modern society, with far-reaching implications for various domains. It needed a broad approach, taking into account not only the economic, but also the many non-economic aspects (legal, fiscal and so on). At the same time he noted a trend in thinking towards theoretical explanations. No doubt, the many contributions by international authors to the volumes were partly responsible for this, as well as the attractions the new field offered to theoretically minded economists. More important, the concept of dynamic competition started to make headway, as we shall see in the next sections.[7]

With regard to the policy inferences to be drawn from the growth of trusts and combinations, economists parted company. Some, like Levy argued that planning by the state comes near to compulsory cartelization and should be avoided because it would (i) expose the state to many risks and responsibilities it could not bear, and (ii) might lead to overconcentration, 'which might have just as fatal results as had had the rationalization craze' (Levy, 1936, p. 265) because the natural tendencies towards concentration are not present, everywhere and at all times and 'sometimes not at all' (ibid., p. 267). Others, like

François de Vries and Jean Marchal, insisted that the structure of the economy which had been determined by individualistic principles was being fundamentally transformed under the influence of associationist movements and that both theory and policy had to be radically transformed.[8]

In the immediate postwar period a very influential line of thinking emerged with the writings of the so-called Eucken school. It added another dimension to the problem. Walter Eucken maintained that one of the central points is the possible divergence in market economies between private and social interests. The treatment of monopoly power requires competition and other policies on behalf of the state which has the obligation to maintain a competitive order. Eucken was less fortunate in postulating as a norm for such a policy the concept of 'full competition', by which he understood, not a market structure but the behaviour of firms – even of oligopolists – who accept the market price as given. The criticisms in the following decades by 'neo-Austrians' on this concept, in which they rightly pointed out that firms in dynamic competition also set prices in the game, nevertheless erred in simultaneously equating private and social interests, as long as those dynamic firms are free to act as they please. That means, as Lenel pointed out, a retrogression from Smith to François Quesnay, with his dubious philosophical concept of a 'natural order' (Lenel, 1975). There is no doubt that the views expressed by the Eucken school contributed to the inauguration of competition policies in West Germany (Lenel, 1962[1], 1968[2]) as well as in the European Community, a historical breakthrough on the continent.

THE FLOWERING OF DYNAMIC MARKET THEORY SINCE 1960

Levy's was not a bad piece of analysis, already formulated in 1911, even in comparison with Schumpeter's which appeared in 1912. It might be argued that the model is not specific enough; although this is true, it has to be balanced against other advantages. If one opts for a dynamic analysis, the gains in realism carry the price of some indeterminism. Also, dynamic analysis can provide for a theoretical framework, encompassing the market process, which is lacking from static analysis. Into such a dynamic framework, market situation models can be inserted and given their place. This is what European economists have done in the postwar period and what differentiated them from the Anglo-Saxon approach using the structure–conduct–performance paradigm. Indeed, many continental Europeans have followed the market growth–decline paradigm, distinguishing between phases of development and the market situations prevailing during those phases.[9] The plausibility of this was strongly underlined by the course of many European industries, which started their growth curves in the postwar years, adopting new products and new technological and organizational processes often originating in the United States. After fast expansion in the 1950s and 1960s, maturity was reached in the 1970s and decline followed in the early 1980s. Naturally, the expansion paths differed in the timing between the sectors. In general, the approach led to the idea that market development phases show different forms and intensities of competition, as firms use alternative competitive parameters (price, advertising, product innovation and variation, takeovers, diversification and so on) suited to differing conditions of demand growth and demand elasticities. Processes of concentration had to be explained by falling back 'on the specific development conditions of an industry or market sector, because a durable growth advantage of large units in all sectors cannot be proved historically. Concentration processes thus have to be seen as industry specific' (Brandt, 1971, p. 280).

These basic ideas were worked on in Germany and the Netherlands starting from the Schumpeterian innovator, and in this way a truly entrepreneurial economics arose. The Schumpeterian view had the great advantage that it freed economic theory from the *homo economicus*, who was central in neo-classical theory. In one stroke, the shackles of the mechanistic view of economic life were broken. But, as Heusz (1965, pp. 9–16) noted, the Schumpeterian entrepreneur has two important limitations:

- first, that he acts only within the context of the economy as a whole, giving rise to innovations and clusters of these, investment waves and various types of cycles, relevant to the total economy; and
- second, that the Schumpeterian entrepreneur was contrasted only with the traditional type of businessman – the non-pioneer.

In addition to this, my main point was that whatever Schumpeterian theory said about motives and types, the continuity and the directions of entrepreneurial moves are left in the dark, whereas this is of fundamental importance for the problems of industrial organization. This naturally leads to research into horizontal, vertical and diversification strategies of firms.

So two routes were chosen. Heusz, in West Germany, developed a typology of entrepreneurs, dividing them into four types:

1. the innovator pioneer;
2. the imitative entrepreneur, showing initiative like the first type but not in a pathbreaking way;
3. the conservative entrepreneur, adapting to the changing market circumstances, initiated by others; and
4. the immobile businessman not even adapting, but simply doing the usual things until he is ousted from the field.

These four types were not meant to be a general typology, reflecting innate human characteristics, but conceptual, analytical instruments, used for explaining the stages of market development. For, as Heusz underlined, entrepreneurial acts are 'mirrored' in the making and unmaking of markets. Production, costs, demand and so on are not simply given, as is maintained in traditional theory, but are the parameters of action, through which market types arise. In one and the same person, therefore, different conceptual types may occur at different times, as for example, with Henry Ford and Heinz Nordhoff in motor cars, who were one-time pioneers, but thereafter remained dedicated to old-fashioned products or methods. Now, two general propositions follow:

1. The entrepreneurial type changes with market development phases.
2. The relationships between these entrepreneurial types shift with either complementary and reinforcing effects or with substitutive consequences.

The first proposition is supported by a probability analysis, in which the supposition is made that among 10 entrepreneurs, one will be of the initiating type and nine will be of the conservative type. Depending on whether the entry of new firms to the industry is supposed to occur (and this is linked to the development phase) and the likelihood that initiating entrepreneurs will shift to successive stages, it follows that sooner or later, the conservative type will come to prevail, and market behaviour will show different characteristics in the course of time. With respect to the second proposition, Heusz's analysis of a number of combinations of similar and different entrepreneurial types shows that, depending on the stage of market development, entrepreneurs may stimulate or block each other's actions. I cannot discuss the intricate analysis here in all its complexity, but one example may suffice: the action of imitative entrepreneurs during the expansion stage will reinforce the pioneer's behaviour, extending the market, bringing prices and costs downwards and so on, whereas the same type will block innovative behaviour during the maturity phase.[10]

There is not enough 'market room' during maturity to accommodate imitation. If, in contrast, the pioneer rivals with conservative and *a fortiori*, immobile types of businessmen, he may continue introducing innovations because these types afford him 'competitive room'.

The picture which emerges from this analysis is that a complementary relationship will prevail if there is sufficient 'room', whereas a substitutive relationship between firms occurs if that is not the case. The 'room' provided depends on market and competitive factors, and both are linked to the development stages of a market. If firms have a tendency to block each other, cartels, mergers and other combinatory moves will follow. But suppose the types diverge very much (for example, one pioneer among many conservative firms), the expansion phase will be held back in its development, whereas the declining phase will be speeded up. This analysis, based on types of entrepreneurs, is preceded by a penetrating research of each development stage and rounded off by bringing into the game the demand and cost factors in one- and multi-product firms (Heusz, 1965, Ch. 5).

One important objection against the Heussian type of analysis may be that it easily gets too complicated, not resulting in testable hypotheses. In fact, the analysis is rich in deductive, probabilistic and mathematically oriented derivations, but short of empirical content. This objection was met by later research, analysing sectors and firm cases (Schlögl, 1972; Kaufer, 1980; Oberender, 1984) from the point of view of a simpler model of market development.

Another objection might be that it leaves the development directions of firms in the dark. The Dutch analysis was oriented towards the directions entrepreneurial moves take, inspired by the growth of large firms like Shell, Unilever, Philips, Sté Générale, and the like.[11]

The basic fact about a market economy is that firms do have relationships with each other, because they cannot avoid each other's actions. Entrepreneurial acts determine the timing and direction of these relationships in order to combine resources with a view to future production and sales. If markets develop according to growth cycles, entrepreneurial acts of a greater or lesser importance are required in every stage of development and not only when founding a new firm or plant, as Schumpeter assumed in his model of 1939. With such acts, responding to new opportunities, entrepreneurs leave their imprint on both the market process and the required structures. The 'right' moves generate profits, the 'wrong' ones losses: both are residuals, arising out of performances, windfalls and power positions.

Market structures are composed out of the working of three basic principles of coordinative behaviour between firms, namely those of a rivalrous, competitive nature, of cooperatively and collusively oriented behaviour, or of a dominating nature (de Jong, 1971b). These principles operate along horizontal, vertical and diagonal lines as entrepreneurs direct their creative and imitative activities towards the improvement of their firm's market position. However, entrepreneurs' freedom of action and their choice of directive strategy are limited by the stages of market development and the related characteristics. This means, for example, that competitive, horizontal rivalry increases during the expansion phase, but subsides and/or changes substantially during the maturity phase of a market, whereas a market in decline normally shows so-called 'ruinous competition' (which should be taken literally, not morally: capacities have to be reduced to a lower level, or scrapped). Similarly, vertical integration and diversification is pursued when the firms reach maturity in their previous activities and are sufficiently profitable to finance takeovers. In expansion there is no need to diversify; in decline there are usually no resources available.

It is worthwhile to underline a few qualifying comments:

1. The theory only predicts tendencies, because individual firms may do nothing, or make the wrong decisions, or be late in adapting themselves. Being a 'thruster' or a 'sleeper' affects performance.
2. Major innovations may distort the sequence of market phases. For example, an important innovation may mean renewed growth for an industry after maturity, or may prolong the expansion phase.
3. The use of action parameters (pricing, advertising, merger activity, location and so on) will shift during market phases, and will be chosen by entrepreneurs in accordance with the prevailing type of market organization.
4. Policy measures as well as general cyclical movements are influential in retarding or accelerating the tendencies and may occasionally shift the direction of market development.
5. Welfare considerations can be applied to this version of the growth-cycle theory. Two examples may illustrate this:

    a. Dynamic market theory implies that governmental policies which sustain mature and/or declining industries by means of protection, subsidies or the permitted formation of structural cartels are seriously mistaken, because they bring about wastage of scarce resources and lead to industrial senility. Economists of the growth-cycle orientation have fiercely opposed such 'aid'. Support for innovative industries can, on the contrary and under certain conditions, be defended as being more sensible (Wijers, 1981. For contrary views see Hindley, 1983).
    b. Kaufer has argued that mergers in the introductory and expansion phases practically always are – *per se* – opposed to the achievement of a net welfare benefit, whereas mergers in the late maturity phase, particularly during stagnation, may well achieve these. He bases this conclusion on the possibility that the latter type of mergers can reduce costs through rationalization and the closing of suboptimal plants (Kaufer, 1980, pp. 305–10). This is what Levy maintained in the 1920s. The main considerations are that introductory phase mergers between market participants (diversification mergers is another matter) do not achieve scale advantages faster

> than internal growth, whereas the interdependency between the investment decision of oligopolists in maturity/stagnation, which threatens deadlock, can be avoided by merger. On the basis of reasonable assumptions, the maturity mergers bringing small savings in costs would be a net benefit, even if the monopolistic price increases were substantial (ibid.).[12]

Analytically, dynamic market theory is an extension of the previously described Mengerian process and of the Levy model. From an innovatory monopoly, the market expands towards fierce competition, ending in the reorganization of the industry by entrepreneurs, who devise combinations (cartels, syndicates, dominating firms through takeovers and mergers) during maturity. When market decline enters, the dialectical pendulum gets reversed: from concentration to ruinous competition, with reorganizations, and, sometimes, splitting-up of firms and de-mergers. Basic innovations are necessary to start the wheel turning again. Mostly, these will imply new growth cycles, either in the same or in different industries.

However, growth-cycle theory is not a perfect description of economic reality. No theory can achieve that. Its main advantage is that it teaches economists that markets are dynamic and that process, structure and performance are interrelated, because of entrepreneurial action.

OPTIMAL COMPETITION DEBATED[13]

Another dynamic theory which has found adherence among European economists is the theory of workable competition, of which the most prominent representation was due to Erhard Kantzenbach[14] (Kantzenbach, 1966). Fierce discussion has followed the introduction of the concept of workable competition in Europe, following the trail set by John Maurice Clark in the United States. Rejecting static equilibrium theory, Kantzenbach described competition as an evolutionary and disequilibrium process, in which rivalry prevails. The rivalrous competition is only an instrument to achieve social welfare goals, of which three are outstanding: the growth of the social product, the optimal distribution and composition of the social product, and the promotion of a flexible adaptation of the economy to changing circumstances.

These goals are not served equally by the two main functions (technical progress and flexible adaptation) which require substantial degrees of monopoly and market imperfection. Consequently, optimal competition is a compromise between the two extremes, and, though difficult to quantify or to measure, is to be found when loose oligopolistic market structures with some degree of product differentiation and market intransparency prevail.

For Kantzenbach, the distinction between potential and effective intensity of competition is decisive. Oligopoly is not general interdependency of sellers, but the dependency of a particular seller on the behaviour of an individual competitor, who may threaten his existence. This creates a high degree of insecurity, which is at a maximum in a homogeneous duopoly situation and very low in polypolistic markets. (Compare the Stackelberg-leading firm.)

The insecurity depends on the divergence of cost functions, relative liquidity reserves as between companies and the short-term demand shifts in the market, which are all difficult to know. Both owner- and management-controlled firms strive for long-term security (be it for different reasons). Potential and effective competitive intensity diverge more strongly the fewer the number of competing oligopolists and the more homogeneous the products sold become.

Stated simply: potential competition intensity rises when fewer and fewer sellers of homogeneous goods threaten to wipe out one of them by means of unforeseen actions. The same facts induce restraints on competition though, because nobody wants to be wiped out. A duopoly will have unlimited potential competition, but the effective degree will be very low. Between six and 12 competitors there might be workable competition, and the optimal degree could be nine competitors.

The six competitors who have effective competition among themselves have a much higher degree of potential competition, so that either they will have some product differentiation or they will practise some restraints of competition that are tolerable. Beyond 12 competitors, the degree of effective competition sinks below the tolerable, and gradually mergers or other restraints of competition would become desirable (obviously, the chosen numbers are artificial and depend on the specific sector). Oligopolistic interdependency is not restricted to horizontal relations between firms, but also relates to vertical liaisons. Schematizing the intensity and the direction of controls between firms, one arrives at the presentation of competitive restraints depicted in Table 3.1 (Kantzenbach, 1966, p. 101), which are further discussed by the author.

Table 3.1 Competitive restraints

Intensity	Direction	
	Horizontal	Vertical
Coordinated behaviour	Group discipline, concerted action	Traditional business relationships
Agreements	Cartels, agreed business conditions	Long-term delivery agreements
Interlocking relationships	Capital participations, syndicates, interlocking directorates	Capital participations, interlocking directorates, co-direction
Mergers, takeovers	Trusts, concerns	Vertical concerns

Source: Kantzenbach (1966, p. 101).

It follows that real markets may have either over- or underoptimal degrees of competition. Competition policy's task is therefore to counter both situations and tendencies in which the intensity of competition potentially is suboptimal (for example, promotion of concentration, the raising of scale of operations and an increase in product differentiation or particular cartel types) or overoptimal (some splitting up of trusts, the prevention of some mergers, or the prevention of oligopolistic price wars in order to avoid the formation of uncontrolled monopolies). Essentially, polypolistic competition lacks dynamic progress, while tight oligopoly carries the dangers of non-functional power battles and/or collusion. Typically, ruinous competition occurs in polypolistic situations, according to the workability theory, because firms are too small, do not have financial means to undertake innovations and behave only traditionally (recall that in the growth-cycle theory, ruinous competition also occurs in recessionary stages between large firms).

As stated before, the workability theory was criticized from various sides.

One criticism of the workability concept (by Erich Hoppmann and others) has pointed out that the inherent antithesis between perfect competition (polypoly), in which there is no progress and monopoly/tight oligopoly in which there is no optimal allocation or distribution, is wrong. There is a dilemma in the goals that competition has to serve only if competition is seen as an instrument to serve general economic goals. If, in contrast, competition is conceived of as a 'discovery process' (Friedrich von Hayek's term), the freedom (equated to an atomistic market structure) to compete and the achievement of desirable results is identical: there will be no dilemma. Exceptionally, Hoppmann says, some natural barriers (economies of scale, exit barriers and so on) may prevent competition altogether. However, this objection assumes an identity of private freedom of action and the resulting advantages with social advantages. Such an assumption is difficult to sustain; by means of competition firms may discover worthwhile economic advantages as well as ways to reduce or eliminate competition itself.

Second, the Dutch Competition Law of 1956 was also based on the theory of workable competition. Reviewing the achievements of 25 years of Dutch competition policy, the President of the Competition Commission remarked that the concept is rather vague: if the intensity of competition is judged by the speed with which a seller's advantage is spoiled, the reactionary move may not be too fast, otherwise the creation of the advantage will not be undertaken, or too slow, so that monopoly will last longer than necessary. But what is 'too' in both cases? In addition, the judgement can only be made *ex post*, which is too late for policy actions. And, finally, what is wanted in present times is the stimulation of price competition, and this is not served by meticulous considerations of 'optimality' (Van der Weijden, 1981). While it is true that in inflationary times more emphasis could be given to price competition in competition policy, the objection with respect to vagueness would not seem to dismantle the structural version of the workability theory. For the theory maintains that in the 'right' structural composition of a market – that is, loose oligopolies – advantages will be created and competed away. As long as both types of action occur, the system does work. The difficulty is to keep the oligopolies in a 'loosely' constructed form, so that no welfare losses occur. In general one could say that analyses of welfare losses due to concentrated market structures (how great are the quantitative losses deriving from concentrated industry structures?) have not been pertinent in Europe.[15]

NOTES

* Some paragraphs, Figure 3.1 and Table 3.1 (on pages 35–45) were taken from *Mainstreams in Industrial Organization*, Book 1, Chapter 3 with kind permission of Springer Science and Business Media. This book was published in 1986 by Kluwer Academic Publishers and edited by W.G. Shepherd and H.W. de Jong.

1. B.H. Slicher van Bath, *De agrarische geschiedenis van West-Europa* (500–1850), 3rd edn, 1976, Utrecht/Antwerp, pp. 197–8 and 272–6.
2. For large-scale producers only exchange valuations are relevant. But it seems opportune to remind ourselves that consumer decisions depending on the determination of the 'economic gravitation point' (Menger), that is, the decision to keep or sell, are pervasive and growing in rich and restless societies: think of secondhand

markets in cars, houses, boats, stamps, coins, animals, clothes, artistic products and so on. Professors who cultivate their own libraries should be the first to concur.

3. Hermann Levy was professor of economics for several decades at the University of Heidelberg in Germany and wrote books on industrial economics between 1909 and 1940. He was, to my mind, a very perceptive economist, who anticipated several points that others came to develop later, for example, the lesser importance of the number of competitors in comparison with their behavioural dynamics, the difference between technical and economic concentration, entry barriers, product differentiation and so on.
4. 'With cartels, in contradistinction to legal monopolies like patents, the rise of new competition by means of the founding of new firms, is never excluded, but always in the background. And it is the more the prospect, that this *latent competition*, this possibility to compete, becomes a fact, the more the cartel exploits its monopoly position by means of high prices and through higher profits gives a special stimulus to the foundation of new firms' (Liefmann, 1930, p. 10, italics added). Before the war (First World War), Liefmann says 'one could observe that even a small rise in profits led to the formation of new competitive firms. But this could not last either, because the more efficient cartel members, willing to remain fully occupied, extended their output, at the cost of weaker rivals ... All longer existing cartels have called forth a very important increase in output and supply', (pp. 131–2).
5. 'In fact both extremes of exchange, monopoly and competition (*freie Konkurrenz*) were never achieved, but both, carried to an extreme, turn into its contrary. ... Competition carried to its extreme leads to monopoly of the remaining strongest. But the same applies in reverse to monopoly, in so far as it is not legally secured: when monopoly positions are exploited and lead to monopoly effects, they attract new competition in the field'. One cannot say that one organizational form is better than another or that economic life has ever been carried on by the one or other principle exclusively; there was always a combination of both (Liefmann, 1930, p. 59). The same idea pervades the works of H. Levy. See his *Monopoly and Competition: A Study in English Industrial Organization* (1911); *Industrial Germany*, Cambridge (1935); and *The New Industrial System: A Study of the Origins, Forms, Finance and Prospects of Concentration in Industry* (1936).
6. Levy (1911, pp. 208ff): 'that an increasing demand is satisfied by a continually decreasing number of firms, the greater productive power of the single unit reducing from decade to decade the aggregate number of firms'. The same arguments, but more broadly worked out, are advanced in *The New Industrial System*, Part III (1936).
7. Both Schumpeter and Kirzner have discussed many aspects of the entrepreneurial role in an illuminating way. Apart from pointing to an absence of recognition of the entrepreneur's role in classical and neo-classical economics, and pursuing the line of thinking of French and German economists in this respect (Schumpeter, 1954), Kirzner discussed the entrepreneurial role in Menger's system. He disagrees with E. Streissler and W. Jaffé, who saw Menger as underlining entrepreneurial activity. Instead he points to the 'entrepreneurial gap' in Menger's principal work. But I fail to see the point, for as Kirzner (1979, pp. 69–70) argues, it is Menger's position that men, by converting goods from a higher order into those of a lower order, create additional value. The first man to do so is, obviously, an entrepreneurial monopolist, expanding the value of goods and their variety. Increasing competition reduces the monopolist's profits in the course of time, until 'Menger's law' (that the value of ends comes to be attached to the means) applies again. This is what Kirzner himself argues in Chapter 10 (especially pp. 162–8). The picture of a market developing from monopoly, via imperfect competition to a state of no profitability, is entirely Mengerian.
8. In the Netherlands, the most prominent economist in the 1920–1950 period, de Vries shifted during the depression from 'freedom of enterprise' towards 'ordening' (that is, private and public regulation of business). And in France, Marchal called for a fundamental revision of theory. See Dullaart (1984) and Marchal (1950–51).
9. A great number of publications have followed this line of thinking, for example, in Germany: Arndt (1952); Heusz (1965); K. Brandt, 'Concentration and economic growth', in Arndt (ed.), (1960/61[1] and 1971[2], pp. 280–88); Krüsselberg (1969); Schlögl (1972); Kaufer (1980); Schmidt (1981). In the Netherlands: de Jong (1971b; 1972[1], 1989[4]), Wijers (1981); van Duijn (1979); Webbink (1984). In France and Belgium: Piatier (1984); Teissier du Cros (1976); de Bethune and Heyvaert (1976); Chevalier (1977). In Italy: Prodi (1971); Aquino (1977).
10. See the analysis of a homogeneous, duopolistic market with a pioneering and imitating firm, that is, a conservative type of firm on pp. 115–17 of Heusz (1965).
11. See de Jong (1971a), chapter on concentration developments in Benelux for an empirical analysis of these firms. I first encountered the growth cycle concept in the late 1950s, when working for a multinational container firm that experienced maturity in the US market, but not in Europe.
12. An important question is whether mergers do indeed lead to rationalization and cost reductions, and if so, do they do so faster than internal growth? On the basis of Dutch evidence, assembled by the Central Statistical Bureau, I previously doubted this and found, on the contrary, that the overwhelming majority of mergers are initiated for market strategic reasons. See 'Theory and evidence concerning mergers: an international comparison', in Jacquemin and de Jong (eds) (1976). An empirical West German research

among 100 firms, taking over other companies during the 1970s, came to similar conclusions: merger intensity rises with the size of the firm; the majority (71–75 per cent depending on the size of firm class) are of a horizontal nature; successes and partial successes of the mergers are severely limited and depend on the type (Möller, 1983, p. 170).

13. This section benefited from remarks submitted by Professor Oberender.
14. Among the numerous writings by Kantzenbach and others only three need be mentioned here, because the first two references contain an extensive literature, in particular with respect to the debates between Kantzenbach and E. Hoppman, *inter alia*, who defend in Germany the sort of freedom of competition approach, reminiscent of the Chicago school in the US: (i) Kantzenbach and Kallfass (1981); (ii) Clapham (1981); (iii) in the Netherlands the Competition Law of 1956 took up a simular position, as Van der Weijden (president of the Dutch Competition Commission) underlined (1981). A good survey of the German discussions is also provided by Schmidt (1981, Part 1). The concept of ruinous competition was extensively discussed by Tolksdorf, both for concentrated and unconcentrated markets (Tolksdorf, 1971).
15. Among the 13 studies, based on branch researches, cited by Böbel (1984, pp. 192–201) only one applies to a European country. For West Germany, Böbel found an efficiency loss of only 1.28 (1.89) per cent for the 1965–73 period, depending on whether sales or added values were used, occasioned mainly by five leading branches (70 per cent) or 10 corporations (66 per cent).

REFERENCES

Aquino, A. (1977), 'Innovazione technologica, spezializzazione internationale e politica industriale', *Rivista di econimia e politica industriale*, no. 3, pp. 417–53.

Arndt, H. (1952), *Schöpferischer Wettbewerb und Klassenlose Gesellschaft*, Duncker & Humblot, Berlin.

Arndt, H. (ed.) (1960/61[1] and 1971[2]), *Die Konzentration in der Wirtschaft*, Schriften des Vereins für Sozialpolitiek, new series, vol. 20, Duncker & Humblot, Berlin.

Böbel, I. (1984), *Wettbewerb und Industriestruktur*, Springer Verlag, Heidelberg.

Brandt, K. (1971), 'Concentration and economic growth', in H. Arndt (ed.), vol. I, pp. 252–301.

Chevalier, J.M. (1977), *L'économie industrielle en question*, Calmann-Lévy, Paris.

Clapham, R. (1981), 'Das wettbewerbspolitische Konzept der Wettbewerbsfreiheit', in H. Cox, K. Jens and K. Markert (eds), *Handbuch des Wettbewerbs*, F. Vahlen, Munich, pp. 129–49.

Damaschke, A. (1922), *Geschichte der Nationalökonomie*, 13th edn, Verlag Gustav Fischer, Jena,

de Bethune, A. and Heyvaert, H. (1976), 'L'innovation dans la politique industrielle', *Anales des Science Économiques*, no. 2, Louvain.

de Jong, H.W. (1971a), *Ondernemingsconcentratie: De ontwikkelingen in Europa, de Verenigde Staten en Japan*, Stenfert Kroese, Leiden.

de Jong, H.W. (1971b), *Marktanalyse en markttheorie*, Stenfert Kroese.

de Jong, H.W. (1972[1], 1989[4]), *Dynamische markttheorie*, Stenfert Kroese, Leiden.

de Jong, H.W. (1988), *Ondernemerschap in Nederland, 1840–1940* [Entrepreneurship in the Netherlands, 1840–1940], Yearbook of History of Business and Technology, Vol 5. Foundation for the History of Business and Technology, Utrecht.

Dempsey, B.W. (1960), *The Frontier Wage*, Loyola University Press, Chicago.

Dobb, M. (1927), *Wages*, Nisbet & Co.: London; (1948) 3rd edn, Cambridge University Press: Cambridge.

Dullaart, M.J.H. (1984), 'Regulation or freedom: Dutch economic thinking in the interwar period', Dissertation, Erasmus University, Rotterdam.

Hall, P. (1966), *Von Thünen's Isolated State*, Pergamon Press, Oxford.

Heusz, E. (1965), *Allgemeine Markttheorie*, J.C.B. Mohr, Tübingen and Zurich.

Hindley, B. (ed.) (1983), *State Investment Companies in Western Europe: Picking winners or backing losers?*, Macmillan, London and Basingstoke.

Hutchinson, T.W. (1981), 'Carl Menger on philosophy and method', in *The Politics and Philosophy of Economics*, Basil Blackwell: Oxford, ch. 6, pp. 176–202.

Jacquemin, A.P. and de Jong, H.W. (1976), *Markets, Corporate Behaviour and the State*, M. Nijhoff, The Hague.

Kantzenbach, E. (1966), *Die Funktionsfähigkeit des Wettbewerbs*, Vandenhoeck & Ruprecht, Göttingen.
Kantzenbach, E. and Kallfass, H. (1981), 'Das Konzept des funktionsfähigen Wettbewerbs-workable competition', in H. Cox, K. Jens, K. Markert (eds), *Handbuch des Wettbewerbs*, F. Vahlen, Munich, pp. 103–29.
Kaufer, E. (1980), *Industrieökonomik*, F. Vahlen, Munich.
Kirzner, I.M. (1979), *Perception, Opportunity, and Profit*, Studies in the Theory of Entrepreneurship, University of Chicago Press, Chicago and London.
Krüsselberg, H.G. (1969), *Marktwirtschaft und Ökonomische Theorie*, Verlag Kombach, Freiburg im Breisgau.
Lenel, H.O. (1962[1], 1968[2]), *Die Konzentration in der Wirtschaft*, J.C.B. Mohr, Tübingen.
Lenel, H.O. (1968), *Die Bedeutung grosser Unternehmen für den technischen Fortschritt*, J.C.B. Mohr, Tübingen.
Lenel, H.O. (1975), 'Walter Eucken's ordnungspolitische Konzeption: die wirtschaftpolitische Lehre in der Bundesrepublik und die Wettbewerbstheorie von heute, *Ordo*, vol. 26, pp. 22–76.
Levy, H. (1911), *Monopoly and Competition: A Study in English Industrial Organization*, Macmillan, London (translated from the German edition of 1909).
Levy, H. (1935), *Industrial Germany*, Cambridge University Press, Cambridge.
Levy, H. (1936), *The New Industrial System: A Study of the Origins, Forms, Finance, and Prospects of Concentration in Industry*, G. Routledge & Sons, London.
Liefmann, R. (1930), *Kartelle, Konzerne und Trusts*, 8th edn, E.H. Moritz, Stuttgart.
Marchal, J. (1950–51), 'La crise contemporaine de la science économique', *Annales de l'Économie Politique.*
Menger, C. (1871, 1968) *Grundsätze der Volkswirtschaftslehre*, 2nd edn, Herausgegeben von F.A. Hayek. J.C.B. Mohr (Paul Siebeck), Tübingen.
Menger, C. (1883, 1963, 1985), *Investigations into the Method of the Social Sciences with Special Reference to Economics*. Translated by Francis J. Nock from the German *Untersuchungun über die Methode der Socialwissenschaften* (1963). Edited with a new introduction by Lawrence H. White (1985). New York University Press, New York.
Menger, C. (1981). *Principles of Economics*, New York University Press, New York (translated by J. Dingwall and B.F. Hoselitz).
Meyer, W. (2002) *Grundlagen des ökonomischen Denkens*, J.C.B. Mohr (Paul Siebeck), Herausgegeben von Hans Albert und Günter Herre, Tübingen.
Möller, W.P. (1983), *Der Erfolg von Unternehmenszusammenschlüssen*, Minerva, Munich.
Oberender, P. (ed.) (1984), *Markstruktur und Wettbewerb in der Bundesrepublik Deutschland*, Verlag F. Vahlen, Munich.
Piatier, A. (1984), *Barriers to Innovation*, Francis Pinter, London.
Prodi, R. (1968), *Concorrenza dinamica e potere di mercato*, Franco Angeli Editore, Milan.
Prodi, R. (1971), *La diffusione delle innovazioni nell'industria italiana*, Il Mulino, Bologna.
Schlögl, H. (1972), *Mehrproduktunternehmung, Marktentwicklung und Wettbewerb*, Atheneum Verlag, Frankfurt/M.
Schmidt, I. (1981), *Wettbewerbstheorie und politik*, G. Fischer Verlag, Stuttgart.
Schumpeter, J. (1952), *Ten Great Economists. From Marx to Keynes*, George Allen & Unwin Ltd, London.
Schumpeter, J. (1912, 1926), *Theorie der wirtschaftlichen Entwicklung*, 5th edn, Duncker & Humblot, Berlin.
Schumpeter, J. (1954), *History of Economic Analysis*, Oxford University Press, Oxford.
Teissier du Cros, A. (1976), *La recherché d'activités et de produits nouveaux*, Editions d'Organisation, Paris.
Tolksdorf, M. (1971), *Ruinöser Wettbewerb*, Duncker & Humbolt, Berlin.
Van der Weijden, C.J. (1981), 'Toestaan of verbieden: een beschouwing rond de wet economische mededinging', *Economisch-statistische Berichten*, 23/30–12.
van Duijn, J.J. (1979), *De lange golf in de economie*, Stenfert Kroese, Leiden.
von Thünen, J.H. (1826, 1842[2], 1850, 1875[3], 1966[4]), *Der isolierte Staat in Beziehung auf Landwirthschaft und Nationalökonomie*, Berlin. The German editions ran between 1826 and 1966 and differ

according to volume and parts as well as place of publication. Von Thünen's work, accessible in English, is in two volumes: vol. 1 of *The Isolated State*, was translated by Carla M. Wartenberg and edited by Peter Hall, Pergamon, Oxford, 1966; vol. 2 has been translated by Bernard W. Dempsey in *The Frontier Wage*, Loyola, Chicago, 1960. Because of this variety I will be restrictive and eclectic in the use of citations.

von Wieser, F. (1927), *Theorie der gesellschaftlichen Wirtschaft*,2nd edn, J.C.B. Mohr, Tübingen.

Webbink, I. (1984), *Innovatie en het midden-en kleinbedrijf*, E.I.M. Publications, Zoetermeer.

White, L.H. (1985), 'Introduction' to Carl Menger's *Investigations into the Method of the Social Sciences with Special Reference to Economics*, New York University Press, New York and London.

Wijers, G.J. (1981), *Industriepolitiek*, Stenfert Kroese, Leiden.

A. HEINRICH VON STACKELBERG (1905–1946)

Peter Oberender and Thomas Rudolf

For a long time von Stackelberg justified National Socialism. He belonged to the many scientists of all disciplines who accommodated themselves with the political relationships of the pre-1945 period. His scientific rank is not disputed, however, in particular with respect to the further development of the theory of market structures.

Von Stackelberg taught in Berlin (1935–40), Bonn (1941–43) and Madrid where he died while working as a guest professor. In 1934 he published *Marktform und Gleichgewicht* (later translated under the title *The Theory of the Market Economy*, 1952). At the heart of von Stackelberg's research was the analysis of oligopolies. He denies the reality of the model of full competition which is at the basis of the general equilibrium theory of Léon Walras and Vilfredo Pareto and which assumes perfect knowledge about products and prices of all market participants. Von Stackelberg maintains that a market is anything but perfectly tranparent. Mostly, one encounters the behaviour of businessmen who influence the market process purposively; equilibrium on these markets is very unlikely because businesspeople link up, make price agreements, form cartels or carry on price wars.

But there might be a market type with equilibrium. Taking Antoine Augustin Cournot's model of a duopoly of mineral water producers as a departure, von Stackelberg supposes not a trial and error process which ends with a market price and a volume of sales which satisfies both contenders but rather he assumes that the one follows the other. The first business will bring that volume to market which assures him, considering the reaction of the second firm, the highest profit. That volume of the first duopolist is called the 'independency supply'. The second supplier will be in a position of dependency: he adapts himself with the sales volume. But he may also choose an independent position with a lower price.

Suppose both duopolists will know all the details, then they will compare the independent and the dependent positions and strive for the one with the highest profit. In the author's model that is the independent position and if both are unwilling to give up, then a 'ruinous' competition will develop. Equilibrium therefore occurs only in von Stackelberg's world of oligopoly if one of the suppliers is independent and the other is satisfied with a follower's position. But why should he do so if he is to earn less?

That will be the case when the independent supplier is much stronger than the dependent one: an asymmetric relationship in von Stackelberg's terminology. The dependent firm will have more profits and a more secure position than if open and fierce price battles are the outcome of (desired or undesired) independent behaviour. The leading firm is called the 'Stackelberg leader' in the literature. The model may influence the strategic decisions of a country in its international trade policy. The higher the number of Stackelberg leaders in a country the more profits will be transferred to the domestic market if the firms are of an international stature. During the 1980s, American economists recommended the payment of export subsidies to leading domestic firms to acquire the leader position and to shift foreign profits to the home country. European countries have sometimes likewise defended a policy of 'national champions'.

Von Stackelberg drew a somewhat different conclusion in his publications. He assigned the role of market leader to the state in agreement with his National Socialistic views.

The state is entitled to interfere with pricing in the market, to change market structures, to order firms to join a cartel and to pursue other goals such as to establish a corporative state. Benito Mussolini's 'Fascist–corporative' state was his lodestar. He considered a democracy unfit to achieve a uniform economic policy; this is prevented by the need to reach compromise in a parliamentary system of democracy. He had already discussed this in his book published in 1934, referred to above.

It is unclear whether von Stackelberg could still be called a National Socialist as time progressed. During his Berlin period he helped a Jewish advanced student; he also tried unsuccessfully to get out of the SS (*Schutzstaffel*). He was a friend of Jens Jessen and participated with him in a wartime class for the study of the economy. The class was closed down in 1943 and Jessen was put to death the following year for having taken part in resistance activities. One of von Stackelberg's teachers, Erwin von Beckerath, became the centre of an independent working group in which many later members of the Freiburg school, which advocated democracy and a free economy, were also active. And in this group he lectured in 1943 on 'The possibilities and limits of state direction of the economy'. This lecture was published in *ORDO*, the yearbook of the Freiburg school in 1949, three years after von Stackelberg's death.

Walter Eucken mentioned this publication in a positive sense in his *Grundsätze der Wirtschaftspolitik* [Principles of Economic Policy] (3rd edn, 1952, p. 271). Apparently, there had grown some 'understanding'.

B. ERNST HEUSZ (1922–)

Peter Oberender and Thomas Rudolf

The effort to mark Ernst Heusz as a representative of a particular school of economics can only fail. Both his academic roots and his life work as an economist are too diversified for this to succeed. But he should be included in this volume because his contributions to oligopoly theory have greatly enriched the discussions about the adequate behaviour of firms in such types of markets. Alongside this area of research, the name of Heusz should also be linked with work in the theory of international economics and with the study of market theory in general.

Heusz studied economics in Leipzig, Berlin and Freiburg from 1940 to 1945. In Freiburg he wrote his PhD thesis with Walter Eucken on 'The rate of interest as a monetary phenomenon'. The book to qualify him as a private lecturer at the university had to be finished in St. Gallen, Switzerland because of the untimely death of Eucken in 1950. He duly qualified in 1954 with the publication of *Economic Systems and International Trade*, delivered on the basis of work on case studies at two Swiss institutions for research on problems of foreign trade and payments.

A Rockefeller stipend brought Heusz to the United States in 1956, where he became acquainted with the problems of antitrust policy in Washington before visiting several universities and meeting leading economists. Returning to Europe he was successively nominated as a private lecturer at St. Gallen, and professor at Nürnberg-Erlangen and Marburg (1966). Ten years later he returned to Nürnberg-Erlangen where he stayed until his retirement in 1990.

Heusz's work always stands in a historical context, the result of his having lived through the last days of the Historical school. The preoccupation with facts from economic history was for him a better approach to the complexity of economic relations as well as creating an enhanced understanding of economic interactions.

The concept of understanding plays a characteristic role in Heusz's way of thinking. Conscious human action presupposes an interpretation of circumstances, relationships and the factors relevant to these, which leads to the building of hypotheses. Following Max Weber, understanding is linked with explanation and an explicit model would clarify the problem. But application to the oligopoly problem is hindered by the multiple number of possible interpretations which can be given to the action–reaction interdependency of oligopolistic situations.

Heinrich von Stackelberg had come to the conclusion that such markets are without equilibrium. However, Heusz says that businessmen act on the basis of experiences they have gone through and will adapt their behaviour to what they may have learned – the more so because it would be unrealistic to assume that business leaders will misinterpret the objectively given action–reaction interdependency. If it is further assumed that there will be a sufficient degree of market transparency to make a rapid reaction possible, it seems unacceptable to agree with Joseph Bertrand that price competition in a duopoly is excluded. Price reductions among the duopolists change expectations and, on the basis of these, behaviour in the market. Suppliers come to understand what division of the market shares is objectively durable; at the end of the learning process they will establish not only *ex post* what has happened but also what is to be anticipated *ex ante*. 'Oligopoly, a determined process' was the title of Heusz's article in the 1960 edition of *Weltwirtschaftliches Archiv*.

The background to Heusz's thinking was made clear in his *Allgemeine Markt-theorie* (1965) which developed the oligopolistic interdependency in the successive stages of the evolutionary market process. The market structures and the conditions which guide the behaviour of the individual firms are seen as the result of the processes in the market which are differentiated in accordance with types of businessmen (innovators, imitators, adaptors and inert movers) and four characteristic market stages. The starting point is an exogenous product innovation which creates a market, and Heusz investigates the competitive processes until their disappearance from the economy. Market development is endogenously explained. The many partial models which are exposed in the book are clothed in verbal, graphical and mathematical presentations and the author also exerts himself to deliver historical evidence. The *Allgemeine Markt-theorie* or general market theory was a landmark in German thinking about the market processes and inspired many younger economists to investigate the consequences of this new approach for a variety of other fields such as business finance, the business cycle, institutional structures and others right to the end of the century.

C. ERICH HOPPMANN (1923–)

Peter Oberender and Thomas Rudolf

Competition theory in the German language area owes much to Erich Hoppmann. Born in Gelsenkirchen, he wrote a PhD dissertation on 'Trading margins as an economic problem'. His *Habilitationsschrift*, *Period Analysis as the Theory of General Economic Dynamics*, was delivered in 1955 (Both were in German.)

Teaching at the university brought Hoppmann successively to Nürnberg-Erlangen (1960–62) and Marburg (1962–68) and finally to Freiburg im Breisgau, where he succeeded F.A. von Hayek. He taught economic policy there until his retirement in 1989, but continued on a more short-term basis at Bayreuth, Jena and Dresden.

Hoppmann was dedicated to the interdisciplinarity of the sciences and valued in particular the exposition of the cohesion of economics and law. In 1993, the University of Tübingen awarded him an honorary degree in law for his work relating to this interest.

For many years the two focus points of Hoppmann's research work as an economist were competition theory and economic organization. Several of his important essays were brought together in the Collected Works. The latest to appear was *Wirtschaftsordnung und Wettbewerb* [The Economic System and Competition] (1988), whose title expressed the double focus.

Increasingly, Hoppmann distanced himself from neo-classical and welfare-theoretical ideas and it is due to him that these are no longer the guiding principles in current competition policy. Market processes occupy the central position. And it is due to his meritorious influence that the cartel law is more oriented towards freedom of competition than towards desired market results. Again, his publications on firm mergers have diverted attention from all efforts to achieve desired market forms.

According to Hoppmann the market is a complex phenomenon, the results of which are not predictable. Interdependencies between the economic and the political order make a planning of the economy or of market processes illusory. It may even distort the free order of society. Market organization is a self-organizing process and competition policy should grow within the context of market and law. That is, it should abstain from arbitrarily overburdening the law and from distancing itself beyond the value preferences of acting persons.

D. ERHARD KANTZENBACH (1931–)

Peter Oberender and Thomas Rudolf

As with Erich Hoppmann, the investigation of competition is central to Kantzenbach's research work. After studying economics at the University of Göttingen, the Free University of Berlin and in North Carolina, Kantzenbach enrolled for a PhD under Professor Andreas Predöhl in Münster. The dissertation was finished in 1959 and entitled 'Möglichkeiten und Grenzen der Konjunkturpolitik in der Europäischen Wirtschaftgemeinschaft' (On the possibilities and limits of business-cycle policies in the European Economic Community).

His *Habilitationsschrift, Die Funktionsfähigkeit des Wettbewerbs* [The Workability of Competition] (1965) became a very influential piece of work. Not only was it one of the most widely read books on economic policy in Germany; it also put its stamp on the scientific discussions relating to practical policy. After a stay in Princeton to carry out research into problems of US antitrust policy, Kantzenbach went to Frankfurt in 1967. This was followed by an appointment at the University of Hamburg where he combined teaching with the directorship of the Institute for Industrial Policy. In his endeavour to engage in the field of competition and competition policy, Kantzenbach was always intent on drawing conclusions for society with a high practical content, derived from theoretical research. This was especially visible in his work on behalf of the Monopolies Commission whose president he was between 1979 and 1986.

In 1994, Kantzenbach became the chairman of the association of German-speaking economists, the Verein für Sozialpolitik (now known as Gesellschaft für Wirtschafts- und Sozialwissenschaften). This was an expression of the high scientific and personal esteem which his colleagues entertained for the man who soon afterwards retired from the University of Hamburg which he had served since 1975.

4. Market theory in the Low Countries

Henry W. de Jong

THE NINETEENTH CENTURY

Napoleonic times were rather disastrous for Dutch industry and commerce though not for the then most important sectors of the economy: agriculture, horticulture, cattle breeding and the dairy and meat industry. Belgian manufacturing, on the contrary, benefited from the so-called 'continental system', introduced by the French emperor to exclude British industrial exports, and became the first business to industrialize on the continent. After 1815, when Restoration followed the European wars, things had fundamentally changed: East European exports depressed grain prices to the detriment of the Amsterdam corn market, the East India Company had failed and the triangular trade pattern of previous centuries, whereby north and east European raw materials, together with Dutch manufactures were sold in southern Europe, Africa and Asia in return for spices, tea, porcelain, gold and other luxury goods, was upset. Consequently, conditions in the Dutch economy were depressed, especially in the cities which claimed a restoration of the guilds and associations. These had been abolished by a Royal Decree of 1818 after a tussle which had lasted for more than 20 years. In France, the guild system was ended in 1791 and the manner in which this was done was the classic one: in the Middle Ages, the cities that wanted permission to institute guilds, paid the Crown an appreciable sum of money; at the dawn of the Revolution the French Republic, being again in dire financial straits, gave freedom of entry to non-guild members to exercise a trade or profession on the payment of a patent tax. In 1818 the Dutch did likewise; but intellectually, this was not a satisfactory solution. One of the scientific associations therefore offered a prize for the best essay on the question of whether the previous guilds were indeed propitious for trade and handicrafts (as it was maintained) and whether a revival of them would counter the prevailing depressed conditions. Professor H.W. Tydeman (1787–1863) won the contest. He was one of the first to teach political economy and descriptive statistics in the Netherlands. At Leiden University, Tydeman was the successor of Adrian Kluit, who lectured in history and diplomatic problems besides political economy between 1778 and 1806. Soon Tydeman had a colleague at the University of Utrecht, J. Ackersdijck, who introduced statistics as a separate discipline and together they founded economics as a distinct academic subject; they were both very good teachers.

Tydeman's Essay

The essay consists of four parts. First, the sources are discussed; these are the Amsterdam Laws and Statutes, which are the most complete and extensively compiled documents relating to the subject in Holland. Second, he makes a comparison of the advantages and disadvantages of the associations, and third, the question is raised whether the dissolution of the associations can be held responsible for the depressed conditions prevailing at the time. This is denied, like the fourth question: can a resurrection contribute to an economic improvement. This approach clearly distinguishes a consideration of the static and the dynamic factors. In the first parts Tydeman gives extensive information about the wages and salaries of the masters and fellows of 30 or so guilds out of the 51 existing at the time, according to a later, painstaking research by Dr van Eeghen (1965).[1] These are compared to the payments which had to be made on entry to the association and the time required for learning the trade. With respect to these, Tydeman recognizes their importance as possible impediments to entry for both youngsters and aliens. But his survey does not bring out such an effect: except for a handful of occupations (brewers, surgeons, pewterers, ribbon-weavers, confectioners) the payments to be made ranged from 4 to 15 per cent of one annual salary and the learning periods were limited to between one and four years (surgeons had an exceptional five years). The surgeons were relatively well paid, but poorly in comparison with the members of the Collegium Medicum, who were the medical doctors qualified at university level.

Entrance to the Collegium was denied to the surgeons who also earned money from beard-shearing and wig-making or had 'fellows' doing the work under their supervision. Frictions between the groups occurred frequently, for example about who was allowed to test and make medicines to cure 'serious illnesses' or to attend confinements using a pair of tongs. One successful surgeon in this skill, Johannus De Bruyn, with a record of 600 out of 900 live births during 38 years of practice was challenged by the Collegium to undergo an examination and (of course) failed. But then Alderman Watrin of the Amsterdam City Board simply changed the rules, installed a mixed examination committee and permitted De Bruyn and a colleague with similar complaints, to be sworn in without further tests. (Van Eeghen relates the story in detail, pp. 93–5.)

The story is symptomatic of the attitude of the rulers towards the guilds. Tydeman refers twice to Philip of Leyden (fourteenth-century author) when he says that the policy of the authorities in the Netherlands of old was to contain the associations. And he points out two other factors limiting the power of associations: first, the public markets which were held at least once per week in cities and towns and where the goods for basic needs could be bought; second, the merchants ordering the ships, equipment and victuals for their business, not only in overseas trade but also for traffic on the extensive Dutch inland waterways system, would restrain the guild's market power. For the rest, the equanimity with which Tydeman views the associations – he recognizes their usefulness as guardians of quality standards and of social support for poor and/or old members – makes it acceptable that he would have agreed with van Eeghen when she emphasized the strong role of competition from outsiders. Of these, two types could be distinguished: the fellows, living in the towns who, for various reasons could not rise to a mastership; and especially the interlopers or dabblers, living outside of town (and therefore not to be penalized by the guilds) who were favoured by consumers because of their low prices and even taken into employment by guild masters, who pocketed the price difference. Stiff penalties limited these practices, however.

As was said earlier, Tydeman sees no merit in the argument about the macroeconomic role of the associations. They are not a cause of the depressed economic circumstances nor will they be able to change them: this he rates as an example of *the post hoc ergo propter hoc* fallacy. Reduced spending by the merchant class because profits and interest receipts are lower, combined with heavy taxation due to the wars are the factors responsible, he says. There may have been some additional labour supply following the abolition of the guilds. But this cause is not an independent factor for its importance depends on the first. Here he is true to the Buridan theory that effective demand is the decisive hinge, though he admits to having to rely on a deductive argument only because the required statistics are not available. Interestingly enough, Tydeman specifies a list of statistical questions, the answers of which were necessary to settle the matter. After all, he was the first professor of statistics in the country.[2]

The Two-handed Economist

Jacob Leonard de Bruyn Kops (1822–87) published the first *Principles of Economics* exactly in the middle of the nineteenth century, in January 1850.[3] He was 27 years old and, by writing this first original book on economics which covered the whole field (in 455 pages), he started a lifelong commitment. Not only did he publish the *Principles* in five editions until the year 1873; he also founded the first scientific journal in economics, *De Economist*, in 1852. It still exists as the official publication of the Dutch Economic Association. De Bruyn Kops was the chief editor of the monthly for 36 years until his death in 1887. As Henk Wilm Lambers wrote on the occasion of its centennial 'this may have been the most fascinating period of the first hundred years because it showed a persuasion which rang through' (*De Economist*, 1952). In 1864 he was nominated to the chair of political economy at Delft Technical University, and in 1857 was one of the founders of the Association for Statistics and its president from 1880 to 1883. Following his election to the Dutch parliament in 1868, where he soon came to be known as 'the economist par excellence', de Bruyn Kops withdrew from his professorship after a collision with the minister for education who considered a professorate incompatible with a parliamentary position. Although this decision was overturned by the minister's successor in 1871 it seems that de Bruyn Kops had had enough, and he left the university two years later. Such a decision fits in with his character which was of a modest, straightforward type, intent on disseminating the truth (as he saw it) in social and economic matters and being of an independent mind. He hailed from a wealthy family of manufacturers and merchants, though he often sided in public behaviour with the lower classes and especially with the poor. De Bruyn Kops criticized the local excises and the taxes on basic necessities throughout the 1850s; to his satisfaction, they were scrapped in 1865.

The Dualistic Economic Science

De Bruyn Kops defines economics as the science that 'teaches how wealth in society originates and is being destructed' (*Principles*, see note 3). He expressly leaves out distribution, in contrast to most handbooks of the time because, he says, distribution or diffusion of wealth is really one of the ways of production if the latter is defined as the increase of exchangeable values. The chain of acts from taking the raw material to delivery to the ultimate consumer of riches is nothing but such an increase, and no room is left for distribution as a separate economic and main constituent. It is in fact related to a set of policy rules and measures; it is a part of the art of governing which is closely connected with the science of economics but should be sharply distinguished. The last 115 pages of the book are devoted to the discussion of topics such as population, wages, poverty and proposals for a different organization of society and the author tries to make it clear what room is left for discretionary measures taking into account 'the laws of economics' exposed in the previous pages.

But de Bruyn Kops is not a classical economist. He is not one who equates wealth or riches with material objects. This is made clear by the maxim on the title page: 'The true wealth of a people is not in the gold and silver, but in the reason, the hearts and the labour of the thousands of rational beings who compose the nation. There and only there is an inexhaustible goldmine'. Following the French economists of his time, de Bruyn Kops includes services as well as physical objects among the varieties of wealth; all labour, which ultimately is the only active producing agent, is differentiated into three types: (i) the productive services of scientists, technologists, engineers and so on who produce knowledge to the benefit of social production, (ii) the services of the entrepreneurs whose function it is to organize the production process and to mobilize the required capital, and (iii) the labourers who bring forth the goods and services. This division is seen as a functional one and will be encountered in all economic branches of activity though in a different composition.

The Right Hand: Competition

The really interesting characteristic of the *Principles* is the contrast between competition on the one hand and monopoly on the other. The first is the dynamic, wealth-producing principle whereas the other is responsible for either the destruction or the retardation of wealth creation (alongside consumption which also 'destroys' produced values). The explanation of the wealth-producing effect of competition rests on a phenomenon which in de Bruyn Kops's *Principles* acquires a compelling force. Income layers in society always form a pyramidical structure. At the top, the income earners are restricted in number although personal incomes are high, and they can buy high-priced goods. The lower layers are more numerous and widen the market substantially if prices can be reduced. The existence of such an income pyramid with layers of purchasing power generates a continuous incentive for producers to save on costs, increase efficiency and lower production prices, for successful producers pocket the difference between the prevailing market price and the reduced production price. The latter may be achieved in various ways: efficiencies of scale, or mass production as can be seen in the production of textiles, furniture, kitchen utensils, basic foodstuffs and so on; or, it may rest on the introduction of new tools, machinery and other aids, such as fertilizers. Also, new needs will arise continuously (people learning to read, creating a book market), transport and communications are improved and so on. Several chapters are used to enlarge on what the author calls 'the resources of production', such as the division of labour, machines, tools, money, credit and banks. This grouping underlines his productivistic bent.

The efficient producer can also share part of the profits with consumers. If he lowers the sales price he gains consumers as his clients by capturing them from competitors as well as attracting new entrants from the next lower income layers. He thereby rewards both consumers and himself:

> This remains so for some time until the improvement is generalized; the efficient producer shares for some time the gains with part of the public until the current price is brought down to the new position of the reduced production costs by the competition and then the advantage is finally secured for the consumers. (*Principles*, p. 46)

De Bruyn Kops clearly distinguishes the initiating, dynamic moves of the efficient firm from the equalizing, imitating actions of competitors and stresses the necessary role of both types: the former causes the advantage, the latter secures it. In the meantime the profits of the initiator are multiplied and that is the lure which spurs him on. Also, the process will not work immediately because there may be time lags: the closing down of a loss-making business will be postponed; suppliers in an overcrowded trade look to each other to give up first; financial resources may delay closures just like the availability of capital is no guarantee that new firms or factories will soon be founded: 'One will first have to be assured that there is a long-term prospect of advantageous prices; and it may be that there is not much idle capital or that, to start the new business, one has to give up other rewarding investments, etc.' (p. 43). The equalizing tendency of profits by means of competition is, properly speaking, never perfect and is only a long-term orientation. Still, it leaves room for the prospect of a large profit, especially for those who come forward with an improvement in the manufacture of a generally used and necessary product. De Bruyn Kops underlines the latter observation by means of italics and an extended paragraph in which the fickleness of luxury and fashion trades is contrasted with the constancy of necessary products; this relates to demand, profits, risks and external events such as wars or natural disasters.

Apart from the long-term face of the competitive process de Bruyn Kops also discusses the short-term movements of demand and supply which influence pricing. Market clearing is exposed by starting from the supply side: a manufacturing firm calculating a production price of a yard of cotton including a managerial reward, and a market where ducks are traded starting from an initial price asked by one of the sellers. It depends on the balance of quantities supplied and demanded *at those initial prices* (emphasized by the author) whether a seller's or a buyer's market develops.[4] This initial price will then be traded up or down until the market is cleared for all those who want to do business at the stated prices. Competition from both sides of the process is involved and the resulting price will not benefit everyone: there may be loss makers on the supply side and dissatisfied persons on the demand side. In particular, our author focuses on expectations and the calculations necessary to anticipate future market prices. This is noteworthy: whereas price anticipations are required in a current market, the producer in a long-term market who wants to be successful should not speculate on future prices but compare the lowest, current production price with the cost price he may be able to secure on the basis of the improved product or process he intends to introduce. This distinction is crucial. The late twentieth-century, neo-Austrian entrepreneur lives and thrives from anticipated price differences in a going market but the Schumpeterian entrepreneur makes a quantum leap, especially if the innovations are in produced means of production with general-purpose applications. De Bruyn Kops makes the comparison: a new lace-producing machine may increase efficiency substantially and lower the price of lace. But book printing on a faster machine will not only reduce the book price; the productivity of all those who apply the knowledge spread through the book itself will be multiplied. This is the reason, he says, why the inventions in telegraphy, steam engines, metallurgy, transport, fertilizers and so on have such wealth-raising effects. They increase incomes but also employment, life expectancy and social standards, be it mostly in the long run only. To cope with the inevitable social costs of the competitive process, later in his book he develops proposals for dealing with poverty and unemployment in which state support for health, retraining and return to the labour process figure prominently.

The Left Hand: Monopoly

The second part of the *Principles* is called 'Hindrances to competition' and is the left hand of the economic process which the author also dubs 'monopoly in its various forms': guilds and similar associations, government interference with the production process, protection against foreign competition and the promotion of domestic power, colonies and their government, and, finally a chapter on the 'monopolization of labour services in history through robbery and suppression, slavery, serfdom, forced services'. This broadly conceived chapter exemplifies the principle of monopoly which the author traces behind the diverging forms mentioned above: monopoly interferes with the fruits of free labour and trade by appropriating them for the benefit of the rulers and/or excludes economic agents from gainful activity by restricting it to the powerful only. It reaps where it has not sown and it excludes others from sowing so that it alone may reap.

This, however, is against the natural order of things under which man works to appropriate the produce for his own use or for exchanging it against the output of other people. The consequences of those hindrances are far-reaching and negative if one keeps to the basic principle that goods and services are always exchanged against other produce. For then one can see that the arresting in its development of whatever branch of activity has lower output as a result, first in those branches which supplied the raw materials and other essential products to the prohibited industry, and second, in the trades which handled the final products of the impeded business. And, indirectly, exchange between sectors is hindered and reduced because the lacking output destroys buying power. Thus direct damage is combined with stunted progress.

A final point: the author acknowledges the exclusive effect of patents though they are awarded to promote inventions and their applications. But he doubts very much the underlying supposition because 'many of the important inventions have been made without there being a prospect on the acquisition of monopoly' (*Principles*, p. 172). His doubts with respect to the necessity of patents were vindicated, at least in the Dutch case, when between 1869 and 1912 the country abolished its patent law and no invention from whatever origin was protected. It was this period which saw the birth and fast growth of the firms and industries which dominated the Dutch economy during the twentieth century: Royal Dutch-Shell, Philips, Unilever, Akzo, DSM, the sugar and textile industries and so on. The effects of the absence of a patent law were different, however. Philips escaped a costly and probably deadly patent litigation in the 1890s, the sugar industry avoided inventor and patent charges of up to 42 per cent when the diffusion process in sugar refining was introduced during the 1870s and the Dutch steel foundry started its business in 1902 on the basis of an exclusive contract with a German inventing firm; this firm was too afraid of revealing its secrets and unduly stimulating the competition.[5] De Bruyn Kops's monopoly theory would seem to be a little too general and dogmatic when he summarizes it as the exclusive right by the strong or rulers to sell or labour for gain (pp. 162–3). The strictures of Tydeman to the formal position of the guilds, for example, were real: alternative institutional markets, outside competition, countervailing power on the demand side, and, last but not least, the mistrust by the rulers of state and cities, mostly prevented an effective exploitation of apparently dominant positions.

Refinement of the Analysis

Following De Bruyn Kops, several economists discussed production cost and market price in their general theories of price and market but, curiously enough, neglected the downward trend of the production cost based on the pyramidical structure of incomes in society. Simon Vissering, for example (1818–88), professor at Leiden University, wrote a two-volume *Manual for Practical Economics* (1860–65) in which a downward-sliding long-run cost curve is depicted together with an oscillating short-run market price (which is applicable to most articles of general use, in particular manufactured products, he says) without telling his readers why that is so. Also, Nicolas Gerard Pierson (1839–1909), the best-known Dutch economist around the turn of the century, discussed the relationship between production cost and market price and stated simply: 'I think that a reduction in production costs in the end always has to reduce the value of goods if there is sufficient competition. This competition is a downward-levelling force which equalizes the profits, achieved in the various firms'.[6] No further explanation is necessary he said, and continued to consider the influence of a rise in cost. Here he differentiated between long-lived, durable goods of an infrastructural type such as houses, factories, canals, railroads and so on, and goods of daily use. In the second category the law of cost prevails but not in the first, he maintains, because the wearing out of such durable goods on a non-profitable basis may prevent their renewal but not their use, provided that the maintenance costs are met.

But these remarks have no general validity, not even in the nineteenth century. First, firms practically never have equal profit rates, notwithstanding fierce competition, if only because the level and structure of costs differ. Second, Vissering pointed out that bakers and butchers seem to work under 'very special circumstances' which 'create a sort of monopoly'. Consumers have special preferences with regard to some products (the 'fresh bread') as well as to the seller (our 'own' butcher or baker); when they buy other goods to satisfy their domestic or daily needs 'our housewives … are clever enough to find the shopkeepers who supply the best goods at the lowest prices' (*Manual*, pp. 331–3). Demand regulates the relationship between market price and production cost even though free competition, as the nineteenth-century economists understood it, prevails. Pierson, in 1864, did not perceive the hybrid sort of monopolistic competition, though Vissering, three years earlier had smelled trouble for established theory. Third, neither saw the dramatic impact of the new industrial competition in the way de Bruyn Kops did, who refused to restrict it to current consumption goods.

Enter the Cartels and Trusts

The final quarter of the nineteenth century saw the rise of the great business combinations: the cartels, syndicates and trusts. In 1883, when the German economist Friedrich Kleinwächter published his well-known book *Die Kartelle*, little was known about their existence, their names, locations, activities or the persons that guided them, as Kleinwächter states. He therefore organized a survey among the leading industrialists in Austria and Germany but was seriously disappointed: the information given was scarce, respondents were reticent with respect to pertinent facts and processes and nearly all insisted on secrecy.

But with their growth during the 1880s and the rising public interest in their activities, a need for apologetics arose. The associations started to publish in order to inform and justify their behaviour. However, 'to explain is to reveal' and a Dutch economist used the German weekly *Die Industrie* (issued by them) and other sources to write a dissertation in 1891 at Leiden University. In his book *Over ondernemers-verenigingen* (*Kartels en Trusts*), Willem van der Schalk (1891, pp. 3–8) dealt analytically and reservedly with the available information, acknowledging possible shortages and one-sidedness, but maintained: 'the secrecy practised relates more to the details, which, however important, will have little influence on the conclusions'. The book of some 190 pages was simply divided into two chapters, one on cartels and one on trusts, with a subdivision of 14 paragraphs followed by two appendices on cartel statistics and the deed of the US Sugar Trust (1887). He used many other sources, particularly in the second part.

Types and Origins

Cartels, the author argues, have to restrain production and/or supply so that prices can be raised or a possible decline stopped. Not all cartel types are equally successful in this and the five types distinguished – namely, the price-and quantity-fixing cartels, those who do both, the regionally sales-distributing organizations and the organizations that allocate sales and practise output sharing by means of a central bureau – show different degrees of effectiveness: the last are the best and comparable to the trusts. However, to bring order to an 'overcompetitive market', import protection is nearly always unavoidable and the domestic price, rewarding even the highest-cost producer required to satisfy demand at the price aimed at by the cartel must include an import duty sufficiently high to keep out foreign suppliers. If no further organization is accomplished, the cartel will mostly succumb because of its own dynamics: efficient producers have an incentive to expand on the high-price domestic market instead of getting rid of the output surpluses abroad at cut-rate prices. German iron wire, quoted at 220 marks per 1000 kilograms on the home market, was sold at 180 marks beyond the borders. Domestic consumers pay for the difference, are victims of monopoly and the foreign processing industry gets an unnatural boost.

Suppose that the protective duties are withdrawn – will the domestic price level revert to a world-market level? Not necessarily, for producers/sellers of various nationalities may unite in an international cartel. But van der Schalk points out the difficulties: of the 11 existing international cartels in 1888, several of them ended in disaster within three years, others disappeared from view and only two proved successful, above all the Nobel Dynamite Trust-Company, a cartel of British and German companies. Cartelized companies in low-tariff Britain – such as the Salt Union, United Alkali and the Metropolitan Bread Company – have tried to raise prices in vain.

Among the reasons why the less-organized types were not likely to succeed were the long preparation time to get joint activity off the ground, the lack of honesty in keeping to the cartel rules and the absence of an effective control procedure. State action at the German coalmines, where inspectors investigate on a monthly basis, or beer brewing where excise-revenues are accurately reported, proved to be cartel friendly. Industries operating with large quantities, and/or under general transparency (because of auctions) such as iron and steel, locomotive works, building and construction may see the rise of cartels. However, a necessary condition may not be a sufficient one, for auctions spread public knowledge about an industry and yet firms collude in the bidding process and entry is made more difficult if they are badly organized. (One hundred and ten years later some Europeans seemed to have forgotten this advice when they held the auctions for mobile telecom licences. Industrial economics needs long memories!)

Wibaut's Contribution

The merit of van der Schalk's analysis can be seen by comparing it with the Dutch monograph which commanded the widest audience during the period from 1900 to 1930: Wibaut's *Trusts en Kartels* (1903). The book asserted as its central theme that modern capitalism is incompatible with competition, because cartels and trusts, being a necessary phenomenon in the development of industry, restore the profitability which competition has eliminated. And these profits are the very rationale of capitalistic industry. Wibaut was a rather prolific writer, his works including a prominent paper on the subject at the meeting of the Dutch Economic Association in 1928. There he repeated his argument that to make a distinction between good and bad trusts or cartels (and still less to condemn them totally) is economically useless: these organizations are an unavoidable accompaniment of present-day capitalism; the challenge is to have their price behaviour guided and controlled by societal power to the benefit of all.[7]

Discussing the trusts, Wibaut referred to the United States, where tough anti-cartel legislation had only furthered the consolidation movement; tough corporate legislation was evaded by the trusts choosing to incorporate in the easygoing states and the tough political rhetoric of President F.D. Roosevelt and others had watered down the longer they were in office. Wibaut – a strong leader himself in the socialist movement and in the governance of the city of Amsterdam – also expressed his long-term outlook for the future. It was a mixture of realism (trusts will also capture the distribution sector and cooperative enterprise is an inadequate response), dogmatism (public firms will in due time improve the distributive imbalance) and, above all, a one-sided view of competition. Competition not only wiped out profits but, as de Bruyn Kops had argued, makes modern industry thrive by the grace of improvements and innovations that serve widening layers of consumers through price reductions in industry after industry.

THE TWENTIETH CENTURY

Nevertheless, as the decades of the new century passed, Wibaut's pertinent question: 'who or what is going to ensure that the actions of the big corporations or combinations will be to the benefit of society?', was increasingly echoed, and eventually, also by academic economists. Wibaut had argued that cartels and trusts are unavoidable because their efficiency far surpassed that of the small, unorganized firms of the nineteenth century. His advice was therefore: 'do not abolish them or reduce them to smaller proportions but hand them over to society', implicitly assuming that nationalized industries would remain equally efficient. Even the control by cooperative buyer or seller organizations would not suffice, he said: at best, as buyers, they can do away with the often large remunerations of middlemen; if they get a grip on the efficiencies of large-scale business by means of producer cooperatives they will, likewise, become profit-maximizing organizations having the same common interests as their rivals. And, these interests are not limited to the pursuit of profits by means of price fixing but extend also to the corruption and bribery of the political and legal system. Typical of his many cases was his reference (1903) to the 'petroleum murders: the low fixation of the inflammation point of petroleum by the oil corporations' (pp. 201–2), and pressure on the legislator which had already prevented, for more than 20 years, the further purification which raised costs of processing. Unnecessary deaths and injuries were the result; in London one per week, in England one per day and countless injuries as in other European countries.

Alfred Marshall had included such things (using child exploitation as an example) under his definition of 'real costs' and argued that the nominal price paid for the product or service did not cover such costs, but in a note he immediately skipped the topic 'as not very closely connected with the subject of this Book'.[8] Dutch economists were still less accessible: Verrijn Stuart, one of the leading Austrians in the field, commenting on a Prussian survey of 1912 in which it was found that industrial workers, especially in heavy industry, had a low chance of surviving past 40 years of age, said that this underlined the urgency for those workers to save from their incomes against the time 'that the productive power because of old age or disability would fail'. What one would expect of an economics professor, even if he had no great fellow-feeling, was at least some sense of elementary logic.[9]

The Pricing Model Discredited

During the first decades of the century the attention of Dutch economists was focused on the model of price formation under competitive conditions. When François de Vries (1884–1958) was appointed at the Rotterdam School of Economics (in 1913 as a reader in industrial economics and in 1918 as a professor) this was changed by his interest in the problem of economic power, especially of business and the trade unions. Initially, de Vries was inspired by Austrian theory, in particular Böhm-Bawerck's article of 1914: 'Macht oder ökonomisches Gesetz?'[10] Whereas Böhm-Bawerck focused on the possession of scarce resources and the combinations on the labour market, de Vries extended the view towards business combinations. These, he said, are not so much motivated for gaining a monopoly position or for achieving the cost savings which cartels and big corporations may secure. What prompts them is the divergence between the enlarged, fixed production capacity and the insufficient absorption capacity of the market. Fixed, relative to variable, costs have risen as a result of the drive for technical optimum and the required response is the limitation of production capacity to given demand by the combinations. Otherwise, entrepreneurs will extend output with every decline of the product price. On top of that, existing capacity of failing firms will be cheaply acquired by financially strong firms, disturbing the market equilibrium still further. The rise of trusts and combinations does not mean the end of free competition, he wrote in 1928. Competition will change its nature: more long-term, stability-oriented, rationalization of output and control of pricing will emerge, but be limited by the ever possible competition of outsiders (new firms, substitute products), insiders and by 'production deviation' (a concept formulated by his colleague

Jan Wisselink). The last, although not so visible, occurs frequently because many smaller firms have a flexible production system which allows them to produce articles or services deviating from those goods for which they are optimally equipped. If the combinations raise prices, their market entrance at higher cost may nevertheless be rewarding and endanger the quasi-monopolists. Examples are fine and coarse fabrics, steel container sheets to be used as boiler bodies and the road and shipping services in the transport sector in competition with the monopolistic railways. It is a form of 'latent competition' as de Vries called it.[11]

But he lost faith in the free competitive system relatively quickly, and in 1935, he pleaded for more regulation by central government, ostensibly because of failing social support for it. No rationalization for this turnaround by means of a new theory was given; nor was it explained whether such regulation should be seen as durable or crisis-induced only; in his lectures de Vries argued that traditional price theory had lost its central position and had fallen apart in a casuistry of cases depending on the conditions prevailing within firms and sectors. Mobility of production factors could not be assumed to bring about market equilibrium; prices in one and the same market could diverge because of preferences and sales costs, or 'stimulation costs' (as he called them); market organization could quickly change with thoroughgoing consequences for pricing and the type of pricing: there might be 'movable' prices and prices 'fixed' by the combinations; even the government might improve the operation of markets by means of price regulation. The paradox of modern markets is that intensifying competition reduces the free competition, he maintained.

After the Second World War, de Vries continued as the grand old man of Dutch industrial economics, having educated scores of academic economists including many professors, but retiring into the prestigious function of being the first president of the Social and Economic Council, the cornerstone of the Dutch postwar *Poldermodel*. If the game could no longer be called harmonious, at least the players could be harmonized under his guidance.

Business Organization and Oligopoly Problems

During the postwar period, competition was long neglected and/or considered to be a self-evident phenomenon. In politics, the debate raged about nationalization of important industries, demanded by the socialists, and the 'organization of industry', the ideal of the Roman Catholic and Protestant political parties and of many trade unionists. The latter type of organization was reminiscent of the ancient guild system with its regulations relating to products, prices and wages, social relations and so on. As we have seen, this topic had been debated recurrently during the previous seven centuries with mixed, and generally speaking, meagre results. The reasons are not difficult to find: the Low Countries have always had an open economy, embedded between the competitors of the large, surrounding countries of Western Europe, and, second, throughout the ages they have had large, internationally oriented firms of their own which were averse to sector organizations that they could not control. So, once again, little eventuated from requests for nationalization or the legally prescribed 'organization of industry': when de Vries died in 1958, no important firms (with the exception of the Central Bank) had been nationalized and only a few sectors of trade and primary industry, harbouring small- and medium-sized firms, had found ways to organize themselves according to the Law of Business Organization (1950). Yet, these developments were not so innocent as might appear at first glance because they fostered the pro-cartel and anti-competitive mentality of important segments of the population.

This was covered up during the quarter-century of fast economic growth (1945–70: 5 per cent volume growth per annum on average); however, with increasing stagnation during the 1970s and 1980s, this mentality became a supporting pillar of industrial rigidities.[12]

Competition policy did not offer a sufficient counterweight. For one thing there was no support in public opinion or in parliament for tough measures; for another, the handful of academic economists who studied competition and the related policies had not developed a market theory suitable to analyse problems of competition or combination in periods of fast growth or long-term stagnation. The void left by de Vries's agnostics was not filled up.

In the 1940s and 1950s a group of young, brilliant economists rose to prominence and concurred in the study of the theme of 'acceptable' or 'workable' or 'effective' competition. That meant the rejection, following the trail of de Vries, of the model of perfect competition as the expression of a natural economic order. At best, this model was, because of its catalogue of required conditions 'a description of a harass which in order to make it impervious has been so stiffened that it can only serve as an ornament' (Lambers, 1950, p. 8).[13] Lambers said that the introduction of the concepts of pure and monopolistic competition (Edward Chamberlin in 1933) was useful but not substantial: the impartial observer had always taken competition to be rivalry between different market partners. More important is oligopoly, but not in the Cournot/Bertrand sense because their models leave out the interdependency between the few. And the problems of oligopoly are those of a group of firms, each of which – it may be assumed with Marshall and Friedrich von Wieser – will strive to realize the integrating principle of continuity in its market strategy. In which the interdependent oligopolistic price is the focus point.

One might ask: are these (official) prices the bastions surrounded by the entrenchments to be extended or given up in line with the course of the battle, as K.W. Rothschild thought? That would imply a primary ranking of internal security, meaning the keeping of mutual relations between the oligopolists. Or is the aim a price meant to keep out the external intruders by setting a limit price just preventing entrance as Joe Bain thinks? Oligopolists will then sacrifice short-term profits in order to safeguard the long-term average profitability. Both positions seem to assume a synchronized behaviour of the oligopolists which may be at odds with their often observed conduct. Why is not every oligopoly the entrance to a cartel agreement, a merger or some other permanent, structural solution? To some extent Lambers sided with the conclusion reached earlier that same year by Fellner: 'In the real world spontaneous coordination shades over into explicit agreement by gradations'.[14]

Ultimately, the limit in such a spectrum of possibilities lies in the entrepreneurial acumen; the desire to remain independent in order to realize cost-saving innovations, product differentiation and new sales stimulation. These are the essential characteristics of competition as rivalrous behaviour.

Yet, even such competition is not without its problems: 'There is an impressive list of factors which hamper the mobility on which competition leans' (Lambers, 1950, p. 20). Such mobility barriers are to be found with entry, exit and the movement of resources within sectors. Governments contribute to them through legally supported arrangements. Friedrich von Hayek's theory of prices in markets, pointing to that 'wonder of telecommunications' through which in one symbol a row of economic changes can be signalled in all directions of the economy, is admirable. But we also know that the signals are often veiled, not so much because of the receivers but also because of the broadcasters.

Published prices do not coincide with transaction prices, quality competition supplants price rivalry and, often, complexes of factors overhang the ephemeral movements of demand and supply.

Schumpeter's theory that the progress of technology requires in a number of cases monopolistic positions may be questioned from two sides (Lambers, 1950, p. 25). First, a large firm may be so devoted to the technology or the product which earlier made it successful that it will have no eye for new developments. Second, there are numerous sectors where technology is not progressive; nevertheless, the alternatives of competition are excluded by the agreements which include the competitors. P. Hennipman's investigation of the same problem a few years later led him to the threefold conclusion that: first, 'the possibility of conquering a monopoly position provides a powerful and often indispensable incentive to adopt innovations'; second, that in so far established, as distinct from potential monopoly is concerned, 'it can plausibly be argued that its net effect is negative'; and third, that the monopolies most dangerous for progress are those that deliberately restrict and suppress competition, 'including that ... from the innovating activity of outsiders and newcomers'. In this way, Hennipman joined the views of the other Dutch competition economists that 'a strictly determinate connection between market structure and performance' should rightly be denied.[15]

Competition Policy: The Law of 1958

When no explanatory theory of the ways in which competition and monopoly influence performance could be found, Dutch economists turned to the other side of the equation and asked whether government could, by means of its intervention in the market, improve the outcomes. Jelle Zijlstra, one of the group of young economists who rose to prominence in the early postwar period, introduced the Law on Economic Competition during his term of office as minister of economic affairs (1952–58). He was also prime minister and governor of the Dutch Central Bank, thus completing a successful career in public office when he retired in 1988. The law was based on the concept of acceptable or workable competition, and incited by the theoretical discussions: if no causal relation between market structure and pricing performance could be upheld and unimpeded entry could not be relied upon to secure 'acceptable' prices, competition policy and pricing control had to be introduced. The general picture being one of a kaleidoscopic variety, the importance of empirical studies to support decision making became manifest.

Looking back in his *Memoirs* (1992),[16] Zijlstra wrote:

> The Law on Economic Competition was, properly speaking, the most beautiful law I have ever been at work on. It was an effort to bring modern views on pricing into practice. The central idea was that free price formation in the market economy should be accepted as the leading principle but that it does not always give acceptable results. Especially through cartelization and other forms of economic power concentration, buyers of products or services may experience great disadvantages. Governments should therefore dispose of corrective means. The law was really well constructed and in the parliamentary debates economists could assail one another with citations from learned manuals. But, unfortunately, the law has not been very effective. Dealing with economic power positions proved to be legally unruly. The fight against unwanted cartel formations is very difficult in our country because the habit, particularly in trade and services, to make agreements on prices, conditions of delivery and so on is deeply rooted.

Because retailers are often involved these things are politically sensitive and the minister has to operate cautiously. By way of a joke I have sometimes said that a visit from bakery employers, with demands regarding the price of bread, worries me more than a visit from the Philips management. There might be parliamentary questions about the bread price, which, if handled carelessly, might be dangerous for the minister. The Philips management or that of other large firms would not be able to achieve that. It is better that the European Economic Commission has also acquired powers in this field, for an effective cartel policy would probably never have materialized in our good country. The law was intellectually a precious toy but policywise a disappointment. (*Memoirs*, p.46)

In Search of the Culprit

Was it really the cartel behaviour of the small firms which undermined the Competition Law? Or was the law itself an ineffective creature because it was based on the abuse principle which obliged the government to detect and prove illicit behaviour? Arguments about correct behaviour, and in particular about pricing, are mostly endless and ephemeral as cases show.[17] Moreover, the criterion for judging abusive behaviour, namely, the general interest, is notoriously vague and will be interpreted differently by the parties concerned as well as by avenues of appeal such as parliament or an administrative court. That the Dutch law (of 1958) contained such criteria, rather than the prohibitions of EEC law (1956) or the more limited German law (1958), was not accidental. They followed from the theoretical view discussed above that government should supervise the formation of 'acceptable' prices and intervene if necessary.

On top of that, decision making was not helped by profound empirical studies. The Department of Economic Affairs barely undertook any, economists of the Competition Advisory Commission had no right of initiative to propose cases and had to get their data material of underlying cases from the department, and university researchers were not encouraged to discuss decisions (which were few) publicly. Whether a case was to be published after a decision was a matter for the minister's discretion. Finally, Zijlstra acknowledged in the second part of the quotation that he was personally involved in negotiations with business interests and no longer felt free to decide objectively. At the time it was known, at least within the Competition Commission, that the civil servants, charged with the execution of the department's decisions would 'anticipate' these: they tried to guess what the head of the department would decide in order not to lose face with their business counterparts in the preparatory talks. Thus, the view that competition policy, when in political hands, is used for political purposes, is not far from the truth. Disappointed, I left the Commission in 1986.

Freedom regained opened up the possibility of writing an article in the widely-read *Economics Weekly ESB*: 'The Netherlands, the cartel paradise of Europe?'. The contents suggested that the question mark should be replaced by a note of exclamation. The article was a bombshell, 'cartel paradise' became buzz words and its impact was soon amplified by the decision of the EC Commission to condemn and fine the nationwide building and construction cartel. Within two years the government proposed a new and remodelled Competition Law which was approved by the Dutch parliament in 1996. Five years earlier, Belgium had modernized its Competition Law of 1960 by changing the abuse principle into a prohibition of conduct preventing, restricting or distorting competition.[18]

Empirical Research

A pioneering study was the first econometric approach to the effects of industrial concentration in the countries of the Common Market, though Germany had to be omitted because of incomparable data (Phlips study).[19] Even for the countries included, the authors acknowledged '[a] heavy burden on empirical work in the field of business pricing problems' due to an absence and a heterogeneity of national price and production statistics. Nevertheless, they came to the conclusion that the degree of concentration appeared to have no influence on upward price flexibility: 'Prices tend to follow increases in unit costs, while market structure does not appear to have any particular influence' (pp. 34–5). But that may have been a premature conclusion and, moreover, only true for the period reviewed (1958–65, using the concentration statistics of 1962).

Between 1958 and 1968 there was rapid economic growth inside the Common Market with increasing interpenetration of trade, due to disappearing tariffs and quantitative restrictions. There was a high proportion of industrial goods and energy in the composition of this trade, rising from 77.5 per cent in 1958 to 81 per cent in 1967. Consequently, export values of the Common Market countries rose hardly at all when the German and Dutch revaluations of 1961 are taken into account: 0.3 per cent on average per annum, much less than consumer, wholesale and domestic industrial goods price increases. The only explanation which fits these facts is the declining effective concentration, as a result of which more intensive competition forced down the sales price of the goods, in particular motor cars and other durable consumer goods, the production costs of which fell per unit because of scale economies and new techniques. After the middle of 1969 this suddenly changed with the cyclical upturn; industrial domestic and export prices rose in tune at the rate of 3.3 per cent on average per annum. In the meantime the merger wave of the second half of the 1960s had changed market structures profoundly in many industrial sectors; the oligopolization of markets enabled large firms to act in concert with regard to their pricing behaviour. The drawback of a cross-section analysis, applied to a dynamic development of growth and structural change as characterized by the institution of the Common Market, is visible here.[20]

Nevertheless, pioneering studies are often valuable as much for the lacunae they lay bare as for what they have discovered and the Phlips study spurred on others to improve industrial statistics and to conduct sector research. With the growth of dominant positions on important EC markets during the 1970s, this proved to be opportune: the first book to appear on industrial economics in the European Community as a whole, after the inclusion of Britain, Ireland and Denmark, could draw on a much improved base in both respects.[21]

Market Size and Growth

The expansion of the Common Market economy and the opening of national markets led Phlips and others to observe that 'Concentration is a decreasing function of relative market size' (see note 19 Phlips et al., 1971, p. 172). Effective concentration, or the intensity of competition could therefore be substantially different from the statistically available ratios. A correction of these being required for adequate measurement, the implication of market widening went much further theoretically. A realistic market theory incorporates both spatial and temporal elements which are influential in determining entrepreneurial behaviour consisting of competitive moves and structural interventions. The causality of structural variables on the dependent performance variables is called into question if widening markets are involved. One is irresistibly reminded of one of Adam Smith's pertinent remarks:

> To widen the market and to narrow the competition, is always the interest of the dealers. To widen the market may frequently be agreeable enough to the interest of the public; but to narrow the competition must always be against it, and can serve only to enable the dealers, by raising their profits above what they naturally would be, to levy, for their own benefit, an absurd tax upon the rest of their fellow-citizens.[22]

However, widening markets and narrowing competition do not run simultaneously. A widening market stimulates expansion by established firms, entry by new firms and vertical forward and backward moves as well as diversifying growth by firms from other sectors. Competition is bound to intensify, prices decline and profits dwindle or, depending on the relative position of firms, disappear altogether. The process is substantially influenced by type of product and the successive innovations in it, by capital intensity, the structure of demand and other factors. It is only when the widening of the market stops or slows down that competition narrows through overt or tacit coordinative actions, and/or mergers and takeovers meant to relieve competitive pressure. Thus, competition for growth widens the market but a market widened to saturation kills the competition just like protection and partition: the urge to merge is fed by the need to compete.[23]

The analytical tool to discuss dynamic markets was found to be the growth or innovation cycle, replacing in the Netherlands the workable competition theory; as we have seen in a previous section, the causal impact of structure on performance being questioned by Dutch economists, some opted for government intervention on (price) performance. But growth-cycle theory denied that this could be successful because it went against the grain of a saturated market where price fixing and price stickiness are the order of the day. Much better would be the prevention of concentrative mergers, the dissolution of nationwide cartels, the refusal of public financial support for (mostly) large firms being phased out and, positively, to create the conditions for new firms to be established and grow in new sectors. Thus, the scenery partially shifted to the meso-economic field and in particular to industrial policy, as we shall see in the last section.

Growth-cycle Theory

There were a number of analytical advantages of growth-cycle theory in comparison with static market theory, though, like every theory, it had to make abstractions. Thus, it was able to explain the economic logic of sector developments.[24]

First, it distinguished various market stages or phases according to rates of growth of sales by competing firms. These were the accelerating and decelerating marginal increases in the innovative and expansionary stages, rising average receipts during saturation and declining absolute sales in the final stage. This method brought market theory much closer to real market proceedings than equilibrium theory would permit. The separate stages could also be distinguished according to structural characteristics, behavioural parameters and performance outcomes. Thereby, distinctions which traditional theory had neglected and which agreed with real processes could be made, for example: the contrasting pricing behaviour of firms in expansionary and stagnationary oligopolies; the different meanings of monopoly in innovative and declining markets and their diverse treatment in competition policy; the rise and types of multi-market firms; and so on.[25]

Second, Schumpeter's brilliant insights into the function of the entrepreneur, applied by him mainly to the explanation of the business cycle, could also, and maybe even better, be applied to the analysis of sector markets. One of the pertinent findings related the surplus capacities arising from decelerating growth of sales after the expansion phase to continuous growth of fixed investments. This proved to be nearly unavoidable because it could not be anticipated. Likewise, a sectoral decline, though partly predictable, if due to substitute products or the rise of a new industrial country, could not be stopped if receding demand occurs.[26] And surely, part of the problem of aging industries has to do with lagging entrepreneurial capabilities as firms grow larger: size necessitates long-term decisions and the uncertainties inherent in these drive managers towards organizational control, the process of internal and external institutionalization, as Lambers had called it in 1958.[27] If market parties are not satisfied with the outcomes of the market process they will substitute it for the creation of 'institutions', that is agreements, procedures, rules and habits: 'It is an effort to add an instrument so that the market can be steered into the direction of desired goals' (p. 766). The institutionalization is 'internal' if it is due to the initiatives of the managers; 'external' if the government or other authorities are involved or take the initiative. Managers conceive their function as one of conserving the existing potential instead of creating new sources of surplus value as entrepreneurs do. So cartelization, merger activity, subsidization of weak firms and calls for an industrial policy were voiced during the 1970s when one sector after another matured or ended in decline.

Third, the theory offered an explanation for the recurrent merger waves which characterized the industrially developed world since the last quarter of the nineteenth century. When sectors mature, competition becomes more intense, which is a major reason for horizontal and partly also vertical mergers. Diversification is stimulated by more adventurous managers and was a growing segment in the postwar period. But sectors mature unevenly; they diverge with respect to duration, scale and regularity of development. So sectoral mergers, takeovers and concentrated joint ventures do not run synchronously, and if events are added an irregular but tendentious wave-like cycle results. Obviously, the importance of leading industries which comprise the merger waves changes in the course of time, and there is no systemic link with the general business cycle.[28]

Fourth, the approach is conducive to the construction of an economy's sector profile in which net or gross added value is used as a measuring rod. If sufficient data are available – such as the EC Commission increasingly provided in the late 1970s and 1980s – the method can be used to gauge the modernity and competitive power of an economy.[29]

The Management of Corporations

Finally, the pathbreaking work of A.A. Berle and G.C. Means on the managerial firm (1932) found an echo and further development in the Low Countries through the contributions of Herman Daems.[30] Daems investigated the reasons why managerial hierarchies replaced market mechanisms and coordinating agreements between firms, first in a joint publication with economic historian van der Wee and later specifically applied to the Belgian form of financial holdings. Those corporations act as financial intermediaries but they were also shown to be able to exert intra- and intersectoral control. The question was raised whether such control had retarded economic development in Belgium (which could not yet be confirmed) or whether other effects in European countries and the United States could be detected. While the verdict remained open ('No easy answer exists', Chandler and Daems, 1980, p. 215; see note 30) at least the problem had been made much more transparent. Also, several penetrating firm studies were made during the 1970s, among others by R. de Lange and A. Wassenbergh on failing firms in the construction and shipbuilding industries.

Restructuring the Economy

With the increasing problems visible since the mid-1960s in industries such as textiles, cloth, shoe and leather production, coal mining, shipbuilding and (later on) steel, another view on economic development seemed to be required. Initially, the reaction had been one of *ad hoc* measures which were sometimes successful because the parties concerned (employers, trade unions and the government) united in a concerted action to restructure the industry or even close it down as in coal. But mostly, the measures lacked sufficient results because the problems had an international origin for which no national solution was available.

Nevertheless, these particular industry problems had a limited effect on the Dutch economy until the end of the 1970s because it could rely on a good number of expansive industries, which paid higher wages than the recessive trades and partly also increased employment. Uneasiness was rather fed by similar problems, but on a much larger scale, in the surrounding countries. Belgium and northern France had troubles in their long-established steel, coal and heavy chemicals trades and Britain experienced deindustrialization on a massive scale, primarily in the large staples trades but also partly, it seemed, due to mishandling more modern industries such as motor cars and electronics. A more comprehensive theory was needed in the view of several economists.

Two candidates were available, namely, the real labour cost theory, developed as a macroeconomic theory by economists from the Central Planning Bureau (CPB) who could use the statistical base gradually built up since Jan Tinbergen founded the institution in the 1940s. This theory held that employment in business (including government firms) is a function of real labour costs; it seemed to seek its foundation mainly on the neo-classical theorem of substitution of production factors in relation to their relative prices.

Growth-cycle economists were opposed to this view and argued that market growth, derived from innovative goods and services, determines employment opportunities in firms, though not necessarily in a strictly proportionate way. Real cost containment, for example by means of wage or price restraint, offers no solution when stagnation strikes or substantially cheaper international competition occurs. It may even worsen things by subdueing expenditures; productivity growth without an increase in market demand wipes out labour and employment opportunities. The Ministry of Economic Affairs sided with this view.[31] Its implied, but also articulated policy design was that, if the overall goal is to increase net added value per employee and to raise the number of gainfully employed, a 'conditioning policy' will be necessary for the innovation and growth phases, encompassing measures such as the elimination of bureaucratic obstacles, the promotion of development credits, the adaptation of the tax system and so on. Second, for maturing industries, policy could investigate and anticipate problems relevant to them in a general sense; for example, environmental, educational or energy questions. Third, the decline phase leaves few other possibilities than consolidation with lower levels of employment and added value. Protectionism is 'very contestable' and does not generate the desired future structures.[32]

One of the main backgrounds to the restructuring crisis of the 1970s was the rise of the service industries. In many quarters, this phenomenon was not recognized. The CPB authors too, held that a rise of productivity through disembodied investments in existing business would be 'improbable'. By extension, the vertical disintegration of those services would not help either. But growth-cycle theorists and the Economics Ministry strongly upheld the value-adding capacity of service industries.

Finally, by using the data of the CPB study for the 23 sectors upon which it was based, but rearranging them in two tables of employment-creating and -expelling industries, it became clear that real cost increases could not be a good explanation of output, changes in the competitive position or price developments. A comparison of two periods, 1953–63 and 1963–73, showed that changes in the capital coefficient did not correspond with wage increases or decreases in the required, inverse way. The CPB itself found for the 1950s a rise in the capital coefficient, though wages were low; since 1963, the coefficient has fallen slightly, but wages 'exploded' (this was the term used for developments during the 1960s). The CPB economists pointed towards a change in the industrial composition which had taken place but had apparently forgotten that their model did not allow for such an explanation (all machines, equally manned, cost the same, it was assumed). The oppositional theory had no problem in explaining these phenomena, for an expansive industry will utilize large-scale production methods and the more capital-intensive processes will go hand in hand with output growth and wage increases. This pattern was repeated in the newer industries of the ensuing decades, for example, production of compact discs or mobile telephones.

Nevertheless, politicians and most macro economists continued to rely on wage restraint as a solution to temporary crises in the next 30 years and the reason is evident: whereas a wage standstill can be negotiated, achieved soon and written on the account of policy makers, a successful innovation policy requires consistency and the application of scarce, intelligent resources. Although the theory battle was won by the market theorists they lost the prize: innovation policy did not get off the ground.

NOTES

1. Henrik Willem Tydeman won the contest and prize, offered by the Zealand Association, with 'an Answer to the Question on the Institutions of Guilds or Corporations'. The Question dated from 1818 and the prize for the 124 pages of the Essay was awarded in May 1821. The essay was published in Middelburg (Eeghen, 1965). The 51 guilds existed in the second half of the eighteenth century, but declined to 37 in 1798. There had been a continuous rise since 1400 (a few); 1486 (19, according to an official count); 1570 (idem: 25); and 1688 (45), a growth partly caused by splitting-ups. The figures are interesting, for they show that the rise and decline of the guilds went hand in hand with fluctuations in Dutch prosperity. See I.H. van Eeghen *De gilden. Theorie en praktijk*. [The Guilds: theory and practice], Fibula reeks No. 5, Van Nishoeck, Bussum.
2. There were, of course, several others who wrote about this subject, some with more pronounced opinions. See C. Wiskerke, *De afschaffing der gilden in Nederland*, H. Paris, Amsterdam, 1938, pp. 90–96.
3. J.L. de Bruyn Kops, *Beginselen van Staathuishoudkunde*, Gebhardt & Co., Amsterdam, 1850. The third edition of 1860 was an extended and revised one and is used here. The book had first and foremost an educational goal: to spread the knowledge of economic principles among the public and the colleges where economics became a compulsory subject. The notes are used mainly to enlarge on topics dealt with in the text, not to refer to other literature. Probably because of this, de Bruyn Kops has been criticized and neglected by academics in the nineteenth and twentieth centuries until the two foremost market theorists at

the centennial of *De Economist* (1952), P. Hennipman and H.W. Lambers, recognized his balanced approach and originality.

4. De Bruyn Kops stated this condition in the third edition (p. 44) or earlier. William Thornton presented it as a novelty in his *On Labour* (first chapter), London, 1869.
5. M. Bakker, *Ondernemerschap en vernieuwing. De Nederlandse bietsuikerindustrie 1858–1919*, NEHA-Serie III, 6, Amsterdam, 1989, pp. 174–91. The book by Bakker about entrepreneurship and innovation in the beet sugar industry, accurately shows the dramatic decline in costs and the inverse rise in output for an industry which stood as an example of de Bruyn Kops's theory and on which he wrote himself in *De Economist* (1877). J.C. Westerman, *Geschiedenis van de ijzer en staalgieterij in Nederland*, Demka, Utrecht, 1948, pp. 190–94. The Dutch firm, De Muinck Keizer paid Fl. 20,000 for the exclusive rights on the use of this invention in the foundry industry, but, of course, had only a monopoly position in the formal sense, because there were solely fiscal import duties.
6. S. Vissering, *Handboek van Practische Staathuishoudkunde*, 2 vols, Van Kampen, Amsterdam, 1860–65. N.G. Pierson, 'Waarde en productiekosten', in *Verspreide economische geschriften*, Vol. 1, F. Bohn, Haarlem, 1910, pp. 104–26 (from *De Economist*, 1866).
7. F.M. Wibaut, *Trust en Kartellen*, A. Soep, Amsterdam 1903; *De betekenis van trusts en kartels voor de volkswelvaart*, Gravenhage, The Hague, 1928, pp. 53–118.
8. A. Marshall, *Industry and Trade*, Macmillan, London, 1919, p. 183.
9. C.A. Verrijn Stuart, *Hoofdtrekken van de leer der maatschappelijke voortbrenging*, 1931, cited from the second edition 1945, F. Bohn, Haarlem, p. 57.
10. E. von Böhm-Bawerck, 'Macht oder ökonomisches Gesetz?', *Zeitschrift für Volkswirtschaft, Socialpolitik und Verwaltung*, 1914, Vol. 23, no. 3–4, pp. 205–71. Translated into English as 'Control or economic law?', in *Shorter Classics of Böhm-Bawerck*, Libertarian Press, 1962.
11. De Vries chaired several investigative commissions, including one about tariffs of the Dutch railway system in the 1930s and one about cartels in the building and construction sector (1956). The assumption that price fixing would be the result of cost rigidities, based on (relatively) higher fixed costs was tested several years later by Verdoorn, who published his findings in 1943. No general increase in the rigidity of production costs was found, but he did not exclude 'that a rise in constant costs, as seen per firm, works in this direction', P.J. Verdoorn, *De ontwikkeling en druk der constante kosten*, F. Bohn, Haarlem, 1943, p. 72. For a summary of de Vries's work and publications, see M. Dullaart, *Regeling of Vrijheid*, Kanters, Alblasserdam, 1984.
12. Macroeconomic policy commanded the attention of politicians and economists because there was a nearly general agreement that the economy could be 'steered' or 'guided' by means of the econometrically clothed models fabricated by Jan Tinbergen's Central Planning Bureau. The fast economic growth was often attributed to the policy prescriptions (including wage restraint) derived from such models. Harold Wincott, a lead writer of the *Financial Times*, during a visit to Holland remarked that in the UK, the dogs [he meant the trade unions] bite the economists, in Holland the economists bite the dogs. With the onset of the stagnation during the 1970s the unanimity disappeared, however.
13. H.W. Lambers, *Marktstrategie en mededinging*, F. Bohn, Haarlem, 1950, pp. 18–24. Lambers, who was a prolific writer on problems of competition, concentration, industrial and competition policy during his long professorship at the Rotterdam School of Economics, was also the first chairman of the Competition Committee, prescribed with the Competition Law of 1958. He died in 2004, 88 years old.
14. W. Fellner, 'Collusion and its limits under oligopoly', *American Economic Review*, May 1950, p. 54. Bain's article was also in the *American Economic Review* of May 1950 and K.W. Rothschild wrote 'Price theory and oligopoly' in the *Economic Journal* of September 1947.
15. P. Hennipman, 'Monopoly: impediment or stimulus to economic progress?', in E.H. Chamberlin, *Monopoly and Competition and their Regulation*, Macmillan, London, 1954, pp. 421–56. Other economists of the workable competition school were W.L. Snijders, who was the first director of competition policy at the Ministry of Economic Affairs and who wrote *Beschouwingen over de theorie der monopolistische concurrentie* (Kemink, Utrecht 1945), and P.B. Kreukniet, professor of economics at the University of Leiden who argued in his *Aanvaardbare mededinging* (F. Bohn, Haarlem, 1951), that such 'acceptable competition' would only be realized if prices were equal to the lowest possible production costs necessary to satisfy demand in a free market. Free entry is indispensable, should be secured by government and, if this were impossible, the authorities should change the market structure. He did not enlarge upon the ways to achieve this goal, however; nor did he apparently see the inconsequence of his precept since the theory stated that causal relationships between structure and price performance did not prevail.
16. J. Zÿlstra, *Per slot van rekening. Memoires*, Amsterdam/Antwerpen, 1992.
17. In the mid-1950s Zijlstra also introduced a new price law meant to 'counter price increases which were considered to be against the general interest'. So the legal apparatus was available. It was mainly used to prevent 'price wars' in small business or to align the pricing behaviour of those firms in times of inflation to the wage restraint imposed on the trade unions. See note 12. Those laws were seldom used against big business and several times proved to be ineffective, for example in the famous case against Hoffmann–La

Roche in the 1970s. To determine the firm's market share in the tranquillizer market (valium and librium) the Competition Commission had asked the minister to make the quarterly surveys of International Medical Statistics (IMS) accessible: the IMS was the European-wide organization assembling and providing the sales statistics from and to the pharmaceutical industry. The answer was that this was considered to be unnecessary. Shortly afterwards the case was lost exactly on this point!

18. The change had already been proposed in 1986 but dissolution of the Belgian parliament caused delays. See *EC Reports on Competition Policy* nos 16, chs 4 and 20, Appendix, Competition Policy in Member States (resp. of 1987 and 1991). The article on the cartel paradise was in ESB or *Economic and Statistical Reports* of 7 March 1990, published by the Nederlands Economisch Instituut, Rotterdam; the Decision by the EC Commission was dated 5 February 1992.
19. L. Phlips and assistants, *Effects of Industrial Concentration: A Cross-section Analysis for the Common Market*, North-Holland, Amsterdam, London 1971. The book was based on a report submitted to the European Commission in 1969.
20. H.W. de Jong, 'Industrial structure and the price problem', in J.M. Blair (ed.), *The Roots of Inflation: The International Crisis*, New York, Burt Franklin & Co., 1975, pp. 165–211. Figures in the text were taken from the tables on pp. 189 and 198.
21. A.P. Jacquemin and H.W. de Jong, *European Industrial Organisation*, London and Basingstoke, Macmillan, 1977. The impact of market structure on price performance was discussed in this book on pp. 146–48.
22. A. Smith, *Wealth of Nations*, Oxford edn 1976, Vol. 1, p. 267.
23. By the middle of the 1970s, European economists from various countries had come to share the view that size and concentration were much less important for achieving good performance than politicians and industrialists thought. See the studies by Philips, Jacquemin, Linda, George, Prais and others in Part Two of *Markets, Corporate Behaviour and the State*, Nijenrode Studies in Economics, Vol. 1, The Hague, Mart. Nyhoff, 1976, edited by A.P. Jacquemin and H.W. de Jong. That, at least, removed the main objection against the tightening of EU competition policy with respect to mergers which was finally achieved in 1989.
24. Growth-cycle theory was prepared by van de Woestijne's demonstration that the Marshallian demand curve is not representative but has to be replaced by a backward-bending curve at the low price level typical of the saturation phase. Empirically, Busé found a growth cycle even in an industry as typical as the Dutch bulb-growing sector with its manifold varieties. W.J. van de Woestijne, *Een algemene vorm van de vraagfunctie*, Leiden, Stenfert Kroese, 1953. H.J. Busé, *De markteconomie van het bloembollenbedrijf*, Nijmegen, De Gelderlander, 1962 (Dissertation, University of Amsterdam).
25. H.W. de Jong, 'Marktanalyse en markttheorie', *De Economist*, 119, no. 2, 1971, pp. 182–205. *Dynamische markttheorie*, Leiden, Stenfert Kroese, 1972. Chapter 4 discussed the effect of widening markets on market structures in a dynamic setting, a topic which attracted the attention of European economists in those years.
26. Marginal revenues of the sector will recede as the income elasticity of total demand and the price elasticity of product demand decline, whereas cross-elasticities between suppliers rise. Interdependencies then drive towards the control of competition and a reorganization of the sector. See de Jong (1972, pp. 116–20), note 25.
27. H.W. Lambers, 'Over de institutionele markt', *De Economist*, no. 11, 1958, pp. 753–75.
28. See the articles on merger waves in Part Two of *Markets, Corporate Behaviour and the State*, op.cit. in note 23, pp. 53 ff. and De Jong (1972, ch. 7); see note 25. 'No systemic link' does not deny that there are mutual influences, sometimes very strong. But the simple proof is that several sectors had no or scant merger events for long periods, notwithstanding the business cycle.
29. See M. Geldens, *De Vennootschap Nederland*, Den Haag 1979, who found a disquieting profile for Dutch industry. This had an echo in the fundamental report organized by A. van der Zwan, (*The Future of Manufacturing* [*Plaats en toekomst von de Nederlandse industrie*], staats-uitgeverij, Den Haag (1980). Together with the Wassenaar Agreement between employers and trade unions (1982) this accomplished a revolutionary change in economic policy. A similar profile was made for the European economy in the 1980s.
30. A.A. Berle and G.C. Means, *The Modern Corporation and Private Property*, Macmillan, New York, 1932. H. Daems and H. van der Wee (eds), *The Rise of Managerial Capitalism*, Louvain University Press and M. Nyhoff, Louvain/The Hague, 1974; H. Daems, *The Holding Company and Corporate Control*, M. Nyhoff, Leiden/Boston, 1978, A.D. Chandler and H. Daems (eds), *Managerial Hierarchies: Comparative Perspectives on the Rise of the Modern Industrial Enterprise*, Cambridge, MA and London, Harvard University Press, 1980.
31. It is impossible to give an adequate survey of this debate within the confined space here available. With numerous variations and intensities it returned when periods of recession became manifest, down to the aftermath of the 'new economy' bubble. Probably the best overview of the various theoretical and policy approaches can be found in A. van der Zwan (ed.), *Investeren, winst en werkgelegenheid*, a collection of essays and articles under the general title: Nederland in zaken, Veen, Utrecht/Antwerpen. (The Netherlands in business; investments, profits and employment), 1985. Professor A. van der Zwan was the economist

who, more than anybody else, focused attention on the persistent restructuring task. In addition he wrote a comprehensive volume, *Grondslagen en Techniek van de Marktanalyse* [Foundations and Techniques of Market Analysis] (Leiden, Stenfert Kroese, 1980).

32. The ministry had published a policy document, *Nota Selectieve Groei*, in 1976. J.W. Hillege, one of its senior officials elucidated the theory of this document in A.W.M. Teulings (ed.), *Herstructurering van de industrie*, Alphen, Samson, 1978, pp. 199–221. In the same volume, M. Brouwer and H.W. de Jong gave the critique of the market theorists against the macro views of H. den Hartog and H.S. Tjan in the CPB Occasional Paper, no. 2, 1974 and the report *De Nederlandse economie in 1980*, by rearranging the data for the set of 23 sectors used by the CPB. In 1976, both van der Zwan and de Jong had voiced their doubts about the real labour cost theory in articles republished by W. Driehuis (ed.) in a collection: *Economische theorie en economische politiek in discussie*, Leiden, Stenfert Kroese, 1977, pp. 163–205 and 133–61.
33. Liefman, R. (1930), *Kartelle, Konzerne und Trusts*, 8th edn, E.H. Moritz, Stuttgart.
34. Robinson, J. (1969), *The Economics of Imperfect Competition*, 2nd edn, Macmillan, London.

A. HENK WILM LAMBERS (1916–2004)

Henry W. de Jong

When Henk Lambers arrived at the Rotterdam School of Economics in 1935, the economy was nearly in ruins and economics nearly completely so. The first had prompted him to study economics instead of his beloved classical literature: 'I was a spirited admirer of Tacitus and the Latin language because one may construct so perfecly in that language'. But his father had died in those years of unemployment and poverty and, moreover, the inquisitive youth was moved to question why so many able people were condemned to obtaining their sustenance from the dole instead of from useful work. This led him into the domain of economics.

The leading theoretical economist of his day, Professor François de Vries, became his teacher and discovered within two years his extraordinary intelligence. De Vries, apart from stimulating Lambers's thinking about the merits and failings of the market economy, also arranged his appointment as a research fellow of the Netherlands Economic Institute in 1937. Although war brought a standstill to his career it could not stop Lambers's intellectual development.

Indeed, it permitted him to prepare for the postwar tasks which followed in quick succession: Reader (1946) and Professor in Economics (1947), Rector of the Rotterdam School of Economics (1950) and President of the Competition Commission (1955). Lambers occupied the position of rector for a total of seven years out of the 41 he spent at the school until his retirement in 1981. He declined the invitation to become the Burgomaster of the city of Rotterdam. This course of events showed him as the economist and educator who generated more than a dozen professors of economics among his pupils, many more who wrote dissertations with him and even more who took the full course of market theory in his doctoral seminars. His lectures, according to a colleague 'were a feast to attend'; being fluent, witty, associative of ideas, illustrating complex problems with realistic examples such as the production planning and locational choice of the ice-cream seller or the cunning tactics of the saleswoman breaking an oligopolistic stalemate. The grand vision did not fail either. Lambers taught, inspired by his favourite authors Adam Smith, Alfred Marshall and Friedrich von Wieser, a meta-economics of markets in which interconnected layers of the pricing process, market structures and the institutional conditions were exposed and shown as the outcomes of acquisitive human behaviour. He called this the 'New Institutional Economics' in an essay in *De Economist* (No. 11, November, 1958). The essay was his favourite means of expression; he was the unequalled master of this style in which he formulated the gist of the problem, contributed rivalling explanations while coining new words or concepts and anticipating possible solutions as he went along.

In a solid article of January 1942, 'Coherence between organizational structures and pricing', Lambers, carefully distinguishing between price formation and price effects, used the words 'potential supply'; purposely as it seemed in contrast to Liefmann's 'latent competition' (1930, p. 10)[33] and Joan Robinson's 'potential competition'(1933, p. 81)[34] because it covers not only the potential but also the actual *suppliers*. Control of the market depends upon the control of supply whatever the form – cartel, collusion or trust – the number of suppliers or their insider or outsider position may be; without such control the prices of commodities will (in Smith's terms) be continually gravitating towards the central price. But a distinction is necessary between the equilibrium price of a model and the equation price of reality.

Moreover, the latter is not a point but a band, embracing fluctuating market price dispersions. By focusing on the conditions of the model, Lambers prevented his students from confusing theory and actual behaviour. His formulation of the methodological dilemma elucidated the tension: 'The paradox of economics is that only by means of a simplification of reality, economic relationships can be demonstrated whereas on the other hand it has to be shown what reality does in fact do' (Lambers, 1963, p. 271). This double requirement prevents both an attitude to be best characterized as *l'art pour l'art* as well as the measurement without theorizing. He was, together with his contemporary and colleague Jan Tinbergen, the educator who inspired this balanced approach to economic problems at the Rotterdam School of Economics. Its rise to be (by far) the largest supplier of economists in the country was no doubt the unintended but inevitable result. Fortunately, this increased supply did not drive the price of economists to a continuously lower level, but it did raise the prize Lambers was awarded on the occasion of his retirement to the highest level that Dutch society is able to give: Commander in the Order of the Netherlands Lion.

Some of Lambers's main publications were (titles translated): *Market Strategy and Competition* (Haarlem, 1950, see note 13); 'On the Institutional Market' (*De Economist*, 1958, see note 27); 'The tough competition', in *The Trading World and World Trade*, Rotterdam, 1963, pp. 261–80 (published in Dutch and English). In this article we find one of Lambers's typical phrases: 'The ubiquity of competition is the protection of the efficiency of the economic process' (p. 275).

5. French political economy about industrial matters

Jacques De Bandt

INTRODUCTION

A preliminary question is, what is industrial economics about, or, more precisely what was industrial economics about, from 1880 to 1980? The answer of course, is a lot of quite different things, over such a long period of time. This century-long period has experienced several rather fundamental changes, with regard to both the economy – the economic system, and more particularly the productive system – and economic thinking. Some of these changes are obviously of some importance from the standpoint of industrial economics.

As far as the economy is concerned, the period has known exceptional secular growth, with at least two Kondratieff growth phases (and two transition or consolidation phases) – not only growth in general, but industrial growth in particular: industrial activities leading the game in terms of growth (both production and productivity) and employment and thus being the main driving force. Ways of doing (and producing value and profits) have been changing continuously. Consumption (mainly mass consumption), production (phenomenal technological progress, cheap energy, economies of scale, automation and so on) and organizational modes (large-scale, self-contained firms, mergers and acquisitions and so on) have been changing dramatically, leading to unprecedented degrees of concentration and levels of market power. The period has also experienced different degrees and modalities of state intervention in industrial affairs, from different forms of industrial policies and different kinds of public enterprise to the strictest forms of central planning. But the period under review ends with some kind of total defeat of the plan rationality model.

In the particular case of France, although some important industrial developments had taken place in the third quarter of the nineteenth century, it still remained an agricultural country for the major part of the period under study, and strong industrial growth came only after the Second World War. Growth – indeed, a catching-up process (industrial growth rates were the highest among OECD (Organization for Economic Cooperation and Development) countries, except for Japan) – then became exceptional, which justifies the fact that this growth period is often referred to as the '*trente glorieuses*'. This happened within the framework of the specific French planning system, with substantial state intervention.

One interesting question, but one that is quite difficult to answer, is to what extent and how these evolutions – in the real sphere of economic activities – have been affecting, in the French case, the representations of the industrial system and the ways it has been analysed and theorized. Of course, the opposite question may also be raised about the possible influence of economic thinking on real economic evolutions: in the previous period, the influence of the Comte de Saint Simon on important economic and, more so, industrial developments in France had been, for a few decades, quite significant.

Other important changes such as demographic (life expectancies, age structures), geopolitical (end of the European empires, rise of the American empire, the emergence of the Third World, the oil shock and so on) and environmental could of course be added.

More important changes still – with regard to both the economy and economic thinking – occurred progressively in the 1970s and even more so since then, for example: at the global level, the development of transnationals and globalization, or the end of the growth of the share of industry and the rise of services and, more so, of informational activities; at the firm level, cooperation agreements among competing firms; at the level of economic thinking, game theory, evolutionary economics and contract theories; and so on. All these changes are here considered as coming only after our period under review.

The century-long period under review has also known different, quite divergent, evolutions with regard to economic thinking. Major economic theories, doctrines and ideologies were developed during this period, even if some of them had emerged earlier. Suffice to mention here Marxism, neo-classical economics, later Keynesian macroeconomics, but also – at some lower level of elaboration and influence – a series of schools of economic and socio-political thinking (such as, in the case of France, protectionism, cooperation, planning and so on). Strong disagreements have been made explicit between various more or less parallel or successive developments.

Speaking of different, or even divergent evolutions, with regard to economic thinking, one could add, at another level, a conflict of opinion which is more directly related to industrial economics, between those who care about industrial realities in all their complexity and concrete diversity (between countries or systems and over time), and those who mainly care about formal modelling and abstract models.

The interesting question again is whether and how these developments in the field of economic thinking have come to influence thinking in the specific field of industrial economics *sensu lato*, in general and more particularly in the French case.

Taking account of all the changes which have characterized our period under review, industrial economics is understood here, in the wider sense of the term, as meaning any kind of economic thinking about industrial affairs. Services are obviously excluded (they will emerge essentially in the 1980s). The distinctive criterion is the object under study: the functioning and the performances of industry and, within the industry, of industrial firms.

The criterion could also be the industrial way of doing, standardizing and rationalizing the production process. It is true that, at that time, whatever criteria we use, we are usually referring to the same domain. But this is no longer the case. In the last decades of the twentieth century it become fashionable to speak of the 'service industries' (for example, the banking, and tourism industries) in order to put the emphasis on the application of industrial methods to service activities. But during the same period, several service or informational activities which had been integrated within industrial firms in the previous period have become progressively externalized.

The presentation of the pioneers in industrial economics (1880–1980), is somewhat paradoxical in the French case. While there existed some strong traditions, with an undisputed worldwide reputation, inherited from the previous period, nothing outstanding happened during the long period under review. However, a distinction has to be made between the periods before and after the Second World War: new, promising, developments have indeed emerged in the period after the war.

TRADITIONS INHERITED FROM THE PREVIOUS PERIOD

The heritage from the previous period (the previous century-long period, from 1780 on, had been very active with regard to economic thinking), consists of three major quite distinct traditions, whose impact – both at the time or in the period following immediately, and on the later evolution of economic thinking – has been totally different.

The Free-market Tradition

The first tradition is the one initiated by Jean-Baptiste Say (1767–1832) – the French 'classical economist', sometimes called the French Adam Smith, even while his work rested on a solid French base, particularly of Turgot,[1] but also, indirectly, of Cantillon,[2] whom he did not know and never mentions – diffusing the basic principles of the free-market economy. Besides his emphasis on 'utility' (as opposed to labour as the basis of value) and his much debated '*loi des débouchés*' (law of markets) pretending to demonstrate the automaticity of full-employment equilibrium (supply creating its own demand), from our standpoint, he is well known for his emphasis on the entrepreneur, as distinct from both the inventor[3] and the capitalist, and (in his last period) on entrepreneurship.

He was himself a businessman (for part of his life), meaning that he had some direct intimate knowledge of such realities himself. He had been impressed by the technological and industrial evolution of England (he stayed in Croydon for some time, at the age of 19), and was convinced of the importance of technological change: for him, the industrial revolution meant the application of science to production activities, and of the division of labour. He was also a proponent – and from that standpoint certainly a pioneer – of 'industrialism', systematically putting much emphasis on industrial activities.

Therefore, because of his business or industrial orientation, Say proposed that his lectures in the Conservatoire would bear the title 'industrial economics' and this was accepted.[4]

While Say was obviously a pioneer with respect to the importance of the role played by the entrepreneur, the exact nature of his entrepreneur is still being debated. Is he mainly a risk taker or a manager? The emphasis seems clearly to be on the management aspects of his role: he uses the terms 'superintendence and administration', which require 'judgment, perseverance, and a knowledge of the world, as well as of business'. Even while some indications, like for instance what he says about the variability of the income of entrepreneurs as opposed to the fixed income of capital, would tend to suggest the opposite, the emphasis is not on risks or uncertainties, but on management and coordination.

Say was at the origin of a long tradition – extending well into the next century – which can be called official, as its representatives were really the 'mainstream economists' of their time, controlling the relevant journals (like the *Journal des Economistes*) and associations (like the Société d'Économie Politique). Say was succeeded at the Collège de France by Rossi[5] and later by Chevalier,[6] who transmitted this tradition faithfully. As we shall see, the strong liberal or free-market tradition,[7] initiated by Say, continued in the next period.

The Socio-economic and Interventionist Tradition

The second tradition is pursued by the work of both Sismondi and Saint Simon. Simonde de Sismondi,[8] is known historically for criticizing David Ricardo – whose writings were labelled as 'chrematistics', the science of wealth – and in turn being criticized by Ricardo and his followers.[9] But his work, which was more or less ignored, has only been recognized much later as containing many useful insights. In addition to his main merit – to have introduced dynamics based on the so-called period analysis of out-of-equilibrium transitions (implying more or less severe social disruptions) – his work contains a rather systematic criticism of the providential Smithian optimism, and called for state intervention.

Parallel to Sismondi, Saint Simon[10] was constantly glorifying and exalting industry (in the rather extensive sense which includes all industrialized producing activities). With reference to a well-known book (Cohen and Zysman, 1987), one could say that his central theme was that 'manufacturing matters'. His 'industrialism' meant that a strong voluntary approach was needed for the development of industrial activities. He was against private ownership, considered as the main cause of the lack of financial resources for the producers, and became a major advocate of banking credit and state intervention. France is seen as one big manufacturing unit (he invented the term 'industrial system') and policy as the science of production aimed at making things as easy as possible for producers. He can be said to have been the originator of industrial policy.

Saint Simon's greatest influence was exerted not through his writings, but by his personal authority on a (progressively well-organized) group of influential men, known as the 'Saint-Simoniens',[11] who became very active in major industrial developments (railroads, banking, the Suez Canal and so on) in the second part of the nineteenth century.

The Mathematicians

A third tradition, of rather secondary importance at the time, but which was much more influential later on, is the one initiated by Dupuit,[12] Cournot,[13] and Joseph Bertrand. Dupuit, an engineer, was rather close to the liberal school (he published in the *Journal des Économistes*), while Cournot was simply ignored by them.[14] Together they are at the origin of much of modern theoretical developments on utility and prices and can be said to be the real forerunners of neo-classical economics.

But the influence of Cournot on 'industrial organization' theory is equally clear. Cournot (contrary to Léon Walras) started from the monopoly case (all suppliers are monopolists), and successively added more suppliers. Cournot's developments on either pure competition, which he called '*indéfinie*' (indefinite), or monopoly, oligopoly and bilateral monopoly had a longlasting influence in industrial organization theory. The term 'Cournot equilibrium' has become a very symbolic catchword in game theoretical developments, although what game theorists, after John von Neumann/Oskar Morgenstern and John Nash, made of it was substantially different (see Magnan de Borgnier, 2000). We should also mention Cournot's insistence on taking account of the whole economic system, thus suggesting the usefulness of macroeconomics. Bertrand is mainly known for his commentaries on Cournot and Walras (two successive articles in *Journal des Savants*, 1883), raising objections against the use of mathematics in economics.

Of course, there were other names and influences, such as Émile Cheysson (1836–1910),[15] in what can be called the engineering vein,[16] or the very influential Pierre Joseph Proudhon (1809–65) in the socialist vein (against private ownership),[17] or Frédéric Le Play in the socio-economic vein (for his consumption budgets), but such additions are not very useful for our purpose here.

Summarizing, one could say that this initial period – up to 1880 – produced quite an abundant literature on industrial realities. While they shared strong views about the necessary promotion of industrialization (the development of industrial activities), these economists, all more or less directly involved with concrete industrial matters, and while representing liberal, interventionist or more technical views, put the emphasis, respectively, on the entrepreneur, on big industrial developments and on competition.

1880–1940

This period must be said first to be characterized by the progessive emergence of Cournot's work from oblivion. This was *per se* important enough, from the standpoint of contributions to industrial economics. Cournot had laid the foundation for most of the partial analysis which Alfred Marshall was to diffuse. But, besides this late recognition of Cournot, the other direct contributions to industrial economics, in this period, cannot be considered as very significant. Nevertheless, some of those contributions were important, even from the standpoint of industrial economics.

Let us consider, successively, the three lines of thought which have been sketched above:

1. *The free-trade tradition* This is an interesting, but somewhat sad, story. We observe a clear continuity in the transmission, from one generation to the other, of classical economics *à la Say*. The Paris group was clearly dominating the scene. Chevalier was succeeded, in the Collège de France, by his son-in-law, Leroy-Beaulieu.[18] They were strongly liberal economists, opposed to any state intervention, very policy oriented, well known for their lectures, but neither of them outstanding economists. They knew business realities better than they were able to analyse them. Joseph Schumpeter insists on the fact that 'when they wrote on practical questions they, like their predecessors and like Marshall, *knew what they were writing about*'. But, even while they were very close to real industrial matters, they were so obsessed by the dangers of socialism, and, for that reason, so ideologically oriented, that their contributions to industrial economics have been negligible.
2. *The socialist tradition* The scene was completely dominated by Marxist theories, and as far as France was concerned, very little happened during this period that may be of interest, at least from the standpoint of industrial economics.
3. *The neo-classical tradition* Of course the French scene (with regard to economic thinking) at that time was somewhat dominated by the development of Léon Walras's general equilibrium theory,[19] even though Walras never succeeded in obtaining a teaching position in France. Although his successor in Lausanne was Vilfredo Pareto – and the term '*Ecole de Lausanne*' has often been used – Walras did not leave a real school as such as a legacy.[20]

What is Walras's contribution to industrial economics, if any? General equilibrium is supposed to rest on microeconomic mechanisms, but there is no consideration of possible alternative organization of (production) units. It is well known that in the long-run equilibrium situation, which is static, the firm has neither profits nor losses. But this is due to the central role of the competitive process, which is supposed to eliminate both losers and profits.

We shall now present three economists who can be seen as having contributed more effectively to parts of industrial economics, though not strictly to industrial organization. Their writings all belong essentially to the late nineteenth and the first part of the twentieth centuries: François SIMIAND (1873–1935); Charles GIDE (1847–1932); and Clément COLSON (1853–1939).

- *François Simiand*[21] is very original and not reducible to any clear-cut category of economists, even while he belongs rather clearly to the socio-economic or interventionist tradition. As a strong opponent of neo-classical economics, he insists on 'positive economics'[22] – his approach being mainly empirical (he is, one could say, a 'radical empiricist') – and on disequilibria. He has studied facts and figures very systematically, and in much detail.

  His main contributions concern long-term wage and price evolutions, and their impact both on economic and social structures and on progress and secular growth. He shows, quite convincingly, that long waves are a necessity from the standpoint of economic progress. This is very close to both Schumpeter's and N.D. Kondratieff's analyses.

  But he may be said to have contributed to industrial economics in the sense that in order to analyse long-term wage and price movements, he feels it necessary to look systematically into the inner workings of the productive system. In order to understand the economy, he typically moved from the micro to the macro level. His analysis starts with the working of enterprises – productive agents – then moves towards the analysis of the workings of industries of different kinds, then finally to the analysis of the global production system, characterized by different market structures or forms of competition. Much of his work here is taxonomic.

  Simiand's empirical work strongly influenced later work of a similar kind by Dupriez[23] in attempts to disentangle and understand the various more or less long (secular), medium (Kondratieff) or short (cyclical) term movements of economic activities. The main emphasis was on price and production evolutions.[24] Following the same type of rather radical empiricism (within a rather Walrasian general framework), some followers were induced to develop monographic analyses of particular industrial realities or specific industrial sectors, including of course the industrial organization aspects.[25]
- *Charles Gide*[26] has contributed, significantly to the study of what he called the 'organization of production', that is, the analysis of competition and concentration. While remaining in the tradition initiated by Say, at the same time he amended the very liberal orientation of this tradition, by taking account of market imperfections and rigidities. Against the strong theoretical and liberal positions, he opposed

more balanced views with regard to both the relative merits and disadvantages of competition and monopoly, and the concentration and development of big firms, recognizing their advantages in terms of cost reductions and innovations. But, because of the disadvantages of concentration, he had a clear preference for small and medium-sized enterprises (SMEs) and also for cooperatives. Gide was the founder of the French 'cooperatist' school,[27] which has been quite influential in the development of production and consumption cooperatives in different sectors of the economy. He may even be said[28] to be, with some others, at the origin of the '*économie solidaire*' (economy based on solidarity principles), which, after a long period of decay, is being resurrected to a significant degree.

The name of Charles Rist is usually closely associated with that of Gide, because together they wrote a well-known and quite successful book on the history of economic thought (see Gide and Rist, 1947). But Rist was mainly a specialist in the field of money and credit.

- *Clément Colson*[29] was an engineer and may be said to belong to the French engineering tradition, going back, as we have seen above, to Dupuit and Cheysson. His major work is on transportation,[30] but he also published lectures on political economy.

  Colson was a point of convergence of different evolutions: the liberal tradition and marginalism, from both the methodological and theoretical points of view. And industrial economics did belong to the domain of applied economics, aiming, inductively, at understanding the complexity of economic reality. His analysis also starts with the firms, as business units, in order to rise to the global economic analysis of society. At the firm level, he develops a kind of multidimensional analysis of production, starting with forms of ownership. He then develops both sectoral studies (transport as already mentioned) and typologies of firms according to levels of concentration. On that basis, it is then possible to study the impact of concentration on enterprise performances. With his theory of market forms, Colson can be said to have assembled many of the basic elements of industrial organization: pure competition, economies of scale, economies of scale with monopoly, natural monopoly, cartels. Optimistically, he considers that monopolies are exceptional and that there are natural limits to the suppression of competition by concentration, thus confirming the superiority of liberalism.

  Going one step further, to the macroeconomic level as it were, he develops a kind of dynamic analysis of industrial structures, showing that technical progress is leading to more concentration. However, notwithstanding his liberalism, he acknowledges that the intervention of the state may be required in the matter of restructuring.

To conclude, these three men may be considered outstanding, very professional, economists, whose contributions have been of much interest and were quite influential. They have contributed, one would say significantly, to industrial economics and even directly, for two of them, to industrial organization – and this was before the industrial organization revolution of the 1930s.

But, while recognizing this, it cannot be said that the contributions of French economists to industrial economics, in this period, have in any sense been remarkable, in that very little has survived.

This raises some interesting questions. After the strong emphasis on industrial realities in the economics literature of the early nineteenth century, these seem to have been largely neglected or ignored in the 1880–1940 period. Why is that so? There are many different explanations, but none of them seems to be totally satisfactory. As already indicated, the leading Parisian group was so obsessed by the dangers of socialism, that they never really tried to do more than to teach – one should say proclaim – free-trade principles. Another interesting explanation is that after the period up to 1870, in which industrial developments were very significant, not much happened in the next period, in a context of rather modest growth. There are again several reasons for this, among which some of a more socio-political type. Another explanation has to do with the diversion of many economists away from mainstream economics towards both socialism and 'social economics'. Interestingly enough, and notwithstanding Cournot, who was rediscovered only much later, there was little sense either of the dangers of economic concentration and market power, or of the necessity and possibility of implementing competition (or market structure) policies.

Quite apart from this – but still in the mathematical or engineering vein which has been highlighted several times – a few words must be said about a very special case, that of Robert Gibrat,[31] whose 'law of proportional effect' (*la loi de l'effet proportionnel*) explains the lognormal distribution, that is, the normal distribution of the logs of the variable which is being measured: the completely asymmetric distribution becomes normal when logs are used. Size distributions of firms (as measured by number of employees) are typically lognormal (but so are income distributions, and others as well). The 'proportional effect' means that the multiple factors at work are influencing their size proportionately. The rate of variation is independent of their size.

This very original piece of work has attracted continuous interest.[32] The questions whether SMEs or big firms are performing better in terms of growth or whether concentration necessarily increases, continuously or not, have always been much debated, and still are; explaining the lognormal distribution by the proportional effect seems to give a simple empirical answer. But things are of course not that simple, and new phenomena do arise (such as new divisions of labour, or new activities, or mergers and acquisitions and so on).

I have suggested (De Bandt, 1970) that the parameters of the lognormal size distribution of firms can best be used for measuring absolute sizes, both representative and small (within a size distribution of firms, the boundary between big and small sizes is defined as the one below that which, when (smaller) firms grow, is reducing the representative size), and concentration, with applications to the evolution of the German mechanical industry. This tends to confirm the earlier insights of Solomon Fabricant (with regard to the median worker for measuring the representative size), and Orris Herfindahl (with regard to concentration or relative sizes).

THE MIDDLE OF THE CENTURY

One has to mention here the very specific contribution of François Perroux (1903–87), who has occupied a central role in French economic thinking for a major part of the twentieth century. He was a powerful, heterodox thinker, quite opposed to neo-classical economics, and particularly to the reductionism of general Walraso–Paretian equilibrium. He has been very influential, not only in the field of economic thinking as such, but also in the field of economic policy thinking and policies (including in many developing countries).

Perroux's contributions to industrial economics or industrial organization can be said to be much more significant. For him, the central issue in economics is economic power or dominance, which is thus given much prominence, but which has a much wider scope than just market power in the usual industrial organization sense of the term. Industrial organization has indeed to do with the ways market structures affect exchanges (or terms of trade) of particular products (goods or services). In the case of Perroux, economic power or dominance concerns not only the exchange (prices and quantities) of particular products, but encompasses the wider complex system of relations and interrelations between the many actors who are more or less directly involved, and which conditions the dynamics of such a system. This was a systematic attempt – indeed, a first attempt – at integrating market structures and power relations within the whole set of interrelations which characterize productive systems, whose obvious multidimensionality is thus highlighted. There are many different dimensions with reference to which power relations can exist: not only price/quality/quantities of products, but also technological and technical knowledge, different types of information, the set of buyer–seller (or inter-industrial) relations, competencies, networks, international links and so on.

His objective being to build a general theory of power or dominance in the economics sphere, Perroux considered both the level of the firm (the case of dominant firms, and/or of monopolies) and the level of countries (the case of dominant countries in the international sphere). In addition, the study of power or dominance implies both the analysis of the links with competition and with monopolistic situations, and the analysis of the dynamics of dominance. On the basis of such developments, he tends to show the 'paradox' of competition without dominance, that is, without strategies, without fighting or without arbitration, or to show alternatively that Edward Chamberlin's theory is a general theory of economic activity.

This tends to show that Perroux did not believe in pure competition not only because of asymmetries and power relations, but also because of the idea put forward – and which was completely original at that time – according to which relations between actors are made of '*luttes-concours*', that is, combinations of competition and cooperation. Cooperation (mainly in combination with competition) is indeed seen as an important dimension of economic life and, more so, of development.

His ideas about development have indeed been interesting. He rightly put forward the concept of development itself (as compared to the concept of growth), insisting on the human or social dimensions: 'development is the combination of mental and social transformations of a population creating its capacities to make the real global product grow cumulatively and over time' (*Économie du XX° siècle*, Presses Universitaires de Grenoble, 1991). But as well, his contributions have highlighted important aspects of the development processes. Starting with economic spaces or territories, Perroux insisted on both driving forces and spatial cooperative dimensions. With regard to driving forces, he came to attribute much weight to 'propulsive firms or industries' (a translation suggested by himself). And with respect to spatial cooperative relations, he put forward the idea of cooperative interrelations on the basis of proximity and developed the concepts of growth and/or development poles. He may be said to have originated the idea of local systems (of production, or of innovation).

Perroux's theoretical contributions – mainly his theory of power relations and dominance and his theory about poles and cooperative interactions as bases of development – have had a considerable influence, for at least three decades, on the French economics profession (and beyond pure economics on some other social sciences as well). In addition to the industrial organization aspect, his contributions have also been quite influential on development thinking (for example, in Latin America).

THE EMERGENCE OF A FRENCH SCHOOL IN INDUSTRIAL ECONOMICS

In relation to the development of industrial economics, both in the US and in Britain, before and after the Second World War, new interest was emerging in France, mainly in the 1950s and 1960s, for concentration and market power issues. The pioneer was Jacques Houssiaux. Under US influence (he had been doing research in Harvard), he introduced the study of concentration in France. In 1958, he published a first analysis of concentration (Houssiaux and Amoy, 1958) and his acclaimed book on monopoly power (Houssiaux, 1958). His approach was mainly empirical and comparative. He became well known due to a contribution, 'Economic concentration outside the USA' in Hearings before the Sub-Committee of Antitrust and Monopoly (90th Congress, Washington, 1968).

He introduced the study of industrial organization, in the strict sense of the term, in France. He persuaded many economists to enter into this domain, which was at that time quite new. Indeed, he convinced them of two complementary things: (i) although concentration had been, not ignored, but neglected, in the past, with the booming economy (France was catching up in the 1950s and even more so in the 1960s) it was fast becoming a really hot issue; (ii) the then dominant structure–conduct–performance (SCP) paradigm was not, or certainly not any more, satisfactory and that better and more comprehensive analyses would be needed. Strong emphasis was thus put both on concentration at the industry level and on big firms (organization, strategies, performances).

His premature death (in a car accident) put a stop to this very promising career. But Houssiaux can be said to have initiated many other French economists into the field of industrial economics. They subsequently created a very lively scientific community, which has been quite influential both in theoretical terms and de facto, in policy matters, mainly in the 1970s and 1980s, and amplified many of his basic ideas. The results of this were quite impressive, as the 1970s experienced an explosive growth of industrial economics in France. In addition to a series of publications,[33] the community of industrial economists was rapidly organized, even institutionally. An association was created in 1976 (ADEFI: Association pour le Développement des Études sur la Firme et l'Industrie), a journal in 1977 (*Revue d'Économie Industrielle*), and a cooperative research structure (GRECO: Groupe de Recherches Coordonnées, en Économie Industrielle) within the National Center for Scientific Research, in 1979.

Because of the intense activity of this community, it has sometimes been called the 'French School of Industrial Economics' (De Bandt, 1991). Many of its characteristics can be said to have been, at least to a certain extent, inherited from Houssiaux and even, through him, from some of the older French traditions. Some of those characteristics are as follows. The importance of empirical approaches, aiming, on the basis of deep and continuous monographic analyses, at some kind of comprehensive knowledge of particular domains of industrial activity. I have asserted above that French industrial economists have always, since Say, had some kind of direct or intimate knowledge or know-how of industrial realities. This tradition has continued through Houssiaux and beyond. A second characteristic has been the attempt to escape from the strict SCP paradigm and to delve more deeply into the complexities and dynamics of industrial realities. This has led in particular to more systemic approaches, integrating a wider set of interactions between agents. Typical of these are many contributions concerning the concept of production '*filière*' (and/or production system). The importance also attached to firms – in contrast to a kind of dualism between the theory of the firm and industrial organization – and particularly both to SMEs and to big firms, with specific strategic designs and behaviours, has led to much attention and research on 'groups' of firms. Another characteristic was the constant emphasis on market power and more generally – following, as we have seen, an older tradition – on economic power and dominance or asymmetric relations. What is said about firms and systems, also means that industrial activities are studied at different levels and attempts are made to make those analyses consistent: at the micro level of the firm, at the meso level of the sector or, better, of some subsystem, and at the global, macro level of the industrial system itself.

On the basis of this presentation of this century-long period, it might appear that more happened in the field of industrial economics in both the period before and the period after. But this would not be a fair interpretation. Significant and very important contributions were made in the preceding period, on the basis of which longlasting traditions have emerged, and strong developments have taken place at the end of and following this period. Nevertheless, the contributions to industrial organization during the period are far from negligible, in particular: (i) the continuation, deepening and extension of empirical industrial organization; (ii) the strong emphasis on concentration, big firms or groups and market or economic power; and (iii) more dynamic and for that reason more systemic approaches to the working and development of the industrial system.

NOTES

1. Anne Robert Jacques Turgot, Baron de l'Aulne (1727–81) was a public decision maker (administrator and politician). His main work *Réflexions sur la formation et la distribution des richesses* was published in 1766.
2. Richard Cantillon (1680–1734) was of Irish origin, but a Paris banker. His *Essai sur la nature du commerce en général* circulated from 1730 on – and was quite influential – but was published only after his death, in 1755. Cantillon was subsequently ignored and then rediscovered, only in 1881, by W.S. Jevons.
3. Say's formulation of a threefold division of productive operations – the production of knowledge, the selection and use of knowledge for practical applications, and knowledge being put to work in the production process itself – is somehow anticipating what will become the so-called 'linear model' of the innovation process, going in successive steps from the production of knowledge (upstream) down to the innovation proper (downstream).
4. As a matter of fact, the Bourbons (*Restauration*) had a strong objection to the term 'political economy' which was seen as being subversive. This facilitated its replacement by another term.
5. Pellegrino Rossi (1787–1848) published his *Cours d'économie politique* in 1840.
6. Michel Chevalier (1806–79), professor, but also involved in politics, published his *Cours d'économie politique*', in 1842–44.
7. The pure or unconditional free-trade tradition, still celebrated to this day, was to be represented somewhat later by Frédéric Bastiat (1801–50), known for his 'optimism' (with regard to the convergence or harmony of class interests). His is often presented as a (brilliant) journalist or even a kind of lampoonist.

8. Jean Charles Léonard Simonde de Sismondi (1773–1842) – simultaneously a farmer, a politician, essentially an intellectual, with a strong propensity for history – published his *Nouveaux principes d'économie politique* in 1819 (after his main work, as a historian, on the Italian republics in the Middle Ages).
9. Two articles written in response to the critiques of the Ricardians are published in the second edition of his *Nouveaux principes*.
10. Claude-Henri de Rouvroy, Comte de Saint Simon (1760–1824) – who was a genuine count, and who had a very adventurous life (including participating in the American War of Independence) – published many books, including *Du système industriel* in 1821.
11. Similar groups, clubs or even sects of 'Saint Simoniens' were created in other countries, particularly in the US.
12. Arsène Jules Etienne Juvénal Dupuit, an engineer, published 'De la mesure de l'utiltié des travaux publics' in 1844 and 'De l'influence des péages sur l'utilité des voies de communication', in 1849.
13. Antoine Augustin Cournot (1801–77), a university administrator, published *Recherches sur les principes mathématiques de la théorie des richesses*, in 1838. For many years, not a single copy of his book was sold. Later, in 1863, he published his *Principes de la théorie des richesses*, which can be seen as a much simplified version of his earlier work – with little more success. It must be added, however, that publications of Cournot in other disciplinary fields – mathematics, philosophy, history, epistemology, and so on were much more successful.
14. The liberals concentrated their repeated critiques on Léon Walras.
15. Cheysson's very detailed microeconomic analyses (*Oeuvres choisies*, 1911) represent an amazing collection of tools and ideas, in particular his 'La statistique géométrique, ses applications industrielles et commerciales' (*Le Génie Civil*, X, nos 13, 14, 1887). See Hébert (1970, 1972).
16. 'If I were willing to use the term School in any other sense than that adopted in this book, I should certainly form a school from those brilliant French engineers in the public services who contributed, and are contributing, so substantially, to scientific economics' (Schumpeter, 1959, p. 842).
17. Best known for his famous 'la propriété c'est le vol', but also for the fierce critique of his work by Karl Marx, who treated him as a 'petit-bourgeois' (meaning a narrow-minded person).
18. Paul Leroy-Beaulieu (1843–1916) published his *Essai sur la répartition des richesses* in 1881. When his term ended (in 1916), the famous chair in the Collège de France was discontinued.
19. Marie Esprit Léon Walras (1834–1910) published his *Eléments d'économie politique pure ou théorie de la richesse sociale* in 1874–77.
20. Except for a few followers, such as Albert Aupetit, Etienne Antonelli and François Oulès.
21. F. Simiand (1873–1935) published his two best-known books, in 1932: *Le salaire, l'évolution sociale et la monnaie*, and *Les fluctuations économiques à longue periode et la crise mondiale*.
22. In 1912, he published *La méthode positive en science économique*.
23. L.H. Dupriez, *Des mouvements économiques généraux*, Louvain, 1951; *Philosophie des conjonctures économiques*, IRES-NAUWELAERTS Louvain, 1959.
24. (L.H. Dupriez, N. Bardos, G. Szapary and J.-P. Peemans, *Diffusion du progrès et convergence des prix*, Etudes Internationales, IRES-Nauwelaerts, Louvain, 1966, J. De Bandt, 'Les redistributions professionnelles sous l'emprise des mouvements longs de prix', *Bulletin de l'IRES*, 1959; C. Reuss, E. Koutny and L. Tychon, *Le progrès économique en sidérurgie: Belgique, Luxembourg, Pays-Bas, 1830–1955*, IRES-Nauwelaerts, Louvain; L.H. Dupriez, *Problèmes économiques contemporains*, IRES, Louvain, 1972.
25. Some of these publications are worth mentioning: L. Phlips, *De l'intégration des marchés*, Nauwelaerts, Louvain, 1962; De Bandt (1962); F. Trappeniers, *Les avantages comparatifs dans le marché commun*, Nauwelaerts, 1967.
26. Charles Gide (1847–1932) published a *Cours d'économie politique*, and with Charles Rist, *Histoire des doctrines économiques*, in 1909.
27. Gide, '*La Coopération*'.
28. Gide, 'L'école nouvelle', in *Quatre école d'economie sociale*, Geneva, 1890.
29. Clément Colson (1853–1939), was a teacher at two major engineering schools: the École des Ponts et Chaussées and the Polytechnique. His lectures were published under the title *Cours d'économie politique*, from 1901 up to 1933.
30. His *Transports et tarifs* was published in 1890.
31. R. Gibrat, *Les inégalités économiques: d'une nouvelle loi, la loi de l'effet proportionnel*, Sirey, Paris, 1931.
32. See for example, M. Kalecki, 'On the Gibrat distribution', *Econometrica*, **13**, 1945, or J. Aitchison and J.A.X. Brown, *The Lognormal Distribution with Special References to Its Uses in Economics*, Cambridge, Cambridge University Press, 1957; H. Simon and Ch. Bonini, 'The size distribution of business firms', *American Economic Review*, September 1958.
33. To mention only a few: A. Bienaymé, *L'entreprise et le pouvoir économique*, Bordas, Paris, 1966; J. De Bandt, *Mesures de la dimension des unités de production*, Cujas, Paris, 1970; A. Cotta, *Les choix économiques de la grande entreprise*, Dunod, Paris, 1970; J. De Bandt, *Les fonctions de production*, Cujas, Paris, 1970; J.

Parent, *La concentration industrielle*, PUF, Paris, 1970; A. Bienaymé, *La croissance des entreprises*, Bordas, Paris, 1971 and 1973; Y. Morvan, *La concentration de l'industrie française*, Armand Colin, Paris, 1972; M. Baudoux, *Les économies d'échelle et leur degré d'exploitation*, Cujas, Paris, 1972; A. Jacquemin, *Économie industrielle européenne*, Dunod, Paris, 1975; P. Weber and F. Jenny, *Concentration et politique des structures industrielles*, La Documentation française, Paris, 1975; G. Triolaire, *L'entreprise et son environnement économique*, Hachette, Paris, 1975; Y. Morvan, *Économie industrielle*, PUF, Paris, 1976; F. Morin, *La structure financière du capitalisme français*, Calmann Levy, Paris, 1974; J.M. Chevalier, *L'économie industrielle en question*, Calmann Levy, Paris, 1977; O. Pastre, *La stratégie internationale des groupes financiers américains*, Economica, Paris, 1979.

LITERATURE

Alcouffe, A. (1991), 'Profits et entrepreneur: Cantillon, Say, Saint-Simon', in Arena et al. (eds).

Arena, R., L. Bensoni, J. De Bandt, and P.M. Romani (eds) (1991), *Traité d'économie industrielle*, 2nd edn, Economica, Paris, pp. 2–12.

Barrere, A. (1994), *Histoire de la pensée économique et de l'analyse économique*, Cujas, Paris.

Blaug, M. (1964), *Economic Theory in retrospect*, Heinemann, London.

Blaug, M. (1999), *La pensée économique*, trans. A. and Chr. Alcouffe, Economica, Paris.

Breton, Y. and M. Lutfalla (eds) (1991), *L'économie politique en France au XIX°siècle*, Economica, Paris.

De Bandt, J. (1962), *Dimension du marché et optimum de production*, Nauwelaerts, Louvain.

De Bandt, J. (1970), *Mesures de la dimension des unités de production: problèmes de méthode*, Cujas, Paris.

De Bandt, J. (1991), 'L'économie industrielle dans le contexte français: développements et spécificités', in Arena et al. (eds), pp. 156–70.

Cohen, Stephen and John Zysman (1987), *Manufacturing Matters: The Myth of the Post-industrial Economy*, Basic Books, New York.

Denis, H. (1999), *Histoire de la Pensée Economique*, Presses Universitaires de France, Paris.

Dos Santos Ferreira, R. and L.A. Gerard Varet (eds) (2000), 'Qu'a-t-on appris sur la concurrence imparfaite depuis Cournot?' special issue, *Cahiers d'Économie Politique*, no. 37, autumn, L'Harmattan, Paris.

Gide, Ch. and Ch. Rist (1947), *Histoire des doctrines économiques*, 7th edn, Sirey, Paris.

Hébert, R.F. (1970), 'A critical evaluation of Émile Cheysson's contribution to economic analysis', PhD thesis, Louisiana State University.

Hébert, R.F. (1972), 'A note on the historical development of the economic law of market areas, *Quarterly Journal of Economics*, **86**(4).

Hébert, R.F. and A. Link (1988), *The Entrepreneur: Mainstream Views and Radical Critiques*, 2nd edn, Praeger, New York.

Houssiaux, J. (1958), *Le pouvoir de monopole*, Sirey, Paris.

Houssiaux, J. and C. Amoy (1958), 'L'évolution de la concentration dans les industries françaises: l'exemple de l'industrie textile', *Revue d'Économie Politique*.

Magnan, J. de Bornier (2000), 'Cournot avant Nash: grandeur et limites d'un modèle unitaire de la concurrence', in Dos Santos Ferreira and Varet (eds), 01–25.

Schumpeter, J. (1959), *History of Economic Analysis*, 3rd edn, Oxford University Press, Oxford and New York.

A. JEAN-BAPTISTE SAY (1767–1832)

Jacques De Bandt

Say's Protestant merchant family, from the region of Nimes, sought refuge in Geneva because of the '*revocation*' of the Édit de Nantes, in 1685. He was successively an insurer, a journalist, a politician, an entrepreneur and, later, a professor.

He became a member of the *Tribunat* (a deliberative assembly, 1799–1804). However, he was expelled because of his lack of support (in his *Traité d'économie politique*) for Bonaparte's fiscal policy. He became the founder and manager of a cotton factory in the northern part of France (1807–1813). At first a flourishing company (with up to 500 workers), it was then badly hit by import duties fixed by Napoleon.

Having discovered political economy by reading Adam Smith's *Wealth of Nations* in 1788, in 1803 he published, his *Traité d'économie politique: Simple exposé de la manière dont se forment, se distribuent et se consomment les richesses*.

His *Traité* – the first such treatise in France – was a real success: besides several editions during his lifetime, it became, for more than a century, the main reference book for the teaching of political economy in France. A shorter version was published in 1815, under the title: *Catéchisme d'économie politique*.

Say became an academic teacher in economics (the first in France), at two well-known institutions : Conservatoire National des Arts et Métiers and the Collège de France and published, in 1828–30, his *Cours complet d'économie politique pratique*, which, compared with the purely theoretical *Traité*, includes a detailed analysis of the various industries and technologies. He also published *Lettre à Malthus* in 1820.

A continuously much debated question concerns the originality and importance of Say in the history of economic thought. He has been much criticized for being too simple or straightforward. Karl Marx used the term '*der fade Say*', referring to his so-called superficiality, Joseph Schumpeter insists on the 'fundamental error that vitiates appraisal of Say's position in the history of economics, namely, with the usual interpretation of his relation to A. Smith' (1959, p. 492). For example, while the division of labour is typically due to Smith, Say can rightly be credited for having deepened the Smithian notion of the division of labour.

Certainly, Say's role has been decisive both for diffusing Smith's basic ideas and for establishing the tradition for the teaching of economics in France. In addition, Say has made several basic contributions, to which many authors and discussions have systematically referred. Three major contributions are attributed to Say, one of which has a direct bearing on industrial economics, namely the central role played by the entrepreneur. The others are the utility theory of value and the '*loi des débouchés*', eliminating the possibility of any overproduction.

B. FRANÇOIS PERROUX (1903–1987)

Jacques De Bandt

François Perroux was an original thinker, very prolific, who has had a deep influence on many economists, in France of course, but also, mainly, in Latin American developing countries. He was a man of many intellectual and scientific debates and conflicts.

As a student of Etienne Antonelli, he became a kind of follower of Léon Walras, whose thinking he presented in his *La Valeur* (1943). A first book on profits (*Le problème des profits*) was published in 1926, followed, in 1936 and 1940, by two publications on the Hitlerian myth and system. He became Professor at the Law Faculty of the University of Lyon, in 1935, and published, that same year, an Introduction to the economic thinking of Joseph Schumpeter, in the French translation of the *Theory of Economic Development* (Dalloz, 1935). He was the founder of ISMEA, the Institute of Mathematical Sciences and Applied Economics, which was to become very influential for most of the second half of the twentieth century, and became professor at the famous Collège de France.

Besides writings on national accounting problems, his major writings were on value, on Europe (*Le Plan Marshall ou l'Europe nécessaire au monde*, 1948, and *L'Europe sans rivages*, Paris, 1954), on economic progress (*Théorie générale du progrès économique*, 1957), on development (*L'économie des jeunes nations, industrialisation et groupement des nations*, 1962), on basic economic principles (*Économie et société, contrainte, échange, don*, 1963, and *L'economie du XXème siècle*, 1969, and *Pouvoir et économie*, 1973). Of special importance, from the standpoint of industrial economics, was his *Industrie et création collective* (1964–70).

We shall end with a quotation from the History of Economic Thought website:

> François Perroux belongs to that small, strange group of unique Frenchmen who, in spite of the Anglophone dominance of economics, still manage to occasionally infect the imagination of the economics world with their novel ideas. ... Like Walras, he was a Cartesian in method, a socialist in sentiment and an evolutionist in vision.

6. Industrial economics in Italy

Patrizio Bianchi

THE RECENT ORIGINS OF INDUSTRIAL ECONOMICS IN ITALY

A brief history of industrial economics in Italy can start in the early 1970s, when the Free University of Trento – a new university sponsored by the local government – established the first chair in industrial economics and public policy in an Italian University.

The first Professor of Industrial Economics and Public Policy was the young Romano Prodi. After studying at the Catholic University of Milan, the London School of Economics and Political Sciences and Harvard University, Prodi focused his research on industrial dynamics and innovation: he diffused the structure–conduct–performance paradigm in Italy, and integrated the international discipline into a rich national context of industrial studies, derived from various theoretical and empirical traditions (Prodi, 1966, 1968).

After a short period in Trento, Prodi went to the ancient and prestigious University of Bologna. At the newly created Faculty of Political Science, he established the Centre of Industrial Economics and Public Policy within that extraordinary Institute of Economic Sciences – founded and directed by Nino Andreatta – which since the beginning of the 1970s has been one of the most dynamic engines of the Italian economic and political culture. The faculty trained a new class of political leaders: Prodi became Minister of Industry in 1979, President of the Instituto per la Ricostruzione Industriale (IRI: Institute for Industrial Reconstruction) in 1983, Prime Minister in 1996 and in 2006 and President of the European Commission in 2000; Andreatta was Minister of Treasury, Budgeting and Defence, and several scholars became members of parliament, members of the Antitrust Authority and leading personalities in both political alliances.

The Faculty of Political Sciences at the University of Bologna was created in the early 1960s by an extraordinary group of young scholars, who founded in the early 1950s, in the most difficult years of the Cold War, a truly bipartisan and free centre of political discussion, called Il Mulino. This association promoted an academic publishing house, which started to diffuse the new social sciences in Italy and to support a new generation of social scientists, trained abroad and interested in developing their research activity in the Italian universities.

The previous Italian academic history was defined either by courses of microeconomics offered in the faculties of economics and commerce, in programmes aimed at training firm accounting experts, or by courses in political economy and public finance, taught in the law faculties.

Economics diffused in the second half of the nineteenth century, mainly thanks to Francesco Ferrara (1810–1900), who brought the marginalist revolution to Italy. The Italian school of economics experienced a boom in the first years of the new century, with

Maffeo Pantaleoni (1857–1924) and Vilfredo Pareto (1848–1923), who both proposed in various ways a strong convergence between partial equilibrium analysis and the theory of general equilibrium.

The rich Italian school of public economics (Luigi Einaudi, Antonio DeViti De Marco) and the school of monetary studies, among which Marco Fanno and the whole group of young economists who managed the Bank of Italy and the economic recovery after the Second World War, both inherited from the teaching of Pantaleoni. The numerous contributions proposed, during fascism and within corporatist economics, an important reflection on the role of the state in the economy and in particular on the role of public firms.

The years of fascism have, however, constituted a long period of closure which interrupted the flow of ideas and people between European universities. The swearing of loyalty to fascism was imposed in Italian universities and Jewish scholars were expelled, with many negative consequences in many disciplines.

Vigorous debate was resumed, immediately after the Second World War, when important discussion on the future of the Italian economy after the years of protectionism and international sanctions took place in the Constituting Assembly. The debate focused on the perspectives of trade openness, the opportunity to reprivatize the firms that had been nationalized during the years of fascism and the necessity to develop the South of Italy. Thus the comprehensive discussions on industrial economics and policy were largely inspired by real questions on the future of the country.

In such a context of recovered freedom of speech and strong social dedication, the so-called 'new social sciences' arrived in Italy. As we said above, the association Il Mulino and its publishing company in Bologna attracted young scholars who had been abroad, in countries such as the United States or the United Kingdom; back in Italy, which had been closed for years, they diffused the new international tendencies in terms of sociology, political sciences and economics.

In the same period, the entrepreneur Adriano Olivetti had created a centre of entrepreneurial culture, the Associazione Comunità, which diffused new studies on the large firm and the ethical values of the modern industrial society, between Turin and Milan, in the heart of the country's industrial area.

In Rome the IRI's research department, the publicly owned company which managed the largest part of heavy industry and services in Italy, became a centre of economic and management studies, the Bank of Italy expanded its analysis on industrial dynamics, and a new Ministry of Economic Planning, which promoted several studies on Italian industry, in particular related to the development of the southern regions, was created in the early 1960s.

In the mid-1960s, a large movement to decentralize the state also started, by establishing the region as an intermediate level of government; this movement was supported by a variety of studies on local economies. Regions were established in 1976 and most of them promoted public centres of applied economic research, and in several cases supported new chairs in industrial economics.

Moreover, from the end of the economic boom (mid-1960s) to the end of the prolonged economic crisis related to the oil shock, the largest companies set up economic research departments, strongly oriented to industrial economic analysis.

All these initiatives created a positive climate for industrial economic studies, a large demand for applied economists, and the opportunity for the new discipline to take root in the Italian academy. New faculties of economics and new research centres were founded during this period of intense intellectual activity: Trento, Bologna, Modena, Ancona, Turin, Milan, Pisa, Naples. The two important journals of the discipline were consolidated in the 1970s: the *Bollettino di economia e politica industriale* (then *Economia e Politica Industriale*) in Milan, directed by Sergio Vaccà, and in Bologna the *Rivista di Economia e Politica Industriale*, founded by Romano Prodi, and merged afterwards with the old prestigious journal *L'Industria*.

The new discipline was incubated in an extraordinary cultural context, but it has developed in the period of dramatic economic and social crisis following the postwar reconstruction and the economic boom at the beginning of the 1960s. A strong need for policy measures to stimulate industrial development pushed the scholars of the new discipline towards an effective applied approach and relevant emphasis on policy issues, fixing the basic features of the Italian tradition of industrial economics and public policy.

This is the context in which the core of industrial economics in Italy has developed from the beginning of the 1970s to the creation of the Italian Society of Industrial Economics and Policy (SIEPI) in 2000.

Nevertheless, most of the topics that the modern discipline identified were taught earlier within lectures of political economy and business economics. A number of courses contributed to the knowledge of the country's industrial structure and to the analysis of the competitive dynamics between firms, before the new science made its official entry into Italian universities.

The elements that contributed to define the new discipline were numerous but some of the most important are:

- the so-called 'industrial technique', related to the work of Pasquale Saraceno at IRI on the management of industrial production and the development of backward regions;
- the studies of large firms, by Franco Momigliano, linked to the experience of Adriano Olivetti;
- parts of political economy, especially the analyses of Paolo Sylos Labini on oligopoly, technical progress and strategic deterrence;
- the vast area of study of economic policy and in particular the work of Federico Caffè linked to the Bank of Italy, and his studies on the role of the state in the economy and on the development of the South of Italy; and
- the extraordinary boom of studies on industrial districts to which scholars of various backgrounds turned their attention; in particular Prodi with his pioneering studies on industrial dynamics and innovation in rapidly growing sectors, such as ceramics (1966), Giacomo Becattini, who made an in-depth and theoretical study of the work of Alfred Marshall (1961), Sebastiano Brusco, who conducted the first studies on the productive externalization of the large firms (1975), and Giorgio Fuà, who studied economic development (1976).

The new discipline consolidated through the convergence of recurrent themes in the Italian debate and has been characterized by the description of a reality which underwent large transformations and where strong peculiarities and diversities started to emerge relative to other countries, especially Anglo-Saxon ones from which the discipline of industrial organization originated.

Italy experienced a much delayed industrial development, having a crucial role for the state in promoting economic growth and industrial organization.

THE DELAYED ORIGINS OF ITALIAN INDUSTRY: THE ROLE OF *L'INDUSTRIA*

Italian industry developed much later than in other European countries. In the years following the unification of the country (1861) there was even a recession. The new Kingdom of Italy was quickly formed, unifying small states with limited productive and commercial structures. The Piedmont had a small productive structure which represented a satellite of the French empire while the Northeast (that is, Lombardy and Veneto) had been a vast and rich region of the Habsburg empire, so that all its flows were oriented towards Vienna. The South had been the Kingdom of the Two Sicilies, politically a satellite of the Austrian empire, but economically oriented towards the Mediterranean sea which was dominated by the UK. The unification implied enormous problems of economic integration between states which were diverse, small and marginal relative to the already established powerful economies of northern Europe (Bianchi, 2002a).

In a first phase the Kingdom of Italy developed strong links with France; the French commercial banks started to invest in Italy, while France imported increasing volumes of agricultural products from the south of the country.

The government which had transformed the small kingdom of Piedmont into the Kingdom of Italy was liberal, with a policy aiming at budget equilibrium and a certain degree of trade liberalization. Economists such as Francesco Ferrara and Maffeo Pantaleoni brought to Italy, through various academic journals such as *Il Giornale degli Economisti*, the new marginalist economy in the last two decades of the nineteenth century.

A reflection on the role of industry in economic development did not come from academia but from industry itself. Thus Alessandro Rossi, a wool industrialist from Vicenza who later became a Senator of the Kingdom, was a leader in advocating the fundamental role of industry in economic development (Avagliano, 1998).

At the end of the nineteenth century, when inflation slowed down, many new firms which have characterized Italian industrial history since then were founded. In the same period the new entrepreneurial class distanced itself from the liberal tradition which had been unable to spur economic development in the country. German banks replaced the French banks, a new political class replaced the old Right Party, and a new policy oriented the country towards the newly created German Reich. From an economic point of view, policy turned towards protection of infant industry on the one hand and strong public intervention by investing in infrastructure, energy, heavy industry and defence, on the other. The young nation also started an imperialist and colonial policy at the end of the 1880s.

The economic journal *L'Industria*, represented the voice of this economic policy stance. The journal was created in Milan in industrialist circles which had also favoured the establishment of the Politecnico (an engineering school still famous nowadays). The debate among journals was acute and led *L'Industria* to sustain protectionist and industrialist ideas against marginalist academic journals (Barucci and Roggi, 1986).

Italian industry experienced a period of strong growth in the first years of the twentieth century, with a government led by Giovanni Giolitti who skilfully managed industrial development. He was supported by new industrial leaders whose culture became the reference in the country: among these, Giovanni Agnelli who founded Fiat in 1898 and strongly supported the government's industrial development policy (Castronovo, 1995). The technical progress related to the adoption of electrical technologies also eased this policy. The Italian regions and especially those located in the Alps area had always used the power of the rivers, developing various technologies for the exploitation of water turbines. The scarcity of coal had induced Italy not to rely on vapour technologies.

The traditional technologies linked to the water mills were used again, this time in the service of electricity generation using the Alpine waterfalls, so that a dynamic school of electromechanics developed in Italy in these years, under the leadership of Galileo Ferraris in the Turin Politecnico.

Turin and Milan became the centres of the new industry and the areas where a new leading class was trained, less oriented towards France and Austria and increasingly towards Germany. This leading class, contrary to the old liberal class close to agricultural traditions, was in favour of protectionism, of support to the newly born industry and to industrialization as the engine of economic development. As already mentioned, *L'Industria* strongly sustained this vision.

While the academic *Giornale degli Economisti* was publishing the elegant proposals of Léon Walras and W.S. Jevons, *L'Industria* referred to John Stuart Mill's work on the strategic protectionism of infant industry or even to Friedrich List's work on the right of the 'new nations' to consolidate their autonomy, even at the cost of closing trade to the more developed countries. This view of *L'Industria* was already consolidated in 1887 with the publication of the work of two parliamentary commissions, the Ellena Commission on the state of Italian industry and the Luzzatti Commission on the social conditions in the country. The vision emerging from these working groups reflected the fragility of the productive structure of the country at that time. Custom tariffs were therefore increased between 1878 and 1887 and remained unaltered until after the First World War. The publications in *L'Industria*, in explicit conflict with the more academic journals, stressed the necessity to accelerate the industrialization which was taking place mainly in the northeastern triangle (Milan, Turin and Genoa) (Zamagni, 1986).

After the First World War a slight opening of trade occurred until the financial crisis of the 1920s which affected Italian banks and urged the Mussolini government to strongly intervene. Indeed, in these years the fascist government defined a type of public intervention which has continued to characterize the country for many years after fascism. The accelerated development of the Italian economy at the end of the nineteenth century had been made possible by the setting up of 'German-type' banks in Italy. These banks collected family savings and invested in industrial activities. The state was the main buyer of the products of these industrial activities and therefore played the role not only of regulator but also of guarantor of the system. During the First World War most firms experienced an exceptionally strong growth but they had difficulty in converting their activities after the war. They chose to acquire the banks they were related to, thereby creating a complex interlaced system that held until the financial crisis.

The financial crisis destabilized the entire system and in order to avoid a collapse of the whole economy, the government asked the Central Bank to acquire a part of the banks' debts. In addition, it founded both a public Credit Institute and the IRI which acquired the stakes of the three main banks in difficulty. Through this acquisition, the IRI also obtained control over most large Italian firms. In the meantime, a new bank act prohibited banks (now mostly public) to invest in firms.

These exceptional measures remained in place until the beginning of the 1990s, at the start of the privatization process which led to the closing of the IRI in 2000. This process turned out to be the largest privatization experience in Europe, including industrial firms and banks.

The man who designed this form of public intervention that characterized Italy from the 1920s to the 1990s was Alberto Beneduce, who spurred a modern view of industrial development especially in the IRI research centre.

ALBERTO BENEDUCE AND THE REORGANIZATION OF ITALIAN INDUSTRY

Beneduce was a technician who led the reorganization of the state institutions regulating the economy. He came to this position in 1919 after a career as a university professor of statistics and demography. He had already collaborated with Prime Minister Francesco Saviero Nitti in the foundation of the Istituto Nazionale delle Assicurazioni (INA: National Institute of Insurance) in 1912. INA was created in response to the crisis of the Cassa Mutua Pensioni (an insurance company) of Turin, and soon became the regulator of this important sector of the economy. Beneduce was asked to design a national insurance monopoly and then, when he directed INA, to design a system not totally replacing the private sector but to be characterized by a leading public firm which could have played a regulating role in the sector through the acquisition of the portfolios of failing firms (Bianchi, 2002a). Subsequently, during the First World War, Beneduce was asked to establish the Opera Nazionale Combattenti (ONC), an organization aimed at finding jobs for veterans of the war.

Beneduce then founded a national bank for public works (CREDIOP – Consorzio di Credito per le Opere Pubbliche) in 1919 and the Credit Institute for works of public interest (Istituto di Credito per le Opere di Pubblica Utilità – ICIPU) in 1924, of which Beneduce remained president until 1939. The aim of these institutions was to guarantee financial resources for public works and for works of public interest, even if conducted by private firms, as in the case of electrical power. These two institutions grew so quickly that in 1936, that is, when the banking reform took place, they managed credits totalling an amount double in comparison with credits managed by the three banks of national interest (Baratta, 1985).

In 1931, Beneduce became a board member of the Istituto Mobiliare Italiano (IMI), the foundation of which he had supported in order to face the crisis of the Commercial Bank in 1933. In the same year he became the first president of the IRI and stayed in office until 1939, managing first the shares in industrial firms obtained through the banks' rescue operations and then the large public industrial assets.

The Banking Law of 1936, which separated ordinary credit operations from special ones and which remained the main pillar of the Italian financial system until the 1990s, was the last step of the reorganization of the Italian economic system, the first step being in our view the establishment of the Bank of Italy in 1894 following the crisis of the French industrial credit institutes.

Beneduce and his colleagues were non-fascist, and at some stage of their life even anti-fascist. They were technicians who conducted a reform of the state to address the problems of fragility of the production system. The measures making up the reform were supposed to be temporary but turned out to have a long-lasting structural effect on the industrial system. Thus the IRI soon abandoned the activity of short-term credit provision and temporarily turned to a privatization policy (abandoned in 1937). The IRI became a permanent body, a public holding that has continued to play the role of regulator of a still fragile and short-term private industrial system (IRI, 1985).

Alberto Beneduce trained most of the technicians, bankers and economists, who managed the postwar reconstruction, recovery and booming of the Italian industry; among them, a special role was played by Pasquale Saraceno.

PASQUALE SARACENO AND THE DEVELOPMENT OF DELAYED INDUSTRY

Saraceno has been one of the most important scholars of Italian industry. He was born in 1903 in the extreme north of the country. During his life he followed the IRI from the early period until his death at the beginning of the 1990s. He promoted a school of study in southern Italy; a school of industrial techniques and economics that is still strong in the University of Venice; and SVIMEZ, the association that taught young people about the problem of delayed development (Vigna, 1997).

Saraceno's first academic activities were in the field of industrial and commercial techniques. This field, together with that of banking techniques, was for long one of the pillars of the preparation in economics and commerce. The analytical base was that of accounting, which represented a general technique for the description of the firm, stylized in stocks and flows. Saraceno accompanied this field of competence with a strong knowledge of political economy and in particular of the Pantaleoni school.

His meeting with Gino Zappa, the founder of modern accounting in Italy, was important but Saraceno in any case had developed an original way of thinking, not only on the theory of the firm, but also and mainly on the links between the industrial firm, its organization, its management and the entire industrial system. He identified the fundamental link between these elements as the organization and management of production. Industrial production is thus the heart of the analysis of the firm in Saraceno's work because industrial production is seen both as the subject and as the instrument of economic development (Bianchi, 2002b).

This link between 'production, the industrial firm, industrial development and economic growth' is examined systematically and in depth in his important book entitled *L'economia dei paesi industrializzati* (The Economy of Industrialized Countries) (1970). The firm as a place of production is considered as the place where technical competencies and material resources are accumulated for the creation of capital and value from productive transformation. This process constitutes the basis for a sustainable development.

The theme of the creation of capital is recurrent in Saraceno's work and is the characterizing element of his vision of Italian development and of the role of the state as a promoter of development. He had an enormous influence on Italian economic literature after the Second World War.

The interest in this issue is understandable, given the characteristics of the Italian economy: problems of capital accumulation, production efficiency, and adequacy between production organization and market extent in an overpopulated country (and therefore with a strong need for development); and product and capital markets not large enough to autonomously create an industrial dynamics able to increase the number of large firms (hence a weak supply of development). In such a context, the risk is the development of an economy based either on firms that are too small (hence, in the case where economies of scale are important, inefficient) or on a few large firms that dominate and monopolize the system. In both cases inefficiency from a social point of view prevails.

Starting from the awareness that development paths are unique and not repeatable and that development requires, whatever the historical trajectory followed, adequate production dimensions, Saraceno proposed an increasingly mature vision of the role of the state in the economy which in Italy takes the form of the IRI, of the state having a stake in industrial firms, of the exceptional intervention in the backward South and of economic planning (Saraceno, 1985; Zoppi, 2002).

The public firm becomes a fundamental pillar for the growth of the industrial system, thanks to its dimension, organization and capacity to accumulate competencies and resources. It is also an essential instrument of economic growth since it avoids the degeneration of the market towards asphyxiated monopoly positions. Here Saraceno views the country as a 'system' that should function according to the same principles of decision making and planning of flows that govern the 'firm as a system', that is, a cornerstone of his reflection on industrial production (1978a).

Saraceno had already addressed the problem of the relation between production dimension and firm behaviour in the publications of the beginning of the 1940s. The core of the relationship between conduct and structure is proposed in *Lezioni di tecnica amministrativa delle aziende industriali* (Lectures on Administrative Techniques of the Industrial Firms, 1940), through the analysis of the accounting problems related to the increase in technical assets strictly connected with production: plants and machinery which incorporate technical progress and imply the risk of fixing today future technological choices. Hence the choice to acquire from outside or producing in-house must also be decided in relation to the existing assets (Saraceno, 1940).

Among the specific choices of the firm is that regarding vertical integration, of which Saraceno analysed the possible advantages in relation to the optimal dimension of the firm, the nature of the productive cycle and the typology of goods produced. The choice depends on historical conditions, structural constraints, market demand and the prefigured strategies.

In this sense Saraceno clearly shows how the tendency to increase a firm's size is essentially determined by the objectives of managers, whose compensations and status are clearly related to dimension and not to performance. Saraceno thus agrees with Robin

Marris and the vast literature on the managerial firm characterized by the separation of management and control.

The large firm thus constitutes a deciding subject that takes decisions under constraints, and that can choose to externalize specific activities which could create rigidities in the productive cycle. As a consequence, if efficiency advantages of dimension exist, they are not absolute but determined by technology and demand. They evolve through time, according to the structural elements that historically define the context in which the firm operates and makes 'bounded rational' choices, implying the *irripetibilità dei modelli di sviluppo* (unrepeatable nature of development models), as stressed by his book of 1978 (Saraceno, 1978b).

Saraceno took a similar approach to the debate of industrial economics that was taking place in the 1940s. He closely followed the international debate and used it in his analysis of the Italian economy, taking the country's specific features into account (Varaldo, 1993).

This approach in any case leads him and other Italian scholars such as Franco Momigliano, to consider the large firm or better, the organizational forms specific to the large firm, as the real engine of development, with the idea that 'planning and development' interlace in the management of the firm where current decisions on fixed capital, skilled labour and managers will constrain the future choices. Therefore, it is necessary to prefigure future strategies today in order to avoid that today's decisions impede future growth.

In this context the constraint represented by the limited extent of the market has to be taken into account (Saraceno 1978a, 1970; Varaldo, 1993). It is in fact obvious that the market must be large enough to enable the growth of a sufficient number of competitive firms, otherwise the local market risks being monopolized. The limited extent of the market can therefore prevent the growth of firms with dimensions and organizations able to sustain the modernization of the productive system and can therefore be a risk factor that generates monopoly inefficiencies.

There is thus a potential conflict which can be avoided only if one accepts the risk of opening markets and is able to sell a large part of production abroad. Hence Saraceno shares the same pragmatic 'europeism' as those who contributed to the opening of the Italian market in the 1950s, a concrete europeism in which trade opening is considered essential for the modernization of the large industry and, with it, of the whole productive system of the country.

The role of the state in the economy is thus a non-ideological but a concrete and pragmatic element of the ways to project the principles of organization defined at firm or country level. Saraceno's approach has nothing to do with Soviet planning or with the French holistic approaches. It is a projection at the country level of the large firm's necessity to avoid improvisation.

Saraceno offers a synthesis or, better, a conceptual map, of his thought in the introduction to the last edition of *La produzione industriale* (Industrial Production, 1978a). Starting from the relationship between scientific research and industrial progress, Saraceno addresses the theme of the link between technical progress and models of development recalling a reflection that, among others, Paolo Sylos Labini brought to the Italian debate through numerous publications. The more important is technical progress, the more the gap expressed in terms of technical, entrepreneurial and financial resources increases and, therefore, the role of a state action to promote development becomes essential. Saraceno thus does not suggest that protecting or guaranteeing the economy is the general solution to the development of backward areas but he emphasizes the need to put the problem of capital formation at the centre of attention in order to initiate and maintain the development process, being aware that the instruments of such action vary according to the historical context and are necessarily more articulated when the technical gap across countries reaches a certain level.

Saraceno inspired a number of scholars who dealt with policy for southern Italy, public enterprise in Rome and business management in Venice. In Rome, Saraceno founded SVIMEZ (Association for the Development of the South) in 1946, as a centre for research and debate on the development of southern regions. For a long time SVIMEZ has had a school of development that is a reference point for all those who studied problems of delayed development and industrial dynamics in Italy. Entire generations of young industrial economists, scholars of development and a political class have been trained there (Zoppi, 2002).

Saraceno has also educated a large number of scholars in the area of industrial technique, first in Milan and then in Venice. One such is Sergio Vaccà, who has worked at the Bocconi University and has been director of both the journal *Economia e Politica Industriale* and the Institute for the Economics of Energy Resurces (Istituto di Economia delle Fonti di Energia, IEFE), two essential elements of industrial economics in Milan. In Venice, that tradition of studies on the industrial firm was developed by a large number of scholars, including Maurizio Rispoli, who also became the rector of Ca' Foscari, the University of Venice.

FRANCO MOMIGLIANO, GIORGIO FUÀ AND ADRIANO OLIVETTI

In the years following the Second World War the intellectual importance of Saraceno persuaded many scholars to choose the study of industrial problems, namely of backward regions and of the creation of an industrial structure based on large firms, for which the role of the public firm is essential in a country where capital is scarce. In the same period, new groups of scholars were formed, specializing in the study of alternative modes of development in the country. In particular, two research centres – both created by two important large Italian firms – played a key role in this respect. First, the public gas company ENI directed by Enrico Mattei founded a research centre that became very dynamic, focusing on problems of energy sources, the new industries and so on. Second, the other cultural pole of research on new industry and on industrial research was the Movimento Comunità of Adriano Olivetti. Olivetti sustained the development of the most innovative Italian firm, generating a whole new culture that he transmitted to generations of managers and scholars.

Olivetti was based in Turin, a city which has been the real industrial capital of the country since the end of the nineteenth century. Besides the presence of large firms like Fiat and Olivetti, Turin has been a centre of technical culture and simultaneously a privileged crossroads of various cultures, due to the arrival of managers (often of Calvinist tradition) from France and Switzerland. Thus, Turin became a centre of Protestant culture in Italy that co-existed with a strong Valdese community and a strong and rich Jewish community.

The political culture was also lively and, after stagnation during fascism, flourished again after the war (Rugafiori, 1999).

This is the context in which Franco Momigliano was trained. He was born in Turin in 1916. He obtained a university degree in 1938 but could not start a university career due to the fascist racial discrimination against Jews. After the war he vigorously launched into the subject of reconstruction, working in Olivetti's economic research and planning office which he directed for many years. Meanwhile, he became increasingly involved at the University of Turin. He published numerous studies on the role of trade unions in the transformation of the industrial system, on economic planning and on the role of large firms in the economy (Momigliano, 1962, 1966). In 1975 he published *Economia industriale e teoria dell'impresa* (Industrial Economics and Theory of the Firm), which was the first Italian textbook on industrial economics.

Turin also hosted the School of Management directed by Ferres Pacces from which the CERIS, that is, the research centre on industrial economics of the CNR (National Council of Research) originates. Some members of this research centre have played an important role in the government of the country, after brilliant academic careers: for instance, Enrico Filippi (then President of the Insurance Control Authority), Giovanni Zanetti (Under-secretary of Industry in the late 1990s) and GianMaria GrosPietro (President of the IRI until the complete privatization of the publicly owned enterprise group, then President of ENI).

Giorgio Fuà has also been closely linked to Olivetti. In Ancona he created a School of Management that has been a reference for decades: the ISTAO, dedicated to Olivetti. Fuà was born in Ancona in 1919 and has devoted his exceptional qualities of researcher to the problems of development, first focusing on the relationship between productive capacity and unemployment and then to the problem of delayed development in Europe (1976, 1985). A school of studies on the development of small enterprises has also originated from his work.

Momigliano and Fuà thus represent the two extremes of the reflection on industrial economics in the 1950s: both had a strong link with the most intellectual Italian entrepreneurs and both shared the view that industrial economics should primarily be applied and thus able to train managers. For Momigliano, the focus was on large firms, agreeing with Saraceno on this point, while for Fuà the focus should be on local small and medium-sized enterprises (SMEs), since he was convinced that development could be initiated by the creation of new firms in the Italian periphery, thereby promoting a different development model.

ECONOMIC PLANNING AND THE ROLE OF PAOLO SYLOS LABINI AND FEDERICO CAFFÈ

While the IRI research centre located in Rome was in the 1950s the reference point of the vast school headed by Pasquale Saraceno, the ENI research centre gathered a group of very young scholars, back in Italy after a period of study abroad. The ENI directed by Enrico Mattei represented a new public firm that claimed to be opposed to traditional private industry in a context of intensification of international competition in the new sectors of oil and energy. It was not only an economic rival of other private firms in the market, but also a political rival, especially of American firms.

The debate on development left the research centres and entered the political arena in the 1960s. The main theme was economic planning, which would be necessary to guarantee a balanced development of the Italian economy. All the important economists of the time, Saraceno, Andreatta, Momigliano, Fuà and so on took part in the debate. They were all involved in the Scientific Committee of the Inter-Ministerial Commission for Economic Planning (Comitato Interministeriale per la Programmazione Economica, CIPE).

In such a fertile Roman context, Paolo Sylos Labini emerged as a key economist. He was born in 1920, was a student of Alberto Breglia and he also studied in the United States with Joseph Schumpeter. In 1957 he published *Oligopolio e progresso tecnico* (Oligopoly and Technical Progress), in which he showed how the technological discontinuities between small, medium and large firms determine various possible market configurations. Commenting on the study of Sylos Labini and on the contemporary study of Joe Bain on entry barriers, Franco Modigliani in 1958 published his famous study on oligopoly, in which he related market dynamics to industrial configurations.

Sylos Labini contributed substantially to the development of economics in Italy, proposing research on economic development problems and the social dynamics involved, and acting as an intellectual stimulus in a country where strong political and social conflict was taking place. Sylos Labini trained entire generations of economists on the problems of oligopoly and innovation, maintaining a role of theorist and of a scholar of political phenomena.

In the meantime, the economic policy school of Federico Caffè was consolidating. Caffè was born in 1914 in Pescara, worked at the Bank of Italy and became Professor of Economic Policy at the Faculty of Economics and Commerce of Rome in 1955. He undertook a rigorous analysis of the presence of the state in the economy, concentrating also on the specific problems of the development of backward regions (1966). This school was not directly connected to the new discipline of industrial economics and policy but played an important role in fixing the elements of the Italian debate by highlighting the problems of a backward economy that experienced an extraordinary economic boom in the 1960s together with a long period of social conflict.

THE STUDIES ON INDUSTRIAL DISTRICTS AND THE DEVELOPMENT OF INDUSTRIAL ECONOMICS

Giacomo Becattini is another scholar who has had a strong influence on the development of industrial economics in Italy, becoming famous for his theoretical studies of Alfred Marshall. From these studies, Becattini elaborated a very innovative view on industrial dynamics in advanced economies, proposing as a reference parameter not the industry but the territory, and in particular the territory characterized by the concentration of small firms that collaborate in the same productive cycle. Using Marshall's terminology, in 1961 Becattini had already proposed a revision of the concept of industry and later reached a complete conceptualization of the industrial district (1990).

A parallel contribution to the new industrial reality came from Sebastiano Brusco who published an article in the *Cambridge Journal of Economics* in 1982 in which he reported an analysis of the industrial structure in the Emilia-Romagna region that later became paradigmatic for numerous studies on SMEs. The reality of SMEs had to be found using instruments of both economic and sociological analysis, given that the process of de-verticalization that characterized the Italian economy implied the development of a new organizational model in which the highly coherent social context guaranteed the social control that the large firm could not ensure.

From the studies of Prodi, Brusco, Becattini and Fuà, the most original Italian line of research in industrial economics arose during the 1980s and 1990s: namely the research on industrial districts and small firms, which also influenced both the analysis of backward countries and the industrial policies proposed by international institutions in developing countries.

The interest for the new model of industrial organization based on territorial diffusion of productive activities grew within a dynamic economic context. The period following the oil crisis experienced a dramatic social and political conflict, exacerbated by an unprecedented occurrence of terrorist attacks on the state. Following the example of Fiat, larger firms adopted a downsizing strategy. Employment in the largest companies halved in the 1980s, from 1,500,000 to 700,000 units. In the meantime, new forms of industrial organization developed rapidly, far away from the traditional industrial triangle.

The focus on SMEs induced a more complex analysis of industrial organization, where the compact vertically integrated model of large firms was destructured in a variety of network of productive and commercial relations, which could adapt more easily to an uncertain and changing demand (Lane, 2002; Quadrio Curzio and Fortis, 2002).

Early studies on industrial districts explored processes of subcontracting in the mechanical factories of the Milan area (Brusco, 1975). Then a wide variety of research, promoted by trade unions, municipalities, trade associations and national government exposed the complexity of the patterns defining an industrial district: Prodi (1966) had already analysed the rapid growth of small firms when they work in a territorial system, favouring individual specialization and collective complementarities.

In any case the decline of the largest companies was balanced by a booming growth of the small firms organized in industrial districts, producing traditional, high valued products, sold in international markets. This model, called 'Made in Italy' offered a successful path to the country, especially after the devaluation of the lira of 1992, but also showed its historic weakness in high-tech sectors and innovation processes based on university research (Barca, 1997).

A new wave of studies deeply analysed this process of social and economic transformation. Recent developments of Italian industrial economics are realized by various scholars and numerous students of the older masters, with particular emphasis on some lines of research, such as technological innovation (Antonelli, Dosi, Orsenigo, Malerba), the organization of the large firm (Pontarollo, Alzona, Gros Pietro, Zanetti, Frigero), the analysis of industrial systems of SMEs (Balloni, Mariti, Santarelli), emerging industrial organization in southern regions (A. Del Monte, Raffa), industrial policy in open economies (Gobbo, Silva, Prosperetti, Ranci, P. Bianchi), the various paths of internationalization of the Italian economy (Onida, Viesti), and the role of energy in industrial organization (Clò, Vaccà).

Several young scholars were involved in the new course of the Italian economy. In the early 1990s a massive process of privatization of the public banks (which accounted at that time for almost 95 per cent of total savings deposits) started and, from the mid-1990s (with Romano Prodi as Prime Minister, and Carlo Azeglio Ciampi as Minister of Treasury) the complete privatization of the IRI (with GianMaria Gros Pietro, as chairman) was completed.

These privatizations – the largest in Europe during the 1990s – give a new shape to Italian industry: new leaders emerged from the districts, and through these privatizations acquired an important position in the national economy. The most interesting case is Luciano Benetton, who in the late 1960s started to organize the textile production in the emerging industrial districts in the northeast; he achieved tremendous success, introducing an innovative model of industrial and distribution organization for high-fashion garments, but he invested massively in privatized companies before finally achieving control of Società Autostrade, the IRI company controlling the Italian motorway network.

Traditional leaders faced dramatic crises, several disappeared, and some repositioned through this privatization and liberalization movement. Pirelli, the traditional tyre producer, acquired the control of Telecom Italia, the past monopolist in the telecommunication sector, and formerly owned by the IRI.

New leaders emerged in innovative sectors, thanks to liberalization of public services, and in some cases, thanks to strict relations with part of the political system, became directly involved in politics as a result of the emergence of new conflicts of interest; the most interesting case is Silvio Berlusconi, who became prime minister in 1994 and again in 2000.

A new set of studies supported this process of industrial reorganization, with an increasing interest in regulation and antitrust issues and in innovation and technology topics (Francesco Silva and Michele Grillo, Luigi Prosperetti, Fabio Gobbo).

In the meantime, a large number of young scholars returning from abroad have massively diffused the new industrial organization paradigm and the theory of game techniques, increasingly integrating the Italian academy in the international science community. Silva, president of the Italian Society of Industrial Economics and Policy (SIEPI), founded in 2000, in the first meeting of the association offered a very broad overview of the discipline in the 1990s (Silva, 2003). His review of recent contributions in industrial economics shows quite clearly the process of convergence of the new scholars into the wider international research trends, but also the vitality of the traditional national approach, stressing the issues related to industrial development and public policy.

Occasions for debating this variety of approaches were not only the publications in the two above-mentioned journals, but also the annual meeting promoted by the journal *L'Industria* that have taken place in various Italian cities since 1976. The annual meeting of *L'Industria* has encouraged the discussion of the themes emerging from industry and also those of the evolution of the discipline, by promoting the new scholars of industrial economics and policy. Alzona et al. (2003), on behalf of SIEPI, analysed the present state of the discipline, as taught in the Italian universities. They identify 156 full and associate professors, lecturers and assistant professors, who offer about 170 courses related to industrial economics in almost all the Italian universities.

In 1976 the present history of industrial economics and policy in Italy began. *La Rivista di Economia e Politica Industriale* (later to merge with *L'Industria*), the journal founded by Romano Prodi, promoted the Annual Congress of Industrial Economics and Policy, providing even today a permanent forum for the national debate on industrial organization and industrial policy. The editorial board of the journal, edited after Prodi by Patrizio Bianchi and finally by Fabio Gobbo, collected scholars such as Giovanni Zanetti, Enrico Filippi, Gianni Gros Pietro, GianLuigi Alzona, PierCarlo Frigero, Enzo Pontarollo, Paolo Mariti, Luigi Prosperetti, Pippo Ranci and Alberto Clò. They all played a crucial role not only in academic life but also serving as ministers, under-secretaries of state, members of antitrust, regulation and privatization authorities, and chairmen of national agencies for regional development. The strong character of the Italian school of industrial and economics policy still remains in the close relations between academic research on structural change and policy implementation, following a path of ancient debate on the delayed development of the country until the recent privatization of IRI (2000) and liberalization of services (2006), both of which occurred under the government of Romano Prodi, prime minister in 1997 and 2006.

REFERENCES

Alzona, G., Frigero, P. and Ninni, A. (2003), 'L'insegnamento dell'economia industriale nelle università italiane', *L'Industria – Rivista di economia e politica industriale*, n.s. **24**(3), 561–80.

Annibaldi, C. and Berta, G. (eds) (1999), *Grande impresa e sviluppo italiano- studi per i cento anni della Fiat*, Bologna: Il Mulino.

Avagliano, L. (1998), *Alessandro Rossi. Fondare l'Italia industriale*, Rome: Edizioni Studium.

Baratta, P. (1985), 'A. Beneduce e la Costituzione e Gestione del CREDIOP e dell'ICIPU', in *Atti della giornata di studio per la celebrazione del 50° anniversario dell'istituzione dell'IRI*, Rome: Edindustria, pp. 53–62.

Barca, F. (1997), *Storia del capitalismo italiano dal dopoguerra ad oggi*, Rome: Donzelli.

Barucci, P. and Roggi, P. (1986), 'I cento anni de "*L'Industria*". La politica economica per l'affermazione della cultura industriale in Italia', *L'Industria – Rivista di economia e politica industriale*, n.s. **7**(3), 355–80.

Becattini, G. (1961), *Il concetto di industria e la teoria del valore*, Turin: Boringhieri.

Becattini, G. (1990), 'The Marshallian industrial district as a socio-economic concept', in F. Pyke, G. Becattini and W. Sengenberger (eds), *Industrial Districts and Inter-form Cooperation in Italy*, Geneva: IILS.

Bianchi, P. (2002a), *La rincorsa frenata. L'industria italiana dalla unità nazionale alla unificazione europea*, Bologna: Il Mulino.

Bianchi, P. (2002b), 'Saraceno, economista industriale ed economista politico', *Rivista economica del Mezzogiorno*, **16**(3), 699–714.

Brusco, S. (1975), 'Organizzazione del lavoro e decentramento produttivo nel settore metalmeccanico', in FLM- Bergamo, pp. 7–87.

Brusco, S. (1982) 'The Emilian model: productive disintegration and social integration', *Cambridge Journal of Economics*, **6**(2), 167–84.

Caffè, F. (1966), *Politica economica. Sistematica e tecniche di analisi*, Turin: Boringhieri.

Castronovo, V. (1995), *Storia Economica dell'Italia dall'Ottocento ai Giorni Nostri*, Turin: Einaudi.

FLM- Bergamo (1975), *Sindacato e piccola impresa*, Bari: De Donato.

Fuà, G. (1976), *Occupazione e capacità produttive: la realtà italiana*, Bologna: Il Mulino.

Fuà, G. (1985), *Problemi dello sviluppo tardivo in Europa*, Bologna: Il Mulino.

IRI (1985), *Alberto Benedice e i problemi dell'economia italiana del suo tempo*, Rome: Edindustria.

IRI (1993), *Pasquale Saraceno e gli studi di economia d'impresa*, Rome: Edindustria.

Lane, D.A. (2002), 'Complessità e interazioni locali. Verso una teoria dei distretti industriali', in Quadrio Curzio and Fortis (eds), pp. 111–40.

Modigliani F. (1958), 'New developments on the oligopoly front', *Journal of Political Economy*, 66, pp. 215–32.

Momigliano F. (1962), *Lavoratori e sindacati di fronte alla trasformazione del processo produttivo*, Milan: Feltrinelli.
Momigliano, F. (1966), *Sindacati, progresso tecnico, programmazione economica*, Turin: Einaudi.
Momigliano F. (1975), *Economia industriale e teoria dell'impresa*, Bologna: Il Mulino.
Prodi, R. (1966), *Modello di sviluppo di un settore in rapida crescita*, Milan: Angeli.
Prodi, R. (1968), *Concorrenza dinamica e potere di mercato. Politica industriale e fusioni d'impresa*, Milan: Angeli.
Quadrio Curzio, A. and Fortis, M. (eds) (2002), *Complessità e distretti industriali. Dinamiche, modelli, casi reali*, Bologna: Il Mulino.
Rugafiori, P. (1999), 'Alle origini della Fiat. Imprese ed imprenditori in Piemonte (1870–1900)', in Annibaldi and Berta (eds), pp. 135–84.
Saraceno, P. (1940), *Lezioni di tecnica amministrativa delle aziende industriali*, Rome: Edizioni Universitarie.
Saraceno, P. (1970), *L'economia dei paesi industrializzati*, Milan: Etas Kompass.
Saraceno, P. (1978a), *La produzione industriale*, 9th edn, Venice: Libreria Universitaria Editrice.
Saraceno, P. (1978b), 'L'Irripetibilità dei modelli di sviluppo', in *Economia e direzione dell' impresa industriale*, Milan: Isedi.
Saraceno, P. (1985), 'L'intervento dell'IRI per lo smobilizzo delle grandi banche', in *Atti della giornata di studio per la celebrazione del 50° anniversario dell'istituzione dell'IRI*, Rome: Edindustria, pp. 111–36.
Silva, F. (2003), 'L'economia industriale in Italia negli anni novanta', in *L'Industria- Rivista di Economia e Politica Industriale*, n.s. **24**(3), 523–60.
Sylos Labini, P. (1957), *Oligopolio e progresso tecnico*, Rome: Edizioni Ateneo, and Turin: Einaudi, 1964.
Varaldo, R. (1993), 'L'economia dell'impresa industriale in Pasquale Saraceno', in IRI, pp. 115–51.
Vigna, G. (1997), *Pasquale Saraceno, L'uomo che voleva unificare l'Italia*, Milan: Rusconi.
Zamagni, V. (1986), 'Il ruolo de "*L'Industria*" nella vita economica italiana: 1887–1942', *L'Industria – Rivista di economia e politica industriale*, n.s. **7**(3), 381–402.
Zoppi, S. (2002), Una lezione di vita. Saraceno, la SVIMEZ e il Mezzogiorno, Bologna: Il Mulino.

7. The contributions of three English economists to the development of industrial economics

Michael A. Utton

INTRODUCTION

For students of industrial economics in the late 1950s there were none of the comprehensive treatises on the subject that are widespread today. There was, it is true, Alfred Marshall's *Industry and Trade*, all 874 pages of it, first published in 1919. For the beginning student, however, or even for those more senior it was a formidable undertaking to read without detailed guidance. What students were frequently recommended were P.S. Florence's *The Logic of British and American Industry* (1953) and E.A.G. Robinson's *The Structure of Competitive Industry* (1931) and *Monopoly* (1941). These works, as we hope to show, were in many ways complementary and although both authors dwell on the overwhelming significance of economies of scale and size, in other respects there is remarkably little overlap. Florence, for example, dealt extensively with types of control and labour relations in the largest private enterprises, while in his second volume, Robinson discussed many of the issues concerning the market conduct of dominant enterprises (such as the manipulation of entry conditions, vertical restraints and localized price cutting) that are still hotly debated today. A conscientious student of their major works would have derived from them a keen sense of the importance of good-quality statistics as well as the need to understand and apply the economic analysis of markets. On the other hand, what a modern student would probably find surprising is the comparative neglect of oligopoly. The neglect is complete in the case of Florence whose focus in any case was on the 'industry' rather than the 'market'. In Robinson there is some reference to the likelihood of near monopoly prices in some cases of concentrated oligopoly but without giving it the same attention or importance that Marshall did in *Industry and Trade.*

ALFRED MARSHALL

Indeed, considering how much of the groundwork for the systematic study of industry had been laid by Marshall and how great their debt to him was, Robinson and Florence actually cite him very infrequently. In *Monopoly* there is one reference to *Industry and Trade* while in *The Structure of Competitive Industry* no direct reference is given, even though it is clear from the subject matter how much of it was inspired by Marshall's work. In

Florence's major work, although a number of references to Marshall are made (usually the adoption of a particular phrase or definition) these are nearly all to the *Principles*. Only three brief references are made to *Industry and Trade*. Yet in that book we can find discussions of practically all of the major themes and issues that have engaged industrial economists ever since. Although our main concern here is with the work of Florence and Robinson it is appropriate by way of introduction to give a brief account of the richness of Marshall's treatment of the field.[1]

Marshall dealt at considerable length with the sources and extent of economies of scale. The scope of his discussion was wide and included not only production economies but economies in the innovation process, raising capital, marketing and product variety. All of these topics, of course, find a place in modern discussions of the economies of size. The notion of minimum efficient scale in production often plays a significant role in antitrust enquiries. Many writers have investigated the importance of large size for innovation. (The results are summarized in Scherer and Ross, 1990, ch. 17). Prais (1976) gives a wealth of evidence on the capital-raising benefits enjoyed by large firms compared with smaller ones, and even economies producing a variety of products (recently re-christened 'economies of scope') are discussed by Marshall in *Industry and Trade* (Marshall, 1921, p. 143). In view of its later prominence in the assessment of entry barriers, Marshall's discussion of marketing economies is especially interesting. While noting the enormous savings that can be made by marketing on a large scale, he regrets the presence of 'competitive advertisements, most of which waste much of their force in neutralizing the force of rivals' (ibid., p. 295). Perhaps his most telling observation on this aspect of the firm is that the economies of size in marketing (broadly interpreted) will frequently exceed by a considerable margin those in production. The size of the representative firm will thus be driven by the needs of marketing. This, of course, was one of the central points made by Comanor and Wilson in their classic analysis of advertising and market structure (Comanor and Wilson, 1974). Marshall's widespread and first-hand experience of many branches of industry convinced him of the overwhelming importance of economies of scale and size and, as we show below, this view also prevails in the writings of Florence and Robinson.

How, then, did this view affect his expectations regarding market structure? Initially he envisaged a self-correcting mechanism illustrated with his famous analogy of the trees in the forest:

> One tree will last longer in full vigour and attain a greater size than another; but sooner or later age tells on them all. Though the taller ones have better access to light and air than their rivals they gradually lose vitality; and one after another they give place to others, which though of less matured strength, have on their side the vigour of youth. (Marshall, 1920, p. 263)

In the later editions of his *Principles*, however, and certainly in *Industry and Trade* he was more cautious. The development and growth of joint stock companies with their ability to hire energetic and talented new managers modified the process:

> a large joint stock company has special advantages, many of which do not materially dwindle with age. ... And even if it be somewhat lacking in energy and initiative, it can utilise ... new ideas and appliances that have been created by independent workers: and it has special opportunities for the introduction of new blood into its management. (Marshall, 1921, p. 316)

He recognized that such advantages could in some cases lead to monopoly but tended to underplay the consequences. The very enjoyment of economies of scale and the decreasing costs that they imply would spur on the monopolist to greater output and this would mean lower prices than if the same commodity were supplied by a multitude of smaller enterprises. Costs would also be lower because duplication of effort (especially in advertising) would be avoided. In addition, a monopolist would also have a stronger incentive to improve methods and machines because of the greater certainty of reaping the full reward of its efforts rather than seeing them dissipated among a host of competitors. In any case Marshall continually emphasized the fragile and conditional nature of all (except natural) monopolies. They are perpetually under threat from the vigorous new entrant, the alternative source of supply and the substitute product or material. In recognition of this contingency, Marshall argued that the monopolist would limit its price not out of altruism but out of a sensible recognition of its own long-term interests.

Monopolies 'hold their sway only "on condition" that, or "provided" that they do not put prices much above levels necessary to cover their outlays with normal profits. If they did, then competition would probably make itself felt; unless stayed by authority, as in the case with patents, copyrights and some rights of way' (ibid., pp. 397–8). As later analysis has shown, of course, how much above the competitive level the limit price may be depends on the size and extent of the impediments to entry.

Marshall reserved some of his most damning criticism for the types of market behaviour that may break out in oligopolies, and there are continued references to issues that exercise modern industrial economists. It is also evident that although Robinson in the second of the volumes considered below discussed many of the same topics, his tone was much more moderate. As Reisman points out, Marshall's analysis of competition among the few centred on two forces which all firms recognized (Reisman, 1986, p. 140): the need to keep interlopers out by whatever means came to hand; and the need to ensure that the insiders remained sufficiently satisfied with their rewards that they did not upset the status quo.

On the first point Marshall was convinced that 'the most malignant features of unscrupulous competition, which recent research has brought to light, have been in the pursuit and maintenance of monopolistic control in industries which might otherwise remain open' (Marshall, 1921, p. 180). The main causes of this anti-competitive behaviour are the large profits that result from the destruction of a competitor and perhaps even more important 'the high prestige for business ability' (ibid.) which modern analysis of predatory behaviour interprets as 'reputation' effects: the perceptions of a potential entrant about the likely profits of a market are adversely affected by the knowledge that a predecessor has been destroyed by an unscrupulous incumbent. 'The largest and most savage developments of destructive competition on record have been incidents in campaigns for crushing inconvenient competitors by a Juggernaut car of combination striving for monopoly' (ibid., p. 653). In such a campaign a whole battery of weapons might be employed. Predatory pricing would be used in a selective way in order to inflict the maximum damage on the entrant while minimizing the loss of revenue to the incumbent. Prices would be cut locally where the entrant had appeared but maintained elsewhere (ibid., p. 533). Fighting brands from bogus independent companies would provide a semblance of genuine competition. In other markets where non-price forms of competition were more appropriate, excessive advertising might be employed to blunt the impact of any new competition. Marshall was also convinced that the need to thwart new entry was regarded as so important that firms would resort to what would now be called 'dirty tricks'. The examples he gives (ibid.) bear a depressing resemblance to those admitted recently by a very distinguished British company (see Carlton and Perloff, 2000, p. 354). Indeed, the whole of his discussion of the strategies employed by incumbents to deter or inhibit entrants is very reminiscent of the strategic behaviour literature which flourished in the 1980s. In contrast there was comparatively little discussion of such concerns in either Florence or Robinson.

In his discussion of the second point, the need to keep insiders happy with their rewards, Marshall was more circumspect. He was prepared to see a number of advantages in the cooperation between firms, partly influenced no doubt by the experience of the First World War which would have been fresh in his mind when he was preparing *Industry and Trade*. Cooperation in the collection and dissemination of information about conditions especially in foreign markets, for example, might well generate economies by enabling firms to share the possibly large overhead costs involved. Such reasoning lay behind the exemption of export cartels from the antitrust laws which the US still provides. He also recognized the possible benefits that could flow from cooperation rather than secrecy in scientific research (Marshall, 1921, p. 583) which modern antitrust provisions in both the US and the EU also allow under certain circumstances.

While recognizing these and other benefits that can flow from cooperation he was also well aware of the negative effects that can result from the too close association between ostensible rivals. In addition to the well-documented effects of restriction on entry which helps to sustain monopolistic prices and the inertia which can result from a more or less guaranteed abnormal return from cartel membership, he also warned of the dangers from tacit collusion: 'Such combinations have often been most mischievous when they have been based on mere implicit understanding, without any explicit and formal agreement' (ibid., p. 280) a problem with which antitrust authorities still have to grapple. Nevertheless his ultimate verdict on highly concentrated industries and collusive behaviour was more reassuring. Like Joseph Schumpeter he placed great faith in the powers of competition from substitutes and innovation. After all, as we have seen, even monopolies are impermanent.

Marshall's canvas was very broad, and like all great masters he has influenced directly and indirectly those who came after him and who often chose a narrower conception of the field of industrial economics. As two of his disciples both Florence and Robinson, in their different ways, conveyed to the reader the complexity and importance of the issues that he had raised and thus helped to ensure their further development.

PHILIP SARGANT FLORENCE

The culmination of Florence's work in industrial economics was *The Logic of British and American Industry* first published in 1953, with a revised edition in 1961. The book was a development of his earlier *Logic of Industrial Organisation* (1933). His interests ranged over a much wider field than is suggested by these works and he was keen to draw on political science, sociology and management science whenever he thought the insights of these disciplines aided our understanding of the structure and development of industry.[2] The central purpose of the book, as the title suggests, was to trace 'the logic that underlies changes and differences in the size of plants and firms and other industry characteristics'

(Florence, 1961a, p. vi). A particular strength was the extensive use of comparative data for the US and Britain. In this respect, as well as many others mentioned below, Florence was a pioneer. Subsequent writers have made more ambitious attempts at international comparisons but all have had to contend with the vagaries of the different authorities responsible for tabulating census returns.

Florence's methodology was to use 'theory as a working hypothesis with attempts at inductive statistical generalisation based on the observed facts of the situation as a whole' (ibid., p. 349). The 'observed facts' were taken largely from the (British) Census of Production and the (US) Census of Manufactures. He expressed surprise that it should have taken economists so long to analyse industry in a systematic fashion given its central importance and, as he said, the firm foundation laid by Marshall's *Industry and Trade*, J.A. Hobson's *The Evolution of Modern Capitalism* (1894), A.A. Berle and G.C. Means's *The Modern Corporation and Private Property* (1932) and Robinson's *The Structure of Competitive Industry* (1931). His explanation for this tardiness was that economists trained in abstract deduction found it difficult to grapple with the real world problems and analysis based on measurement of the facts and on the behaviour and motives of actual persons (ibid., p. xii).

A major conclusion from the data on US and British plant and firm-size distributions, discussed in the first two sections of his 1953 book and indeed in contributions made to the *Economic Journal* and the *Statistical Journal*, was the enormous efficiency gains that could be made in many branches of industry by operating on a large scale. At the *plant* level the principles of bulk transactions, massed reserves and multiples were used to explain this phenomenon and, of course, similar explanations can be found in modern treatises on industrial economics.[3] At the *firm* or organization level, Florence made much of the recent advances in scientific management which allowed for the seemingly unlimited growth of firms: 'Most of those who have made a special study of organisation … come to the conclusion that no limit is set to the size of organisation, if correct principles are adopted to enable the single leader to delegate control' (ibid., p. 142). He contrasts this conclusion with that of 'the economists', citing E.A.G. Robinson and Nicholas Kaldor in particular, who saw limits to the coordinating ability of the management as the factor setting an upper limit to the growth of firms. If there was no definite limit to the size of firms there could not be, of course, a competitive equilibrium. There are clearly echoes here of the famous controversy that had surfaced in the inter-war period over the laws of returns.[4] In contrast, Florence argued that their conclusion was not based on actual experience of business. To reinforce his point he refers to top decision making by government ministers or army generals, where the organization involved was frequently much larger than that of even the largest business enterprise.

He was convinced that the powerful forces making for economies of scale were far from being fully realized in many industries. A major factor preventing their attainment was the vagaries of consumer preferences. It is probably his treatment of consumer demand that the modern reader would find most idiosyncratic. Consumers' desires for variety and new versions of established products often forced manufacturers to produce on a scale that was 'technically' inefficient. If consumers could be persuaded to narrow their demands to a smaller range of products with less frequent modifications, this would improve production planning and allow producers to achieve greater economies, resulting in lower costs from which consumers would benefit. As a result, believed Florence, a more 'logical' match between production and consumption could be achieved.

Even as a student in the late 1950s the present author felt a little uneasy at the apparent contradiction that lay at the heart of sections II and III of Florence's treatise. Florence not only felt that consumers inhibited producers from realizing the full extent of scale economies by their thirst for increased product variety but he also believed, along with J.K. Galbraith whose *American Capitalism* (1952) was published not long after, that much consumer demand was artificially created by the wiles of advertising agents:

> Consumers react to emotional appeals and sentimental clap-trap, and are influenced by telling posters with bright colours and snappy wise-cracks, and are gulled by half truths flashily presented ... The demand is artificial in the sense that it is built upon high pressure advertising 'copy' that has little relation to the real qualities of the product. (Florence, 1961a, p. 119)

Since producers (of final consumer products) were thus responsible for stimulating consumer taste for greater product variety, presumably producers were also ultimately to blame for the non-achievement of all technically possible scale economies. Florence looked forward to the time when the 'modern spirit of scepticism, coupled with wider education' would ensure that consumers made more logical choices on the basis of quality and cheapness. Ironically he believed that advertising could be used in this process 'to stimulate the consumer to demand the article which by large scale methods is the most efficiently produced, and gradually to get trade into fewer hands, thus enabling each to produce on an ever larger scale' (p. 120). Given the very large number of firms then in existence, he did not expect this desirable process to end in monopoly.

Although he envisaged that the trend may result in a number of industries having only a few firms, there is practically no mention of oligopoly and certainly no analysis of the competitive process in oligopoly. In fact the term 'competition' is used for the first time on page 116 and then merely *en passant.* A modern reader is bound to be struck by the continued reference to 'industries' and an almost complete absence of any use of the concept of a market. The focus on industries flows naturally from his use of census data to describe and compare manufacturing in Britain and the US. Relating such information to 'market structure' was left to later authors such as Evely and Little who in their imaginative use of similar data in *Concentration in British Industry* (1960) presented a comprehensive analysis of 'markets' in Britain which formed the basis for much later work in the market structure–conduct–performance tradition. Kaysen and Turner had published a similar analysis for the US in the previous year (1959).

With the benefit of hindsight we catch tantalizing glimpses of concepts and ideas which were being or would be developed by later researchers. One example in Florence's discussion of efficiency measurement is his reference to 'survival'. 'A distribution of the sizes of plants existing at any one time in various industries ... is a review of the survivors and of growth; and this process of growth in sizes (or decline) was directly traced for American industries between 1909 and 1939 and for British industries between 1935 and 1948' (Florence, 1961a, p. 53). This idea was, of course, to be developed much more fully by Stigler (1958) and other writers in the 1960s and 1970s when the survivor technique was widely used to estimate economies of scale.

Other examples occur in his discussion of integration both vertical and conglomerate (or 'lateral' to use his preferred term). Having earlier taken theoretical economists to task for an over-reliance on the simplifying assumption of the single-product firm, he argues that integration depends largely on three factors: common costs; technical factors particularly in distribution; and risk and uncertainty (Florence, 1961a, p. 74). There is much in the subsequent discussion that a modern reader of Baumol et al's (1982) analysis of economies of scope would find familiar. Similarly in his references to management extending product lines and seeking out all means to ensure that productive factors are all used to capacity rather than allowed to remain partially idle, one is reminded of the subsequent development of this (and many other) ideas by Penrose in her *The Theory of the Growth of the Firm* (1959).

In his central work (Florence, 1961a) although he spends a great deal of time discussing the factors making for economies of large-scale operation as well as the importance of a scientific approach to internal organization and control, in contrast with modern treatments of industrial economics, he had little to say about price determination. A large part of the explanation for this was his intention to set out a factual comparison of industrial *structures* of the two countries. However, it was also a reflection of his focus on *industries* (essentially firms having similar technologies and using similar methods) rather than *markets*. Thus, whereas a modern treatment will spend much time analysing price determination in, say, oligopolistic or dominant firm market structures, he made scarcely any mention of how prices emerge from the competitive process. One of the few references is to the 'full-cost' principle and then only in passing:

> Though decisions on prices involving real thought may be made in a crisis, prices may normally be determined by a fixed rule as to the margin to be charged above average costs – a 'ritual' with 'priestly' and 'lay' codes (strict and less strict) discussed by English economists as alternatives to profit maximisation. (ibid., p. 148)

At this point he cites P.W.S. Andrews whose *Manufacturing Business* was published in 1949 at the height of the controversy over cost–plus pricing and the principle of profit maximizing.[5] Perhaps rather surprising in view of his lack of emphasis on price determination and market structure, is his (albeit casual) reference to the theory of games, in the early 1950s still in its relative infancy. Having noted that large firms had been extending their scope through internal growth and acquisition, he conjectures that:

> The colourful model of two (or a few) large scale strategists playing a game (like red versus white chessmen) is now challenging the (greyly) imperfect competition model which a decade or so ago, displaced the two alternative models of (black) monopoly or (white) perfect competition between numerous suppliers. (Florence, 1961a, p. 126, footnote reference to von Neumann and Morgenstern (1944) omitted)

The scope of Florence's work was both broader and narrower than modern students would expect. Thus Chapter V of *The Logic* contains an extensive discussion of the role of the shareholder in the large firm and what would now be termed issues of 'corporate governance'. These were questions more fully explored in his 1961b study of *Ownership, Control and Success of Large Corporations*. Today texts on industrial organization may make passing reference to these topics, especially when dealing with mergers, but detailed treatments tend to be left to more 'managerially' oriented works such as Milgrom and Roberts's *Economics, Organization and Management*. On the other hand, although Florence devotes a lengthy chapter to the government and control of nationalized and cooperative enterprises, there is no treatment of antitrust policy, except to note that it was more developed in the US than in Britain. Although this was true, the omission is surprising because by the time of the revised edition of *The Logic* in 1961 there had been a large number of detailed reports by the British Monopolies and Restrictive Practices Commission, as well as the establishment of a special branch of the High Court to hear cases against restrictive practices. Economists were quick to realize that these reports and proceedings provided an additional rich source of material on market conduct and performance. There is no reference to it, however, in Florence's work.

Perhaps because the formative time of his career was in the inter-war period, dominated by widespread unemployment in the 1930s and then by the planning required by the war economy, he did not consider monopoly a problem. Indeed, he concluded that 'Monopoly obtained by combination … has attractions' (p. 340) not least because it would allow the full exploitation of technical economies. His emphasis on the potential efficiency of large organizations and the consequent need for planning within them, leads him to a conclusion which Galbraith was to develop in his *New Industrial State* (1967) and the concept of the 'technostructure'. Thus Florence concludes:

> The trend towards greater mechanisation and larger plants and firms requires the attention to be shifted from the higgling of the market to the policy (particularly the investment policy) of large firms and their internal organisation. Investment implies, in logic and fact, more fixed costs, and planning to meet trade fluctuations, with an increase in staff, office workers and middle management. (1961a, p. 341)

EDWARD AUSTIN GOSSAGE ROBINSON

How does this atheoretical, highly fact-based approach, compare to that of his slightly younger contemporary who apart from a brief absence during and immediately after the Second World War, remained in Cambridge throughout his career?

Robinson and Florence had had a lively exchange in the pages of the *Economic Journal* in the 1930s.[6] Students of industrial organization, however, would have had their first contact with Robinson's work in two monographs he wrote for the renowned Cambridge Economic Handbooks series, *The Structure of Competitive Industry* (first published in 1931) and *Monopoly* (1941). Both can still be read with profit today but the first has the greater resonance. A large part of the *Monopoly* volume consists of a review of the competition laws in the US, Britain and Germany, and is necessarily dated. The central focus of *The Structure of Competitive Industry* (hereafter *SCI*) is a detailed analysis of the factors determining the optimum size of firm. Robinson's method is in the Marshallian tradition, with many illustrations from British and American firms and industries. Compared with Florence he made little, if any, use of the kind of data collected in the Census of Production or Manufactures.

His discussion of the five forces which determine the best size of the business firm – technical, managerial, financial, marketing, and risk and fluctuation – remains a classic and is still frequently cited in modern treatments (for example, Tirole, 1988 and Scherer and Ross, 1990). The factors underlying technical economies of scale, the fact that the different forces will frequently have quite different impacts on the optimum size of the entire unit, and in particular, the recognition that economies of scale in marketing may play a central role in overall size, all had an important bearing on much subsequent empirical work.

He agreed with Florence (although in rather less colourful language) that while some advertising was desirable 'in very many cases it is purely wasteful' (*SCI*, p. 63). More significantly, in his later volume he recognized that 'goodwill' frequently built up 'by effective sales talk and the pressure of advertisement yields in some cases a monopoly power that is far from negligible, and the great expense of competitive advertising can be used by a large concern as a very effective weapon in preventing the growth or expansion of small companies' (*Monopoly*, p. 44). This insight anticipates the classic study by Bain on *Barriers to New Competition* (1956). From his detailed case studies, Bain concluded that product differentiation (in which advertising plays an important part) was the most significant source of high entry barriers, greater that is, than economies of scale or absolute cost advantages (ibid., p. 216). Robinson underlines the importance of the selling part of the organization by arguing that the economies of scale in this function will tend to determine the lower limit to the size of the optimum firm. In contrast, without attempting an empirical analysis he was nevertheless confident that technical economies, with a few notable exceptions, were not determinative of overall size: 'the technical optimum, though it establishes a minimum scale of efficient operation, contributes hardly at all to the fixing of a maximum point beyond which growth will lead to progressively increasing output' (*SCI*, pp. 32–3). In this regard, too, he anticipates much later work in the 1960s and 1970s which attempted to determine the extent of production economies, as opposed to other economies of size (Goldschmid et al., 1974; Scherer and Ross, 1990). The context then, as when Robinson was writing, was how far market concentration needed to proceed to ensure the achievement of all productive economies of scale. While Europeans tended to believe that the state needed to do all it could to encourage firm growth (through merger, for example) to compete with their larger US competitors, the Americans were growing increasingly concerned that market concentration had gone beyond what was necessary to achieve all available economies and that some downward correction was necessary.

Both Robinson and Florence were convinced, however, that when all factors, not just technical ones, were taken into account, the overall advantages of size were very great and that further substantial savings in resources were to be made by concentrating production (in the UK) into fewer, much larger units. Robinson acknowledges, by citing Florence's work and that of others, that British firms were on average no smaller when measured in terms of manpower employed, than American firms. UK firms, however, were more diversified than their US counterparts and hence sacrificed economies. Robinson's explanation for this difference was in terms of the character of the US market: 'the willingness of the American consumer to accept standardisation, and in the determination and power of the American producer and retailer to coerce him [sic] by sales pressure than in the straight and simple economies of mere size of the market' (*SCI*, p. 117).

In his chapter entitled 'Intervention to improve efficiency', Robinson sets out the central point very clearly: 'it is hoped, by a scheme of rationalisation, to concentrate production in those works which are best equipped to undertake it, and to close down the less efficient plants. By operating the surviving plants at full capacity, it is hoped to secure economies and reduce costs and prices' (ibid., p. 148). Undoubtedly a large part of this optimistic expectation arises, as in the case of Florence, from having seen the disastrous effects of the Great Depression especially on the old 'staple industries' of textiles, coal, steel and shipbuilding. Painstaking empirical work carried out shortly after the Second World War by Rostas (1948) showed the enormous gap in productivity between many US and British industries. The same point about comparatively low British productivity has been made at regular intervals ever since, right up to the present. The current UK government remains as concerned as its predecessors about a productivity gap which resists correction by even the most imaginative policy measures.

We mentioned above the importance Robinson attached to what he termed 'goodwill', created in large part by advertising, in his discussion of entry barriers in *Monopoly*. In fact throughout this volume there are many references to issues that have concerned later writers. He has an extensive discussion of the four main factors making entry difficult (legal prohibition, control of factors of production, goodwill and scale economies) including a reference to what would now be called 'raising rivals' costs': 'To raise wages to a level that can only be paid by a large and efficient organisation may, moreover, make the invasions of smaller men doubly difficult' (*Monopoly*, p. 171). In a chapter devoted to 'devices for establishing or prolonging monopolies' he argued that on close analysis 'the majority of these devices will be found ... to be methods of preventing or impeding the entry of new firms into the industry concerned by making the minimum scale of possible or effective competition larger than it would otherwise have been' (p. 63). He placed particular emphasis on the effects of vertical integration where his discussion anticipates many of the issues still aired in the literature, especially his conclusion that 'the power to prevent the distribution of a product through the ordinary channels of the trade is likely to be a most effective limitation to new entry' (p. 66). Empirical support for this proposition has recently been found among studies highlighting the main variables incumbent firms may use to maintain their position (Smiley, 1988; Singh et al. 1998).

His interpretation of monopoly was broad and encompassed not only the single-firm case (including natural monopoly) but also collusive agreements and concentrated oligopoly. In common with Chamberlin (1932) he expected that markets with few firms may well be able to arrive at a non-collusive equilibrium close to the monopoly level. Having discussed the problem of price competition in oligopolies (without actually using the term) he concludes:

> [M]onopoly price is fully as much a consequence of the attitude of a small number of firms to each other, of the assumptions that they make regarding each other, as of formal or informal agreements. We cannot assume that where there is no agreement, even of a tacit nature, competition exists. It all depends upon what one manufacturer thinks another manufacturer is going to do. (*Monopoly*, p. 29)

He follows this immediately with a passage that the officials of the European Commission might wish they had read before embarking on the notorious *Woodpulp* case:[7] 'It follows, therefore, that what we call the detective story approach to the study of monopoly, the search for mysterious hidden agreements, is really a waste of time. Their existence may prove something, their non-existence proves nothing' (ibid., p. 30).

He also had a lesson for those writers who in the recent extensive debate about predatory pricing argued that it was irrational for a dominant firm to employ such a tactic because, given their extensive market share, they would suffer heavier losses than an entrant. Consequently they would refrain from predatory pricing (Bork, 1978; McGee, 1980). He makes the obvious (to most observers) point that:

> [T]he smaller firm is unlikely to be competing with equal intensity throughout the whole area of the market, or throughout the whole range of products of the larger [firm]. A drastic cut of price by the larger firm in *some small part of the territory* will thus greatly injure the smaller competitor, while leaving the larger able to earn monopoly profits elsewhere. (*Monopoly*, p. 74, emphasis added)

He illustrates this point with various examples from Britain and the US where the dominant firm used a 'fighting brand' as the vehicle for its strategy. In the UK early reports by the newly established Monopolies and Restrictive Practices Commission provided further examples in the 1950s.[8]

At the time Robinson was working on *Monopoly* the famous article on the same subject was published by Hicks with its widely quoted conclusion that: 'The best of all monopoly profits is a quiet life' (Hicks, 1935, p. 8). Robinson elaborates the same point and thus anticipates by some 25 years or so the concept of X-inefficiency which has now become part of the mainstream of industrial organization:

> For the comparatively greater ease with which profits may be earned [by a monopolist] may lull a management into the torpor of routine, or provide insufficient spur to the achievement of the highest efficiency ... Not a few monopolies would appear to reap their monopoly gains not in the form of exceptional profits, but in a laxity of organisation and a conservation in technique. (*Monopoly*, p. 129)

However, he does not give any illustrations of this point or direct the reader to those monopolies where such laxity may be found. Florence does not refer to this idea, perhaps because he was aware that it would be very difficult to demonstrate empirically.

Both writers, as we have indicated, were convinced of the substantial economies of size still to be realized by British industry. Largely for this reason, Robinson in particular was generally in favour of 'consolidations' or mergers. He quotes with approval US data which showed that 'industrial consolidations have not impeded technical progress. On the other hand they have been amongst the foremost leaders in experimenting with and introducing time-saving methods of production' (ibid., p. 105). Furthermore, contrary to earlier beliefs, consolidations had been more successful, on average, than the general run of firms.

Confidence in the extent of untapped economies of size plus the experience of inter-war depression influenced Robinson's conclusions about the significance of competition or antitrust policy. While he was certainly in favour of the control of restrictive practices either by a single firm or a colluding group (although he was sceptical of the suitability of courts for such proceedings) he was doubtful about structural remedies: 'If we discover a condition of monopoly it is highly unlikely that we can with any certainty re-establish a condition of competition merely by breaking up that monopoly into a few constituent parts' (ibid., p. 30). Furthermore, because of the distinctive form of competition in concentrated oligopoly and the likelihood that price may often approximate the monopoly level, breaking up oligopolists will also fail to restore competition: 'where willing co-operators have been turned by law into unwilling competitors, such harmony of policy as would produce this result [that is, a monopoly price] would not be improbable. It is thus extremely uncertain whether the policy of disintegration can in any case achieve the intended result' (ibid., p. 180). With a few spectacular exceptions (for example, AT&T in the early 1980s) antitrust authorities, even in the US, have been reluctant to order the dismemberment of their largest (and highly successful concerns). Although the lower court proposed such a remedy in the *Microsoft* case, it was rejected by the Court of Appeal.

A student of the work of Florence and Robinson was bound to be struck by their different approaches. Florence examines a multitude of propositions about industrial structure strictly in the light of the facts available for the US and the UK. In his attempt to understand and explain, he was prepared to draw freely on the related disciplines of economics, sociology and management science. In contrast, Robinson closely following the example of Marshall, derives his conclusions about the structure of competitive industry and monopoly from the application of economic analysis but with numerous short case studies drawn largely from British experience.

While both achieved their stated objectives and stimulated much later work, neither provided an overarching framework within which subsequent students could place the many strands of their work. The first tentative steps in this direction were already being taken by Clark (1940) and Mason (1937 [1957]) leading to the development of the market structure–conduct–performance framework and the empirical studies of the 1960s and 1970s.

NOTES

1. Much more detailed discussions can be found in Andreano (1965), Gonce (1982) and Reisman (1986).
2. An indication of the breadth of his interests is given by the titles of his major works: *Economics of Fatigue and Unrest* (1924), *Overpopulation, Theory and Statistics* (1926), *Economics and Human Behaviour* (1927), *Sociology and Sin* (1929), *Statistical Methods in Economics and Political Science* (1929), *Investment, Location and Size of Plant* (1948), *Labour* (1949) and *Ownership, Control and Success of Large Corporations* (1961).
3. Most extensively in Scherer and Ross (1990).
4. The contrasting contributions from J.H. Clapham, A.C. Pigou and D.H. Robertson were brought together in G.J. Stigler and K.E. Boulding (eds), *Readings in Price Theory* (1953).
5. A survey of the controversy is given in R.B. Heflebower (1955), 'Full costs, cost changes and prices', in National Bureau of Economic Research, *Business Concentration and Price Policy*, Princeton University, Princeton, NJ.
6. Robinson's paper in the *Economic Journal* for 1934 was entitled 'The problem of management and the size of firms'. Florence's reply appeared later in the same year.
7. The Commission found that a large number of companies from several countries had operated a 'concerted practice' in woodpulp markets. However, the Court allowed the companies' appeal on the ground that the facts of the case could sustain a quite different interpretation. The case is discussed in Van Gerven and Varona (1994).
8. A review of these cases is given in Utton (1979, ch. 5).

REFERENCES

Andreano, R.L (1965), 'Alfred Marshall's *Industry and Trade*: a neglected classic in economic history', in Andreano, R.L. (ed.) *New Views on American Economic Development*, Shenkman, Cambridge, MA.

Andrews, P.W.S. (1949), *Manufacturing Business*, Macmillan, London.

Bain, J.S. (1956), *Barriers to New Competition*, Harvard University Press, Cambridge, MA.

Baumol, W.J., Panzar, J.C. and Willig, R. (1982), *Contestable Markets and the Theory of Industry Structure*, Harcourt Brace Jovanovich, New York.

Berle, A.A. and Means, G. (1932), *The Modern Corporation and Private Property*, Macmillan, New York.

Bork, R.H. (1978), *The Antitrust Paradox*, Basic Books, New York.
Carlton, D.W. and Perloff, S.M. (2000), *Modern Industrial Organization*, 3rd edn, Addison-Wesley, Reading MA.
Chamberlin, E.H. (1932), *The Theory of Monopolistic Competition: A Re-orientation of the Theory of Value*, Harvard University Press, Cambridge, Mass.
Clark, J.M. (1940), 'Toward a concept of workable competition', *American Economic Review*, **30**, pp. 241–50.
Comanor, W.S. and Wilson, T.A. (1974), *Advertising and Market Power*, Harvard University Press, Cambridge, MA.
Evely, R. and Little, I.M.D (1960), *Concentration in British Industry*, Cambridge University Press, Cambridge.
Florence, P.S. (1952[1], 1961a[2], 1971[3]), *The Logic of British and American Industry: A Realistic Analysis of Economic Structure and Government*, Routledge & Kegan Paul, London.
Florence, P.S. (1961b), *Ownership, Control and Success of Large Companies*, Sweet and Maxwell, London.
Goldschmid, H.J., Mann, M. and Weston, J.F. (eds) (1974), *Industrial Concentration: The New Learning*, Little, Brown, Boston, MA.
Gonce, R.A. (1982), 'Alfred Marshall on Industrial Organisation: from *Principles of Economics* to *Industry and Trade*', in Cunningham Wood, J. (ed.) *Alfred Marshall: A Critical Assessment*, Vol. iv, Croom Helm, London, pp. 327–72.
Hicks, J.R. (1935), 'Annual survey of economic theory: the theory of monopoly', *Econometrica*, 3, pp. 1–20.
Hobson, J.A. (1894), *The Evolution of Modern Capitalism*, (1926 reprint), Walter Scott Publishing, London.
Kaysen, K. and Turner, J.S. (1959), *Antitrust Policy*, Harvard University Press, Cambridge, MA.
Marshall, A. (1920), *Principles of Economics*, 8th edn, Macmillan, London.
Marshall, A. (1921), *Industry and Trade*, 3rd edn, Macmillan, London.
Mason, E.S. (1937 [1957]), *Economic Concentration and the Monopoly Problem*, Harvard University Press, Cambridge, MA.
McGee, J.S. (1980), 'Predatory pricing revisited', *Journal of Law and Economics*, **23**, October, pp. 289–330.
Milgrom, P. and Roberts, J. (1992), *Economics, Organization and Management*, Prentice-Hall, New Jersey.
Penrose, E.T. (1959), *The Theory of the Growth of the Firm*, Blackwell, Oxford.
Prais, S.J. (1976), *The Evolution of Giant Firms in Britain*, Cambridge University Press, Cambridge.
Reisman, D. (1986), *The Economics of Alfred Marshall*, Macmillan, Basingstoke.
Robinson, E.A.G. (1931, revised 1935, 1958), *The Structure of Competitive Industry*, Cambridge Economic Handbooks, Cambridge University Press, Cambridge.
Robinson, E.A.G. (1941), *Monopoly*, James Nisbet & Co., London.
Rostas, L. (1948), *Comparative Productivity in British and American Industry*, Cambridge University Press.
Scherer, F.M. and Ross, D. (1990), *Industrial Market Structure and Economic Performance*, 3rd edn, Houghton Mifflin, Boston, MA.
Singh, S., Utton, M. and Waterson, M. (1998), 'Strategic behaviour of incumbent firms in the UK', *International Journal of Industrial Organization*, **16**, pp. 229–51.
Smiley, R. (1988), 'Empirical evidence on strategic entry deterrence', *International Journal of Industrial Organization*, **6**, pp. 167–180.
Stigler, G.J. (1958), 'The economies of scale', *Journal of Law and Economics*, **1**, pp. 54–71.
Stigler, G.J. and Boulding, K.E. (eds) (1953), *Readings in Price Theory*, Homewood, IL, R. Irwin.
Tirole, J. (1988), *The Theory of Industrial Organization*, MIT Press, Cambridge, MA.
Utton, M.A. (1979), *Diversification and Competition*, Cambridge University Press, Cambridge.
van Gerven, S. and Varona, E.N. (1994), 'The *Woodpulp* case and the future of concerted practices', *Common Market Law Review*, **31**, pp. 575–608.
von Neumann, J. and O. Morgenstern, (1944[1], 1953[2], 1953[3]), *Theory of Games and Economic Behavior*, Science editions 1964, Wiley & Sons, New York.

A. ALFRED MARSHALL (1842–1924)

Henry W. de Jong

In his *Memoirs* of 1924, written on the death of Marshall, John Maynard Keynes says that Max Planck, the originator of the quantum theory, once remarked that he had thought of studying economics but had found it too difficult. Something akin to that must have moved Marshall. He came late to economics, having tried several other subjects, was moved more by social considerations than by intellectually persuasive reasons, was a hesitant writer, retarding his publications sometimes for decades and said towards the end of his life: 'If I had to live over my life again I should have devoted it to psychology. Economics has too little to do with ideals' (Keynes, *Essays in Biography*, Rupert Hart-Davis, London, 1951, p. 176).

Yet, Marshall was a pioneer who invented several concepts or names for concepts which were half-understood and which influenced the profession, and market theory in particular, for at least half a century. He has been compared to Adam Smith in the breadth of his approach. The new things which flowed from his pen were concepts such as consumer rent, elasticity (of wants or demand and of supply), and substitution at the margin. Although important, these innovations were sometimes only new in name (the idea of consumer surplus went back to Jean Buridan in the fourteenth century), or of limited operational validity or simple a half-truth. For example, Marshall wrote in the *Principles* (8th edn, 1920, Macmillan, London, p. 515) that the principle of substitution adjusts the employment of each agent so that its cost is proportional to the additional net product (at the margin). The role of the alert businessman is to be the medium through which this principle works, he states.

This principle is founded upon the presence of diminishing returns and diminishing product utilities. For industries where these conditions do not apply or are even reversed – think of growth industries based on technological innovations – substitution is of small importance in comparison with the cost reductions achievable through new methods or systems of production or new types of products. Marshall did argue that these are also substitutions; that may be true but in a different context. The Japanese *Kanban* system of motorcar production, the introduction of shipping containers or the supermarket revolution were not adjustments at the margin but fundamental adaptations of the production structures.

Of course Marshall was not blind to these things. Even more than with Adam Smith they occurred under his nose in English industry and he tried to cope with them by means of the introduction of time as an analytical element and concepts such as 'internal' and 'external' economies. Both were first-rate improvements, in particular because they were not tied to irrelevant chronological time but to economic time.

Generally, it is said that the distinction refers to the long and the short period, but it seems more true to distinguish, as Marshall did, between the instant period, the short and the long and the structurally determined periods, depending on the time necessary for supply to adapt to shifts in demand. Although Marshall was quite right in stressing the inadmissibility of devising sharp classifications 'where Nature has made none' (Preface, *Principles*, 1890): 'For the element of Time, which is the centre of the chief difficulty of almost every economic problem, is itself absolutely continuous' (p. vii).

Whether that sentence remains true when supply forces itself on demand is doubtful. The continuity of time seems broken when periods of intense competition alternate with gigantic consolidations, when old-time industries are decimated if not disappearing altogether, when new nations become the workshop of the world within one quarter-century, or when managerial revolutions like the conglomerate movement or the information technology new age, uproot all that is sacred only to crash immediately afterwards.

Towards the end of the *Principles*, Marshall discusses the wider aspects of the distribution and growth of the national dividend (that was his way of naming what we call the national income). In Chapter 7 of Part VI he comes to distinguish between the two classes of 'employers and other undertakers', namely those who open out new and improved methods of business, and those who follow beaten tracks. The services which the latter perform for society 'seldom miss their full reward: but it is otherwise with the former class'. He seems to intimate here (pp. 597 ff.) that businessmen who pioneer new paths have mostly not been rewarded in accordance with the benefits they conferred on society. Yet he states that it is the struggle for survival that tends to make the new business methods prevail; being cheaper they will supplant the older ones. That may well be true in fact, at least in some industries and in certain times. What is less convincing is that Marshall makes the law of substitution a special case of the law of survival of the fittest. The first law was exposed earlier in the book within the context of the stationary state in order to demonstrate the proportionality of the cost of each agent with the additional net product at the margin. Here, the struggle for survival operates within a developing and dynamic economy and – says Marshall – the proportionality has gone.

Is an industrial economist excused if he thinks that competition to substitute is not the same as the competition to survive?

The first variety serves equilibrium or – as Marshall calls it 'the famous fiction of the Stationary State' (p. 366). The second type of competition is supposed to serve 'organic growth of real society' (p. 461). Here the great economist would seem to overtax our comprehension. As a Dutch economist wrote with subtle irony: 'The concepts "organism" and "mechanism" are not a well-balanced pair' (G. Kool, *Statica en Dynamica*, H.J. Paris, Amsterdam, 1935, p. 53).

8. Industrial economics in Scandinavia, 1880–1980

Nicolai J. Foss and Peter Møllgaard

INTRODUCTION

In the span of time covered by this chapter, the Scandinavian countries produced numerous famous economists, notably Knut Wicksell, Gustav Cassel, Erik Lindahl, Gunnar Myrdal, Bertil Ohlin, Frederik Zeuthen, Ragnar Frisch, Tryggve Haavelmo and Leif Johansen. However, none of these saw themselves as contributors to 'industrial economics' (however defined), although at least Cassel (1901), Zeuthen (1929, 1930) and Frisch (1941a/b) made the occasional contribution that can be argued to lie within the interstices of industrial economics. Indeed, some of these have often been cited in the industrial economics literature (Zeuthen's 1930 work on bargaining). Moreover, the majority of the famous Scandinavians in economics did their main work prior to or immediately after the Second World War, that is, largely prior to the emergence of industrial economics as a distinct and recognized field in economics in the 1950s.

Still, as we show in the following, the Scandinavian countries did produce interesting work in industrial economics, although there was comparatively little of it and much was written in the national languages. Specifically, in the ensuing pages, we map industrial economics in the Scandinavian countries – Denmark, Norway and Sweden – in the 1880 to 1980 period. For each country, we offer a broad survey of the state of industrial economics in the period, highlighting the contributions of the three to four leading economists in the field. We also discuss the relative performance of the Scandinavian countries, as well as their distinctive peculiarities.

METHODS AND DATA SOURCES

In this section, we briefly discuss the definition of industrial economics, and present our methods and data sources.

Defining Industrial Economics

We adopt a broad definition of industrial economics as the 'disciplined application of economic principles to explain and predict real-world behaviour of firms, markets and industries' (vision statement of the editors of the *Journal of Industrial Economics*). This includes the economics-based study of the 'nature of competition, the determinants and welfare effects of market structure, the variety of products that will be produced, and the price and sales policies of suppliers' (Krouse, 1990: xi). As Tirole (1988: 3) observes, the frontiers of industrial economics are 'fuzzy,' and a precise definition is impossible to forward because the field strongly overlaps with microeconomics and because it has strong implications for macroeconomics.

Observe also that the fuzziness may extend to what is meant by the 'disciplined application of economic principles'. Thus, modern industrial economists may not think of the use of economics by the first wave of industrial economists as particularly 'disciplined' (see Tirole, 1988; Krouse, 1990). Morever, if by the notion of 'economic principles', is meant contemporary standard theory, this is definitely too narrow, first, because the pioneers simply did not have access to contemporary tools, and, second, because, contributions were made to what we would like to think of as industrial economics by contributors who thought of themselves as being outside of the economic mainstream. In Scandinavia, Swedes Erik Dahmén and Bo Carlsson are two prominent examples.

Methods and Data Sources

We have relied on a broad spectrum of methods to identify Scandinavian industrial economics contributions in the relevant period. These are briefly discussed in the following.[1]

E-mail questionnaire

An e-mail was distributed to 10 economics departments in Scandinavia, requesting responses to questions relating to key persons in industrial economics prior to 1980 and relating to their main contributions. About 10 responses were returned.

Search in relevant journals

We searched all volumes of the following journals for articles on industrial economics by Scandinavian authors: *Nordisk Tidsskrift for Teknisk Økonomi* (*Nordic Journal for Technical Economics*; 1935–55), *Nationaløkonomisk Tidsskrift* (*Journal of the Danish Economics Society*; 1873–), *Ekonomisk Tidskrift* (*Scandinavian Journal of Economics*; 1899–), and *Journal of Industrial Economics* (1952–). These journals were selected because publishing activity in the relevant period was still a fairly local affair, so that national journals would for many be a first choice. The *Journal of Industrial Economics* was included because it is the only specialist journal in the relevant period.

There are obvious limitations of this procedure. Most notably, the sample of journals is small – and it may well be *too* small. For example, we cannot entirely exclude the possibility that we have overlooked Scandinavian industrial organization (IO) papers in journals such as the *Economic Journal, Economica, Zeitschrift für Nationalökonomie*, or more obscure journals. However, we are confident that the procedures we have followed have resulted in a high probability of identifying Scandinavian IO contributions to at least the major journals. One reason for this is that an IO publication in a major journal is likely to make a splash in the relevant local economics community that is remembered, even years after.

Library search

We performed an extensive search in the Royal Library in Copenhagen, and in the libraries of the Copenhagen Business School and the economics departments at the University of Copenhagen. Inputs into the search were those names that we had identified through searching the above-mentioned journals or names that our key informants had provided us with.

Key informants

On the basis of responses to the questionnaire, a number of key informants were selected. These were:

- Norway: Professor Einar Hope, Department of Economics, Norwegian School of Economics and Business Administration
- Sweden: Professor Lennart Hjalmarsson, School of Economics and Commercial Law, Gothenburg
- Denmark: Professor Bjarke Fog, Copenhagen Business School

DENMARK

Microeconomics has always been an important topic for Danish economists, especially in the area of general equilibrium theory. Kærgård (1983, 1996) argues that marginal analysis had already penetrated Danish economic thinking in the 1870s, that is, simultaneously with the independent discoveries of Carl Menger, Stanley Jevons and Léon Walras, sometimes even preceding them. These Danish economists (for example, Frederik Bing, Julius Petersen and Harald Westergaard) were adamant about the use of mathematics in economics and quick to adopt Jevons's thinking in particular. The dissemination of the ideas of the marginalist revolution was rapid in Denmark, not least because it quickly got connected with economic policy, for example, issues concerning the determination of the 'rational wage'.

By 1880, Denmark was thus 'equipped' with mathematical economists with knowledge of and interest in microeconomics and marginal analysis. It thus seemed well situated to take on industrial economics. In fact, four persons can be identified as pioneering Danish IO in the twentieth century: Frederik Zeuthen started off on oligopoly, bargaining and general equilibrium. He inspired Winding Pedersen to work on price theory, Hans Brems to work on monopolistic competition (among other subjects) and Bjarke Fog to study pricing empirically.

Frederik Zeuthen

Frederik Zeuthen (1888–1959) was in many ways an excellent example of an early Danish professor of economics. He was interested in many different areas and covered both economic theory and social policy (Philip, 1976: 367). He was one of the very few Danish full professors of economics at that time, and had broad interests. However, he distinguished himself from his peers by contributing to three strands of the international economic literature (Brems, 1976: 347–8): Monopolistic competition and a reinterpretation of A. Augustin Cournot including 'business stealing effects' in a sort of Bertrand model of differentiated goods; bilateral monopoly as a 'dynamic game' of 'alternating' offers;

and Walrasian equilibria with non-negativity constraints. We focus here on the first two contributions that fall within industrial economics.

Arguably, Zeuthen's best-known contribution was to the literature on imperfect or monopolistic competition. His first paper on this was in Danish and appeared in 1929, just after (and referring to) Hotelling (1929) and preceding the contributions by Chamberlin (1933), Robinson (1933) and von Stackelberg (1934). He made this contribution available in English in his monograph, *Problems of Monopoly and Economic Warfare*, which was first published in 1930 with a preface and a recommendation by Joseph Schumpeter.

Zeuthen's view of monopolistic competition was surprisingly modern. He defined monopolistic competition as:

> the instance in which several entrepreneurs have at the same time so great a share in the production that they may be, and are, interested in influencing the price even at the cost of some reduction of their own sales … The actions of one entrepreneur will be adjusted to those of the others, and vice versa. Many economists, therefore, think that no stable equilibrium can be obtained in this instance, but others are of the opposite opinion. The different points of view depend, however, on the choice of hypotheses. (Zeuthen, 1930: 24)

Today we would describe this situation as *oligopolistic* rather than monopolistic competition and Zeuthen was indeed thinking of competition *à la* Cournot (as 'further explained by Wicksell', p. 26), Joseph Bertrand and F.Y. Edgeworth. He explains the difference in approaches as stemming from different assumptions as to the degree to which a unilateral reduction of the price extends the firm's business by 'taking customers from the other party' (diversion[2]) or 'by capturing some of the unsatisfied consumption' (business growing) (Zeuthen, 1930: 41). Zeuthen thinks of Cournot's duopolists as price setters (!) and uses the parameterized ratio of 'diversion' to 'business growing' as an explanation why different oligopoly models reach different results. He thus arrives at a reinterpretation of Cournot equilibria (differentiated Bertrand) that is novel (Brems, 1976: 355) and based on rigorous, but graphical, analysis.

Zeuthen's other contribution within the field of IO dealt with the determination of prices in bilateral monopoly, that is, the 'case when two monopolistic concerns face one another as buyer and seller' (Zeuthen, 1930: 64). In today's terminology and following Brems's (1976) exposition, Zeuthen defined the threat point utilities that up- and downstream firms[3] would obtain in the case of a breakdown of negotiations. Denote these u and d. He defined the probability q that a breakdown would occur and the price p of the intermediate good in the case of successful negotiation. Let $U(p)$ and $D(p)$ be the payoff or utility to each party in the case of agreement on a price p. At round t of the negotiations, the upstream firm offers to sell at $p_u(t)$ and the downstream firm offers to buy at $p_d(t)$. The upstream firm can accept $p_d(t)$, thus obtaining utility $U[p_d(t)]$ or reject the offer which means that with probability q it gets payoff u and with probability $1 - q$ it gets payoff $U[p_u(t)]$ since the upstream firm accepts its offer. Thus the upstream firm will be indifferent between accepting and rejecting if q takes the value $q_u(t)$ that satisfies the indifference condition:

$$U[p_d(t)] = q_u(t)u + [1 - q_u(t)]\ U[p_u(t)].$$

Similarly, the downstream firm will be indifferent between accepting the offer of the upstream firm or rejecting it, if q takes the value $q_d(t)$ that satisfies:

$$U[p_u(t)] = q_d(t)d + [1 - q_d(t)]\ U[p_d(t)].$$

Zeuthen assumed that firm j would accept if the actual $q > q_j(t)$ since the risk of conflict was too large and would reject if $q < q_j(t)$ where $j = u,d$ denotes whether the up- or the downstream firm is in focus. Thus $q_j(t)$ is the maximum 'probability of conflict to which they are willing to expose themselves by maintaining an ultimatum' (Zeuthen, 1930: 110). Zeuthen then assumed that the party to cave in at round t would be the one with the lowest $q_j(t)$. Caving in, however, did not mean accepting the counterpart's offer but making a new offer at round $t + 1$. He further assumed that both parties would revise their offers in the next round such that the new set of offers would be less favourable to the party with the lowest $q_j(t)$ of the previous round and more favourable to the other party. This process would ensure convergence on an agreement. The last couple of assumptions were clearly *ad hoc* to ensure the convergence and not founded in fundamentals, the main problem being that the two firms do not see continued rounds of bargaining as an option when setting up the indifference conditions. Thus, Zeuthen did not treat the problem as fully dynamic. However, the setup is ingenious and is an early version of a dynamic bargaining problem that was finally solved by Ariel Rubinstein (1982) in terms of a fully dynamic model of sequential alternating-offers bargaining. This was more than 50 years later and the solution exploited all the progress in the field that arose from the rigorous incorporation of game theory.

In 1939, Zeuthen organized the 9th European meeting of the Econometric Society in Elsinore, Denmark. In P. de Wolff's (1940) account of the meetings in *Econometrica*, the first day of the meeting was chosen to coincide with the last day of the annual meeting of the Society of Nordic Economists. However:

> on account of the political situation of the moment, most non-Scandinavian members were prevented from attending … This, however, had the advantage that nearly all participators in the meeting of the Nordic Economists were present during all the lectures of the Econometric meeting. (de Wolff, 1940: 284)

At the meeting, many topics of IO or of marginal interest were discussed: Børge Barfod of Aarhus contributed a paper on the theory of advertising; Professor E. Schneider of Aarhus discussed price policy of firms in periods of depression; Thorkil Kristensen of Copenhagen discussed a multi-product monopolist for which demands were interdependent; and Professor Winding Pedersen of Copenhagen discussed problems of monopoly, arguing that duopoly pricing is indeterminate because the 'solution depends entirely on the assumption made about the entrepreneurs' opinions about their mutual policy. … [S]uch a solution can be given only by a dynamical theory' (ibid.).

At the Econometric Society meeting, Zeuthen discussed price theory, arguing that the study by Hall and Hitch (1939) that showed that firms use full-cost pricing (rather than the marginal principle, see below) was not theoretically satisfying since the profit margin is determined by an arbitrary (unmodelled?) collective pricing policy. '[Zeuthen] underlined the importance of the publications of Winding Pedersen and Thorkil Kristensen, treating different forms of price policy and their consequences and showing that, even in the case of several competing enterprises, deviations from the liberalistic thesis may occur' (de Wolff, 1940: 284). Brems (1951c) elaborated on Zeuthen's critique of Hall and Hitch (1939) and provided a reinterpretation of full-cost pricing as consistent with the marginal principle in the long run.

While being one of the first Danish economics professors with a formal training in mathematics, Zeuthen was no great believer in too complicated maths as a tool in economics (Brems, 1976: 359). He also developed an interest in managerial economics and was open to collaboration on cost theory with engineers (Ivar Jantzen) and economists of other countries, notably Erich Schneider of Germany. But he was generally well connected internationally; witness the preface by Joseph Schumpeter, the fact that Bertil Ohlin was one of the discussants of this doctoral dissertation, and his organization of the European meeting of the Econometric Society. And he inspired younger Danish economists such as Brems, Fog and Winding Pedersen.

H. Winding Pedersen

Hans Winding Pedersen (1907–99) could be said to be the grand old man of Danish antitrust economics. He contributed many books and articles in Danish on price theory and competition and participated in the Trust Commission that prepared the Monopolies and Restrictive Practices Act of 1955; see Trust Commission (1953) and Winding Pedersen (1953) for the political economy of the proposal. He also served for many years as a highly respected member of the Monopolies Council that decided antitrust cases according to this act.

Winding Pedersen (1936) compared and analysed the decline of competition, comparing the American antitrust tradition represented by Burns (1936) with von Stackelberg's (1934) work on oligopoly. He concluded that imperfect competition will lead to stable prices rather than extra volatility. In his 1939 treatise on modern price theory, he formulated a hypothesis of indeterminacy of oligopoly prices and argued that rivals' conjectures are important in resolving this problem. He further concluded that the importance of conjectures necessitates a dynamic approach to finding the equilibrium since firms will react to each other's actions with a lag.

His later books were mainly textbooks: his 1965 work treats the structure, conduct and performance of manufacturing and was intended for use in a course on industrial and trade policy. Winding Pedersen (1976) deals with price theory and competition, focusing on oligopoly, buyer power and full-cost pricing and was intended to supplement Bain (1972).

Hans Brems

Hans Brems (1915–2000) was mainly known for his work on the history of economic thought and quantitative modelling, but he also worked on issues of industrial economics. After receiving his doctorate from the University of Copenhagen on 'Some problems of monopolistic competition' in 1950, Brems taught at the University of California at Berkeley, before joining the University of Illinois in 1954. Early on he was interested in the micro foundation for macroeconomics – a passion he maintained through his career (for example, Brems, 1944, 1947, 1952a).

In 1970, Brems was awarded an honorary doctorate from the Swedish School of Business in Helsinki, Finland, for his contribution to the theory of monopolistic competition. He also received an honorary doctorate from Copenhagen Business School in 1992 for the same contributions.[4] Examples include Brems (1948, 1949, 1951a, 1953) but he also analysed oligopolies (1951b), and cost and production functions with indivisibilities (1952b, 1964) tracing his ideas back to engineer-turned-economist Ivar Jantzen (1928, 1948).

In terms of prestigious international publications, Hans Brems is certainly the most successful of the Danish economists that dealt with IO. He maintained contact with Scandinavia and often returned to give talks in Denmark and Sweden.[5]

Bjarke Fog

Bjarke Fog (1921–) was doing traditional industrial economics research in more than four decades after the Second World War, and doing it at an international level. He received his master's degree in economics in 1946, was a non-matriculated student at Harvard University in 1947, and took up academic positions in Aarhus (Denmark) the same year. In 1949, he joined the Copenhagen Business School where he became full professor in 1958, the year in which he defended his doctorate. His opponents were Frederik Zeuthen (1958) and H. Winding Pedersen (1958). In contrast to his more theoretical colleagues, Fog's approach was based on hands-on experience as a member of several boards and as a consultant to numerous firms.[6]

Even his very early work was written in English. Fog (1946) dealt with dynamic oligopoly pricing using an adaptive-expectations reaction function duopoly with conjectural variations. The article was based on a talk given at Harvard University and the author thanks Wassilij Leontieff of Harvard and Hans Brems for comments. The article's point of departure is a model of Winding Pedersen (1939).

Fog (1948) dealt with a recurrent problem of his research: to what extent is price theory descriptive of what businessmen do? Do businessmen use the marginal principle when setting prices? His doctoral dissertation (1958, 1960) has a long discussion of this and sets out to investigate the problem empirically. Based on semi-structured interviews, he describes the pricing policies of 139 Danish manufacturing companies. As in the study of the UK that inspired him (Hall and Hitch, 1939), he found full-cost pricing (or average-cost pricing) to be the most dominant pricing policy but also that the margin to be added to average costs might vary, for example due to changes in demand. He concludes that while businessmen do not think that they use the marginal principle in the short run, this does not preclude that their pricing is consistent with the marginal principle in the long run. This study is much cited, for example, by Scherer and Ross (1990) and Hay and Morris (1979).

Another much-cited work, (Fog, 1956) describes how cartel prices are negotiated between members of a cartel. At the time, formal price-fixing agreements were not immediately illegal and Fog interviewed members of six cartels and found that cartel agreements often do not express cordial cooperation but are rooted in distrust, necessitating the signing of formal contracts. One of the sources of internal conflicts in cartels was found to be that some firms were more short-sighted than others. In today's wording we would say that the discount factor of some firms was too low to allow cartels the full benefits of cooperation. Fog's work on cartels has been cited as recently as by Connor (2001).

In sum, Fog built an international recognition of his work on topics that were central to IO and his research methodology fell within the mainstream at the time. His monograph from 1994 represents the accumulated knowledge of a life-time of research of empirical IO.

Summing Up

As the above shows, Danish research in industrial economics had a strong theoretical orientation in the 1930s, and was pioneered by Zeuthen, followed by Winding Pedersen and Hans Brems in the 1950s. Bjarke Fog epitomizes empirical IO in the 1950s. In the 1960–80 period very little happened, although a few researchers published working papers on oligopoly pricing (Mossin, 1978) and articles on dynamic models of entry deterrence (Waagstein, 1982, 1983), mergers and acquisitions in Danish industries (Øhlenschlæger Madsen, 1983), or competition in quality space for industrial goods (Hjort-Andersen, 1981, 1988).[7]

NORWAY

In Bergh and Hanisch (1984) – a history of economics in Norway from about 1835 to 1980 – no explicit mention is made of industrial economics or anything resembling it. Norwegian economics research appears to have evolved around distributional and macroeconomic issues, often with a very close link to bureaucrats and politicians.

However, some pockets of industrial economics research did exist, notably at the Norwegian School of Economics and Business Administration (NSEB; Norges Handelshøyskole) in Bergen and, from about 1950, also at Bergen University. Norwegian research efforts in industrial economics were therefore commonly referred to as the 'Bergen group' (*Bergen-miljøet*). Most of the Norwegian industrial economics research, with a few exceptions constituted by Frisch (1941a/b) and Munthe (1959, 1960, 1961), appears to have been strongly descriptive and much focused on individual industries. A peculiar manifestation of this is the establishment of professorships that were (and to some extent still are) designed to address the economic concerns of particular industries, notably shipping and fisheries. In spite of the relatively atheoretical character of much of this work, it still owes a peculiar debt to a particular theoretical emphasis in Norwegian economics, namely the fundamental work of Ragnar Frisch on production and investment theory; thus, much of it may be seen as an attempt to make empirically concrete Frisch's heavily theoretical work.

Ragnar Frisch

Ragnar Frisch (1895–1973) made seminal contributions to a number of fields, for which he (jointly with Jan Tinbergen) was awarded the first Nobel Prize in economics in 1969. One of the areas to which Frisch made very significant contributions was production theory. In fact, a case can be made that much of what today is called 'neoclassical production theory' is, in fact, the brainchild of Frisch, although for a long time much of this work circulated only in the form of memos. Although Frisch began his work on the fundamental theory of production in the mid-1920s, and soon produced a Norwegian volume on the subject, Frisch's perfectionism did not allow him to publish an English language book-length statement of his theory of production until four decades later (Frisch, 1964). The book impresses by its magisterial quality, but there was probably relatively little in it that was new when it was published.

It is open to some debate whether Frisch may be classified as an industrial economist in the modern sense of that term. His concern with production seems ultimately to have been motivated by his interest in macroeconomics and business-cycle theory rather than in constructing a foundation for industrial economics.[8] However, Frisch published one paper that explicitly deals with a classical industrial economics topic, namely his 1941 paper on horizontal price agreements. Moreover, he lectured on forms of competition (1941a), giving – for the time – an advanced treatment of alternative competitive forms, and explicitly dealing with, and introducing, the notion of 'conjectural variations' as an important aspect of what he called competition in 'polypolies'. The direct Norwegian descent of this kind of work is represented by the work of Preben Munthe about two decades later.

Moreover, it is arguable that Frisch's emphasis on the theory of production influenced subsequent work on issues relating to firm-level production, although most of this later work can be categorized as either business economics (for example, Coward, 1937, 1944; Hellern, 1940) or empirical analysis of the cost and production characteristics in specific industries (Wedervang, 1965; Hope, 1967).[9] Frisch himself had published an early exemplar of this kind of research, namely the 1935 paper, 'The principle of substitution: an example of its application in the chocolate industry'!

Preben Munthe

The Norwegian economist who comes perhaps closest to the traditional concerns of the industrial economics area is Preben Munthe (1922–), who after studying at NSEB and Oxford University received his doctorate from NSEB and later became a professor at the University of Oslo where he is still active as an emeritus. Munthe was in regular contact with Bjarke Fog in Denmark. Although his early research was strongly theoretically informed, and thus in some ways closer to the concerns of Danes Winding Pedersen and Brems than to Fog's strongly empirically driven approach, Munthe was also interested in using industrial economics to throw light on empirical phenomena, such as sales cartels in whaling, dental manufacturing and rubber footwear (Munthe, 1961). In fact, like Fog he was interested in applying industrial economics to the understanding of firm strategies, rather than in understanding the aggregate welfare implications that may follow, given assumptions about firms' behaviours.

Although Munthe later broadened his research interests very considerably (for example, to doctrinal history), his early work, mainly published as monographs, dealt with such favourite industrial economics topics as entry conditions (1959), vertical relations (1960) and horizontal cartels (1961).

The last is Munthe's doctoral thesis. Using diagrammatical analysis, Munthe analyses the necessary conditions for the formation of cartels (that is, the expectation of gains from forming the cartel), the conflicting incentives of cartel members, and the resulting chiselling. A slightly earlier work (1960) is taken up with vertical relations, in particular how a producer's advertising decisions relative to end consumers is influenced by whether he can fix retail prices or not. Thus, Munthe treats a topic that after the publication of, in particular, Yamey (1954) conquers centre stage at the time. Surprisingly, however, he refrains from drawing any welfare and antitrust conclusions. His main aim seems to be to give an economics-based interpretation of how pricing may interact with marketing decisions, thus staying closer to the concerns of Arne Rasmussen (1955) in Denmark than to the traditional antitrust concerns of most industrial economists.

Frøystein Wedervang

Frøystein Wedervang (1918–?) was the the son of influential economist Ingwar Wedervang (1891–1961) (see Bergh and Hanisch, 1984). Frøystein Wedervang studied at NSEB, but received his doctorate in statistics from the University of Oslo. He returned to NSEB as a Professor in Business Administration. While at NSEB he wrote his major work, *Development of a Population of Industrial Firms* (1965). The monograph is a major study of the evolution of a large subset of the population of Norwegian firms in the period from 1930 to 1948. The main interest lies in tracing major structural characteristics of this population, such as the number of employees and the value of fixed capital in establishments (taken to be a proxy of firm size), and the capital–labour ratio and the ratios between added value and each of the input factors (gross labour productivity and gross capital productivity, respectively). Also, C4 concentration ratios, rates of entry and exit by sectors, and much else are calculated. This is done in painstaking detail, and is by itself quite impressive, given the computing power and the data sources of the time.

However, the overall purpose of this major statistical exercise is not entirely clear. Although findings on the size distribution of Norwegian firms and how this changes over time is compared to findings such as those of Simon and Bonini (1958), there is no overall attempt to ground such population dynamics in an overarching perspective (as in Downie, 1958). The overall impression is somewhat negative; for example, Wederwang finds that it is not possible to fit a Cobb-Douglass function to the data, and he also observes that Gibrat's law is contradicted by his findings. However, this does give rise to much theoretical reflection on his part. Wederwang does not seem to have published any of his findings from the study in an international journal (that is, there are no hits in the *Journal of Economic Literature* database).

Einar Hope

Einar Hope (1937–) spent two years as a graduate student at the University of Minnesota in the mid-1960s, and his 1967 PhD thesis *Kostnader og bedrifsttørrelse* (Costs and the size of firms) (Hope, 1967) bears a strong US imprint with respect to its references and its econometrics approach. However, in analysing the cost structure of a single industry it may be argued to be directly in the Norwegian tradition of concern with production and cost characteristics of single industries. Hope's thesis is an attempt to clarify whether and to what extent increasing returns to scale characterizes Norwegian banking. Because of data limitations, Hope begins from cost functions rather than production functions, and finds, using standard regression techniques, that increasing returns do indeed characterize the banking industry. He explicitly chooses not to discuss any possible efficiency implications of this finding.

Most of Hope's professional career has taken place at NSEB, where he has been instrumental in developing the teaching of industrial economics and where he served for some time as the director of the Institute for Industrial Economics. Hope has also been the Director General of the Norwegian Competition Authority (1995–99), and has served on many government committees. He produced numerous contributions to industrial economics through the 1970s, many of which were highly descriptive and some of which were taken up with the methodology of industry analysis (Hope, 1977). Hope's interest in electricity markets pushed his research interests in the direction of energy economics (he is professor of energy economics at NSEB), although he continued to be a prolific contributor to industrial economics.

Summing Up

To sum up, Norwegian research efforts in industrial economics were relatively scant, and had a mainly empirical orientation. Apart from Munthe´s work, very little or no theoretical work appears to have been undertaken. Internationalization also came late to Norwegian research.

SWEDEN

Around the turn of the century (1900), Sweden was endowed with four great economists: Knut Wicksell of Lund/Stockholm (1851–1926); Gustav Cassel of Stockholm (1866–1945); David Davidson of Uppsala (1854–1942) and Eli F. Heckscher (first Uppsala then Stockholm; 1879–1952). They were to some extent rivals, eagerly debating utility theory, Walrasian general equilibrium models, marginal productivity and international trade. Like in Denmark, the preconditions for applying microeconomics to problems of industrial organization were good, but somehow the interest was never really sparked in Sweden – until the 1970s.

Hans Thorelli

Hans Thorelli (1921–), wrote a doctoral thesis half a century later (Thorelli, 1954), appraising the early development of the American federal antitrust policy and dealing with 'a broad range of problems in the field of industrial economics and public policy in relation thereto' (p. viii). Thorelli offers 'a synthesized social science interpretation of the origination and institutionalization period of [the federal antitrust policy]' (p. vii). At the University of Stockholm, Thorelli was a student of Gunnar Heckscher, the son of Eli F. Heckscher. He moved on to Northwestern University and through numerous teaching and research institutions, ending his career at Indiana University's Kelley School of Business, where he is now a distinguished professor emeritus. During the 1960s, Thorelli's research interests changed to strategic management and marketing, and he developed simulation systems to facilitate strategic decisions in a multinational world.

Erik Dahmén

Erik Dahmén (1916–2005) provided a detailed study of the development of Swedish manufacturing between the two World Wars (Dahmén, 1950). In addition to being a professor at the Stockholm School of Economics, he was director of the Industrial Research

Institute in Stockholm, 1948–50.[10] Dahmén's main influence appears to lie in coining the notion of 'development block' in the context of his inquiry into the evolution of Swedish industry (Dahmén, 1950). The notion is an important early anticipation of contemporary ideas on the role of complementarities in economic development. The main inspiration for it appears to be the ideas of Joseph Schumpeter.

Bo Carlsson and Lennart Hjalmarsson

More recently, Bo Carlsson and Lennart Hjalmarsson have been pioneering Swedish industrial economists. They shared an interest in the measurement of efficiency, tracing their roots back to Eli Heckscher's (1918) work on Swedish problems of production in which he presented a diagram that preceded the Salter (1960) diagram by 42 years.[11] Their academic ancestors also include Gustav Åkerman (1931) who investigated the distance between best practice and average practice in Swedish saw mills and Ingvar Svennilson (1944) who followed in the same track.

Bo Carlsson

Carlsson received his BA from Harvard University in 1968 and his MA and PhD from Stanford University (1970 and 1972, respectively). Today he is E. Mandell de Windt Professor of Industrial Economics at Case Western University and has published widely on industrial dynamics and technological systems. His early work (Carlsson, 1972) on the measurement of efficiency in production was awarded the David Davidson Prize in Economics. Carlsson (1987) measured efficiency in 26 Swedish manufacturing industries and found that 'tariffs adversely affect efficiency and that the four-firm concentration ratio is positively and strongly associated with efficiency'. He argues that the latter result shows that 'the concentration ratio reflects economies of scale and specialization rather than the market power of the largest firms'. In a report for the Industrial Research Institute, Carlsson (1980) analyses technical change and productivity in Swedish industry in the postwar period. Later articles appeared among others in the *Journal of Industrial Economics*, the *Journal of Economic Behavior and Organization* and the *International Journal of Industrial Organization*. In one of these, his Presidential Address to the European Association for Research in Industrial Economics, Carlsson (1987) makes an interesting attempt to separate what he calls 'industrial dynamics', a more evolutionary/Schumpeterian approach, from supposedly more static mainstream industrial economics. His later research has clearly concentrated on elaborating the industrial dynamics programme, leading to publications in, for example, *Research Policy* and the *Journal of Evolutionary Economics*.

Lennart Hjalmarsson

Hjalmarsson (1944–) received his PhD in economics 1976 from the University of Gothenburg. His thesis was entitled *Studies in a Dynamic Theory of Production and its Applications* and his supervisor was Professor Leif Johansen of the University of Oslo. By that time he had already published in the *Swedish Journal of Economics* and in the *European Economic Review*. In Førsund and Hjalmarsson (1974) he initiated a productive collaboration with Norwegian economist Finn Førsund of the University of Oslo. In this article, they use static efficiency measures for inhomogeneous production functions in a dynamic setting of structural change. They argue that from a policy point of view the problem is not to force the current structure close to the best-practice frontier but rather to optimize an ongoing process.

In another early study, Førsund and Hjalmarsson (1979) analyse technical progress in Swedish dairy plants in terms of the production function. Shifts of the production function are translated into a reduction in unit costs (a generalization of Salter's (1960) measure) and further split into constituent parts consisting of proportional technical advance, factor substitution and increase of optimal scale. They are able to trace the changing efficiency frontiers from 1964 to 1973 and show that it is a movement of the frontier along a ray towards the origin that is responsible for a 9–13 per cent reduction of unit costs at the optimal scale. Hjalmarsson is the author of numerous articles in very prestigious journals since 1980 and has ventured into energy economics along with his Norwegian co-author, Finn Førsund.

Summing Up

As the above shows, Swedish research in industrial economics was rather sparse and scattered until around 1970. In the 1970s, Bo Carlsson, Lennart Hjalmarsson and their Norwegian colleague Finn Førsund did an impressive amount of work of a high quality, especially in the area of efficiency measurement. It is also noteworthy that with the exception of Hjalmarsson, the major early contributors to industrial economics either did not have industrial economics as a major research area, or took industrial economics into distinctly non-orthodox and usually Schumpeterian directions (Dahmén, Carlsson, Gunnar Eliasson). In fact, for a long period in the 1980s and 1990s, the Stockholm-based 'Industriens Utredningsinstitut' (see, for example, Dahmén and Eliasson, 1980) became a hotbed for these kinds of ideas.

CONCLUDING DISCUSSION

The Relative Performance of the Scandinavian Countries

There are some remarkable differences in the way that industrial economics developed in the Scandinavian countries. Thus, while the Danish research had a strong leaning towards a more formal approach – arguably a Zeuthen legacy (and perhaps going back even earlier) – Norway was almost completely dominated by empirical, industry-specific inquiry, in spite of the strong emphasis on formal methods that the 'Frisch revolution' (Bergh and Hanisch, 1984) marked in Norwegian economics. There were no Norwegian counterparts to Zeuthen, Brems and Winding Pedersen of Denmark. In fact, much of the relevant Norwegian research is so much characterized by meticulous industry studies that 'industrial economics' may be a bit of a misnomer, at least as that term is understood today. The Frisch influence was often indirectly present in such work, namely in attempts to fit specification of production function to the data. Still, some contributions exist that may be categorized as industrial economics proper, the names of Preben Munthe, Frøystein Wedervang and Einar Hope being representative.

Sweden presents a picture rather similar in some respects to that of Norway. Swedish research in economics has historically been almost completely dominated by monetary economics, trade theory and general equilibrium theory, and until the 1970s, very little research in industrial economics appears to have been undertaken. A distinct Swedish peculiarity is the importance of Schumpeterian ideas, notably in the work of Dahmén and Carlsson.

In terms of internationalization, Denmark appears to have been the first mover. However, in spite of having the two advantages of some emphasis on formal methods and some internationalization of the relevant research already around the Second World War, Danish research in industrial economics did not take off in the sense of building a research group. Research was largely concentrated on two professors, namely Winding Pedersen and Bjarke Fog, and the perhaps most internationally prolific Dane, namely Hans Brems, who had already emigrated to the United States in 1951.

What Explains the Scandinavian Research Effort in Industrial Economics?

One may speculate that a reason for the relatively little interest in industrial economics in the Scandinavian countries has to do with, first, the relatively lax antitrust regimes that have historically characterized these countries: because of the nature of these regimes, there were simply rather few antitrust cases into which an economist could sink his analytical teeth. Another possible reason has to do with the strong dominance of research in macroeconomics and general equilibrium, the former tendency no doubt being partly prompted by (and lending partial legitimacy to) the ongoing development of the Scandinavian welfare states.

One may further speculate that in the absence of these historical peculiarities, industrial economics could have gained more momentum. This is not least because of the existence of one important institution that could have organized research efforts in industrial economics, namely the *Nordisk Tidsskrift for Teknisk Økonomi* (*Nordic Journal for Technical Economics*) (1935–55). As Tjalling Koopmans (1977: 261) noted in his Nobel Prize speech, this journal provided an internationally recognized 'important medium' for discussions of production theory and of ways of conceptualizing and measuring the internal efficiency of firms. However, the journal never seriously took industrial economics on board. In fact, it closed its operation in 1955, at about the time when industrial economics became recognized as a field in economics.

Later Developments

Since 1980 there has been an upsurge of research in industrial economics. In Norway, Lars Sørgard of the Norwegian School of Economics and Business Administration in Bergen has been the prime driver of research in industrial economics. In Sweden, Norwegian Tore Ellingsen has an impressive track record. Lennart Hjalmarsson and Finn Førsund have continued their cross-border collaboration with good results. Danish economists who have contributed to industrial economics in the last 25 years include Morten Hviid, Svend Albæk, Per Overgaard and Christian Schultz. What they have in common is that they base their research on the international literature and that they are not 'burdened' by the legacy of the pioneers of the preceeding century. The link is missing.

NOTES

1. In addition to those methods mentioned in the following, we also performed searches on Google and the *Journal of Economic Literature* database. However, these searches were, on the whole, fruitless, except for tracking a few publications by Swedish and Norwegian industrial economists in the 1970s.
2. Diversion as a concept is used to calculate the unilateral effects of mergers. The diversion ratio shows the fraction of demand for a certain brand that is captured by a rival brand (the ratio of the cross-price to the own-price elasticity), see, for example, Shapiro (1996).
3. Zeuthen was mostly interested in applying the theory to the labour market so he phrased his theory in terms of a workers' union and an employers' confederation.
4. The official reason was the importance of Brems's contribution to the theory of monopolistic competition, a body of theory that was central to the development of the distinct approach to marketing developed by Barfod (1937) and Rasmussen (1955).
5. Indeed Brems (1954) provides an overview of the state of competition policy in all three Scandinavian countries.
6. Brems (1950) and Fog (1950) is a debate of what 'free competition' means, whether there is any competition left in Denmark (given its lax competition rules and pervasive postwar regulation), and in what dimensions competition may take place (price, advertisements, quality). It is very clear that Brems is a theoretician and that Fog is based on the empirical side of the divide.
7. This research was by and large undertaken in the late 1970s.
8. However, it is noteworthy that the Department of Economics at Gothenburg University has singled out as one of its main research areas, 'the Scandinavian approach to industrial economics, developed by Ragnar Frisch and Leif Johansen in Oslo'.
9. However, the work of Finn Førsund, briefly discussed in connection with Lennart Hjalmarsson, is very clearly in the formal Frisch tradition.
10. The Industrial Research Institute was founded in 1939 by the Federation of Swedish Industries and the Swedish Employers' Confederation with the aim of conducting research 'on economic issues of importance for long-term industrial development in Sweden' (www.iui.se). One of the major research programmes deals with industrial organization and many Swedish academics have spent time at the Institute in Stockholm, which in this way assembles the largest concentration of industrial economists in Sweden.
11. The (Heckscher-)Salter diagram shows a ranking of the different unit costs of different plants starting with the lowest and ending with the highest. The abscissa measures the capacity of the different plants and the ordinate the unit cost.

REFERENCES

Åkerman, Gustav (1931), 'Den industrielle rationaliseringen och dess verkningar' (Industrial rationalising and its effects), SOU 1931: **42**, Stockholm.

Bain, Joe S. (1972), *Essays on Price Theory and Industrial Organization*, Boston, MA: Little, Brown & Co.

Barfod, Børge (1937), *Reklamen i Teoretisk-Økonomisk Belysning*, Copenhagen: Schønberg.

Bergh, Trond and Tore J. Hanisch (eds) (1984), *Vitenskab og Politik: Linjer I Norsk Socialøkonomi Gjennom 150 År*, Oslo: Aschehoug.

Brems, Hans (1944), 'Prisstivhed', *Nationaløkonomisk Tidsskrift* 82: 341–61.

Brems, Hans (1947), *Monopoly and Employment*, Copenhagen: Association for Education of Young Businessmen, Copenhagen Business School.

Brems, Hans (1948), 'The interdependence of quality variations, selling effort and price', *Quarterly Journal of Economics*, **62**: 418–40.

Brems, Hans (1949), *Some Problems of Monopolistic Competition*, Copenhagen: (no publisher information available).

Brems, Hans (1950), 'Er den frie konkurrence død? I: Indlæg', *Det Danske Marked*, **9**: 216–27.

Brems, Hans (1951a), *Product Equilibrium under Monopolistic Competition*, Cambridge, MA: Harvard University Press.

Brems, Hans (1951b), 'On the theory of price agreements', *Quarterly Journal of Economics*, **65**: 252–62.

Brems, Hans (1951c), 'Omkostninger og prispolitik. Nogle nye britiske bidrag og et forsøg på fortolkning', *Nationaløkonomisk Tidsskrift*, **89**: 1–20.
Brems, Hans (1952a), 'Employment, prices, and monopolistic competition', *Review of Economics and Statistics*, **34**: 314–25.
Brems, Hans (1952b), 'A discontinuous cost function', *American Economic Review*, **62**: 577–86.
Brems, Hans (1953), 'Foreign exchange rates and monopolistic competition', *Economic Journal*, **63**: 289–94.
Brems, Hans (1954), 'Monopoly and competition in Scandinavia', in E.H. Chamberlin (ed.), *Monopoly and Competition and Their Regulation*, New York: International Economic Association.
Brems, Hans (1964), 'Cost and indivisibility', *Journal of Industrial Economics*, 12: 142–50.
Brems, Hans (1976), 'Frederik Zeuthen', in Socialøkonomisk Samfund, pp. 347–66.
Burns, Arthur R. (1936), *The Decline of Competition*, New York: McGraw-Hill.
Carlsson, Bo (1972), 'The measurement of efficiency in production: an application to Swedish manufacturing industries 1968', *Swedish Journal of Economics*, **74**(4): 478–85.
Carlsson, Bo (1980), *Technical Change and Productivity in Swedish Industry in the Post-War Period*, IUI Research Report No. 8, Industriens Utredningsinstitut: Stockholm.
Carlsson, Bo (1987), 'Reflections on "industrial dynamics"', *International Journal of Industrial Organization*, **5**: 135–48.
Cassel, Gustav (1901), 'Kartell- og trustväsendet från socialekonomisk synspunkt' (Cartel and antitrust authorities from an economics viewpoint), *Ekonomisk Tidskrift*, **3**: 475–502.
Chamberlin, Edward H. (1933), *The Theory of Monopolistic Competition*, Cambridge, MA: Harvard University Press.
Connor, John M. (2001), '"Our customers are our enemies": the lysine cartel of 1992–1995', *Review of Industrial Organization*, **18**: 5–21.
Coward, Dag (1937), 'Standardisering af Industrielle Selvskostendeberegninger i Norge', *Nordisk Tidsskrift for Teknisk Økonomi*, **3**: 121–41.
Coward, Dag (1944), *Kostnadsregning i Industribedrifter*, Oslo: Aschehoug.
Dahmén, Erik (1950), *Svensk industriell företagarverksamhet* (Swedish manufacturing), Stockholm: Industrial Research Institute (IUI).
Dahmén, Erik and Gunnar Eliasson (eds) (1980), *Industriell Utveckling i Sverige*, Stockholm: Almqvist & Wiksell.
de Wolff, P. (1940), 'Report on the Elsinore Meeting, August 25–26, 1939', *Econometrica*, **8**(3): 279–88.
Downie, Jack (1958), *The Competitive Process*, London: Duckworth.
Fog, Bjarke (1946), 'Dynamic price problems under monopolistic competition', *Nordisk Tidsskrift for Teknisk Økonomi*, **22**: 257–70.
Fog, Bjarke (1948), 'Price theory and reality', *Nordisk Tidsskrift for Teknisk Økonomi*, **12**: 89–94.
Fog, Bjarke (1950), 'Er den frie konkurrence død? II: Svar', *Det Danske Marked*, **9**: 227–32.
Fog, Bjarke (1956), 'How are cartel prices determined?', *Journal of Industrial Economics*, **5**: 16–23.
Fog, Bjarke (1958), *Priskalkulation og prispolitik: en analyse af prisdannelsen in dansk industri*, Copenhagen: Einar Harcks Forlag.
Fog, Bjarke (1960), *Industrial Pricing Policies: An Analysis of Pricing Policies of Danish Manufactures*, Amsterdam: North-Holland (translation of Fog, 1958).
Fog, Bjarke (1994), *Pricing in Theory and Practice*, Copenhagen: Handelshøjskolens Forlag.
Førsund, Finn and Lennart Hjalmarsson (1974), 'On the measurement of productive efficiency', *Swedish Journal of Economics*, **76**(2), 141–54.
Førsund, Finn and Lennart Hjalmarsson (1979), 'Frontier production functions and technical progress: an application to milk processing in Swedish dairy plants', *Econometrica*, **47**(4): 883–900.
Frisch, Ragnar (1935), 'The principle of substitution: an example of its application in the chocolate industry', *Nordisk Tidsskrift for Teknisk Økonomi*, **1**: 12–27.
Frisch, Ragnar (1941a), *Polypolteori*, A summary of Professor Frisch's Lectures at Oslo University, Oslo.
Frisch, Ragnar (1941b), 'Priskartellisk prisdannelse', *Statsøkonomisk Tidsskrift*, **55**.
Frisch, Ragnar (1964), *Theory of Production*, Dordrecht: Reidel.

Hall, R.L. and C.J. Hitch (1939), 'Price theory and business behaviour', *Oxford Economic Papers*, **2**: 12–45.
Hay, Donald A. and Derek J. Morris (1979), *Industrial Economics: Theory and Evidence*, Oxford: Oxford University Press.
Heckscher, Eli F. (1918), *Svenska Produktionsproblem* (Swedish production problems), Stockholm: Bonniers.
Hellern, B. (1940), 'Industriens behov for produksjonsteknisk forskning', *Nordisk Tidsskrift for Teknisk Økonomi*, **6**: 93–103.
Hjort-Andersen, Christian (1981), 'Price and quality of industrial products: some results of an empirical investigation', *Scandinavian Journal of Economics*, **83**(3): 372–89.
Hjort-Andersen, Christian (1988), 'Evidence on agglomeration in quality space', *Journal of Industrial Economics*, **37**(2): 209–23.
Hope, Einar (1967), *Kostnader og bedrifsstørrelse*, PhD dissertation, Bergen: Samfundsøkonomisk Institut ved NHH.
Hope, Einar (1977), 'Industry studies in theory and practice', in *Festschrift to Professor Olav Harald Jensen: Business Administration in Theory and Practice*, Oslo: Bedriftsøkonomens Forlag.
Hotelling, Harold (1929), 'Stability in competition', *Economic Journal*, **39**: 41–57.
Jantzen, Ivar (1928), 'Voxende Udbytte i Industrien', *Nationaløkonomisk Tidsskrift*, **62**: 1–62.
Jantzen, Ivar (1948), 'Laws of production costs', *Econometrica*, **16**: 44–8.
Kærgård, Niels (1983), 'Marginalismens gennembrud i Danmark og mændene bag', *Nationaløkonomisk Tidsskrift*, **121**(1): 20–42.
Kærgård, Niels (1996), 'Denmark and the marginal revolution', *Research in the History of Economic Thought and Methodology*, **14**: 247–58.
Koopmans, Tjalling (1977), 'Concepts of optimality and their uses', *American Economic Review*, **87**: 261–74.
Krouse, Clement (1990), *Theory of Industrial Economics*, Oxford: Basil Blackwell.
Mossin, Axel (1978), 'A theory of oligopolistic price formation', *Blue Memo*, **71**, Institute of Economics, University of Copenhagen.
Munthe, Preben (1959), *Freedom of Entry into Industry and Trade*, Bergen: Skrifter fra Norges Handelshøyskole.
Munthe, Preben (1960), *Produsentenes vertikale markedspolitik som pristeoretisk problem*, Bergen: Skrifter fra Norges Handelshøyskole.
Munthe, Preben (1961), *Horisontale karteller*, Bergen: Skrifter fra Norges Handelshøyskole.
Øhlenschlæger Madsen, Ole (1983), *Virksomhedsovertagelser og fusioner i dansk industry*, Copenhagen: NNF.
Philip, Kjeld (1976), 'Socialpolitikeren Frederik Zeuthen', in Socialøkonomisk Samfund, pp. 367–75.
Rasmussen, Arne (1955), *Pristeori eller Paremeterteori*, Copenhagen: Einar Harcks Forlag.
Robinson, Joan (1933), *The Economics of Imperfect Competition*, London: Macmillan.
Rubinstein, Ariel (1982), 'Perfect equilibrium in a bargaining model', *Econometrica*, **50**(1): 97–110.
Salter, W.E.G. (1960), *Productivity and Technical Change*, Cambridge University Applied Economics Monographs.
Scherer, Frederick M. and David Ross (1990), *Industrial Market Structure and Economic Performance*, 3rd edn, Boston, MA: Houghton Mifflin.
Shapiro, Carl (1996), 'Mergers with differentiated products', *Antitrust*, 23–30.
Simon, Herbert A. and Charles P. Bonini (1958), 'The size distribution of business firms', *American Economic Review*, **48**: 607–17.
Socialøkonomisk Samfund (1976), *Danske Økonomer* (Danish Economists), Copenhagen: Samfundsvidenskabeligt Forlag.
Svennilson, Ingvar (1944), 'Industriarbetets växande avkastning i belysning av svenska erfarenheter', *Studier i ekonomi och historia tillägnade Eli F. Heckscher 24–11–1944*, Stockholm.
Thorelli, Hans (1954), *The Federal Antitrust Policy. Origination of an American Tradition*, Baltimore, MD: The Johns Hopkins Press.
Tirole, Jean (1988), *The Theory of Industrial Organization*, Cambridge, MA: MIT Press.

Trust Commission (1953), *Foreløbig betænkning vedrørende en lov om konkurrencebegrænsning og monopol*, Copenhagen: S.I. Møllers Bogtrykkeri.
von Stackelberg, Heinrich (1934), *Marktform und Gleichgewicht*, Vienna and Berlin: Verlag von Julius Springer.
Waagstein, Thorbjørn (1982), 'Fixed costs, limit pricing and investments in barriers to entry', *European Economic Review*, **17**(1): 75–86.
Waagstein, Thorbjørn (1983), 'A dynamic model of entry deterrence', *Scandinavian Journal of Economics*, **85**(3): 325–37.
Wedervang, Frøystein (1965), *Development of a Population of Industrial Firms*, Oslo: Universitetsforlaget.
Winding Pedersen, H. (1936), 'Konkurrencens Tilbagegang', *Nordisk Tidsskrift for Teknisk Økonomi* **2**(5): 119–34.
Winding Pedersen, H. (1939), *Omkring den moderne pristeori*, Copenhagen: Nielsen & Lydiche.
Winding Pedersen, H. (1953), 'Konkurrencebegrænsning og monopolkontrol. Foredrag i Nationaløkonomisk Forening d. 17. nov. 1953' *Nationalokonomisk Tidsskrift* **91**: 299–314.
Winding Pedersen, H. (1958), 'En disputats om priskalkulation og prispolitik' (A thesis on pricing policies), *Nationaløkonomisk Tidsskrift*, **96**: 133–40.
Winding Pedersen, H. (1965), *Industriens struktur og sammenslutninger*, Oslo: Universitetsforlaget.
Winding Pedersen, H. (1976), *Træk af pris- og konkurrenceteorien*, Copenhagen: Akademisk Forlag.
Yamey, B.S. (1954), *Economics of Resale Price Maintenance*, London: Pitman.
Zeuthen, F. (1929), 'Mellem konkurrence og monopol' (Between competition and monopoly), *Nationaløkonomisk Tidsskrift*, **67**: 265–305.
Zeuthen, F. (1930), *Problems of Monopoly and Economic Warfare*, London: Routledge & Sons. Reissued 1967 by Routledge & Kegan-Paul.
Zeuthen, F. (1958), 'En disputats om priskalkulation og prispolitik' (A thesis on pricing policies), *Nationaløkonomisk Tidsskrift*, **96**: 141–8.

PART II

Pioneers of the field in the USA and Canada

9. Introduction to the pioneers in North America

William G. Shepherd

INTRODUCTION

From the 1870s to the 1980s, scholars in the United States and Canada made a brilliant array of innovations. Some new ideas were basic and broad, such as the very nature of 'effective' competition, and the harms or benefits of monopoly. Others ranged down to small and technical points; for instance, certain pricing tactics, or indexes of concentration. Some involved pure theory and arcane symbolism, whereas others focused on hotly debated facts or complex econometric methods. Still other new ideas were about public policies such as antitrust or regulation.

The pioneering was often irregular and faltering, rather than steady and smooth. Many authors excitedly extolled 'new' ideas which were, in fact, never accepted. Other innovations were accepted for a while but then soon faded out. Even so, some fundamental concepts have now been well settled for over 100 years, and they may last for centuries more.

Here I sum up this North American history, showing how the various pioneers fitted into the long waves and brief ripples of new ideas and scholars. There were a series of distinct eras, each lasting one or several decades (for example, the 1900–30 period, then the 1930s, then the 1940s). I sum up each period in a few paragraphs and then present the individual pioneers whose new ideas came out then.

After this introductory chapter, I present the individual profiles of the 43 most prominent pioneers, in a long section. Here in this Introduction, those 43 pioneers are mentioned briefly, but only to show where they fit in the flow. The details of their innovations, training and best writings are saved for the later write-ups about them.

Each of the full write-ups of the 43 pioneers, and the shorter mentions of the 52 others in this Introduction, has a length and details that reflect the relative importance of the ideas. The lengths are only approximate. My suggested page lengths to authors were my best judgment, but there is room for debate about them. And some authors strayed from my suggested lengths. Even so, the whole array of profiles is probably a reasonably good guide.

Also, there is some room for debate about the sequence; where each innovator should be located in the whole series. I have tried to place each one when their main ideas began to take hold, though of course some pioneers kept making innovations over many years. In any event, I hope that the whole sequence is at least approximately correct.

THE MAIN IDEAS AT THE CORE OF THIS FIELD

Before I start the review decade by decade, remember that there is a dominant organizing topic of the field: how competition and monopoly may affect the efficiency and innovation that occur in markets. That whole subject divides into a large series of detailed points and debates. Early pioneers quickly clarified many of these large and small points, even before 1900. Other innovations continued, right down to the mid-1980s when this survey ends. They have been targets for spirited debates, and rightly so.

The following list itemizes the whole field's main categories of ideas and methods.[1] It is a matrix for the field's literature, into which the innovators have placed their ideas, trying to answer all the deep questions as well as the many technical points:

1. The meaning of '*effective competition*' in *correctly defined economic markets*. This involves the defining of genuine and relevant markets; the true nature of competitive processes (dynamic, static, short run, long run or other); the specific equilibrium conditions reached by competition; and the variety and severity of imperfections that can infect markets.
2. How the *specific market features* and structures may take effect. This especially includes companies' own market shares. They may give market dominance by one firm or concentration that is jointly held by the several largest firms. It can also be important how the several biggest firms interact with each other. Tight oligopolists may coordinate with each other rather than compete, while loose oligopolists usually fight hard.
3. The *economies of scale*. They are often shown by how steeply the average cost curve slopes down, to reach its lowest point at minimum optimum scale. There also may be diseconomies of scale at larger sizes. Also, the various methods for measuring the economies and diseconomies; no methods are robust, but some methods are much more reliable than others.
4. The *nature of enterprises* of all sizes. This includes their managers' alternative motivations (short- and long-run profits, company size, risk avoidance and so on); and transactions costs for settling the arrangements that are made externally, among companies, and internally, among the parts inside companies.
5. *Mergers* of all types (horizontal, vertical, and conglomerate). Also, friendly mergers as distinct from hostile takeovers; the motives and quality of merger planning; which mergers raise market power, or instead reduce it; and the economic impacts of mergers on efficiency and innovation, including the impacts of hostile takeovers.
6. *Vertical conditions and actions* of all types, including vertical integration, vertical economies, vertical restrictions, and other vertical exertions of control. The main problems of defining and measuring these vertical conditions.
7. '*Potential competition*' from outside of the market. This includes whether and how the potential competition might be measured; new entry (what it really is, and how it might be measured); and barriers against new entry (what are they, and how might they be measured?). How to define and estimate the many sources of entry barriers (both the many possible 'exogenous', fundamental sources, and various 'endogenous' voluntary sources, particularly strategic pricing and related entry-preventing actions).

8. The *benefits of competition* and the *effects of monopoly power*. These impacts include: (i) financial outcomes, for example, price levels, profitability and price discrimination; and (ii) such real economic outcomes as allocational efficiency, X-efficiency, the rate of innovation, fairness and other effects of monopoly. The meaning and testing of the 'efficient structure hypothesis'.
9. Concepts of *innovation*: the measurement of innovation's speed, scale and effects; and how competition and monopoly may affect innovation.
10. Important *other values* that competition promotes, including freedom of choice, fairness, stability, democracy and so on.
11. *Industry studies in all sectors of the economy*, ranging from primary materials and agriculture to manufacturing, services, military supplies and others.
12. Game theory, mathematical versions of theory, and modeling of all kinds. Experimental studies of the choices made by firms, rivals, consumers and policy makers under controlled situations.
13. *Antitrust policies*, of the three main types: toward market dominance, toward mergers, and toward collusion on prices and other conditions. Criteria for finding which actions are truly anti-competitive: for example, some price discrimination, 'predatory pricing' and actions, 'raising rivals' costs', mergers and alliances, and other devices.
14. *Public regulation policies* since the 1880s. Regulation as a social contract; with constraints on prices and profits; the protection of monopoly positions; various effects on efficiency and investment; and other critical and favorable theories of regulation.
15. The *deregulation* of various industries in the US and elsewhere; conditions favoring the removal of constraints; the various successes and failures of deregulation. Natural gas, banking and equity markets, airlines, railroads, telecommunications, postal, electricity, water and so on.
16. *Public enterprise and not-for-profit 'third sector' firms* of various types. Defining publicness by degrees of public ownership, control and subsidies. Varieties of non-profit and social enterprises.

All these 16 main areas and their subtopics add up to a very wide range of complicated subjects. Moreover, each area has several levels: the theory and concepts of the ideas; the facts and patterns in real situations; and the methods for studying those ideas and facts.

The pioneers' work has improved understanding in all of these areas during the 1870s to 1980s, but of course the innovations have varied hugely in their timing, importance, style and impact. Every new idea and method has been controversial in some degree, amid debates about their relative importance, their validity and their value. These are difficult questions, and we can only present our best judgments about the pioneers and their writings.

In this review, the 43 leading pioneers' names are set in capital italics; their details are given in individual profiles, in the next section. The 52 less-prominent pioneers (in italics) are noted along the way here, in capsule summaries.

THE 1870s–1900s: CLARIFYING THE BASIC CONCEPTS AND METHODS

The modern pioneering in this field began in the 1870–1900 decades, as neo-classical economic theory became dominant in Europe and the United States.

Americans had long favored competition and had resisted controls over markets, by monopolists and price fixers. After the 1870s, the focus on competition became even clearer. The new microeconomic theory stressed with precision that competition drove markets toward efficient allocation.

But at the same time, fierce struggles in real, rugged industrial markets were reducing actual competition in many parts of the booming and changing US economy. For example, the new Standard Oil trust captured monopoly power, as also did the US Steel trust of 1901 in the steel industry. Western railroads gained great monopoly power by 1890, and so did heavy metals producers, farm equipment makers, the new electricity and telephone monopolies, and scores of other new near-monopoly 'trusts' in US industries during the first great merger wave of 1897–1901. These problems were intensified not only by the rising flood of mergers, but also by a variety of abuses that many dominant firms were inflicting on their small rivals.[2]

So the up-beat competitive concepts were being developed in this field just as industrial turmoil was creating a counter-reality, with intense needs for new policy lessons and tools. The clash between bright theory and destructive reality forced the leading scholars to reach complicated judgments and policy choices. Americans had long resisted monopoly and industrial abuses in small local markets. Now the 1870–1900 tumult brought much larger needs, on a national scale.

The earliest modern innovators tackled and clarified many of competition's basic issues. By 1900 they had made major progress throughout much of the 16 main areas listed above.

These pioneers engaged in intense debates over the correct theories and methods of research. They also focused on the real conditions of real markets, even though the basic types of data were scarce back then (such as about costs and profits, production levels in firms and industries, and the market share of companies). By 1900–1910, the main foundations of the field were in place.

The earliest American pioneer was *CHARLES ELLET, JR* (1810–62). He was the first American mathematical economist, who clarified demand and cost functions, and pricing, as early as 1839 – though with little recognition.

Then in the 1870s–1880s, a handful of energetic new scholars and economics departments emerged, including a few important pioneers. At the University of Michigan, *HENRY CARTER ADAMS* (1851–1921) pioneered before 1890 the early theory of monopoly's effects and the nature of increasing and diminishing returns, of natural monopolies, and of the basis for public policies.

JOHN BATES CLARK (1847–1938) soon became the leading US economist writing on the new neo-classical theory. He drew optimistic lessons that the competitive system was both efficient and fair, even if it had 'trusts', monopolies, upheavals, and extreme rich–poor contrasts.

Richard T. Ely (1854–1943) at Wisconsin pushed further the analysis of natural monopoly and of market abuses in the turbulent emerging electricity industry.[3]

JEREMIAH W. JENKS (1856–1929) of Cornell did the first detailed studies of industries that were monopolized by 'trusts' (dominant firms). He also clarified the economies of scale, effective competition, efficiencies and wastes.

Many others – including spectacular popularizers and muckrakers like Ida Tarbell – also wrote and debated the effects and facts, but these few were the most prominent scholars.

THE 1900–1930 PERIOD: FURTHER INDUSTRIAL TURBULENCE STIRS NEW IDEAS AND ACTIONS TOWARD NEAR-MONOPOLIES LIKE STANDARD OIL AND AMERICAN TOBACCO

Summary

The main issues of the 1870–1900 debates now played out in antitrust battles and new regulatory experiments.

During the 1890s, the issues had gathered force with the merger flood, creating near-monopolies in a wide range of major industries. The supposed 'mandates of modern technology' favoring large size (that is, economies of scale) were widely claimed, but they were disputed at length, along with the various harms of monopoly. There was much debate about whether the new electric and telephone companies were actually 'natural monopolies'. All these struggles continued after 1900, with the added heat of public outrage over plutocrats' excesses and legions of hapless victims.

During 1906–15, major antitrust cases were launched against six of the ten largest US industrial companies. These spectacular cases stirred extensive disputes about the true extent of the markets, what the anti-competitive abuses were and how severe their impacts were, and whether the monopoly profits were enormous. During 1911–13 there were major antitrust decisions, remedies and compromises by the Supreme Court, involving Standard Oil, American Tobacco, AT&T and others. Later there was research on the impact of those cures, especially in the oil industry.

Telephones and electricity stirred extensive debate about regulation and other possible cures, and the first state-level 'regulatory commissions' were created.

The 1920s brought a number of deeper analyses of costs, pricing and profits in complicated large firms. The 1920s also engendered the roaring and unstable merger boom, which included the corrupt pyramiding of controls over electricity systems.

In 1903, *Charles J. Bullock* (1869–1941) gave a thorough critique of the claims that mergers created huge new efficiencies, showing that instead most of them were exaggerated.[4] Bullock anticipated much of the concepts and facts that John Moody presented in 1904, in his extensive popular book, *The Truth About the Trusts*. Moody's book surveyed, profiled and extolled the new dominant firms formed by mergers in many scores of large industries.

Further critiques of the great 1897–1901 merger wave were done by *William Z. Ripley* (1867–1941) and others.[5]

JOHN MAURICE CLARK (1884–1963), the son of John Bates Clark, made large innovations with his 1923 book on overhead costs. In 1940 he offered the idea of 'workable competition': a set of ten indicators or conditions which might show the strength of competition.

Eliot Jones (?–1971) provided early 'industry studies', with concepts and evidence about leading problem industries such as railroads, petroleum, steel and copper. He mainly criticized the idea of 'ruinous pricing'.[6]

GEORGE W. STOCKING (1892–1975) made contributions from 1925 to the 1950s on the inefficiencies caused by market power, and antitrust in many industries, especially oil and steel.

MARTIN G. GLAESER (1888–1967) published in 1927 a landmark book on the mainstream methods for regulating utilities, advancing the concepts of costs and pricing.

INNOVATIONS IN THE IMPORTANT 1930s: LARGE FIRMS, OLIGOPOLY THEORY AND EVIDENCE, THE STRUCTURE–CONDUCT–PERFORMANCE LOGIC, 'WORKABLE COMPETITION' AND UTILITY REGULATION

Summary

The 1930s brought a dramatic enlargement of new ideas and research, as well as upheavals to antitrust and regulatory policies.

Berle and Means dramatically restated the nature of large corporations, and Chamberlin and Robinson then offered new theories of oligopoly. Many of the field's leaders shifted toward using theoretical models and greater abstraction.

But government sources and some scholars also presented new research into large firms, new statistical data, the detailed study of industry conditions, and the ways that each market's structure may influence the performance of firms in that market. New data on four-firm concentration in the US began to be produced and analyzed.

The mainstream structure–conduct (behavior)–performance logic of causation emerged, saying that a market's structure tends to influence its behavior and performance. This logic continued to lead the field's thinking on into the 1970s. It was tested and supported by logic, statistical studies, and detailed industry research.

Vertical integration and price discrimination also drew attention. AT&T's large and deep vertical monopoly (tying its equipment-supplying Western Electric company to its monopoly of local telephone operating companies) was critiqued at length. Other vertical problems were hotly debated, especially the rapid growth of grocery chains like A&P and other discounters as they wiped out thousands of small local stores. The discounters used their monopsony power to force down the wholesale prices of the goods that they bought and then resold to the final consumers.

Antitrust and regulatory policies also went through spectacular changes, first fading and then rebounding.

GARDINER C. MEANS (1896–1988) explored in 1932 (with A.A. Berle) the changing nature of large corporations. Means also studied the effects of concentration on price cooperation, and he advanced the idea of 'administered prices'.

EDWARD H. CHAMBERLIN (1899–1967) published in 1933 *The Theory of Monopolistic Competition*, often praised as the leading innovation in the field during the important 1930s decade.

It was paralleled by *Joan Robinson*'s (1903–83) book of 1933 on imperfect competition, though there were significant differences.[7] Always writing with sophistication, she originated the marginal-revenue curve, which is crucial to analyzing monopoly's effect on price. She also enlarged the analysis of price discrimination and its competitive effects.

'The oligopoly problem' was intriguing, but it drew attention away from the much more acute problem of single-firm dominance for at least the 1930s–1950s period.

JAMES C. BONBRIGHT (1891–1985) developed further the concepts of consumer benefits and natural monopoly as the basis for rate-base regulation of utilities.

In the 1930s, *Frank H. Knight* (1885–1972) and *Henry C. Simons* (1899–1946) led the original 'Chicago school' of the 1930s and 1940s, with a sophisticated view of competition and many harms of monopoly.[8] In the 1920s, Knight had pioneered the analysis of profit and risk. In the 1930s, Knight and Simons stressed the wider values of competition, beyond pure static-allocation efficiency. They also urged the importance of protecting competition because it promoted innovation, healthy democracy, and broader social values, going well beyond narrow efficiency. This Chicago school approach was radically reversed in the 1950s, toward a rosy optimism that all markets are essentially perfect, that market power is insignificant, and that monopoly firms always deserve their control over their markets.

Ronald H. Coase (born 1910) began in England but spent most of his career at the University of Chicago.[9] In 1937, he advanced his theory of the nature of the firm. It explored the conditions that would encourage the firm to enlarge its scope so as to coordinate its actions internally, versus relying on market transactions to achieve coordination with outsiders. His 1960 article, 'The problem of social cost', argued that private actions could eliminate many harmful externalities, abuses and 'social' problems. This favored minimal government and encouraged the emergence of the 'law and economics' field.

Abba P. Lerner (1903–82) also began in England but spent most of his career in the US. He proposed a simple 'index of monopoly' in 1937: the ratio of price minus marginal cost to price.[10] It soon became a fixture in the literature. The difficulties of defining and measuring marginal costs (and for that matter, measuring prices) has limited its practical uses.

HAROLD HOTELLING (1895–1973) originated the theory of spatial location, and he provided the logic of duopolists tending to choose adjacent locations in product space.

The young *Paul M. Sweezy* (1910–2004) presented in 1938 the idea of a 'kinked demand curve', to explain how oligopolists might set uniform and unchanging prices.[11] He assumed that oligopolists were timid, because they fear the worst from either cutting or raising their prices. So they would neither cut nor raise prices. Their resulting two-part demand curve would have a kink, and the unchanged prices would be 'sticky'. Though Sweezy was the leading Marxist economist in the US, he did not make research innovations in this field's areas.

EDWARD S. MASON (1899–1992) joined J.M. Clark in advocating complex criteria for competition. He also formed the 'Harvard' group that did various industry studies, and he promoted the structure–conduct (behavior)–performance logic.

In 1940 *Clair Wilcox* (1898–1970) published the first comprehensive survey of competition and monopoly in the US economy.[12] He noted that most of the US economic activity took place in 'effectively competitive' markets, but large market power existed in markets with about 20 percent of the economy. His appraisals considered both concentration and companies' behavior and profitability. The study became a landmark for commentary and later research.

Horace M. Gray (1898–1986) in 1940 declared that the regulation of utilities had already shown fatal economic weaknesses.[13] This early critique made him the first major advocate of deregulation, a change which gained force only in the 1970s.

IN THE 1940s: SCHUMPETER AND GAME THEORY

Summary

The 1940s brought a new emphasis on the 'good' role of dominant firms, and it also saw the creation of game theory.

Schumpeter defended large firms with the idea of 'creative destruction', where competition was a rough, dynamic process rather than a set of precise equilibrium results. Dominant firms, he said, would generate innovations, rather than merely raise prices and retard creative progress.

The 1940s also brought more oligopoly theorizing. Von Neumann and Morgenstern's creation of game theory in 1944 enlarged oligopoly theory and enhanced the role of mathematics. Yet Fellner showed that words could still clarify oligopoly. Adelman praised price discrimination for its pro-competitive role. And Edwards criticized extreme diversification by large firms.

JOSEPH A. SCHUMPETER (1883–1950) advanced in 1942 his view of competition as a dynamic process, which would promote innovation even if it sacrificed static efficiency.

In 1944, *John von Neumann* (1903–57) and *Oskar Morgenstern* (1902–77) published *The Theory of Games and Economic Behavior*, with its extensive technical analysis that immediately created game theory as a new field.[14] It had relevance for numerous areas like war gaming, and also for the two-firm version of oligopoly. It also enlarged the role of mathematics in all market theorizing, including oligopoly.

In contrast, *William J. Fellner* (1905–83) enriched and extended in 1949 the analysis of oligopoly situations, using analytical words and judgments rather than mathematics.[15] In 1951, Fellner also wrote a classic paper arguing that competition would tend to increase the rate of innovation. Both his oligopoly book and the innovation paper became fixtures in the literature, but he then moved on to other economic areas.

Corwin D. Edwards (1901–79) helped to create the Robinson–Patman Act of 1936, which attacked price discrimination by large firms.[16] He also studied and censured the spread of highly diversified firms, both in the US and in the vast Japanese conglomerate combines. They combined market power from many financial and industrial sectors, resulting cumulatively in greater total political power. With that power, as Edwards and others noted, the combines had strengthened Japan's militarism and its ultimate role in the Second World War. He later wrote extensively about price discrimination, which he regarded as mostly anti-competitive.

Eleanor M. Hadley (born 1916) was a key young staff official in the Allied Occupation Forces in postwar Japan.[17] She worked aggressively and effectively in helping to break up the leading financial and industrial conglomerates; Japanese officials often referred to her as the 'Dragon Lady'. In 1969 she published a definitive account of the industrial break-ups.

MORRIS A. ADELMAN (born 1917) was the true originator of many free-market ideas, involving price discrimination, concentration and vertical integration. After 1960, he became a leading expert on the world oil industry.

THE 1950s: NEW RESEARCH IDEAS ON TIGHT OLIGOPOLY, BARRIERS TO ENTRY, COUNTERVAILING POWER AND MEASUREMENTS

Summary

The 1950s greatly enriched the field's variety of concepts and methods.

Adelman led the effort to disprove any rise of US industrial concentration. Galbraith advanced the idea of countervailing power, and Harberger produced empirical suggestions that monopoly's harms might be tiny rather than important. Marginal-cost pricing was advanced by J.R. Nelson in the US, as well as by French and British specialists.

Big business assigned itself credit for much of the US 1950s' economic boom, when the 'structure–conduct (behavior)–performance' logic of this field was dominant. But the large oligopolies in steel, automobiles and so on, usually raised prices once each year, after labor-union bargaining was set, and then held them steady. This stair-step pattern looked like the 1930s' 'administered prices', rather than determined by flexible, competitive pressures.

Also, there was testing of the Berle–Means thesis from 1932, that large-firm managers often pursue other motives – sheer size, growth, risk avoidance, personal amenities and so on – which deviate from maximizing the firms' profits.

In 1956, Bain's major book shifted attention out to the edges of the market, where 'potential competition' and 'entry barriers' may be important. Such barriers would supplement – or perhaps displace – the dominance and concentration that could create market power at the center of the market.

In contrast, Kaysen and Turner said in 1959 that 'tight oligopoly', with four-firm concentration above 70 percent, was really 'shared monopoly', which needed correction by antitrust policy actions. Oligopoly was now analyzed with several distinct models (including theoretical models and game theory, kinked demand curves, price leadership of various sorts, and tight oligopoly 'shared monopolies').

A major 1959 book also explored competition in the transport industries, especially railroads. And by 1960 Shubik and others had tried but failed to apply game theory to real industries.

JOHN KENNETH GALBRAITH (born 1908) advanced a theory of war-time price controls in 1948. The government's controls could be tighter over few-firm oligopolies than over the many scrappy firms in unruly competitive markets. In 1952 he originated the idea of countervailing power, and later in the 1960s he analyzed and deplored the military–industrial complex.

In 1951 *John Nash* (born 1928) wrote his main ideas about the theory of games, which later gained prominence in the game theory literature.[18]

Fritz Machlup (1902–83) published in 1952 two thorough books, on monopoly pricing and on patents.[19] His discussion of price discrimination was detailed and sophisticated, noting that discrimination could be pro- or anti-competitive, depending on the setting.

ALFRED E. KAHN (born 1917) and *Joel Dirlam* (born 1915) proposed in 1954 that 'fair competition' be made the goal and criterion for antitrust policy. This would consider a firm's behavior and intentions, not just its market position and profit rates. In 1959 Kahn co-authored (with Melvin de Chazeau) a major study on vertical integration in the US oil industry.

Dirlam later joined in the important 1958 study of diverse managerial motivations in large firms.[20] It showed that disparate motives like large size, risk avoidance and personal amenities were widespread. He was also the co-author in 1966 with *WALTER ADAMS* of two strong critiques of the US steel industry, for its pricing rigidity (which was caused by excess vertical integration) and its poor innovation. In the 1960s, Dirlam pioneered by studying Yugoslavia's shift toward less-controlled markets and its unique worker-managed enterprises.

In 1954 the theorist *Arnold Harberger* (born 1924) analyzed some data for 1926, concluding that market power in the US economy back then had only a tiny effect in reducing efficient allocation.[21] Various downward biases in his methods were soon shown by several writers, and a variety of later estimates were substantially higher. But Harberger did initiate this line of research.

WALTER ADAMS (1922–98) and Horace M. Gray in 1955 attacked needless regulation for blocking the beneficial effects of competition, especially in transportation industries. Adams also presented a textbook of industry studies, and (with Joel Dirlam) in 1966 he criticized the tight oligopoly in the steel industry. In the 1980s he criticized the merger mania.

Jesse W. Markham (born 1916) published industry studies on rayon in 1952 and the fertilizer industry in 1958.[22] Perhaps his best-known innovation was about price leadership. He noted that price leaders might raise prices as benign 'barometers', which merely reflected the underlying cost trends and other causes, rather than exerting any separate effects to raise prices.

Gideon Rosenbluth (born 1921) has been a Canadian innovator who published extensive analyses of Canada's industrial concentration.[23] Rosenbluth put this in book-length form in 1957, and in 1970 he mounted a pathbreaking study of foreign control in relatively small countries like Canada, 'small' in economic totals, compared at least with the US.

JOE S. BAIN (1912–93) urged the importance of potential competition, entry barriers and limit pricing. He also elaborated more on the mainstream SCP (or SBP) approach, and in the 1960s he published an international comparison of industrial structures in several Western nations.

A thorough study of managers' actual motivations was published in 1958 by Kaplan, Dirlam and *Robert F. Lanzillotti* (born 1920).[24] Applying extensive research to the Berle and Means hypothesis of managerial control, it showed that many managers strayed significantly from strict profit maximizing. This anticipated much of the large-firm literature of the 1960s.

Edith Tilton Penrose (1915–96) presented in 1959 a pathbreaking analysis of *The Theory of the Growth of the Firm*.[25] It stressed that new pockets of various managerial skills and excess resources might naturally emerge within firms, leading to further growth and change. It tied into Marshall's earlier study of firms' evolution, and it anticipated much of the later discussion of firms' internal conditions. After some time, it came to be seen as a classic, with seminal status. Because Penrose had to be peripatetic with her husband's career, she lacked a firm academic platform for building and enlarging on her innovations.

WILLARD F. MUELLER (born 1925) co-wrote with George W. Stocking in 1955 an influential critique of antitrust standards in the *Cellophane* case decision. He greatly enhanced the quality and influence of economics in the Federal Trade Commission (FTC) in the 1960s, developing many lines of research.

William Vickrey (1914–96) also concentrated on marginal-cost pricing, developing concepts for using it in road pricing and other local transportation.[26] In 1971 he offered proposals for 'responsive' pricing of utility services.

James R. Nelson (1917–85) critiqued in 1958 the regulation of transportation, particularly railroads, for blocking competition and flexible pricing.[27] In 1963 he published *Marginal-Cost Pricing in Practice*; his applied focus was an advance on the pure theories of marginal-cost pricing. Nelson dealt especially with French electricity pricing, including translations and commentary by Nelson on the major French writings.

CARL KAYSEN (born 1920) applied oligopoly theory creatively in 1951–52; published in 1956 a major case study of the *United Shoe Machinery* case; and urged in 1957 a wider standard for evaluating the impacts of large corporations.

In 1959 he joined with *DONALD F. TURNER, JR* (1922–94) in rethinking 'tight oligopoly' and antitrust policy. They surveyed industry structures in the US economy, arguing that tight oligopoly held harmful market power and needed an antitrust cure. Later, both as a scholar and as the Antitrust Division chief in 1965–68, Turner dealt with a wide range of antitrust issues. His Areeda–Turner rule (1975) changed antitrust policies toward 'predatory pricing'.

GEORGE J. STIGLER (1911–91) had advocated strict criteria for competition and antitrust during 1947–52; but by 1958 he reversed this viewpoint, finding virtually all markets to be competitive. He promoted the survivor method for estimating scale economies, and in the 1960s he developed theories of oligopoly and of regulation.

WILLIAM J. BAUMOL (born 1922) urged in 1959 that sales or growth maximizing was important in many large firms. He later suggested a 'stay-low' rule for curing 'predatory pricing'. With colleagues, he discussed in 1979 the 'sustainability' of 'Ramsey prices', and he offered in 1982 (with colleagues) the idea of 'contestability'.

Merton J. Peck (born 1925) contributed to assembling the detailed concentration data on tight oligopolies in the 1959 Kaysen–Turner book.[28] He also participated as a co-author in the landmark 1959 book (by *JOHN R. MEYER* (born 1927), Peck, John Stenason, and Charles J. Zwick), which analyzed how competition might improve efficiency in the regulated railroad industry. In 1962 Peck analyzed (with *F.M. SCHERER*) why the military's weapons purchasing process created large wastes. He also published in 1962 a case study of the aluminum industry. In 1969 he co-authored (with *ROGER G. NOLL* and John J. McGowan) an innovative analysis of regulation and future of the television industry.

Martin Shubik (born 1926) was deeply involved with game theory in the 1950s, developing new technical features of it.[29] He also tried to apply it to real markets. But in his 1959 book *Strategy and Market Structure*, Shubik admitted that game theory could not be applied to real markets. Real cases were simply too complicated to fit to games models of duopoly. Game theory faded in interest and attention, but in the 1970s many young theorists turned to it again. Game theory still lacked practical uses, but theorists spoke of its 'insights' and 'suggestions' and 'rigor'. Shubik led and joined that rebirth, and his *Market Structure and Behavior* (1980) (with R.E. Levitan) was a significant contribution to the 'new' game theory literature.

THE 1960s: EVEN RICHER VARIETY, WITH NEW ATTENTION TO INNOVATION, DATA ON CONCENTRATION, X-INEFFICIENCY IN LARGE FIRMS, AND DOUBTS ABOUT REGULATION

Summary

The 1960s expanded the diversity of research methods, to use pure theory, various kinds of cross-section empirical studies, and analyses of antitrust and regulation.

The analysis of antitrust and regulation became increasingly critical. New econometric studies of structure and performance drew on the fast-growing power of computers, which could crunch far more detailed numbers on industrial concentration, price–cost patterns, and mergers. The causes, types and benefits of innovation became a major research topic. Critiques of regulation's economic impacts began to expand, especially about the regulation of transportation industries like airlines and railroads.

Chicago school and other free-market advocates began to defend monopoly more aggressively, and their resistance to antitrust policies hardened. As for large firms, they blossomed as a research field. The idea that large firms might often have great 'X-inefficiency' became influential.

As part of the rising attention to technological change, *Richard R. Nelson* (born 1930) supervised two major NBER (National Bureau of Economic Research) studies (in 1961 and 1962), dealing in depth with the measurement and analysis of innovation.[30] He and Sidney G. Winter also researched how an evolutionary process might cause changes in firms and markets.[31]

Norman Collins and *Lee E. Preston* (born 1930) showed in 1961 how unstable the ranks of the largest US corporations might be.[32] Then in 1968 they used census price–cost margins to test market power's effects in raising prices.

Edwin Mansfield (1930–98) was a leader in the 1960s in the practical measurement of innovation's dimensions and monopoly's influence on it.[33] He tested monopoly power's effect in retarding innovation, as William J. Fellner had predicted theoretically in 1949. In contrast, Galbraith had suggested that tight oligopolies facing vertical pressure would innovate rapidly. Mansfield found mixed patterns; market power showed some slowing of innovation, but certain conditions could reverse the effect.

RICHARD E. CAVES (born 1931) published in 1962 a pathbreaking critique of US airline regulation. Later he applied econometric methods to many hypotheses, especially about international aspects of competition. His research also extended into numerous fields beyond industrial organization.

Michael Gort (born 1923) provided in 1962 an extensive factual analysis of diversification and integration in US industries.[34] He stressed the role of the firm's endowment of human capital; it determines the choices whether to diversify and/or to integrate vertically. In 1963 he analyzed the stability and change of market shares over time, with a focus on concentration patterns. He explored how innovations have changing roles over the life-stage of an industry; at first, innovation promotes entry, while it retards entry in the later stages.

Richard M. Cyert (born 1921) and *James G. March* (born 1929) extended the analysis of large firms' internal tendencies toward bureaucracy and inefficiency.[35] The concepts expanded the ideas begun by Berle and Means in 1932, Ronald Coase in 1937 and Edith Penrose in 1956.

LELAND L. JOHNSON (born 1930) published in 1963 (with Harvey Averch) a pathbreaking analysis explaining why regulated monopolies tend to indulge in bloated costs and too much investment.[36] They also explained why the constrained monopolist will try to capture and monopolize adjacent markets, using subsidies from the regulated market, as AT&T had done and continued to do in the 1970s.

Almarin Phillips (1925–2006) published studies in 1962 covering a range of collusive and cartel pricing behavior.[37] Phillips also led a 1975 collective study of regulation's possible economic harms in a variety of sectors (this extended the work of Adams and Gray in 1955).

LEONARD W. WEISS (1925–94) began with case studies, then measured concentration and its effects on wages, prices, discrimination and advertising.

John M. Blair (1916–76), a prominent congressional economist and later academic scholar, argued that industrial concentration caused large costs and dangers.[38] As Chief Economist of Senator Estes Kefauver's Senate Subcommittee on Antitrust and Monopoly during 1956–70?, he produced research evidence about market and total concentration in the 1950s–1960s, and also about administered prices. In the 1960s he led the subcommittee's investigations of monopoly in drug markets. He also worked with census officials to expand US industrial concentration data, and he clarified the adjustments for fitting arbitrary census 'industries' to true market boundaries.

Franklin M. Fisher (born 1934) was a co-author in an early group study (1962) into oligopoly's effect in raising the frequency and costs of US automobile model changes.[39] Later he and colleagues criticized the use of accounting profits. They said that profits data had no value in antitrust cases involving IBM (he led IBM's economics team in the 1970s, helping IBM to defeat some 20 antitrust challenges).

Donald J. Dewey (1922–2002) was an early innovator in using price theory to assess the research on concentration and its effects.[40] Though trained at Chicago, he held independent views, urging 'realism rather than romance' in antitrust policy, avoiding the perfect-markets attitude. Among his creative discussions: challenging the possible correlation of concentration with profitability, the importance of free entry, the harms of collusion, and the claims of Robert H. Bork. He relied on neo-classical price theory, in deflating traditional claims for antitrust and other public policies.

JACOB SCHMOOKLER (1918–67) deepened in 1966 the analysis of technology's progress, exploring its historical sources and stressing the role of competition.

FREDERIC M. SCHERER (born 1932) studied military waste, dominant-firm innovation, mergers and economies of scale; he also wrote a 1970 landmark textbook on the field.

WILLIAM G. SHEPHERD (born 1936) analyzed the actual levels and effects of market concentration, the efficiency of public enterprises, the 'survivor test', marginal-cost pricing, racial and gender discrimination, dominant-firms' profits, the trend of US competition, the central role of market share, and 'contestability' theory.

HARVEY J. LEIBENSTEIN (1922–92) created in 1966 the important concept of 'X-efficiency'.

WILLIAM S. COMANOR (born 1935) created studies (with Thomas A. Wilson) that explored how intensive advertising might tend to raise market power. Comanor also clarified drug-industry innovation, vertical restrictions, and (with Robert H. Smiley) he estimated monopoly's impact on the distribution of wealth.

Paul M. Sweezy joined with Paul A. Baran in 1966 in publishing a Marxist book about *Monopoly Capital*. They asserted that financial controls over industrial concentration were pervasive, but they did not present evidence.

OLIVER E. WILLIAMSON (born 1932) did early-1960s research on large firms, eventually developing the idea of 'transactions costs'. In 1968 he explored the possible 'trade-off' between mergers' monopoly effects in raising prices and the possible economies of scale that might reduce prices.

HAROLD DEMSETZ (born 1930) extended the new Chicago school's free-market approach in two ways. He argued in 1968 that franchise regulation could replace price regulation. He also favored reversing the mainstream SCP (or SBP) logic of causation.

Seymour Melman (1917–2004) first showed by 1954 how management costs related to firm sizes. Later he focused on the 'permanent war economy', with its industrial market power.[41] Extending Galbraith's work on the military-industrial complex, Melman stressed in the 1960s and later that 'Pentagon capitalism' was distinct from normal competitive markets; it was driven by monopoly, vertical collusion, and other special conditions.

Radical political economists are a puzzling case of Marxian innovations that did *not* occur. Karl Marx had provided in *Das Kapital* (1883) a deep left-wing challenge to the mainstream ideas in this field, which treated markets as mostly competitive. Marx predicted that ownership and power would become ever more concentrated, eventually 'in a few hands'. Monopoly would prevail. Until the 1960s, Marxist economists were few, and only two of them, Paul M. Sweezy and Paul Baran, continued to urge Marx's predictions.[42] Their restatement of them in 1966 amounted to a type of pioneering step at that time.

In the 1960s sharp dissent cropped up in the US, and a new echelon of radical economists formed sizeable groups at several campuses (especially the University of Massachusetts, the New School for Social Research, and the University of California at Riverside).[43] They focused on labor problems, social issues and Third World development. But they ignored the applied questions of actual industrial concentration and market power. Therefore they missed the chance to do innovative research in this field.

THE 1970s: MORE RICH VARIETY, BUT WITH A SHIFT TOWARD FREE-MARKET THEORY, GAME THEORY AND A CAMPAIGN FOR DEREGULATION

Summary

The 1970s brought further enrichment of the field, but also a rapid spread of game theorizing. And free-market advocates grew more influential.

Econometric studies tested the effects of individual firms' market shares, mergers and innovations. Large-firm conditions were explored further by Williamson, especially 'transactions costs'. Experimental studies of duopoly were developed further by Friedman and others. The free-market challenge to the mainstream SBP approach gathered force, relying mainly on theory rather than on thorough factual research. Game theory spread, and research about regulation's possible harms proliferated further, favoring the growing campaign to remove regulation from a variety of 'utility' sectors.

PAUL W. MACAVOY (born 1934) partitioned and criticized the effects of natural gas regulation, helping make the case for the deregulation of that industry. He critiqued (with Stephen Breyer, born 1938) the regulation of electricity. And he suggested that OPEC (Organization of the Petroleum-Exporting Countries) raised oil prices in the 1970s only moderately above the effect of rising long-term scarcity.

HARRY M. TREBING (born 1927) restated regulatory economics and applied it to telecommunications.

John J. Siegfried (born 1945) defended concentration ratios; and did numerous empirical studies, including one which tested firm size and market structure as determinants of antitrust actions to raise competition.[44] He also tested how market power could influence political activities and actual policies.

Stanley E. Boyle (1927–84) was a leading economist at the FTC in the 1960s, working with Willard F. Mueller to enlarge FTC research.[45] In the 1970s he and Mueller founded the Industrial Organization Society to foster applied research, and in 1974 he began publishing the *Industrial Organization Review*, which was renamed the *Review of Industrial Organization* in 1984.

DENNIS C. MUELLER (born 1940) explored with econometrics the determinants of corporate mergers, the persistence of dominant-firm profits in the long run, and the welfare costs of market power.

Morton I. Kamien (born 1938) and *Nancy L. Schwartz* (1937–81) studied the possibilities that competition would lead firms to invest in innovation by either too much or too little; too little, because they cannot capture all the benefits of innovations, or too much because of pressures in the race to prevail by innovating first.[46] Kamien and Schwartz also modified the analysis of limit pricing to assume that entry was related to the incumbent's price level.

ROGER G. NOLL (born 1940) joined early analysis of deregulation (1971), co-authored an early exploration of television regulation and deregulation (1973), and pioneered economic research into the sports industry (1974).

SAM PELTZMAN (born 1940) analyzed controls and entry in commercial banking in 1965, finding them ineffective. Later he evaluated the regulation of the drug industry in the 1960s, and in 1976 he offered a general theory of regulation.[47]

Kenneth G. Elzinga (born 1942) extended Walter Adams's earlier point that many successful antitrust cases turn out to be 'Pyrrhic victories'; winning the formal case but losing when no good remedy is applied.[48] He also co-authored a criterion (with Thomas F. Hogarty) for defining geographic markets, such as for coal or beer. This test used data on the ratio of shipments into and out of a local area to find if that area was a true market.

James W. Friedman (born 1936) developed early experimental studies of duopoly, working with groups of students.[49] His work analyzed the numerous dimensions and behavior of leading firms in oligopoly markets.

RICHARD SCHMALENSEE (born 1944) did research on advertising's effects, market power in the cereals industry and advertising, the nature of market power, and the various causes of high profitability.

Robert T. Masson (born 1944) analyzed the motives of large-firm executives, relating them to stock-price performance. He also showed distortions caused by the public regulation of milk markets.[50]

A. MICHAEL SPENCE (born 1943) studied monopolistic competition and possible excess product variety, and also the power of signalling.

Kenneth D. Boyer (born 1949) disaggregated the informational and persuasive components of advertising, while estimating how advertising influences profits.[51] He showed that differing sizes of firms could make it difficult to define markets clearly. He also became a leader in applying rigorous concepts to the economics of transportation.

The theorist *ROBERT D. WILLIG* (born 1947) joined W.J. Baumol in much of the work on sustainability and contestability. He also explored definitions of predation (1981).

1980–1985: FURTHER EMERGENCE OF PURE THEORY AND FREE-MARKET IDEAS

Summary

Free-market ideas gained political advantage in the Reagan administration, both in antitrust and deregulation efforts. Game theorizing also spread further.

Christopher Green (born 1937) of Canada's McGill University, wrote the first comprehensive study of the Canadian field of industrial organization.[52] This early 1980s' book also covered the actual competitive conditions, as well as Canada's antitrust and regulatory policies.

Stephen Martin (born 1948) showed in the early 1980s that market structure can be partly endogenous in empirical structure–conduct (behaviour)–performance studies using industry data.[53] His 1983 monograph suggested that the positive market-share-profitability association reflects more than efficiency. This finding was affirmed by his 1988 study.

JOSEPH E. STIGLITZ (born 1943) studied asymmetric information, risk, insurance and the theory of market structure.

John E. Kwoka (born 1946) applied statistical analysis in 1979 to relate individual firm's market shares – especially the third-largest firm – to the price–cost margins of the entire market.[54] Kwoka also joined in FTC research on the professions, showing that market power reduced quality and raised prices in those important sectors.

Steven C. Salop (born 1946) defined 'raising rivals' costs' (with David T. Scheffman), a device which firms may impose to put their rivals at a disadvantage.[55] He also analyzed theories of price variations, strategic entry deterrence, consumer information and oligopoly coordination.

Paul M. Joskow (born 1947) wrote in 1983 (with Richard Schmalensee) an extensive analysis of the prospects for competition in the regulated electricity industry.[56]

JOHN R. MEYER and others explored the effects from deregulating US airlines in 1978.

NOTES

1. The shape of the field's literature can be seen in Joe S. Bain, *Industrial Organization*, rev. edn, Wiley, New York, 1968; F.M. Scherer and David Ross, *Industrial Market Structure and Economic Performance*, 3rd edn, Houghton Mifflin, Boston, MA, 1990; William G. Shepherd, *The Economics of Industrial Organization*, 5th edn, Waveland Press, Prospect Heights, IL, 2005; and for recent technical directions, Richard Schmalensee and Robert D. Willig (eds), *Handbook of Industrial Organization*, North-Holland, Amsterdam, 1989.
2. See Ralph L. Nelson, *Merger Movements in American Industry, 1895–1956*, Princeton University Press, Princeton, NJ, 1959; and Naomi Lamoreaux, *The Great Merger Movement in American Business, 1895–1904*, Cambridge University Press, Cambridge, 1985.
3. BA Columbia College, 1876. Professor of Economics, University of Wisconsin, 1892–1922. Also Founder and President, American Economic Association, 1900–02.
4. BA Boston University, 1889; PhD University of Wisconsin, 1895. Professor of Economics, Harvard University, 1903–35. See his 'Trust literature: a survey and criticism', *Quarterly Journal of Economics*, February 1901, pp. 167–217.
5. BA MIT, 1890; MA, PhD Columbia University, 1892, 1893. Professor of Economics, Harvard University, 1901–33. See his *Railroads – Rates and Regulation*, Ginn, Boston, MA, 1912; and Ripley, W.Z. (ed.), *Trusts, Pools and Corporations*, Ginn, Boston, MA, 1916.
6. See Eliot Jones, 'Is competition in industry ruinous?', *Quarterly Journal of Economics*, May 1920, pp. 484–5.
7. MA Cambridge University, 1927. Lecturer to Professor of Economics, Cambridge University, 1932–71. See her *Economics of Imperfect Competition*, Macmillan, London, 1933.
8. Frank H. Knight, 1885–1972. BA Milligan College, 1911 and University of Tennessee, 1913; PhD Cornell University, 1916. Professor of Economics, University of Chicago, 1928–55; also at Cornell University and the University of Iowa. See his *Risk, Uncertainty and Profit*, Macmillan, London, 1921, and, at the University of Chicago Press, Chicago, Chicago, *The Economic Organization*, 1933, *The Ethics of Competition*, 1935 and *Freedom and Reform*, 1947.

   Henry C. Simons, 1899–1946. BA University of Michigan, 1920. Professor of Economics, University of Chicago, 1927–46; also at the University of Iowa, 1920–27. See especially his *Economic Policy for a Free Society*, University of Chicago Press, Chicago, 1948.

9. BCom, DSc University of London, 1932, 1951. Professor, University of Chicago, 1964–79. Reader at the London School of Economics, 1935–51; Professor, University of Buffalo, 1951–58 and University of Virginia, 1958–64. Recipient of the Nobel Prize for Economics in 1991. See his 'The nature of the firm', *Economica*, November 1937, pp. 386–405; and 'The problems of social cost', *Journal of Law and Economics*, October 1960, pp. 1–44.
10. BSc, PhD University of London, 1932, 1943. Professor of Economics, New School for Social Research, 1942–47; Roosevelt University, 1947–59; Michigan State University, 1959–65; University of California, Berkeley, 1965–71; and Queen's College, New York, 1971–78. See his 'The concept of monopoly and the measurement of monopoly power', *Review of Economic Studies*, June 1934, pp. 157–75.
11. BA, PhD Harvard University, 1931, 1937. Instructor and Assistant Professor, Harvard University, 1934–46; Co-editor, *Monthly Review*, 1949–2004. See his 'Demand under conditions of oligopoly', *Journal of Political Economy*, August 1939, pp. 568–73.
12. BS University of Pennsylvania, 1919; MA Ohio State University, 1922; PhD University of Pennsylvania, 1927. Assistant Professor to Professor of Economics, Swarthmore College, 1927–68. See his *Competition and Monopoly in the American Economy*, Monograph 21, Temporary National Economic Committee, US Government Printing Office, Washington, DC, 1940; and *Public Policies Toward Business*, 4th edn, Richard D. Irwin, Homewood, IL,1970.
13. BS 1922, MS 1923, PhD 1926 all at the University of Illinois. Assistant Professor to Professor, University of Illinois, 1927–66. See his 'Passing of the public utility concept', *Journal of Land and Public Utility Economics*, **8**, February 1940, pp. 16–35.
14. John Von Neumann, PhD University of Budapest, 1926. Professor at Princeton University Institute for Advanced Study, 1933–57. See *Theory of Games and Economic Behavior*, Princeton University Press, Princeton, NJ, 1944.

    Oskar Morgenstern, Dr. University of Vienna, 1925. Professor of Economics, Princeton University, 1938–70.
15. Diplome (Chemical Engineering) Federal Institute of Technology, Zurich, 1927; PhD University of Berlin, 1929. Professor of Economics, University of California, Berkeley, 1939–52; and Yale University, 1952–73. President of the American Economic Association, 1969. See his *Competition Among the Few*, Norton, New York, 1949.
16. BA, BJ, University of Missouri, 1920, 1921; Diploma in Economics, BLitt, Oxford University, 1922, 1924; PhD, Cornell University, 1928; Rhodes Scholar, 1921–24. Edwards spent most of his career in staff positions at the Federal Trade Commission and various congressional committees, but he was also Professor of Law, University of Oregon, 1963–71. He wrote a massive study of the Japanese combines in 1945, based on research he did in Japan immediately after the Second World War. See also his *Maintaining Competition*, McGraw-Hill, New York, 1949; *The Price Discrimination Law*, Brookings Institution, Washington, DC, 1959; and *Cartelization in Western Europe*, Department of State, Washington, DC, 1964.
17. BA Mills College, 1934; MA Radcliffe College, 1943; PhD Harvard College, 1949. Associate Professor of Economics, Smith College, 1956–65; Adjutant Professor, George Washington University, 1972–84; Group Director, International Division, US General Accounting Office, 1974–81; Lecturer, University of Washington, 1984–. See her *Antitrust in Japan*, Princeton University Press, Princeton, NJ, 1971.
18. BS, MS Carnegie-Mellon University, 1948; PhD Princeton University, 1950. Instructor, MIT, 1951–59. Awarded the Nobel Prize in Economics, 1994. See his 'Noncooperative games', *Annals of Mathematics*, September 1951, pp. 286–95. Featured in the major movie *A Beautiful Mind*, 2003.
19. Dr. Rer. Pol. University of Vienna, 1923. Professor of Economics, University of Buffalo, 1935–47; Johns Hopkins University, 1947–60; Princeton University, 1960–71; and New York University, 1971–83. President of the American Economic Association, 1966. See his *The Economics of Sellers' Competition*, Johns Hopkins University Press, Baltimore, MD, 1952; and *The Political Economy of Monopoly*, Johns Hopkins University Press, Baltimore, MD, 1952.
20. BA, PhD Yale University, 1936, 1947. Professor of Economics, University of Connecticut, 1952, 1956–63; University of Rhode Island, 1964–81; and Visiting Professor, University of Paris, 1969–70. Consultant, US International Trade Commission, since 1981; research on Yugoslav enterprises, 1959–73.

    See A.D.H. Kaplan, Joel B. Dirlam and Robert F. Lanzillotti, *Pricing in Big Business: A Case Approach*, Brookings Institution, Washington, DC, 1958; Adams and Dirlam, 'Steel imports and vertical oligopoly power', *American Economic Review*, March 1966, pp. 160–68; and Adams and Dirlam, 'Big steel, invention and innovation', *Quarterly Journal of Economics*, May 1966, pp. 167–89.
21. MA (International Relations), PhD University of Chicago, 1947, 1950. Associate Professor to Professor of Economics at the University of Chicago, 1953–91. See his 'Monopoly and resource allocation', *American Economic Review*, May 1954, pp. 77–87.
22. BA University of Richmond, 1941; MA, PhD Harvard University, 1947, 1949. Professor of Economics, Princeton University, 1953–68; Harvard University, since 1982. See his 'The nature and significance of price leadership', *American Economic Review*, December 1951, pp. 891–905; *Competition in the Rayon Industry*,

Harvard University Press, Cambridge, MA, 1952; and *The Fertilizer Industry: Study of an Imperfect Market*, Vanderbilt University Press, Nashville, TN, 1958.

23. BA University of Toronto, 1943; PhD Columbia University, 1953. Professor at University of British Columbia, since 1962. President, Canadian Economic Association. See his 'Measures of concentration', in George J. Stigler (ed.), *Business Concentration and Price Policy*, Princeton University Press, Princeton, NJ, 1955; *Concentration in Canadian Manufacturing Industries*, Princeton University Press, Princeton, NJ, 1957; and 'The relation between foreign control and concentration in Canadian industry', *Canadian Journal of Economics*, February 1970, pp. 57–95.
24. Robert F. Lanzillotti, BA, MA, American University, 1947, 1948; PhD, University of California at Berkeley, 1953. Professor and Chair of Economics, Michigan State University, 1961–69; Professor of Management and Dean, School of Business, University of Florida, since 1969. Commissioner, US Price Commission, 1971–72. See A.D.H. Kaplan, Joel B. Dirlam and Robert F. Lanzillotti, *Pricing in Big Business*, Brookings Institution, Washington, DC, 1958.
25. BA University of California, 1936; MA, PhD Johns Hopkins University, 1951. Lecturer, Johns Hopkins, 1951–59; Professor of Economics, SOAS, 1964–78; and Professor of Political Economy, INSTEAD, Fontainebleau, France, 1977–84. She served on numerous British Commissions of Enquiry and councils on overseas development matters. See her *The Theory of the Growth of the Firm*, Basil Blackwell, Oxford, 1959, rev. edn, 1995.
26. BS Yale University, 1935; MA, PhD Columbia University, 1937, 1947. Professor of Political Economy, Columbia University, 1950–79. President of the American Economic Association, 1992; awarded the Nobel Prize in Economics, 1996. See his *The Revision of the Rapid Transit Fare Structure of the City of New York*, Financial Project, Mayor's Commission Management Survey, 1952; and 'Responsive pricing of utility services', *Bell Journal of Economics*, 1971.
27. BA 1938, Oberlin; PhD 1941, Harvard. Professor of Economics, Amherst College, 1948–84. See his *Marginal-Cost Pricing in Practice*, Wiley, New York, 1963.
28. BA Oberlin College, 1949; MA, PhD Harvard University, 1951, 1954. Professor of Economics, Yale University, 1962–81. See *Competition in the Transportation Industries* (with John R. Meyer, John Stenason and Charles J. Zwick), Harvard University Press, Cambridge, MA, 1959, *Competition in the Aluminum Industry*, Harvard University Press, Cambridge, MA, 1962, and *Weapons Acquisition: An Economic Analysis* (with F.M. Scherer), Harvard University Press, Cambridge, MA, 1963, *Economic Aspects of Television Regulation* (with Roger G. Noll and John McGowan), Brookings Institution, Washington, DC, 1973.
29. BA (Maths), MA University of Toronto, 1947, 1949; MA, PhD Princeton University, 1951, 1953. Professor of Economics and Organization, 1960–75, of Mathematics and Institutional Economics, Yale University, since 1975. See his *Strategy and Market Structure*, Wiley, New York, 1959, and *Market Structure and Behavior* (with R.E. Levitan), Harvard University Press, Cambridge, MA, 1980.
30. BA Oberlin College, 1952; MA, PhD Yale University, 1954, 1956. Professor of Economics, Yale University, 1968–86; Professor of International Public Affairs, Business and Law, Columbia University, since 1986. See Nelson (ed.), *Government and Technical Progress: A Cross-Industry Analysis*, Pergamon, Oxford, 1982.
31. See their *An Evolutionary Theory of Economic Change*, Harvard University Press, Cambridge, MA, 1981.
32. Lee E. Preston, BA Vanderbilt, 1951; MA, PhD Harvard University, 1953, 1958. Professor, School of Business Administration, University of California at Berkeley, 1958–69; Professor, School of Management, State University of New York at Buffalo, 1969–79; Professor, College of Business and Management, University of Maryland at College Park, 1980–. See Collins and Preston, 'The size structure of the largest industrial firms', *American Economic Review*, December 1961, pp. 986–1011; and their 'Price–cost margins and industry structure', *Review of Economics and Statistics*, August 1969, pp. 271–86.
33. BA Dartmouth College, 1951; MA, PhD, Duke University, 1953, 1955. Assistant and Associate Professor, Carnegie-Mellon University, 1955–63; Professor of Economics, University of Pennsylvania, 1963–98. See his *Industrial Research and Technological Innovation*, W.W. Norton, London, 1968, and *The Economics of Technological Change*, W.W. Norton, London, 1968.
34. BA Brooklyn College, 1943; MA, PhD Columbia University, 1951, 1954. Professor of Economics, State University of New York, Buffalo, NY, since 1963. See his *Diversification and Integration in American Industry*, Princeton University Press, Princeton, NJ, 1962; 'Analysis of stability and change in market share', *Journal of Political Economy*, **71**, February 1963 pp. 51–61; and 'Time paths in the diffusion of product innovations', *Economic Journal*, **92**, September 1982 (with S. Klepper), pp. 640–42.
35. Richard M. Cyert, BS University of Minnesota, 1943; PhD Columbia University, 1951. Professor of Economics and Industrial Administration, Carnegie-Mellon University, 1948–72, President, Carnegie-Mellon University, after 1972. See his 'Oligopoly price behavior and the business cycle', *Journal of Political Economy*, February 1955, pp. 41–51, and (with James G. March), *A Behavioral Theory of the Firm*, Prentice-Hall, Englewood Cliffs, NJ, 1963.

    James G. March, BA University of Wisconsin, 1949; MA, PhD Yale University, 1950, 1953. Professor of Economics, Carnegie-Mellon University, 1953–64; University of California at Irvine; and Dean of the School of Social Sciences, 1964–70, Professor of Higher Education, Management and International Management, Stanford University, 1970–95.

36. BA, University of Oregon, 1952; MA, PhD Yale University, 1953, 1956. Senior Economist, RAND Corporation, 1963–. See 'Behavior of the firm under regulatory constraint', *American Economic Review*, December 1963, pp. 1052–69.
37. BS, MA, University of Pennsylvania, 1948, 1949; PhD Harvard University, 1953. Associate and Full Professor, University of Virginia, 1956–63; University of Pennsylvania, 1953–56, 1963–91?. See his *Market Structure, Organization and Performance*, Harvard University Press, Cambridge, MA, 1962; and Phillips (ed.), *Promoting Competition in Regulated Markets*, Brookings Institution, Washington, DC, 1975.
38. BA, ? PhD,? Starting 1938, he did research reports on industrial concentration, especially in the oil industry. He was Assistant Chief Economist at the Federal Trade Commission during 1947–56, doing many reports on concentration. See John M. Blair, *Economic Concentration*, Harcourt, Brace, Jovanovich, New York, 1972; and *The Control of Oil*, Pantheon Books, New York, 1976.
39. BA, MA, PhD Harvard University, 1956, 1957, 1960. Professor of Economics, MIT, since 1962; Visiting Professor, Tel Aviv University, 1973–80. Clark Medal, American Economic Association, 1973; Vice-President and President, Econometric Society, 1977–79. See his 'The costs of automobile model changes since 1949' (with Zvi Griliches and Carl Kaysen), *Journal of Political Economy*, **70**, October 1962, pp. 433–51, and *Folded, Spindled and Mutilated: Economic Analysis and U.S. v. IBM* (with John J. McGowan and Joen Greenwood), MIT Press, Cambridge, MA, 1983.
40. BA University of Chicago, 1943; MA University of Iowa, 1947. Professor of Economics, Columbia University, New York, 1960–92?; Associate Professor, Duke University, 1950–60. See his *Monopoly in Economics and Law*, Rand-McNally, Chicago, 1959, 1964. *The Theory of Imperfect Competition: A Radical Reconstruction*, Columbia University Press, New York, 1969. *The Antitrust Experiment in America*, Columbia University Press, 1990, which contains his main articles.
41. BSS City College, NY, 1939; PhD Columbia University, 1949. Professor of Economics, 1948–63; Professor of Industrial Engineering, 1963–95, Columbia University. See his 'Administration and production cost in relation to size of firms', *Application Statistics*, March 1954, *The Peace Race*, Ballantine, New York, 1961, and *The Permanent War Economy*, Simon & Schuster, New York, 1974.
42. See Paul M. Sweezy and Paul Baran, *Monopoly Capital: An Essay on the American Economic and Social Order*, Monthly Review Press, Washington, DC, 1966.
43. I was closely involved with them as a fellow faculty member at the University of Massachusetts in 1986–2002.
44. BS Rensselaer Polytechnic Institute, 1967; MA Pennsylvania State University, 1968; PhD University of Wisconsin, 1972. Professor of Economics, Vanderbilt University, since 1972. See his 'Economic power and political influence: the impact of industry structure on public policy', *American Political Science Review*, September 1977 pp. 1026–42).
45. BA, MA Washington State College, 1954, 1955; PhD University of Wisconsin, 1959. Economist, Bureau of Economics, FTC, 1959; Division Chief, FTC, 1963–69; Professor of Economics, Virginia Technical University, 1969–84.
46. Morton I. Kamien, BA City College of NY, 1960; PhD Purdue University, 1964. Professor of Economics, Kellogg Graduate School of Management, Northwestern University, 1970–; also Carnegie-Mellon University, 1963–67. See *Market Structure and Innovation* (with Nancy L. Schwartz), Cambridge University Press, Cambridge, 1982.

    Nancy L. Schwartz, BA 1960, Oberlin College, 1960; MS, PhD Purdue University, 1963, 1964. Professor of Economics, 1970–81; and Chair, Managerial Economics and Decision Sciences, Kellogg School of Management, Northwestern University.
47. BBA City College, NY, 1960; PhD University of Chicago, 1965. Professor of Economics, Graduate School of Business, University of Chicago, since 1978; and University of California, Los Angeles, 1967–73. Member, Council of Economic Advisers, 1990–92. See his 'Entry in commercial banking', *Journal of Law and Economics*, October 1965; 'An Evaluation of consumer protectiion regulation: the 1962 drug amendments', *Journal of Political Economy*, September–October 1973; and 'Toward a more general theory of regulation', *Journal of Law and Economics*, August 1976.
48. BA Kalamazoo College, 1963; MA, PhD Michigan State University, 1966, 1967. Professor of Economics, University of Virginia, since 1967. See his 'The antimerger laws: Pyrrhic victories', *Journal of Law and Economics*, April 1969, pp. 43–78; 'The Problem of geographic market delineation in antimerger suits' (with Thomas F. Hogarty), *Antitrust Bulletin*, Spring 1973, pp. 45–81.
49. BA University of Michigan, 1958; MA, PhD Yale University, 1960, 1963. Professor of Economics, University of North Carolina at Chapel Hill, since 1985; and at the University of Rochester, 1968–83. See his *Oligopoly and the Theory of Games*, North-Holland, Amsterdam, 1977, and *Research in Experimental Economics: An Experiment in Noncooperative Oligopoly* (with A. Hoggatt), JAI Press, Greenwich, CT, 1979.

50. BA University of California, Santa Barbara, 1966; MA, PhD University of California, Berkeley, 1967, 1969. Professor of Economics, Cornell University, since 1976; and Northwestern University, 1969–74. See his 'Executive motivations, earnings, and consequent equity performance', *Journal of Political Economy*, November–December 1971, pp. 1278–92, and 'The social cost of the government regulation of milk' (with R.A. Ippolito), *Journal of Law and Economics*, April 1978, pp. 33–65.
51. BA Amherst College, 1970; MA, PhD University of Michigan, 1973, 1975. Professor of Economics, Michigan State University, since 1975. See his 'Information and goodwill advertising', *Review of Economics and Statistics*, November 1974, pp. 541–8; 'Minimum rate regulation, modal split sensitivities and the railroad problem', *Journal of Political Economy*, July 1977, pp. 493–512; 'Degrees of differentiation and industry boundaries', in Terry Calvani and John Siegfried (eds), *Economic Analysis and Antitrust Law*, Little, Brown, Boston, MA, 1979; and 'Are there scale economies in advertising?' (with Kent M. Lancaster), *Journal of Business*, July 1986, pp. 509–26.
52. BA University of Connecticut, 1959; MA, PhD University of Wisconsin, 1962, 1966. Professor of Economics, McGill University, 1969–. See his *Canadian Industrial Organization and Policy*, McGraw-Hill Ryerson, New York, editions of 1980, 1985 and 1990.
53. BA (Math) Michigan State University, 1970; PhD MIT, 1977. Professor of Economics, Michigan State University 1977–88; European University Institute (Florence, Italy), 1988–95; University of Copenhagen, 1995–99; and Purdue University School of Business, since 1999. See his 'Advertising, concentration, and profitability: the simultaneity problem', *Bell Journal of Economics*, Autumn 1979, pp. 639–47; and 'Market structure and trade flows' (with Anthony Y.C. Koo), *International Journal of Industrial Organization*, September 1984, pp. 173–97.
54. BA Brown University, 1967; PhD University of Pennsylvania, 1972. Professor of Economics, George Washington University, 1981–2001; Northeastern University since 2001. See his 'Effects of market share distribution on industry performance', *Review of Economics and Statistics*, **LXI**, February 1979 pp. 101–109; and 'Advertising and the price and quality of optometric services', *American Economic Review*, **79**, March 1984, pp. 211–16.
55. Steven C. Salop, BA University of Pennsylvania, 1968; MPhil, PhD Yale University, 1971, 1972. Professor, Law Center, Georgetown University, 1981–; Assistant Director, Bureau of Economics, FTC, 1978–81.
56. BA Cornell University, 1968; MPhil, PhD Yale University, 1971, 1972. Professor of Economics and Management, MIT, since 1972. See Paul L. Joskow and Richard Schmalensee, *Markets for Power: An Analysis of Electric Utility Deregulation*, MIT Press, Cambridge, MA, 1983; also Joskow, M. Baughman and D. Kamat, *Electric Power in the United States: Models and Policy Analysis*, MIT Press, Cambridge, MA, 1979.

SECTION 1

Individual pioneers in the USA and Canada

10. To the 1930s

A. CHARLES ELLET JR

F.M. Scherer

Innovations
Calculus-based theory of the firm's profit-maximization problem with explicit demand and cost functions; concepts of reservation price and 'charging what the traffic will bear'; advantages of price discrimination in railroad and canal price-setting; showed tendency for vertically stacked monopolies to charge more than an integrated monopolist; foundations of spatial economics.

Personal history

Born 1810, Penns Manor (Indiana County), PA, USA; died of combat wounds in 1862 as a colonel in the Union army.

Education Self-taught plus formal studies at the École des Ponts et Chaussées, Paris, 1830–32.

Principal positions Bridge, canal and railroad engineer.

A graduate student at the University of Chicago is said to have rushed into the office of Professor Jacob Viner reporting excitedly that he had discovered an unknown nineteenth-century mathematical economist. 'Oh', said Viner, 'You must mean Charles Ellet Jr'. 'Yes', said the student, 'but how did you know?'. 'Because he is the only unknown nineteenth-century mathematical economist', was Viner's reply.

Since then Ellet has been rediscovered, but his stunningly original contributions are still undervalued relative to those of his contemporaries and economists who wrote during the second half of the nineteenth century.

Ellet ventured into economics because he perceived errors in the policies adopted by his employer, the James River and Kanawha Improvement Association, in the pricing of canal and eventually rail connections between Richmond, Virginia, and the Ohio River through the Allegheny Mountains. These errors, he concluded, prevented his employer from maximizing its profits and influenced the spatial pattern of US economic development. His insights were reported in an 1839 book, in a series of short articles published during the ensuing five years, and in diverse later papers.

While better-known contemporary economists (other than Augustin Cournot) were treating the demand for goods and services in muddled ways, Ellet saw clearly the quantity demanded as an explicit declining function of the price charged for transportation services. He recognized that too high a price could choke off demand altogether, and for bulky commodities of relatively low value, he argued, transport rates should fall discriminatorily with distance shipped rather than being invariant per ton mile as long as the marginal costs of transportation were covered. In this and in recognizing that higher-valued items could pay higher freight charges, he anticipated the concept of 'charging what the traffic will bear'. He saw that there was a difference between the maximum price that would be paid for a service – the reservation price – and costs, and he showed that with linear demand functions, profits were maximized by equating what we now call marginal revenue with marginal cost at a quantity where costs were half the reservation price. For passenger fares, he recommended two rate classes, one for travellers desiring economy and a higher one for those with a preference for luxury.

Many transportation lines, he observed, fed into one another, each with monopoly power over its individual segment. Ellet demonstrated that the price charged by a unified service monopoly would yield higher total profits and permit a higher quantity of service than the prices the individual segments would charge if they myopically maximized their profits. In this he anticipated the 'double marginalization' proof by Joseph Spengler 110 years later. Ellet recognized that many rate setters, with imperfect understanding of the 'laws of trade', set prices above the profit-maximizing level and that in order to correct this error, which was also disadvantageous to the general public, legislative intervention might be required. In a series of articles published in the *Journal of the Franklin Institute*, Ellet worked out a mathematical theory of railroad costs, among other things distinguishing among costs varying with distance, with tonnage carried, and those independent of both variables. He recognized that fixed costs vary in the longer run and worked out a trade-off between the costs of climbing steep gradients and increasing line length. Among other things, he viewed as one cost of shipment the interest cost of capital invested in goods in transit. He compared the predictions generated by his theoretical estimates with actual cost data for 17 rail lines and found in most cases a close correspondence.

Many of Ellet's insights and methodological innovations paralleled those published in 1839 by Cournot. Ellet's were specialized to transportation services, while Cournot's claimed wider generality, which probably explains why Cournot's fame is greater. There is no indication in Ellet's publications that he was aware of Cournot's work, and so, without new evidence, it would appear that the two economists' contributions were, as is often the case, simultaneous but independent.

Most relevant publications

(1839), *An Essay on the Laws of Trade in Reference to the Works of Internal Improvement in the United States*, Richmond, VA: Bernard; Reprinted by Augustus Kelley, 1966.

(1840), 'The laws of trade applied to the determination of the most advantageous fare for passengers on railroads', *Journal of the Franklin Institute*, **30** (new numbering system), 369–79.

(1842–44), 'Cost of transportation on railroads', *Journal of the Franklin Institute*, **34** (1842), 145–7, 228–33 and 304–11; **36** (1843), 316–24 and 361–70; **37** (1844), 1–8 and 73–82.

(1842), 'On the value of time', *Journal of the Franklin Institute*, **34**, 361–7.

B. HENRY CARTER ADAMS

Harry M. Trebing

Innovations

Landmark analysis of the role of the state in the public control of economic activity. Adams established the conceptual framework within which many of the Progressive and New Deal reforms dealing with the regulation of public utilities and transportation took place in the first half of the twentieth century.

Personal history

Born 1851, Davenport, IA, USA; died 1921.

Degrees Bachelor's Degree Iowa College, 1874; PhD Johns Hopkins University, 1878.

Principal positions Professor of Political Economy and Finance, University of Michigan, 1887–1921. Lecturer in Political Economy at Johns Hopkins University, 1880–81. Lecturer at Cornell University and the University of Michigan, 1880–87. (Adams was forced out of Cornell because of his radical economic teaching.) President of the American Economic Association, 1895–97. From 1887 to 1897, Dr. Adams also held various administrative positions with the newly created Interstate Commerce Commission.

Henry Carter Adams stands as a major figure in the development of economic thought in the US from the late nineteenth century into the early twentieth century. As one of the founders of the American Economic Association, he sought to bring economic theory and its policy uses to bear on the real-world problems of industrial power.

Adams sought to develop a completely different system of thought for defining the nature and concept of economic regulation and competitive action. His landmark paper, 'Relation of the state to industrial action' (1887), placed this major set of innovative ideas squarely in the fledgling literature of the new American Economic Association (AEA). He rejected both English *laissez-faire* and the German concept of the state. He argued that 'the fundamental error of English political philosophy lies in regarding the state as a necessary evil; the fundamental error of German political philosophy lies in its conception of the state as an organism complete in itself' (Adams, 1887, p. 494) In Adams's view, the role of the state would be to determine the playing field for competitive action, permit social realization of the efficiency gains from monopoly, and establish a social harmony between economic sectors by extending the duties of government.

As a part of this process of defining the role of the state, Adams introduced a pioneering analysis of the concepts of constant returns, diminishing returns, and increasing returns, with direct state control focusing primarily on the latter. Where increasing returns prevailed, he argued, the benefits of competitive markets could never be realized through the uncontrolled play of private interests. Rather, state intervention would be necessary to achieve effective economic results. At the same time, the public would be denied the benefits of increasing returns without public control in those industries where these natural-monopoly cost characteristics prevailed. Unless there were strong and thorough public regulation, the public would be denied benefits inherent in cases where monopoly organization yielded the greatest efficiency. Adams was intensely skeptical and practical, as well as being a gifted theorist.

Further, he believed that a well-organized society would include no extra-legal monopolies of any sort. Rather, society must be secured against the oppression of exclusive privileges administered for personal profit. Adams held a variety of high-level assignments at the new Interstate Commerce Commission. In those, and throughout his long and distinguished career, he was able to engage in the pioneering applications of statistics and accounting as regulatory tools. Adams deserves great credit for developing the Uniform System of Accounts that would permit the classification and valuation of assets, the determination of operating revenues, the calculation of operating expenses, and the estimation of net operating income. This conceptual framework would also lend itself to the disallowance of expenses and charges not properly assigned to the ultimate consumer. Over time, this system of accounts created a valuable database for rate base/rate-of-return regulation. Private accounting was totally inadequate to this task and clearly vulnerable to fraudulent manipulation.

A century later, the accounting scandals that culminated in the bankruptcy of Enron and WorldCom (America's two largest bankruptcies) demonstrated the wisdom of Adams's argument in favor of public accounting oversight. Regrettably, these accounting controls were summarily dismissed in the 1990s by the proponents of deregulation.

Adams also had a great interest in the interrelationship of economics and law. In his AEA presidential address, 'Economics and Jurisprudence' (1896), he reaffirmed this interest and incorporated a role for labor through arbitration and collective bargaining in the structure of modern industry. Professor Joseph Dorfman believes that John R. Commons's *Legal Foundations of Capitalism* (1924) was 'an expansion of Adams's doctrines' (Dorfman, 1954, p. 172).

Most relevant publications

(1887), 'Relation of the state to industrial action', *Publications of the American Economic Association*, **1**(6), January, 465–549.

(1905), 'Commercial valuation of railway operating property in the United States', 1904, *United States Bureau of the Census Bulletin* No. 21, Washington.

(1908), 'The administrative supervision of railways under the twentieth section of the Act to Regulate Commerce', *Quarterly Journal of Economics*, **22** (May), 375–6.

(1910), 'Valuation of public service utilities', in *Publications of the American Economic Association*, 3rd series (Cambridge MA), April, **11**, 193.

(1954), *Relation of the State to Industrial Action and Economies and Jurisprudence – Two Essays by Henry Carter Adams*, edited with an Introductory Essay by Joseph Dorfman, New York: Columbia University Press.

C. JOHN BATES CLARK

John Howard Brown

Innovations
Developed marginal productivity theory of wages, potential entry as substitute for competition in an industry.

Personal history

Born 1847, Providence, RI, USA; died 1938.

Principal position Professor of Economics Columbia University.

Other Cofounder American Economic Association (1885), serving as its president (1893–95).

John Bates Clark whom Henry (1995) characterizes as, 'the first United States economist to reach a position of prominence within this profession' (p. 1) produced an immense body of professional work. (Henry's bibliography lists over 100 publications dating from 1877 to 1935.) That work extends well beyond industrial organization, including pioneering work in marginal productivity theory and the economics of war and peace.

In industrial organization, Clark was concerned with the problem of trusts. He praised large-scale business organizations for their economies: 'The machine – and particularly the locomotive – has been what we may call a great promoter; it has been a great consolidater [sic] of business establishments and has caused large shops to be so economical as to drive out a multitude of small ones' (1904, p. 15). However, he notes that not all of the advantages of large firms are socially beneficial: 'such ... as getting special rates for freight on the railroads which the small shop cannot get' (p. 17) or erecting barriers to entry: 'Can they ... club or frighten off, or in their own rough way, send off, the competitors who enter the field ... but if competitors do not dare to come, if the few that do come have severe lessons taught them, and others, in prudence, stay out, the trust has a clear possession of the field' (p. 31). Among the 'clubs' Clark mentions are cutting prices locally (p. 35) or on varieties of goods (p. 36), or exclusive dealing arrangements inhibiting the distribution (p. 36) of smaller competitors.

However, Clark was optimistic about the control of trusts. He placed great emphasis on potential competition: 'In the selling of goods and services the best competition has always been in the potential form' (p. 112). The example he cites is of a village blacksmith who has the structural characteristics of a monopolist as a sole supplier but can never exert monopoly power because of entry. He concludes: 'That is an instance of potential competition, and this is the variety which ought forever to survive. That implies that it ought to be made to survive, even after the formation of great trusts' (p. 112). Henry (1995, p. 67) notes that this is essentially the notion of contestability proposed by William J. Baumol and others in the 1980s.

John Bates Clark occupied the middle ground in the 'gilded era' debate regarding appropriate response to the developing dominant firms in manufacturing. He did not feel that dissolution of such monopolistic powerhouses was desirable because of the substantial economies they achieved. However, his faith in the discipline of potential competition was tempered by the fear that 'bullying' tactics by incumbents could indefinitely prevent the emergence of competitors to limit monopoly power.

Clark held that legal restrictions on firm tactics limiting potential competition were more effective than attempting to restore competition to industries not capable of an atomistic structure: 'The trust can get a monopolistic price because, by virtue of these different clubs which it holds in its hands ... What sort of legislation do we want if we are going to keep the trust, make it a useful thing and take away its power for evil?' (1904, pp. 36–7). He felt that the common law doctrine of restraint of trade which was the primary contemporary tool was irrelevant to the requirements of modern industry.

Later, in the revised edition of *The Control of Trusts* (1912) written with his son, the equally distinguished John Maurice Clark, Clark senior's notions of the beneficial contributions of large-scale enterprise and potential competition were tempered by Clark junior's acceptance of a larger governmental role in supervising competition. Joseph Dorfman (1971) in his introduction to the reprint, judges that: '*The Control of Trusts* played a formative historical role in policy making, for it provided the most systematic exposition of the view on trusts that was embodied in 1914 at President Wilson's urging in the Clayton Act and the Federal Trade Commission Act' (p. 17).

The Clarks begin with an open acknowledgment of their advocacy: 'The purpose of the work is entirely constructive, since it advocates a positive policy for controlling trusts' (p. v). Their proposal is: 'regulating competition. It would cut off entirely an abnormal type of [competition] by forbidding and repressing the cut-throat operations by which the trusts often crush their rivals' (p. vi). This represents a more interventionist stance than John B. Clark had advocated earlier.

An important difference between Clark senior's previous positions and the 1912 book is a focus on the dynamic contribution of large firms instead of their economies. The Clarks agree: 'We do not here retract anything that has been said as to the economy of large production . ... The trusts have saved wastes and added to the productive power of labor and capital' (p. 14). They go on to assert that: 'It is not a large present social income that is the chief desideratum but a constantly enlarging income. Progress is in itself the *summum bonum* in economics, and that society is essentially the best which improves the fastest' (p. 134, emphasis in original).

This revised edition of *The Control of Trusts* also emphasizes the historical importance of new entry, 'in the eighties of the last century ... trusts went through a hard experience' (p. 25). That experience was: 'When prices are raised beyond a certain point, owing to the too grasping policy of some trusts, the thing still happens which happened more frequently in the early history of combinations' (pp. 25–6).

Extrapolating from this historical experience leads to the assertion: 'A merely possible mill which as yet does not exist may forestall and prevent monopolistic acts. If the way is quite open for it to appear, the trust may refrain from keeping prices at a high level' (p. 121). However, 'the influence of this latent competition cannot be trusted as it could in earlier days' (p. 27). As John B. Clark emphasized in his *The Problem of Monopoly*, 'because the possible competitor does not become an actual one as promptly as he should. The trouble is that he has not a fair chance for his life when he appears on the scene. He is in danger of being crushed by the trust' (p. 27). The situation was made worse because: 'his [the entrant's] plant is a specialized one' (p. 172), or as put more colorfully earlier in the same discussion: 'He enters ... burning his bridges behind him' (p. 171). Thus Clark recognized sunk costs as a barrier to potential entry well before the debate on 'contestability'.

The elder Clark's earlier position changed in two significant, if subtle, ways. First, 'The only sure evidence that rival mills can be built and run with safety is the fact that some of them have been built and are running' (p. 121). Thus actual entry into a market is now more emphasized than potential entry in assessing the state of competition.

Also, reflecting the professional work of John M. Clark on overhead costs, is an added appreciation of the role of such costs in price discrimination. Entry in some industries involves a substantial addition to capacity, 'the would-be competitor ... must build a big plant or none at all' (p. 172). For these: 'industries are more likely to find themselves equipped with power to produce more goods than the market will take at a living price' (pp. 172–3). Where entry has occurred and there is excess capacity, the firms find themselves in 'a fierce struggle for business' (p. 173), since incremental orders permit firms to further spread their overhead costs.

Thus, even though the Clarks condemn discrimination as unfair competition, they recognize that conditions of modern industry make some discrimination inevitable. What policy do they propose against these trust abuses? They first establish their yardstick: 'the supreme test of measures for regulating trusts is that which tells us whether they will accelerate technical progress or retard it – whether they will make the world as a whole grow richer or poorer' (p. 3).

They contrast two widely held views, either that: 'in large-scale business competition has failed completely and monopoly has come to stay. The large plant is more efficient than the small one, the combination is more efficient than the independent, competition is wasteful and unnatural and monopoly the inevitable outcome' (p. 141), or that which 'consists of those which would merely destroy monopoly and make competition free' (p. v). The first view tends to 'legalize monopoly, and in place of free competition as a regulator of prices ... will place the decrees of a public commission' (p. 143). The second view holds 'that the monopolistic powers of the trusts are accidental and not inevitable, that they are built upon privileges that can be removed, powers that can be withdrawn and predatory acts that can be forbidden' (p. 143).

Neither opinion is without difficulties. Regarding the trust-busters, they note that the task is Sisyphean: 'we may attack the various forms of combined control, as we have done in the past; but like the sorcerer in the story they take new shapes and elude us' (p. 144). Although they concede: 'We know today that we can dissolve the trusts – that we can break up the big corporations into smaller ones and this is distinctly more than we once knew' (p. 3).

Price regulation by commission is likewise no panacea: 'We cannot afford to remove or seriously reduce the incentive to improvements. Any change involves risk, and capital takes no chances unless lured by hope of rewards above the safe interest' (p. 161). They then argue presciently against the limitations of rate of return regulation.

The way forward is to combine elements of both, competition is to be maintained, not by breaking up efficient businesses, but by outlawing practices that support exploitative monopoly. The regulatory commission ought to regulate not prices but unfair practices.

The Clarks advocate the imposition of FOB (free on board) pricing for all manufacturers. This would eliminate both predatory price discrimination and railroad favoritism that allegedly represented the major advantages realized by the 'trusts'. They also suggest a test for monopoly: 'Has every consumer a choice of efficient and independent producers to buy from? If so, there is no monopoly, even if one combination should control three quarters of the output' (pp. 184–5). Their other prescription is more conventional: more publicity regarding the trusts affairs (both to protect investors and stimulate entry). This is a common theme in gilded age/progressive era responses to monopoly.

References

Clark, John B. (1904), *The Problem of Monopoly*, Columbia University Press, New York, Macmillan.

Clark, John M. and John B Clark (1912), *The Control of Trusts: rewritten and enlarged edition*, Reprinted 1971, Augustus M. Kelley, New York.

Henry, John F. (1995), *John Bates Clark: The Making of a Neoclassical Economist*, St. Martin's Press, New York.

D. JEREMIAH WHIPPLE JENKS

John Howard Brown

Innovations
Empirical analysis of price–cost margins in industries dominated by trusts.

Personal history

Born 1856, St Clair, MI, USA; died 1929.

Degrees BA, MA University of Michigan, 1878, 1879; PhD University of Halle, 1885.

Principal position Professor of Economics, Cornell University, Ithaca, NY, 1891–1912.

Other Positions at Mt. Morris College, Knox College, Indiana State University, New York University (1912–29).

Jenks deserves recognition as an important precursor of the contemporary economic field of industrial organization. Jenks pioneered a style of statistical empiricism that would not be out of place in modern industrial organization. He also proposed an analytical scheme that anticipates the structure–conduct–performance paradigm proposed in the late 1930s by Edward S. Mason.

Jenks's own assessment of his accomplishments, in the final edition of his classic, *The Trust Problem* (1900) shortly before his death in 1929, begins with his conclusion 'that the question of the Trusts was likely to be one of the two most prominent subjects of legislation in the near future' (p. 3). He approached the problem with, 'personal investigation of large corporations through contact with their officers and workmen ... and also from such statistical data as seemed to be trustworthy' (p. 3).

The investigation he refers to in the quotation above was one of the first attempts to study an industry (other than railroads) by an American economist, reported in his article, 'The Michigan Salt Association' (1888). In this article he considers the attempts of salt manufacturers in Michigan to establish a stable collusive arrangement. He followed this article with 'The development of the Whiskey Trust' (1889), also on the theme of developing a sustainable collusive arrangement.

The two industries were similar in their production processes since both involved joint production that made individual firms reluctant to reduce production. There were also potential competing sources of supply. Jenks provides a detailed history of each industry and the painful steps toward developing a 'trust'. In each case, the trust was formed after an extended period in which prices had been too low. The first step was a marketing 'pool' where the respective producers used a joint market agency to distribute their output. This was of limited effectiveness so long as the individual firms in the industry retained control of productive capacity. Thus the ultimate step was forming a single entity in trust or holding company form to control the assets of the producers and restrict output to keep prices high.

In the Whiskey Trust article, Jenks provided a chart comparing the behavior of whiskey prices with corn prices and the margin between them. The time periods during which collusion was practiced were identified and the effects of these collusive episodes on the margins analyzed. As Jenks notes (Jenks et al., 1929, p. 6), 'This has proved to be the most effective method of showing clearly the course of price and of exposing many of the fallacious conclusions drawn from merely grouping over a series of years prices of the finished products or by using groupings of selected years of the marginal differences'. Jenks claimed to have been the first to use this empirical technique and the first to employ index numbers for comparing the effects of combination in the steel industry on prices (ibid., p. 6).

Jenks applied this tool again in 'Trusts in the United States' (1892) where he analyzed the price–cost margins in sugar and petroleum refining. In his investigation for the Industrial Commission, he extended the analysis of price–cost margins in two dimensions. He added international comparisons of the margins between raw and refined sugar and analyzed the pricing in several segments of the steel industry relative to a price index. Jenk's s statistical, empirical approach to the trust problem was unprecedented and unparalleled by his contemporaries. It foreshadows the development of empirical industrial organization almost half a century later.

Jenks also held views that are surprisingly close to the modern analysis of the effects of market structure. He recognized that the conditions of production such as economies of scale limited the number of firms in a market and altered the nature of competition. Thus:

> If the amount of capital which must of necessity be invested in a fixed plant for the successful production of any class of goods is large, the nature of the competition differs materially from that of an industry in which a small amount of fixed capital is sufficient to enable one to work to good advantage. In the first instance the number of competitors is likely to be much smaller than in the latter. (1900, p. 16)

This led him (1894) to speak of a 'capitalistic monopoly' which was, 'a qualified monopoly maintained within rather narrow limits by the sheer force of large capital' (Jenks et al., 1929, pp. 5–6). Jenks claimed this term as yet another of his doctrinal innovations. In modern terms this is an absolute capital barrier to entry. The concept was controversial when Jenks proposed it, since the economists had held that only government franchise created monopoly.

Other barriers he recognized were:

> those industries ... in which the product is uniform in its nature and the productive work of a routine character; those in which the product is bulky and there is a wide distribution of freight; or ... somewhat similar characteristics ... such as very expensive advertising, patents, etc., serve to encourage the combination of capital. (Ibid., p. 208)

Jenks here highlights structural aspects of the markets which produce concentration of output in limited numbers of firms. Advertising expenditures for product differentiation and patents have been recognized as barriers to entry which limit the degree of competition since at least the 1950s (Bain, 1956).

Jenks contrasts these oligopolistic industries with, '[a]n industry which requires but small capital to carry it on, will encourage hundreds, or more likely thousands or tens of thousands, of individuals to engage in it' (Jenks et al., p. 18). He further observes: '[i[t is the consideration mainly of industries of this type (i.e. competitive ones) that has given rise to theories of normal price, a marginal price, etc., as a safe basis for economic reasoning, and many writers in speaking of competition think of this kind only' (ibid., p.18). Jenks likewise disparaged what he characterized as the 'common assumption' that competition is free. He noted:

> The 'friction' of competition is most readily noticed in the retail trade. Careless customers, ignorant of prices, call for goods which please them, and often purchase without striving to get the lowest price. ... The convenient location of his store, or his pertinacity in soliciting custom, often enables a dealer to sell for more than the lowest market price, so that competition, from the point of view of price, is far from being free, or at least from being efficient. (1900, p. 11)

Thus Jenks recognized something quite like the modern notion of monopolistic competition. He also claimed that implicit collusion among members of a trade within a city was a near constant in commercial life, echoing Adam Smith's famous opinion about such 'conspiracies against the public'.

In concentrated industries, Jenks recognized that:

> [A dominant firm] certainly is exercising and can exercise for a considerable length of time a really monopolistic power. It is also, however, true that in fixing prices so as to secure under the circumstances the greatest net returns, he has to take into consideration this third factor – that of potential competition ... (ibid., p. 61)

> [Under these circumstances] it may perhaps keep prices somewhat above former competitive rates, it must keep them low enough so that the temptation for competitors to enter the field will not be great, and it must be able to put them without absolute loss lower than it would be possible for an ordinary rival to manufacture and sell. (Ibid, pp. 62–3)

This passage anticipates the famous 'limit price' analysis of Joe Bain in the 1950s (see Bain, 1956).

Although Jenks agreed that potential competition was useful, he was somewhat more pessimistic about its effects than many other figures of the era:

> Those, however, who take the position that potential competition will prevent prices from going at all above former competitive rates, overlook the fact that new capital is not at all likely to be invested under such circumstances, unless the profits of the combination are put very high indeed. (1900, pp. 65–6)

He also noted the significant efficiencies that could be attained by large-scale production, although he carefully noted that a firm need not be a trust to achieve many of these: 'One ought not to lose sight of the distinctions between production on a great scale and production under monopoly' (ibid., p. 21). In terms of policy responses to monopoly power, as early as 1892, Jeremiah Jenks was critical of antitrust legislation for failing to recognize: 'that without combination financial ruin was imminent, and that organization was merely a means of safety. Free competition had proved disastrous' (ibid., p. 72).

He urged the abolition of unfair competitive methods, particularly the various forms of discrimination:

> When unfair and illegal methods of competition are employed ... Such unfair and illegal methods put the question rather into the field of criminal law or social ethics. Such practices are under no circumstances to be justified or defended. (Ibid., p. 200)

In a later article (1908) Jenks argued that the dissolution decrees against Standard Oil and American Tobacco were ill-considered since: 'although there might be a reorganization in form, they would still remain combinations in fact' (p. 355). Jenks concluded that even if competition were restored in these industries, 'we should still question whether the remedy were in the public interest [since] the application of this remedy must result in a loss of industrial efficiency' (p. 355).

For Jenks the appropriate role for government in the economy was entirely a matter of pragmatic adaptation to the ever-changing conditions of the market economy and society at large. In his 1907 Presidential Address to the American Economic Association, he argued that the nature of some industries was such that they ought to be managed by the government.

In other cases, Jenks asserts: 'A legislature or an executive may lay down fixed rules for certain lines of industry, and a commission or an inspector may apply these rules in special cases' (ibid., p. 15). In either of these capacities, government can set an example for private establishments (ibid., p. 16). It can also fix the limits of competition, either by operating enterprises that compete with private monopolies or through 'inspection and supervision' (ibid., p. 17). However, this is conditioned upon 'the fact that competition affords on the whole the best stimulus to effort, to originality of thought, and to the development of personality in enterprise' (1908, p. 17). As a consequence, 'The government should simply see to it that the competition in all directions is kept within fair and just limits' (ibid., p. 17).

As the final word on Jenks's scholarly activity in industrial organization, we can take his own words from the Introduction to *The Trust Problem* (1900, pp. 8–9):

> An effort has been made to explain these Trusts, and not to rest content with calling them the product of evolution, and assuming that, therefore, they are both inevitable and in the long run helpful rather than harmful . ... with that view of economic evolution, as something requiring further explanation before being either approved or condemned, the book has been written.

References

Bain, Joe S. (1956), *Barriers to New Competition*, Harvard University Press, Cambridge.

Jenks, Jeremiah (1888), 'The Michigan Salt Association', *Political Science Quarterly*, **3**(1), March, 78–98.

Jenks, Jeremiah (1889), 'The development of the Whiskey Trust', *Political Science Quarterly*, **4**(2), June, 296–319.

Jenks, Jeremiah (1892), 'Trusts in the United States', *Economic Journal*, **2**(5), June, 70–99.

Jenks, Jeremiah (1894), 'Capitalistic monopolies and their relation to the state', *Political Science Quarterly*, **9**(3), September 486–509.

Jenks, Jeremiah (1900), *The Trust Problem*, McClure, Phillips & Co, New York.

Jenks, Jeremiah (1908), 'The principles of government control of business', *American Economic Association Quarterly*, 3rd Series, **9**(1), Papers and Discussions of the Twentieth Annual Meeting, Madison, WI, December 28–30, 1907, April, pp. 1–20.

Jenks, Jeremiah and Walter E. Clark with John J. Quigley (1929), *The Trust Problem*, 5th edn, Doubleday, Doran & Company, Inc, Garden City, New York.

E. JOHN MAURICE CLARK

William L. Baldwin

Innovations

Intensive analysis (with J.B. Clark) of antitrust policies in light of scale economies. Path-breaking complex analysis of costs, including overhead costs in the presence of high capital density. Workable competition. Competition as a dynamic process.

Personal history

Born 1884, Northampton, MA, USA; died 1963.

Degrees AB Amherst College, 1906, PhD Columbia University 1910.

Principal positions Served on the faculties of Colorado College (1908–10), Amherst College (1910–15), the University of Chicago (1915–26), and Columbia University (1926–57), where in 1951 he was appointed to a chair named in honor of his father, the John Bates Clark Professorship of Political Economy.

Other Over the course of his long and distinguished career, other honors include his election as President of the American Economic Association (AEA) in 1935 and award of the Francis A. Walker Medal for distinguished service, the highest recognition given by the AEA. He received honorary degrees from Amherst College, Columbia University, the University of Paris, the New School for Social Research and Yale University.

Noting that John Maurice Clark (JMC) was a 'prolific writer', Jesse W. Markham wrote in the *International Encyclopedia of the Social Sciences*, vol. 2, pp. 508–11 (New York: Macmillan, 1968):

> Clark's writings include treatises on virtually every economic problem that loomed large in his lifetime. Although he is chiefly recognized for his contributions designed to close the gap between the abstractions of statics and the realities of dynamics, he published works concerned with the business cycle, the economic costs of war, wartime controls and demobilization, public works, the labor market, education and a host of other problems.

While the sheer volume and significance of his published scholarship would have won JMC a prominent place among the leading economists of the twentieth century, the web of interconnections tying his varied works into an integrated whole over an active career of nearly 60 years is a unique feature of his work that adds to his luster.

A strong professional relationship with his father, John Bates Clark (1847–1938), marked JMC's early career. The elder Clark, a founding member and third president of the AEA, was one of a handful of economists of the previous generation whose development of marginal productivity and distribution theorems had led to the marginalist 'revolution' which transformed economics in the post-Civil War era.

The close association between father and son became sealed when John Bates Clark served as an advisor to JMC on the latter's doctoral dissertation, *Standards of Reasonableness in Local Freight Discriminations*, published in 1910 by Columbia University Press. It was reinforced in 1912 when the two Clarks co-authored a revised and enlarged edition of an original work by J.B. Clark alone, *The Control of Trusts* (New York: Macmillan). In the preface to the revised edition, JMC is given credit for most of the new material, although both authors share in the revisions. Harsh criticisms of the antitrust laws in the first edition were removed from the second. In light of the aftermath of the Supreme Court's 1911 dissolution decrees against the Standard Oil Company and the American Tobacco Company, the Clarks wrote: 'We know to-day than we *can* dissolve the trusts – that we can break up the big corporations into smaller ones – and this is distinctly more than we once knew' (p. 3, italics in original). However, simply because dissolution was possible did not mean that it was advisable. Rather, the Clarks continued to oppose a widespread dissolution policy. The trusts had been of benefit to the nation in several ways, notably checking cut-throat competition and promoting technical progress. If the large trusts stagnated, the Clarks contended, they would be far worse than if they raised prices and restricted output. The large trusts that were true monopolies in the most fundamental sense of the word, that is, because they feared no competition, either existing or latent, should be dissolved. The Sherman Antitrust Act should be strengthened to constrain anti-competitive practices. The Clarks wrote:

> America is the natural home of the trusts; but if we can draw the fangs of the monster and train it to good uses, we can get therefrom an advantage over other nations and realize all the benefits it is possible to get out of material civilization ... namely abundant wealth, honestly gained, widely dispersed among the people and ensuring a high level of life, intellectual and moral as well as physical. (p. 22)

'Drawing the fangs', for JMC, meant identifying their sources and then formulating public policies to extract or blunt them. The primary sources such as he saw them were the accelerator effect, overhead costs, and price discrimination. Appropriate public policies included enforcing antitrust laws aimed at promoting effective or workable competition, both static and dynamic.

In 1917 JMC published an article, 'Business acceleration and the law of demand: a technical factor in economic cycles' in the *Journal of Political Economy*, in which he developed a principle that subsequently became central to macroeconomic models of the business cycle. The core of this accelerator is a relationship between demand for consumer goods and the demand for capital goods derived therefrom in which a change in the level of increase in the demand for consumer goods leads to a proportionately greater change in the demand for capital goods. JMC recognized that business firms of all sizes, as well as farms, might well be capital intensive and thus be vulnerable to magnification of fluctuations in consumer demand, but he noted that the large firms with monopoly power, that is, the trusts that had sprung up in the post-Civil War era, were particularly capital intensive and therefore had the most plausible reason for stabilization of demand even if it involved agreements or understandings with rivals.

JMC's long-standing interest in the effects of capital intensity and overhead cost led to his major contribution to that area in 1923, when his book *Studies in the Economics of Overhead Costs* (Chicago: University of Chicago Press) appeared along with a four-part journal article, 'Overhead costs in industry' in the *Journal of Political Economy*. But JMC's continued intellectual ties to his father were made clear in his dedication to the book where he noted that '[my] greatest debt of all is to my father, who started me in this field of inquiry as a graduate student' (pp. xi–xii).

JMC defined overhead costs as those which did not vary with output or could not be traced to units of output, and he observed that these costs were crucial in modern processes of production. (For this reason he thought that improvements in cost accounting were of great importance in an industrialized economy as they would give business managers a better idea of what effects they would have on their market in setting prices intended to cover full costs.) He maintained that a meaningful economic theory must be built around the consequences of high overhead costs. He emphasized the fact that the problems raised for the firm were not limited to the trusts but were endemic to business in an industrialized nation. JMC's basic concern was that high overhead costs could lead to ruinous competition as overhead costs remained constant, in the short run, even as variable costs fluctuated. In terms of the marginal analysis to which John Bates Clark had contributed immensely, in a short-run profit-maximizing equilibrium every factor of production would be employed up to the point where the value of its marginal output was equal to its marginal cost to the firm. But in the short run, marginal overhead cost is zero, and the firm will continue to produce as long as the marginal revenue of its product is greater than or equal to marginal short-run, or variable, costs. In the long run, of course, the firm must cover overhead costs or go out of business, but JMC thought that short-run pricing was widespread, and where it existed it could drive rivals to match prices below full cost, resulting in cut-throat and possibly ruinous pricing. Further, static equilibrium theory was of little or no help in explaining or analyzing the observed phenomena.

The problem was compounded by the possibility of price discrimination. If lower prices could be charged to some but not all customers, 'spreading the overhead' became more feasible but made retaliatory pricing by other firms more likely. In *Studies in the Economics of Overhead Costs*, JMC wrote:

> Since unchecked competition is suicidal and cannot continue, can anything continue which deserves the name of competition, or are we living in a regime of combination and monopoly, and is monopoly essential to the life of private industry? ... The answer appears to be that business rivalry still exists, subject to checks in the way of understandings and standards of fair tactics ... group ethics of the business community ... [and] a lively sense of the need of common self-preservation. (p. 435)

In a 1926 book, *Social Control of Business* (Chicago: University of Chicago Press), JMC discussed both the economics of concentration and monopoly and the ethical, legal and political issues involved in government regulation of industry. Arguing that the law, although constrained by precedent, is 'a means to a social end', JMC noted with approval that the courts were condemning only clear-cut antisocial behavior by the large combinations while paying no attention to indiscriminately broad prohibitions included in the antitrust laws. On this basis he welcomed these laws.

JMC's introduction of the concept of workable or effective competition in a 1940 *American Economic Review* article, 'Toward a concept of workable competition' (vol. 30) is generally regarded as on a par with, as well as complementing, the significance of his analysis of overhead costs. The basic thrust is the author's 'realization that "perfect competition" does not and cannot and presumably never existed. ... What we have left is an unreal or ideal standard which may serve as a starting point of analysis and a norm' (p. 241). There were two features of the model of perfect competition that might lead to the most egregious errors. First, it was static, whereas the real economy was dynamic, that is, subject to irreversible change, and the causes and results of such change are much more important to our understanding of what the real world is like than are equilibrating forces. Second, many of those features which render the model of perfect competition irrelevant or incorrect, such as immobility of resources, lack of full knowledge, economies of scale relative to market size and differentiation of product, may make generalization impossible: that is, analysis must be inductive rather than deductive. For this reason JMC never attempted to formulate a complete and uniformly applicable definition of workable competition. Anticipating the theory of second best, he posited an industry with all of the attributes of perfect competition and argued that these attributes could be so interdependent that if any one was taken away the others would be unable to sustain workable competition.

In the preface to his last major work (*Competition as a Dynamic Process*, Washington, DC: Brookings Institution), JMC wrote:

> The present volume is an elaboration of a line of inquiry dating from the author's [1940] article 'Toward a Concept of Workable Competition'. ... I have become increasingly impressed that the kind of competition we have, with all its defects ... is better than the pure and perfect norm, because it makes for progress. ... Thus the inquiry goes back to my father's basic conception that the analysis of static equilibrium, for which he is chiefly known, is properly not an end but an introduction to the study of dynamics, in which it should find its fulfillment.

Bibliographic notes

Extensive lists of the published works of John Maurice Clark are to be found in Jesse W. Markham, 'John Maurice Clark, *International Encyclopedia of the Social Sciences*, vol. 2, pp. 508–11 (New York: Macmillan, 1968) and in C. Addison Hickman, *J.M. Clark* (New York: Columbia University Press, 1975).

I have also drawn on my unpublished PhD dissertation, 'Changing concepts of the large firm and antitrust enforcement' (Princeton University, 1958).

F. GEORGE WARD STOCKING

Willard F. Mueller

Innovations

Critiques of antitrust legal–economic rules using industrial organization theories and empirical analyses. Conducted numerous empirical studies of international cartels, domestic monopoly and anti-competitive practices. Served as an advisor and active participant in the enforcement of the antitrust laws and as an advisor to many other government agencies. He was an imaginative academic administrator and inspiring teacher.

Personal history

Born 1892, Clarendon, TX, USA; died 1975.

Degrees BA Clarendon College, TX, 1918; BA, MA University of Texas, 1918, 1921; PhD Columbia University, 1925.

Principal position Research Professor and Chair, Department of Economics and Director of Research in the Social Sciences at Vanderbilt University, 1947–63.

Other Dartmouth College, 1925; University of Texas, 1926–47. Technical Advisor, US Labor Board, 1933–35; Chairman, Petroleum Labor Policy Board, NRA, 1933–34; Member, Consumers Advisory Board, NRA 1933–35; frequently served as consultant to Antitrust Division of the Justice Department and served as co-chair of the Consent Decree Section of that department, 1942–43; Member, War Labor Board, 1943–46; Director, Federal Reserve Bank, San Antonio, TX, 1943–46. President of the Southern Economic Association (1951) and the American Economic Association (1958).

The hallmark of George Stocking's professional career was to improve understanding of American capitalism and to develop antitrust policies improving competitive markets. His thinking about these matters was influenced by his mentors at Columbia University, Thorstein Veblen and Wesley Clair Mitchell. Although he admired Veblen's insights into the institutional characteristics of American capitalism, Stocking rejected Veblen's view that the system of private business enterprise would pass away in the course of time. He embraced Mitchell's belief that the institutional matrix in which economists find themselves determines the problems economists think about and the way they think about them.

Although public policy fashions often changed during his lifetime, Stocking consistently advocated reliance on antitrust policies to promote competitively structured markets. To this end he applied the disciplines of economics and law in evaluating the origins and implications of economic power. His life work involved (i) empirical studies of specific industries and business practices and (ii) analysis and formulation of legal rules governing competitive behavior.

His early research reflected his previous life in Texas, where he had worked as a 'roughneck' in the western Texas oilfields. His first published research was *The Oil Industry and the Competitive System* (1925); his last major work was *Middleast Oil: A Study in Political and Economic Controversy* (1970).

Stocking's most ambitious research accomplishment was a six-year study of the interrelated problems of domestic monopoly and international cartels. The studies were sponsored by the Twentieth Century Fund and were directed by Stocking and his long-time friend, Professor Myron W. Watkins. Their first volume, *Cartels in Action* (1946), provided a detailed factual account of cartel arrangements in eight fields. The second volume, *Cartels or Competition?* (1948), provided an appraisal of international cartels and their influence on industrial stability, employment, technological progress and the growth of investment. These seminal works often became the genesis of subsequent studies of international cartels.

The third volume, *Monopoly and Free Enterprise* (1951), addressed the monopoly problem in the American economy. It examined the relation between the concentration of economic power and the theory and practice of 'free enterprise'. It also examined the laws designed to ensure that the system served the public interest. The book became a popular textbook for courses in public policy toward business.

Stocking's second area of accomplishment involved his active participation in the regulatory process. Following enactment of the National Recovery Act of 1933, Stocking was appointed to the Consumers Advisory Board of the National Recovery Administration (NRA). But he and his fellow board members were no match for the industrialists that enforced the NRA codes that fixed prices of numerous industrial products. Stocking often regaled his students with his frustrations during this period as his 'years of spitting in the wind'. But the experience proved rewarding by demonstrating the dangers inherent in abandoning antitrust enforcement.

During the subsequent antitrust revival in 1938 with President F.D. Roosevelt's appointment of Thurman Arnold as head of the Antitrust Division, Stocking served as an economic advisor to Arnold. In the 1950s, Stocking became a leading critic of the concept of 'workable competition' conceived by Edward Mason and John M. Clark as an appropriate test of socially acceptable market arrangements. In essence, the approach proposed that the legality of competitive practices be judged by an industry's performance rather than its structure and business practices. Stocking believed that competitively structured markets best fostered satisfactory business performance.

These conflicting approaches clashed in 1953 when the Attorney General appointed a National Committee to Study the Antitrust Laws. Stocking was invited to serve on the committee, but demurred. The committee was chaired by S. Chesterfield Oppenheim, who had urged injection of the concept of workable competition and the rule of reason into the antitrust laws. Stocking's worst fears were realized when the committee's final report contained a chapter on the 'Economic indicia of competition and monopoly' that embraced the concept of 'workable competition' and included numerous economic criteria for identifying the nature of competition in a market. In consultation with Arnold, Stocking prepared a lengthy law review article attacking the committee's report.

What especially rankled Stocking was that the committee embraced an essentially Sherman Act 'rule of reason' standard for the enforcement of the recently enacted Celler–Kefauver Act. Moreover, the committee endorsed a Federal Trade Commission

(FTC) decision in the first merger challenged under the Celler–Kefauver Act, *Pillsbury Mills.* F.T.C. Dkt. 6000 (1953).

Stocking believed that the FTC's legal standard requiring 'a case-by-case examination of *all* relevant factors' was ambiguous and contrary to the language and legislation history of the Celler–Kefauver Act. He predicted that the standard would, at best, greatly prolong litigating merger cases. Subsequent events confirmed Stocking's prophecy. The *Pillsbury* case remained in litigation until 1963, when an appellate court once again remanded the case to the FTC to decide what steps should 'now be taken in view of both the lapse of time and the present state of the law applying Section 7'. The Commission vacated the case for lack of public interest.

Stocking continued to conduct research of business practices and antitrust policy for the rest of his life. Many of his works are included in a book, *Workable Competition and Antitrust Policy* (1961). In addition to educating his students and other scholars, Stocking was adept in influencing policy makers. Two articles he co-authored were cited with approval in important Supreme Court decisions in the 1950s and 1960s. One critiqued the initial decision in the *DuPont Cellophane* case of 1954 and the other examined the potential competitive problems of reciprocal trading among large corporations.

Finally, Stocking established prominent economics departments at the University of Texas and Vanderbilt University. At Vanderbilt he attracted substantial research grants, graduate students, and a prestigious group of industrial organization economists: William H. Nicholls, Jesse W. Markham, and James W. McKie.

Most relevant publications

(1946), *Cartels In Action* (with M.W. Watkins) (Twentieth Century Fund, New York).
(1948), *Cartels or Competition?* (with M.W. Watkins) (Twentieth Century Fund, New York)
(1951), *Monopoly and Free Enterprise* (with M.W. Watkins) (Twentieth Century Fund, New York).
(1955), 'The *Cellophane* case and the new competition' (with W.F. Mueller), *American Economic Review*, **65**, March, 29–63.
(1955), 'The Attorney General's Committee report: A businessman's guide through antitrust', *Georgetown Law Review*, **44**(1), November, 1–57.
(1957), 'Business reciprocity and the size of firms' (with W.F. Mueller), *University of Chicago Journal of Business*, **30**, April, 73–93.
(1961), *Workable Competition and Antitrust Policy*, Vanderbilt University Press, Nashville, Tenn.
(1970), *Middle East Oil: A Study in Political and Economic Controversy* (Vanderbilt University Press, Nashville, Tenn).

G. MARTIN G. GLAESER

Harry M. Trebing

Innovations

Glaeser formulated comprehensively much of the economic content of utility regulation. He analyzed the interrelationships among differential pricing, cost and operational characteristics of public utilities, technological advance, and the move toward greater industry concentration. He concluded that these factors required an evolving pattern of government intervention and control for public utility industries. He critically examined the components of the regulatory process, ranging from the determination of revenue requirements to the design of rates and proposed ratemaking guidelines to promote efficiency and control the exercise of market power. Glaeser analyzed changing technology in these industries, and advanced the analysis of common and joint costs.

Personal history

Born 1888, Tepliwodau, Germany; died 1967.

Degrees AB University of Wisconsin, 1911; PhD Harvard University, 1925.

Principal positions Professor of Economics, University of Wisconsin, 1919–67. He initially joined the Wisconsin faculty in 1917 working with Richard T. Ely and John R. Commons. Glaeser held a variety of positions at the Wisconsin Public Service Commission (1911–18), and he was executive secretary for the Public Utility Acquisition Committee studying regulation or municipal ownership of the Milwaukee electric utility (1920–25). He served as special adviser to the Tennessee Valley Authority (TVA) from 1933 to 1936, and Chief Power Planning Engineer for TVA from 1937 to 1938. Glaeser served as a commissioner with the Wisconsin Commission for the last four years of his life.

Martin G. Glaeser devoted much of his professional career to the study of public utility industries – both at the academic and governmental levels. He received an introduction to the problems of the railroads and the regulation of corporate power as a student of William Z. Ripley and Roscoe Pound while completing a PhD at Harvard. At the University of Wisconsin he was a youthful colleague of Richard T. Ely and John R. Commons, who were heavily involved in implementing the 'LaFollette Idea' which sought to integrate academia with state government to introduce public policy reform. He served as a special adviser to the Tennessee Valley Authority (1933–36) and as Chief Power Planning Engineer (1937–38), where he played a pivotal role in shaping the policies of TVA, which had become one of the jewels of the New Deal reform program. He also served as a member of the Wisconsin Commission. All of this was combined into almost 40 years of teaching as an institutional economist at Wisconsin.

Glaeser's perception of public utility industries as a separate sector in need of state control or regulation was set forth in *Outlines of Public Utility Economics* (1927) and *Public*

Utilities in American Capitalism (1957). He analyzed the origin of the concept of public utility status and the evolution of different patterns of social control as these industries moved from competition to monopoly status, and then to regional or national infrastructure networks. He incorporated this pattern of evolution into the four economic dimensions of efficiency that characterize these industries. These are economies of the load factor, diversity factor economies, economies of scale and economies of joint production.

Glaeser described the public utility sector as quite distinct from traditional government functions where collective interests are supported by taxes (for example, national defense and the administration of justice), and the unregulated market sector. Public utilities perform quasi-public functions where collective interests and common benefits are dominant, but special benefits accrue to individuals in a fashion that can be rationed by price. The public interest is promoted through collective action (that is, state intervention and regulation) that liberates individual action and enhances consumer choice. Glaeser noted that the zone between public utility functions and competitive markets can be characterized by oligopolistic behavior and administered pricing. Here, he says, 'we meet some of the most perplexing problems of modern capitalism' (Glaeser, 1957, p. 11).

In his approach to the study of public utilities, Glaeser adopts a broad evolutionary approach that is much more comprehensive than that developed by Henry Carter Adams or James Bonbright. He traces the origin of the concept of public utility status back to the doctrine of just price. He then proceeds to describe both the evolution of public utility industries and the institutional arrangements for social control through four distinct epochs. The first was the promotional epoch that was characterized by government promotion and subsidization of public utilities and transportation. The second was the competitive epoch where primary reliance was placed on promoting inter-firm rivalry to constrain the behavior of suppliers. During this period, considerable reliance was placed on the issue of multiple franchises to encourage entry. The third epoch emerged when monopoly replaced competition. In part, the monopoly epoch was the result of mergers and consolidations when capital-intensive suppliers faced conditions of excess capacity and demand instability. It also reflected growing acceptance of the natural monopoly concept by government as the most efficient method for providing service. In this period, the independent regulatory commission replaced franchise and legislative regulation. The fourth epoch was characterized by Glaeser as a period of planning and coordination. Government would assume greater planning responsibility and there would be greater acceptance of more diverse options for providing utility-type services. Interconnection of networks and integration of systems would also grow in importance. When the provision of public utility service became monopolized, the producer would have control over a common necessity, and that market power would have to be curbed by the political power of the state.

For Glaeser, this required commissions to apply rate base/rate-of-return regulation utilizing the Uniform System of Accounts as a database together with supplemental monitoring for quality of service. He discusses each of these components of the regulatory process at length and he devotes special attention to the incentive to achieve full utilization of fixed plant through pricing strategies. His 1927 book contains a pioneering discussion of price discrimination. He noted that the classification of customers on the basis of different demand elasticities and charging them differential class prices permits the monopolist to 'invade what might otherwise be either a consumers' surplus or competitive profit' (1927, p. 627).

Glaeser believed that public utilities should be permitted to compete for different classes of customers, but not at the expense of placing additional burdens on current customers. If there were surplus revenues through differential pricing, Glaeser argued that: (i) prices on all units should be reduced, (ii) output should be increased, or (iii) prices should be lowered for existing customers and output expanded to new customers at a lower price: 'The objective is that public purpose and not private goals should control the disposal of surplus profits' (ibid., p. 635). He also added that regulatory approval of additional capacity does not imply that the state should underwrite the associated risks.

Throughout both the 1927 and 1957 books, Glaeser discusses at length four economic dimensions of efficiency that are of unique importance in the public utility industries. These are economies of the load factor, economies of the diversity factor, economies of scale and economies of joint production. He gave particular attention to economies of joint production where 'it would be cheaper to turn out two or more services from one central process or structure than to produce them separately' (1957, p. 177). He points out that joint costs associated with such production are difficult to segregate among different products or components of the enterprise. In 1927, he noted that those services where demand is highly elastic will bear the smallest portion of the total joint costs.

Glaeser's experience with the TVA and the need to reconcile the joint costs of multiple purpose of river basin projects led him to formulate a fascinating theory for handling this problem. Glaeser's alternative justifiable expenditures theory would proceed as follows. First, the direct (avoidable) cost of each service would be subtracted from the total system cost. This would yield the joint/common costs. These joint/common costs would be assigned to each service on the basis of the relative benefit which that service derived from being included as a part of the integrated utility supply system. The relative benefit is measured by the difference between each service's direct and stand-alone cost. Each service could then be assigned its direct plus its allocated joint/common cost. If this consolidated cost is less than its stand-alone cost, then pervasive system-wide economies exist and that service or activity benefits by being an integral part of the network. Where no such economies exist because the stand-alone cost is equal to or less than the combined cost of providing the service over the system network, then there would be no cost-based rationale for including it as an integral part of the utility-based supply system. Glaeser's theory could be applied to prescribe the revenue contribution of each service of activity. It would be far preferable to relying on demand-based price discrimination to determine each service's proportional contribution.

Since Glaeser stressed the evolutionary nature of public utility services and regulation, it is reasonable to assume that he would agree that the form and scope of regulation should change over time. Proponents of deregulation could argue that the Energy Policy Act of 1992 and the Telecommunications Act of 1996 became the embodiment of his government planning function. Only this was planning to replace regulation with markets wherever possible. Clearly, this is not what Glaeser had in mind. His emphasis on the dominance of collective over individual interests, the need for regulation to liberate individual action, and the potential abuses inherent in monopoly costing and pricing leave no doubt that deregulation was not his objective. He would admit that the zone between public utilities and the unregulated market will change, but it is difficult to envisage that he would concede that the latter would supplant the former. Quite the contrary, his approach to the treatment of joint costs provides an intriguing solution for the problem of preventing cross-subsidization between regulated and deregulated markets when repeal of the Public Utility Holding Company Act leads to the proliferation of new holding companies.

Glaeser's argument on the need for collective action by the state stands in sharp contrast to the deregulation movement of the past two decades. He provides a conceptual and historical framework for a critical examination of deregulation that strongly suggests deregulation will not yield pervasive competition but rather greater concentration and greater market power.

Most relevant publications

(1927), *Outlines of Public Utility Economics*, London: Macmillan.
(1939), 'Those joint TVA costs', *Public Utilities Fortnightly*, **24**, August, 259ff.
(1957), *Public Utilities in American Capitalism*, London: Macmillan.

11. The 1930s

A. GARDINER C. MEANS

John Howard Brown

Innovations
Separation of ownership from control in modern corporations, concept of 'administered prices', concentration ratios as a measure of market structure.

Personal history

Born 1896, Windham, CN, USA; died 1988.

Degrees BA (Chemistry) Harvard University, 1918; MA and PhD Harvard (Economics) 1927, 1933.

Principal position Non-academic, government.

Gardiner Means deserves to be considered as at least the most important forerunner, if not the founder, of modern industrial organization. His influential and creative scholarship during the crucial decade of the 1930s helped to set the research agenda which dominated the early field of industrial organization.

Means's contribution was predominantly empirical. With Adolph Berle, Means (1932) documented the gradual erosion of the rights of shareholders. This led to the notion that there had emerged a 'separation of ownership and control'.

As they note in the 1967 edition of *The Modern Corporation* one of the consequences of their book was the Securities Exchange Act of 1933. Within the economics profession, the vast literature of agency, the market for corporate control, and executive compensation proceeds from Berle and Means. At the same time the early twenty-first-century corporate scandals point to the continued relevance of the concept of the separation of ownership and control.

Berle and Means assert that the changes are significant, because '[t]he separation of ownership from control produces a condition where the interests of owner and of ultimate manager may, and often do, diverge, and where many of the checks which formerly operated to limit the use of power disappear' (1932 [1967], p. 7). At the same time, the giant size and all encompassing nature of modern firms changes the very nature of capital, so that:

> To an increasing extent it is composed not of tangible goods, but of organizations built in the past and available to function in the future. Even the value of tangible goods tends to become increasingly dependent upon their organized relationship to other tangible goods ... of these great units. (pp. 45–6)

These organizations exert what they characterize as a 'centripetal attraction' causing ever larger organizations. It also has consequences for the 'social control of business'. They observe: 'a society in which production is governed by blind economic forces is being replaced by one in which production is carried on under the ultimate control of a handful of individuals. The economic power in the hands of the few persons who control a giant corporation is a tremendous force' (p. 46).

The major conceptual revolution of Berle and Means's work is the notion of 'control' as something distinct from either ownership or management (p. 66). They define control as 'for practical purposes (that) control lies in the hands of the individual or group who have the actual power to select the board of directors (or its majority)' (p. 66). They go on to identify and quantify the various methods of control ranging from control by a single dominant shareholder to control by the incumbent management with little or no shareholding. Of this last category they observe: 'Where ownership is sufficiently subdivided, the management can thus become a self-perpetuating body even though its share in the ownership is negligible' (p. 82).

They examined the ownership structure of the 200 largest corporations and conclude: '[that] 65 percent of the companies and 80 per cent of their combined wealth should be controlled either by the management or by a legal device involving a small proportion of ownership indicates the important extent to which ownership and control have been separated' (p. 110).

They acknowledged a very definite limitation on the 'control' of the corporation, the power of public markets. According to them, the growing corporation is, 'dependent on new capital' (p. 247) so that: 'The bulk of their growth came almost entirely from new issues of stock or other securities'. The corporation's dependence upon capital markets, 'sets a very definite limit on the extent to which those in control can abuse the suppliers of capital'.

Another of Means's contributions to industrial organization was the notion of administered price. Working as an Economic Advisor to Henry Wallace the Secretary of Agriculture, Means examined the behavior of prices as a part of the implementation of the Agricultural Adjustment Act. Thus he followed his bombshell, *The Modern Corporation* with yet another incendiary, his theory of 'administered prices' (1935a). Hamilton (Hamilton et al., 1938, p. vii) cites the creation in the 'summer of 1934' of a Cabinet Committee on Price Policy which was to investigate the pricing policies of various industries. It is not clear whether this committee predates Means's memo to Secretary Wallace.

Means defined an administered price as, 'one which is set by administrative action and held constant for a period of time' (1935a, p. 1). This differs from market prices 'that are made in the market as the result of the interaction of buyers and sellers' and also to the traditional distinction between competitive and monopoly prices. The distinguishing characteristic of administered prices which gives them their considerable economic significance is that they are 'rigid' and 'sales fluctuate with the demand at the rigid price' (1935b, p. 401).

As Means puts it, 'The main point ... is that inflexible, administered prices have acted as an impediment to that automatic readjustment which is supposed to occur through price change and which is supposed to keep our economy in approximate balance with full use of economic resource' (1936, p. 33). According to Means, 'technology and economic concentration have brought about a change in the demand curve faced by the individual producer. In a great body of cases he faces a demand curve which slopes up to the left' (pp. 33–4). Thus the producer in an oligopolistic industry has the discretion to control prices, and does.

Means's thesis is well known. In competitively structured industries, prices fell dramatically at the onset of the Great Depression. In more concentrated industries the tendency for prices to change was substantially more muted. In a flurry of theoretical and statistical analyses in 1935–36, Means showed that sectors of the economy had responded differently to the onset of the Great Depression. He further identified 'administered prices' as a source of the American economy's unsatisfactory performance in the period.

For statistical evidence he used the Bureau of Labor Statistics' monthly survey of wholesale prices over the 1926–33 period (1935a,b). He first counted the number of changes reported in the price of one of the commodities sampled. The number of price changes experienced by a commodity proved to be widely variable (1935b, Chart 1).

Means divided the commodities into ten groups based on their frequency of reported price change. The behavior of prices for each of these groups was described, first from 1926 to 1933 (1935a), subsequently from 1929 through 1936. The results were dramatic. Commodities with the most flexible prices dropped the most during the recession of 1929–33 and then rose the most in the subsequent recovery (1936, p. 24). Means linked the differences in price flexibility to the extent of output adjustment in the respective industries. Inflexible prices were closely associated with large reductions of output during the recession. In contrast, flexible price industries maintained output at almost unchanged levels during the recession and the subsequent recovery.

In the first of the three papers (Senate Document 13, 1935a) the links to Means's earlier work with Berle are most evident. He asserts that administered prices were caused by the rise of large-scale firms so that where once: '[b]alance between the actions of individuals was maintained ... by the impersonal forces of the market and the law of supply and demand. Through the market, the apparently unrelated activities of individuals were made to mesh into a single coordinated whole' (1935a, p. 9), now there arose an economy where: 'more and more of economic coordination has been accomplished administratively'.

As Means notes: 'More than half of all manufacturing activity is carried on by 200 big corporations while big corporations dominate the railroad and public-utility fields' (p. 10). There were benefits to this since: 'This development of administrative coordination has made possible tremendous increases in the efficiency of industrial production within single enterprises'. However, it also eliminates flexibility in adjusting to changing demand. Because decision-making power in the economy has been concentrated in the hands of a few managers, 'individuals have a direct control over industrial policy which they exercise in making business policy for their own enterprise' (p. 10). This is a distinct change from *laissez-faire* principles. Instead, since in many industries the number of competing units has, 'been reduced to a relatively small handful', industrial policy is 'no longer made wholly by the market but in part by individuals. Industrial policy become subject to administrative control even though there is no monopoly or collusion'.

Unfortunately, the incentives for the individual businessman are such that in making industrial policy, 'he almost necessarily makes wrong industrial decisions'. This is the case since the businessman must 'make business policy in a way to maximize the profits of his own enterprise'. This 'frequently requires him in the presence of falling demand to hold price and curtail his production even though this means idle men and idle machines' in consequence, 'The net effect of business control over industrial policy is, therefore, to aggravate any fluctuations in economic activity and prevent any necessary readjustments'. This is 'no necessary reflection on either his character or his intelligence'.

Means's work on pricing inspired and contributed to the wave of investigations of pricing during the 1930s. Edward Mason's 'Price and output policies' (1939), usually considered the founding document of industrial organization, represents a logical extension of this literature. Means's role in sparking the literature on pricing is the reason that this author ranks him, and not Mason, as the founding father of industrial organization. However, Means's contribution to the development of industrial organization was not complete.

A third contribution is found in, *The Structure of American Industry* (Natural Resources Committee, 1939). This massive volume was nothing less than a case study of the entire American economy. Means was the head of the research division of the Natural Resources Committee. This was a bureau within the Interior Department charged, as the name suggests, with examination of patterns of resource use in the United States.

Each chapter outlines one aspect of the national economy. Chapter Seven contains the material related to the current field of industrial organization. It is the first study to use the four-firm concentration ratio of an industry to establish the degree of oligopolistic dominance in the industry (Lee, 2001). This measure is a stalwart of empirical industrial organization.

Nor was Means done with the concept of administered prices in the 1930s:

> In 1959, my pamphlet, *Administrative Inflation and Public Policy*, reported the discovery of a wholly new kind of inflation in which prices increase perversely in response to a fall in demand, thus producing simultaneous inflation and recession, an impossibility under traditional theories. Study of this finding showed that the new inflation does not arise from too much money chasing too few goods but from normal administrative decisions which carry an inflationary bias and that it cannot be controlled by monetary and fiscal measures. (Means's autobiographical summary in Blaug, 1999, p. 762)

According to Means, this administered price inflation, unlike conventional inflation, was not subject to the ordinary levers of fiscal and monetary policy.

Bibliography

Berle, Adolf and Gardiner Means (1932), *The Modern Corporation and Private Property*, Macmillan, New York, reprinted 1967, Harcourt, Brace & World, New York.

Blaug, Mark (ed.) (1999), *Who's Who in Economics*, 3rd edn, Edward Elgar, Cheltenham, UK and Northampton, MA, USA.

Hamilton, Walton, Mark Adams, Irene Till, Albert Abrahamson, George Marshall and Helen Everett Meiklejohn (1938), *Price and Price Policies*, McGraw-Hill, New York.

Lee, Frederic S. (2001), personal communication, April 4.

Mason, Edward S. (1939), 'Price and output policies of large scale enterprise', *American Economic Review*, Supplement, **29**(1), pp. 61–74.

Means, Gardiner C. (1935a), *Industrial Prices and Their Relative Inflexibility*, Senate Document 13, 74th Congress, 1st session, Washington, DC.
Means, Gardiner C. (1935b), 'Price inflexibility and the requirements of a stabilizing monetary policy,' *Journal of the American Statistical Association*, **30**(190), June, 401–13.
Means, Gardiner C. (1936), 'Notes on inflexible prices', *American Economic Review*, **26**(1), 23–35.
Means, Gardiner C. (1959), *Administrative Inflation and Public Policy*, A. Kramer Associates, Washington, DC.
Natural Resources Committee (1939), *The Structure of the American Economy*, Government Printing Office, Washington, DC, reprinted 1966, Augustus M. Kelley, New York.

B. EDWARD HASTINGS CHAMBERLIN

William L. Baldwin

Innovations

The theory of monopolistic competition in oligopoly markets where the leading firms understand their mutual dependence.

Personal history

Born 1899, La Conner, WA, USA; died 1967. On the death of his father, his mother moved the family to Iowa City, Iowa, where he completed his high school education and graduated from the University of Iowa.

Degrees BA University of Iowa; MA University of Michigan, 1922; PhD Harvard University, 1927; his doctoral dissertation was awarded the David H. Wells prize for the academic year 1927–28.

Principal position He remained a member of the Harvard faculty until his death, by which time he had been appointed the David H. Wells Professor of Political Economy.

For six years Chamberlin devoted his attention virtually exclusively to his 1933 book *The Theory of Monopolistic Competition: A Re-orientation of the Theory of Value* (TMC) (Cambridge, MA: Harvard University Press), drawn from his dissertation. In the following years Chamberlin wrote over 30 published scholarly works in the general field of microeconomics, but his focus remained largely on the theory of monopolistic competition.

Jesse W. Markham noted in the *International Encyclopedia of the Social Sciences* (vol. 18, pp. 117–21 at p. 119, New York: Macmillan, 1979), '[T]here are eminent scholars whose fame rests on a major contribution and whose professional lives are devoted to elaborating and perfecting it'. Chamberlin, he concluded, was *par excellence* such a scholar. Indeed, Markham observed, 'It is a ... high tribute to the results of his tenacity that *Monopolistic Competition* and [Keynes's] *General Theory* are often identified as the two most influential economic treatises of the twentieth century' (p. 120). Or, as William J. Baumol commented in the 1964 *American Economic Review Papers and Proceedings* (vol. 54, May, p. 52), Chamberlin's book was 'the most influential single work ever produced by an American economist'.

But not all American economists subscribed to quite such a glowing opinion of this book. In one text, A *History of Economic Theory and Method* by Robert B. Eckelund, Jr and Robert F. Hébert, the authors wrote 'Practically every text in principles of economics and in intermediate microeconomic analysis devotes space to Chamberlin and his ideas'. However, '[A] large and ever-growing coterie has come to defend an expanded model of perfect competition as a more consistent and useful approach to microeconomic problems' (New York: McGraw-Hill, 3rd edn, 1990, pp. 494, 495). This division of opinion may be described and assessed in three major areas: basic concepts such as demand curves and mutual dependence recognized; analysis; and policy implications.

Prior to the publication of TMC – and simultaneously of Joan Robinson's *The Economics of Imperfect Competition* (London: Macmillan, 1933) – economists tended to simplify their analyses of market structures and pricing by assuming that firms were either price makers (monopolies) or price takers (in competition). In the case of a monopoly a firm was assumed to have no competitors, with perhaps its ability to raise price to a very high level constrained by the potential entry of others, but with much of the downward-sloping Marshallian demand curve facing the monopolist being identical with the market demand. The firm in competition, by contrast, was assumed to be so small, and the number of these firms in a given market so large, that no firm could alter the supply-and-demand determined price by raising or lowering its rate of output. Such a firm would face a horizontal or perfectly elastic demand curve showing price as independent of any one firm's output. The standard approach by economic theorists of the late nineteenth and early twentieth centuries was to develop models of pure monopoly and pure competition and compare the two. Economists of the marginalist revolution were well aware of and dissatisfied with the simplistic dichotomy between the two, but had been unable to go any further than to note factors which might temper both monopoly and competition. As Chamberlin observed in introducing the concept of mutual dependence recognized:

> When a move by one seller evidently forces the other to make a counter move, he is very stupidly refusing to look further than his nose if he proceeds on the assumption that he will not. ... He must consider not merely what his competitor is doing now, but also what he will be forced to do in the light of change which he himself is contemplating. (TMC, 8th edn, pp. 46, 47)

This concept is the core of Chamberlin's theory and what distinguishes his contribution most distinctly from Joan Robinson's. Essentially, the demand curve becomes a subjective construct, or what the firm *thinks* is most likely to be the relation between its price and output. In one limiting case, the monopolistic seller assumes correctly that it faces the market demand curve. At the other limit, each of the many competitive firms accounts for so many rivals and so small a share of the market that it is impossible for any one to think through the likely ramifications of a price or production rate change, or correctly it assumes that its impact on the market would be so minor that others would ignore it. As a result, the competitive firm takes the existing price structure as given. The concept could be applied as a continuum to intermediate markets; that is, mutual dependence fully recognized, partially recognized and ignored. But, as Chamberlin warned repeatedly throughout his book, such flexibility made it necessary to neglect, hold constant or assume away so many elements of real-world industries and markets that each case had to be treated *sui generis*. Among these are number and size distribution of firms, product differentiation, risk, entry conditions, frictions, imperfections of knowledge and brand loyalties. In his discussion of the theory Chamberlin wrote: '[T]hese variations will give no real difficulty in the end. Exposition of the group theory is facilitated, however, by ignoring them for the present. We therefore proceed under the heroic assumption that both demand and cost curves for all the "products" are uniform throughout the group' (ibid., p. 82).

While the mutual dependence model was without doubt a great improvement over the monopoly/competition dichotomy, it has its problems, notably in the case of mutual dependence fully recognized in oligopolistic markets. Under Chamberlin's 'heroic assumption' mutual dependence recognition fully recognized in such markets will lead to the same price, output and profit as pure monopoly. This may come about through either overt or tacit collusion. However, early work in game theory made it clear that the mutual adoption and maintenance of joint maximizing strategies involved extremely difficult problems, even in the duopoly case, notably in the absence of direct communication (that is, the prisoner's dilemma) or in a repeated game with a finite time horizon (the final round problem). It appeared that Chamberlin had attributed abilities to at least some business decision makers in tight oligopoly situations that were well beyond the skills of economic theorists to model.

In Chamberlin's basic analytical model the firm in oligopoly faces two subjective demand curves. The first, labeled DD' for graphical purposes, is the curve for mutual dependence fully recognized; and the second, labeled dd', is that for mutual dependence ignored, or assuming that competitors' prices and outputs are held constant. Both have negative slopes, but clearly, dd' is more elastic than DD' and intersects it from below and to the left. Assuming that the firm's price and output are shown at the point of intersection of these two curves, the firm faces a constant temptation to cut price on the assumption that it can get away with the cut without triggering any response from its rivals – that is, dd is the relevant demand curve. But it is often not so, for this reason having been labeled an 'imaginary' demand curve. The result is that the firm's rate of output is determined by the less elastic DD', or dd' has slid down DD' to a new short-run equilibrium at which all firms in the industry are worse off. From time to time such slides occur and are reversed by restoration of mutual recognition, but over time the number of firms and the differentiation of products increase and mutual dependence is ignored. A long-run equilibrium in this case is determined by tangency of dd' and long-run average cost.

At this equilibrium, however, even though the rate of profit has been reduced to zero, the rate of output is below the optimum and price is above optimum. This equilibrium, in which oligopoly has been replaced by monopolistic competition, is illustrated by the tangency of a downward-sloping demand curve with a U-shaped cost curve. Such a tangency must by construction lie to the left of the minimum point of the cost curve, indicating that there are too many firms of suboptimal scale. At the same time Joan Robinson came to the same conclusion, illustrating with virtually identical graphs. In her view, this misallocaton of resources reflected an inefficiency of free-market capitalism, although later she was quoted, curiously enough in a volume edited by Chamberlin, as saying: 'I make no apology for having written my book twenty years ago, but I find it shocking that people still read it' (*Monopoly and Competition and Their Regulation*, Papers and Proceedings of a Conference Held by the International Economic Association, London: Macmillan, 1954, p. 507). Chamberlin, on the other hand, held that variety in products offset much if not all of the social costs of monopolistic competition:

> [E]ven where possible, it would not be desirable to standardize products beyond a certain point. Differences in tastes, desires, incomes, and the locations of buyers, and differences in the uses which they wish to make of commodities all indicate the need for variety and the necessity of substituting for the concept of a 'competitive ideal' an ideal involving both monopoly and competition. How much and what kinds of monopoly, and with what measure of social control, become the questions. (8th edn, pp. 214–15)

Chamberlin's formulation of mutual dependence recognized quickly replaced the concept of monopoly as limited to a single or overwhelmingly dominant seller and in 1956 was adopted by the U.S. Supreme Court, which defined monopoly as 'the power to control prices or exclude competition' (*United States v. E. I. du Pont & Company*, 351 US 377, 391). Monopoly power is now understood by economists and lawyers alike to be a matter of degree. Mutual dependence fully recognized among a small group of oligopolistic firms with similar costs and products may lead to collusion, whether overt or tacit, yielding virtually the same results as single-firm, or pure, monopoly. As the number of firms increases or differences in cost or product grow, the degree to which mutual dependence is recognized, and hence monopoly power, is likely to fall. But the courts have had difficulty with the concept which the judiciary has labeled 'conscious parallelism', but which in truth is hard to distinguish from recognition of mutual dependence.

In 1946, the Supreme Court upheld the conviction of three major cigarette manufacturers on charges of conspiracy both to restrain trade and to monopolize. These three had in total at one time accounted for approximately 90 percent of cigarette production in the US. The evidence presented was almost entirely of parallel behavior in setting prices, particularly during the Depression. In its opinion the Supreme Court stated:

> 'No formal agreement is necessary to constitute an unlawful conspiracy. Often crimes are a matter of inference deduced from the acts of the person accused and done in pursuance of a criminal purpose. ... The essential combination or conspiracy in violation of the Sherman Act may be found in a course of dealings or other circumstances as well as in an exchange of words. (*American Tobacco Company v. United States*, 328 U.S. 781, 809–10)

In a series of subsequent cases the courts adopted the term conscious parallelism, and the antitrust enforcement agencies sought to convince the courts that the *American Tobacco* decision outlawed tacit as well as overt collusion. But in a 1954 case, the Court stated its reluctance to rely solely on consciously parallel business practices, asserting:

> This Court has never held that proof of parallel business behavior conclusively establishes agreement or, phrased differently, that such behavior itself constitutes a Sherman Act offense. Circumstantial evidence of consciously parallel behavior may have made heavy inroads into the traditional judicial attitude toward conspiracy; but 'conscious parallelism' has not yet read conspiracy out of the Sherman Act entirely. (*Theater Enterprises, Inc. v. Paramount Film Distributing Corporation*, 346 U.S. 537, 541)

As Galbraith had viewed the issue on the eve of the *Theater Enterprises* decision:

> To suppose that there are grounds for antitrust prosecution wherever three, four or a half dozen firms dominate a market is to suppose that the very fabric of American capitalism is illegal. This is a notion which can seem sensible only to the briefless lawyer. (*American Capitalism: The Concept of Countervailing Power*, Boston, MA: Houghton Mifflin, 1952, p. 55)

Isaiah Berlin has quoted a line from the Ancient Greek poet Archilochus, 'The fox knows many things, but the hedgehog knows one big thing' (*The Hedgehog & the Fox: An Essay on Tolstoy's View of History*, New York: Touchstone, 1986, p. 1). E.H. Chamberlin exemplifies the best in Berlin's hedgehog, with 'one big thing' which made fundamental contributions to both microeconomic analysis and public policy toward business.

Bibliographic notes

An extensive list of the published works of Edward H. Chamberlin is to be found in Jesse W. Markham, 'Chamberlin, Edward H.', *International Encyclopedia of the Social Sciences*, vol. 18, pp. 117–21 (New York: Free Press, 1979).

I have also drawn on my unpublished PhD dissertation, 'Changing concepts of the large firm and antitrust enforcement' (Princeton University, 1958).

C. JAMES C. BONBRIGHT

Harry M. Trebing

Innovations

Bonbright presented a comprehensive analysis of the case for public utility regulation, setting forth the conditions for public control of enterprise, the components of economic regulation, and an analysis of the broader market structure within which such control must function. With respect to the latter, he demonstrated the need for structural reforms that would be forthcoming in the Public Utility Holding Company Act of 1935.

Personal history

Born 1891, Evanston, IL, USA; died 1985.

Principal positions Professor of Finance, Graduate School of Business and Department of Economics, Columbia University (1927–60). He initially joined the Columbia faculty in 1920. He was a trustee of the Power Authority of New York from 1931 to 1946, and was a member of the Governor's Commission on New York State Power Resources in 1959.

Degrees BS Northwestern University, 1913; PhD (Economics) Columbia, 1921. He was awarded an Honorary LLD from Northwestern University in 1956.

Bonbright wrote extensively on public utility problems over a long professional career. He taught at Columbia University from 1920 to 1960, wrote four major treatises on public utility regulation, and served as chair of the New York Power Authority from 1920–1960. His continuing goal was the refinement and improvement of the institution of economic regulation.

He accepted and articulated the concept of public interest regulation. In defining a 'public utility', Bonbright believed that an enterprise should not be regarded as a public utility unless it was subject to direct controls over the rates charged for service. However, he believed that price control alone was not sufficient to confer public utility status. Bonbright emphasized that the primary purpose of regulation must be the protection of the public in the role of consumer rather than in the role of producer or taxpayer. Accordingly, a public utility is any enterprise subject to price regulation of a type designed primarily to protect consumers. As he noted, 'What must justify public utility regulation is the necessity of regulation and not merely the necessity of the product' (Bonbright 1961, p. 9).

On the topic of market structure, Bonbright recognized that although public utilities may face severe competition in selected markets they are still essentially monopolistic. What favors regulation, he believed, was not that the enterprise operates under increasing returns, but rather that it involves a close connection between the plant-supplying service and the ultimate consumer. Interestingly, Bonbright, in collaboration with Gardiner C. Means, wrote a critical assessment of the holding company movement in 1932. Both authors believed that the holding company system was conducive to waste and inefficiency, financial manipulation and exploitative service fees that could be shifted forward to the consumer.

Bonbright and Means argued against the diversification of utilities into non-utility activities since this would be damaging to the ratepayer because it would menace the credit of the public utilities. For them, the appropriate industry structure was composed of autonomous operating entities, unencumbered by holding company affiliates and diversification programs. Clearly Bonbright would have vigorously opposed efforts in 2005 to repeal the Public Utility Holding Company Act and to eliminate regulation of the holding companies by the Securities and Exchange Commission.

Much of Bonbright's writing was devoted to the application of base rate/rate-of-return regulation to public utility enterprises. This included both the calculation of revenue requirements and the appropriate design of price or rate structures. He wrote a two-volume study on the valuation of assets which is an integral part of determining revenue requirements (Bonbright, 1937). In 1961, he wrote an authoritative analysis of rates, which remains a classic for regulators applying base rate/rate-of-return regulation (Bonbright, 1961).

Bonbright distinguished between total revenue requirements reflecting historic and current costs and the design of rates reflecting anticipated or escapable costs. To determine revenue requirements he would rely upon base rate/rate-of-return regulation. To design prices he would rely upon marginal cost analyses. Bonbright noted that between revenue requirements and rate design there would be an intermediate standard reflecting the cost of serving a particular class or group of customers. He called this a 'class rate standard'. Class rate standards would determine whether charges for a specific service were compensatory or non-compensatory, and accordingly would serve as a standard for judging internal cross-subsidization.

For Bonbright, class rate standards should be based on differential or incremental costs and not on absolute accounting costs. However, if a total cost apportionment were required, Bonbright suggested that: 'fully apportioned costs should reflect cost relationships, not absolute costs ... a relationship of direct proportionality suggests itself, and is perhaps the most generally useful one for rate-making purposes' (Bonbright, 1961, pp. 340–41). In effect, Bonbright was proposing an apportionment of total costs or revenue requirements reflecting relative or proportional relationships rather than an estimate of absolute cost by service.

Bonbright continued his discussion of pricing behavior by responding to the critics of regulation who argued that rates in the long run will be higher with than without regulation, and that profit-maximizing firms would experiment with rate reductions which would be impeded under commission regulation. Bonbright believed that when freed from controls, utilities would not follow a practice of lower prices to maximize profits. Instead, these utilities would be more apt to follow a policy of price discrimination with high prices for inelastic markets and low prices for elastic markets. He believed that there would be no incentive for this type of rate structure to conform to cost-of-service standards.

Bonbright advocated public utility regulation so as to promote efficiency. Like Henry Carter Adams and Martin Glaeser, Bonbright sought to capture the efficiency inherent in the cost characteristics of public utilities and pass them forward to the ultimate consumer. While he felt that public utility status involved more than increasing returns, he clearly believed that a single public utility supplying a given market would do so more cheaply than two or more companies operating in direct competition. He noted that even when the utility supplies output under conditions of increasing unit costs, 'the single company can secure the maximum advantages of economies of scale and density, while it is no more subject to the diseconomies of enhanced output ... than two or more companies ... called upon to supply the region with the same total output' (ibid., pp. 15–16). In a sense, he anticipated the subadditivity argument that came more than a decade later.

Critics of regulation will argue that the Bonbright model is limited to static situations where classic conditions of natural monopoly prevail. They will argue that the cost of this approach is the resultant stability that produces little or no innovation. They might point to possible examples in telecommunications. However, this does not mean that rapidly innovative market structures will not satisfy the need for consumer protection which was Bonbright's principal criterion for regulation. How to adapt the regulatory model to dynamic conditions remains a challenge for the future.

Most relevant publications

(1932), *The Holding Company* (with Gardiner C. Means), New York: McGraw Hill.
(1937), *The Valuation of Property*, 2 vols, New York: McGraw-Hill.
(1948), 'Utility rate control reconsidered in the light of the *Hope Natural Gas* case', *American Economic Review*, **38**, May, 465–82.
(1961), *Principles of Public Utility Rates*, New York: Columbia University Press.

D. HAROLD HOTELLING

John Howard Brown

Innovations

Spatial product differentiation; theory of marginal cost pricing.

Personal history

Born 1895, Fulda, MN, USA; died 1973. He spent much of his youth in Seattle.

Degrees BA (Journalism) University of Washington, 1919; master's (Mathematics) University of Washington, 1921; PhD (Mathematics) Princeton University, 1924.

Principal position 1931–46 Columbia University, where he was a central figure in the creation of the statistics department.

Other Stanford University; University of North Carolina at Chapel Hill, where he was a professor of mathematical statistics, associate director of the Institute of Statistics and a professor of economics.

Harold Hotelling is best known in economics today for his 1929 article, 'Stability in competition'. This article, in fact, represents an important milestone in the development of modern theories of industrial organization. However, Hotelling's contributions extend substantially beyond this much-cited work. He was also an important and pioneering statistician, responsible for the development of statistics education at both Columbia University and the University of North Carolina at Chapel Hill. In addition he published a work often considered as a foundation of resource economics (1931) and substantial work on the theory of marginal cost pricing.

In his 'A general mathematical theory of depreciation' (1925), Hotelling first develops the modern economic view of depreciation. That is, 'the owner wishes to maximize the present value of output minus the operating costs of the machine or other property. This quantity is, in fact, the value of the property' (1925, p. 341). This allows depreciation to be, 'defined simply as rate of decrease of value' (ibid.).

Hotelling's 1929 paper, 'Stability in competition', represents a first systematic attempt to model product differentiation. Hotelling begins by noting the gap in economic analysis arising from cases lying between the monopoly case where market and firm demand are identical and the competitive case where demand is perfectly elastic. The famous Hotelling model is offered as an example of one form of product differentiation. The article develops the notion of product differentiation much further than is generally appreciated.

The starting point of Hotelling's analysis is that: 'If the purveyor of an article gradually increases his price while his rivals keep theirs fixed, the diminution of volume of his sales will in general take place continuously rather than in the abrupt way which has been tacitly assumed' (1929, p. 41). This characteristic, associated in modern thought with product differentiation, was Hotelling's key to the puzzle of whether competition among duopolistic firms could ever achieve stable equilibrium. He considers the literature of duopoly stemming from Augustin Cournot (considered in Chapter 2) and including Joseph Bertrand and Francis Edgeworth's criticisms of the instability of the model. Hotelling then asserts that economic theory has failed to take notice of this characteristic of demand for individual firms (that is, their demand curves are not perfectly elastic) (p. 44). He concedes that these cases violate the law of one price but notes that: 'the doctrine is only valid' where the commodity is standardized and its market is a single point in space (pp. 44–5). As a consequence, '[b]etween the perfect competition and monopoly of theory lie the actual cases' (p. 44).

It is at this point that he introduces the justly famous 'Hotelling's model' which uses physical location as an analogue of the various types of actual product differentiation. The mathematical details of the model, being well known, need not delay us. More important are the results derivable from the model. The first is that the model converges to a stable equilibrium in a manner similar to Cournot's. Hotelling also notes both the possibility of implicit collusion among the duopolists to emulate the monopoly outcome and the inherent instability of such understandings. One important point of difference that Hotelling asserts is that prices will never stay below the equilibrium, contradicting Bertrand's assertion that prices tend to the competitive level in duopoly.

The other result in Hotelling's paper runs contrary to the conventional result that differentiation driven by the pursuit of profit results in too much product variety. Instead, where relocation is costless, Hotelling notes the tendency of suppliers to cluster, offering insufficient differentiation of products. In this result, he explicitly extends the analysis to product varieties as well as physical location (p. 54). Hotelling's model represents a substantial innovation in industrial organization by developing a method of incorporating product differentiation in modeling of competition.

Hotelling's subsequent work was largely concerned with the proper mathematical specification of demand systems. It is in this context that his work in marginal cost pricing arose. In his 1938 article, 'The general welfare in relation to problems of taxation and of railway and utility rates', Hotelling first demonstrates that any departure from marginal cost pricing results in a decrease in general welfare or what he refers to as 'dead loss' (p. 254). This is coupled with the formula that was subsequently applied by Arnold Harberger in calculating the welfare costs of monopoly. Following a discussion of the case of pure monopoly (a bridge), he discusses railroad rates and their relationship (or actually their lack of a relationship) with marginal costs and vigorously argues the merits of adopting marginal cost based tariffs (p. 264).

In the following section, he recognizes that marginal cost depends on the extent of capacity utilization of a facility. He further suggests that tariffs based on marginal costs ought to include a surcharge when capacity is approached. In modern terms these capacity surcharges are recognized as a component of the marginal costs of the services. Given the high level of mathematical sophistication Hotelling's work usually displays, it is surprising that he did not determine the appropriate welfare-maximizing surcharge.

A final section of this remarkable paper notes that the criterion for socially worthwhile investment in facilities with large fixed costs is different from the conventional breakeven constraints. Instead, he specifies that: '*if some distribution of the burden is possible such that everyone concerned is better off than without the new investment, then there is a prima facie case for making the investment*' (p. 267, emphasis in original). His final passionate argument for marginal cost pricing is:

> it will be better to operate the railroads for the benefit of living human beings, while letting dead men and dead investments rest quietly in their graves, and to establish a system of rates and services calculated to assure the most efficient operation. When the question arises of building new railroads, or new major industries of any kind, or of scrapping the old, we shall face, not a historical, but a mathematical and economic problem. The question then will be whether the aggregate of the generalized surpluses … is likely to be great enough to cover the anticipated cost of the new investment. (p. 269)

Most relevant publications

(1925), 'A general mathematical theory of depreciation', *Journal of the American Statistical Association*, **20**(151), September, 340–53.
(1929), 'Stability in competition', *Economic Journal*, **39**(153), March, 41–57.
(1931), 'The economics of exhaustible resources', *Journal of Political Economy*, **39**(2), April, 137–75.
(1938), 'The general welfare in relation to problems of taxation and of railway and utility rates', *Econometrica*, **6**(3), July, 242–69.
(1939), 'The relation of prices to marginal costs in an optimum system', *Econometrica*, **7**(2), April, 151–5.

E. EDWARD S. MASON

William G. Shepherd

Innovations
Mason led in establishing the underlying 'structure–behavior–performance' logic of the field, and in defining effective competition; also he led the creation of detailed 'industry studies'.

Personal history

Born 1899, Clinton, IA, USA; died 2002.

Degrees BA University of Kansas, 1919; MA, PhD Harvard University, 1920, 1925.

Principal position Professor of Economics, Harvard University, Cambridge, MA, USA, 1936–69.

Other President, American Economic Association, 1962.

From the 1930s to the mid-1950s, Mason presided at Harvard as a leader shaping the field. He interpreted the new oligopoly theory of E.H. Chamberlin and Joan Robinson, as well as the ongoing public debates about market power. Mason explained and helped to establish the 'structure–behavior–performance' logic of causation, in defining market power and its effects. He also developed the criteria for effective competition and monopoly's impacts, in responding to J.M. Clark's idea of 'workable competition'.

His 1939 paper, on 'Price and production policies of large-scale enterprises', is regarded as a landmark, if not the foundation itself, in the creation of the field of industrial organization.

Always an applied thinker and clear writer, Mason developed the 'industry study' approach to the field, creating and leading a group of young scholars who produced detailed studies of specific industries. In the 1940s and 1950s at Harvard, the group eventually included Joe S. Bain (petroleum), William Nicholls (tobacco), Jesse W. Markham (rayon and fertilizer), Merton J. Peck (aluminum), Richard E. Caves (airlines), Samuel Loescher (cement), Richard Tennant (cigarettes) and James W. McKie (metal cans).

Mason stressed the importance of antitrust policies in shaping industries; also that the policies were open to industrial pressures. The leading companies, after all, were determined to prevent government limits and to defeat the government agencies' every case against them. He discussed the repeated waves of self-interested advocacy for bigness in business (in the 1890s, 1920s and 1950s), which claimed that very large businesses were inherently superior to small-scale firms and unruly competition. These advantages of bigness supposedly justified reducing or even eliminating antitrust enforcement. Those waves have, of course, continued since then and will probably recur into the indefinite future.

Most relevant publications

(1939), 'Price and production policies of large-scale enterprises', *American Economic Review*, March, 64–74.
(1949), 'The current state of the monopoly problem', *Harvard Law Review*, June, 1265–85.
(1959), *Economic Concentration and the Monopoly Problem*, Cambridge, MA: Harvard University Press.

12. The 1940s and 1950s

A. JOSEPH A. SCHUMPETER

F.M. Scherer

Innovations
The impact of technological innovation on economic growth, the key role of entrepreneurship in innovation, the relationship between innovation and business cycles, market structural conditions favorable to innovation, and 'creative destruction'.

Personal history

Born 1883, Triesch (now Třešt), Moravia; died 1950.

Degree Doctor of jurisprudence, University of Vienna, 1906.

Principal position Professor of Economics, Harvard University, 1932–50.

Other Attorney, Cairo, Egypt, 1907–08; dozent, University of Czernowitz, Moldavia, 1909–11; professor, University of Graz, Austria, 1911–18; State Secretary of Finance, Austria, 1918–19; bank president, 1920–24; professor, University of Bonn, Germany, 1925–32.

By the time Joseph Schumpeter was a university student during the first decade of the twentieth century, enormous strides had been achieved in articulating the theory of general competitive market equilibrium. But the theory, summarized and evaluated meticulously in papers written during Schumpeter's doctoral studies and his Habilitation Monograph, was essentially static. It provided no satisfactory explanation of how real income per capita had advanced so dramatically in industrialized nations during the nineteenth century. Filling this void was the goal he set after taking his first teaching posiiton at Czernowitz. The result, his *Theory of Economic Development* (1912, 1934) was critically acclaimed throughout the economically literate world.

Schumpeter begins his analysis, carried through without the use of formal mathematics, by focusing upon equilibria changing only gradually – a condition he called the 'circular flow'. What jolts economies out of essentially static equilibria is innovation – significant and discontinuous change in the quality of goods or production processes, or the opening of new markets, or the tapping of new supply sources, or new forms of business organization. Important innovations simultaneously create surplus value or rents for the firms implementing them while undermining the profitability of competitors mired in the circular flow. As the innovator succeeds, other firms imitate it in an increasing 'swarm', propelling a burst of new capital investment and the erosion of temporarily elevated prices, with consumers as the ultimate beneficiaries. In Schumpeter's original view, success in one important innovation created preconditions favorable to other innovations. The clustering of innovations and the investment they precipitated led in the aggregate to business-cycle upswings. In a later (1939) book, Schumpeter elaborated on this macroeconomic theme, recognizing among other things how differences in market structure could lead to aberrations in business-cycle phenomena.

In his *Theory of Economic Development*, Schumpeter sharply distinguished the role of entrepreneurship – undertaking 'new combinations' – from invention, narrowly defined, and the provision of risk capital to finance innovations. The entrepreneur was the central actor in his scheme of economic development – a captain of industry type who departed radically from accepted technological or organization norms. Entrepreneurs were distinctive in recognizing the opportunity for new combinations and making the key strategic decisions to act upon them. Their motivation was profit: they innovated to tap latent profit opportunities. In this sense the central feature of Schumpeter's scheme of economic development was profit-seeking behavior. And since it was driven by the desire for profit, the economic changes to which it led were endogenous, quite different from inventions that appeared like manna from heaven through scientific advances or a stroke of genius. As Schumpeter emphasized (1934 translation, p. 88):

> Economic leadership in particular must hence be distinguished from 'invention.' As long as they are not carried into practice, inventions are economically irrelevant. And to carry any improvement into effect is a task entirely different from the inventing of it, and a task, moreover, requiring entirely different kinds of aptitudes. ... It is, therefore, not advisable, and it may be downright misleading, to stress the element of invention as much as many writers do.

In Schumpeter's 1912 schema, innovations tended to come from firms outside the circular flow – that is, from new and initially small firms, not from established enterprises. Schumpeter recognized the existence of monopolies and trusts but considered them too hidebound to innovate. That successful innovations often gave rise to monopoly positions, and that the lure of monopoly profits motivated entrepreneurs, was clearly recognized in his original 1912 book. But in a 1942 book written for a more popular audience, which among other things quantified the substantial gains in real per capita income resulting from technological progress, he changed his view radically. Innovation, and especially high-technology innovation, had become so complex and expensive that large-scale oligopolistic enterprises enjoyed powerful advantages in undertaking it by virtue of their financial resources, their command over superior talent, the scale economies they realized, and the stable platform their positions provided for planning and investing in long-range schemes. As he concluded (1942, p. 106):

> What we have got to accept is that [the large-scale establishment or unit of control] has come to be the most powerful engine of that progress and in particular of the long-run expansion of total output not only in spite of, but to a considerable extent through, this strategy which looks so restrictive when viewed in the individual case and from the individual point in time. In this respect perfect competition is not only impossible but inferior, and has no title to being set up as a model of ideal efficiency. It is hence a mistake to base the theory of government regulation of industry on the principle that big business should be made to work as the respective industry would work in perfect competition.

Nor was Schumpeter fearful of adverse consequences that might come from tolerating or encouraging monopolies to achieve more rapid economic progress. Monopoly positions themselves were subject to an ever-present threat of displacement in what he called 'the process of creative destruction'. He argued (ibid., p. 84):

> But in capitalist reality as distinguished from its textbook picture, it is not [price competition] which counts but the competition from the new commodity, the new technology, the new source of supply, the new type of organization (the large-scale unit of control for instance) – competition which commands a decisive cost or quality advantage and which strikes not at the margins of the profits and the outputs of the existing firms but at their foundations and their very lives. This kind of competition is as much more effective than the other as a bombardment is in comparison with forcing a door ...

Schumpeter's conceptual innovation stimulated a swarm of studies by economists attempting through mathematical theory, statistical analysis, and case studies to determine what kind of market structure was in fact most conducive to economic progress. The weight of the evidence appears to support a conclusion that Schumpeter overstated the advantages of large-scale enterprises and monopolistic positions. But not all have been persuaded, and some nations – especially many leading European nations – remained in the decades following the Second World War committed to industrial policies stressing the cultivation of 'national champion' enterprises able to hold their own technologically against what were perceived to be more powerful corporations based in the large US market.

Although Schumpeter viewed modern capitalism as a spectacular success in generating economic growth, he was skeptical that it could survive. On one hand, the increasingly formal organization of corporate research and development laboratories would so routinize innovation that the Schumpeterian entrepreneur's essential function would be undermined. On the other hand, business cycles, including depressions, unemployment and considerable inequality of income were seen as natural concomitants to the processes of capitalistic growth. Intellectuals whose position owed much to capitalist prosperity would react to these evils by successfully advocating steeply progressive taxation, the support of labor unions, price controls, bank regulation, antitrust and a host of other government interventions that demoralized the remaining cadre of entrepreneurs and made them less willing to take risks. Writing in his 1942 book following the traumatic experience of the Great Depression of the 1930s and when the wartime US economy was tightly controlled from Washington, and again in his presidential address to the American Economic Association (1950), he feared (he expressly disclaimed predicting) that the consequence of these developments would be a march into some form of socialism. On this he has, at least thus far, been more wrong than right. But others of more conservative persuasion than the author might disagree.

Most relevant publications

(1912), *Theorie der wirtschaftlichen Entwicklung*, Berlin: Duncker & Humblot; English version translated by Redvers Opie, *The Theory of Economic Development*, Cambridge, MA: Harvard University Press, 1934.

(1939), *Business Cycles*, New York: McGraw-Hill.

(1942), *Capitalism, Socialism, and Democracy*, New York: Harper.

(1950), 'The march into socialism', American Economic Association Presidential Address, *American Economic Review*, **40**, May, 446–56.

(1954), *History of Economic Analysis* (edited by Elizabeth Boody Schumpeter), Oxford: Oxford University Press.

B. MORRIS A. ADELMAN

William G. Shepherd

Innovations

He explained that price discrimination will often intensify competition, both by horizontal and by vertical effects; he showed that industrial concentration scarcely rose during the 1930s–1950s; he clarified the dimensions and effects of vertical integration; and he analyzed the world oil industry after 1960.

Personal history

Born 1917, New York, NY, USA.

Degree PhD Harvard University, 1948.

Principal position Professor of Economics, MIT, Cambridge, MA, 1960–.

Especially in the 1950s, Morris Adelman led the analysis of vertical practices and structures, as well as the more complex pricing processes. Always a thorough but lively writer, he noted forcefully in 1949 that price discrimination could be a crucial device driving real competition forward, as competitors make selective price cuts in order to attract sales. This pricing device attacks monopoly-affected prices, driving them down. He stressed the dynamic nature of the process, in contrast to the static inverse-elasticity structure of discriminatory prices set by monopolists.

In 1954, Adelman showed that US industrial concentration had scarcely been rising since the 1930s; if at all, then only at a 'glacial pace'. The finding countered Karl Marx's prediction in *Das Kapital* that capitalism would become increasingly concentrated, reaching extreme levels.

In 1955 Adelman published a major restatement of the economics of vertical integration, including the problems of measuring it reliably.

In 1959, he published a comprehensive defense of the A&P against antitrust claims of 'unfair competition'. A&P had led the rise of the new supermarket grocery chains, from the 1930s on. It used lower prices (mostly based on requiring lower input prices from its suppliers) – in addition to convenience and the wider array of choice – to defeat the traditional small, local grocery stores. Using thorough and detailed evidence, Adelman argued that A&P's lower retail prices largely reflected true cost advantages, not anti-competitive pricing and unfair cost advantages. Therefore, he said, A&P was functioning in pro-competitive and pro-efficiency ways. A&P's victory in the case led not only to a massive spread of supermarket chains but also to the rapid growth of discount chains in many other retail sectors.

Adelman then turned in the 1960s to the world petroleum and gas industry, doing his most extensive and sustained research during the next several decades. Among many specific topics, he analyzed the opposed fundamental tendencies that determined oil prices:

increasing physical depletion raised the costs of crude oil. But that could be offset by the increasing knowledge of geology and engineering, plus improved technology.

Most relevant publications

(1949), 'Effective competition and the antitrust laws', *Harvard Law Review*, **62** 1289–350.
(1955), 'Vertical integration', in George J. Stigler (ed.), *Business Concentration and Price Policy*, Princeton, NJ: Princeton University Press, pp. 281–322.
(1959), A&P: Cost–Price Behavior and Public Policy, Cambridge, MA: Harvard University Press.
(1972), *The World Petroleum Market*, Baltimore, MD: Johns Hopkins University Press.

C. JOHN KENNETH GALBRAITH

William G. Shepherd

Innovations

He advanced in 1952 the phenomenon of countervailing power; he noted oligopoly's benefits in promoting rapid innovation, and also its compliance to wartime price controls; and he stressed in the 1960s the links of big business and military overproduction.

Personal history

Born 1908, Iona Station, Ontario, Canada.

Degrees BA Ontario Agricultural College, Guelph, 1931; PhD (Agricultural Economics) University of California, Berkeley, 1934.

Principal positions Professor of Economics, Harvard University, Cambridge, MA, USA 1946–75; Paul M. Warburg Professor 1975–.

Other Deputy Administrator, US Office of Price Administration, 1941–43; Director, US Strategic Bombing Survey, 1945–46; US Ambassador to India, 1961–63. Chairman, Americans for Democratic Action, 1967–69; President, American Economic Association, 1972; President, American Academy of Arts and Letters, 1984–87.

One of America's most provocative and interesting economists, Galbraith began as an agricultural economist from Canada and then, improbably, became leader of the US effort to control prices during the Second World War. Drawing on that experience as the head of the Office of Price Administration, Galbraith noted in a 1952 book that high concentration would help price controllers to put an effective lid on prices in oligopoly industries, which were dominated by only a few firms. His officials were able to control the price of tight ologopolies much more easily than the prices of highly competitive industries, which are fragmented among many small, unruly firms.

In 1952 Galbraith published *American Capitalism: The Concept of Countervailing Power*, which found that both efficiency and innovation would occur when high horizontal concentration faced strong vertical monopsony power. This amounted to praise for tight oligopoly, which was then under attack for its collusive tendencies. Tight oligopolists would be able to innovate rapidly because they were large enough to reach large-scale economies of innovation. But they were also under competitive pressure from each other, and they were under vertical pressure from their few large customers, such as large supermarket chains or other discounters.

That countervailing power would also nullify any attempts by tight oligopolies to raise their prices. Powerful discount retailers (a leading recent example is Wal-Mart) would neutralize and prevent the sellers' attempts to raise prices.

Under criticism, Galbraith conceded in 1954 that countervailing power would not always automatically arise to nullify the market power of large sellers. But Galbraith's idea had strengths, it gave more weight to the older concept of monopsony, and it remains a significant part of the literature.

Galbraith took a broad view of industrial power, urging that market power could arise outside the specific technical market conditions of high market shares and concentration ratios. Also, he was disturbed by the post-Second World War rise of large US military and industrial interests. There, he said, was very large power indeed. He extended in detail the analysis of a large interlocking system of the government and the Pentagon, the array of weapons-producing companies, and leading university research interests.

Most relevant publications

(1952), *A Theory of Price Control*, Cambridge, MA: Harvard University Press.
(1952), *American Capitalism: The Concept of Countervailing Power*, Boston, MA: Houghton Mifflin.
(1967), *The New Industrial State*, Boston: MA, Houghton Mifflin.

D. ALFRED E. KAHN

William G. Shepherd

Innovations

He proposed 'fair competition' as a behavioral standard for antitrust. His landmark textbook (1971) restated and expanded the economic content of regulation and deregulation. He chaired the New York Regulatory Commission (1974–77), applying thorough economics; he quickly abolished US airline regulation in 1978 (as Chair of the Civil Aeronautics Board), and he later joined at length in debates about the deregulation of many sectors.

Personal history

Born 1917, Paterson, NJ, USA.

Degrees BA, MA New York University, 1936, 1937; PhD Yale University, 1942.

Principal positions Professor of Economics, and Dean, Cornell University, Ithaca, NY, USA, 1947–89.

Other Chairman, NY State Public Service Commission; Chairman, Council on Wage and Price Stability; Adviser to President Carter on Inflation, 1978–80.

Kahn has been a restless and creative encyclopedist, in applying new thinking and evidence to many of the most important industrial, antitrust and regulatory topics. Both the intellectual breadth of his interests and the time-length of his pioneering interval have been extraordinary.

His earliest work clarified the economics of patents. He also made early industry studies on cartels in the chemical industries.

Then in 1954 he proposed (with Joel B. Dirlam) a complicated and nuanced behavioral standard of 'fair competition' for antitrust, to replace the traditional structural evidence of market power and anti-competitive actions. The factual tests for 'fair competition' proved to be difficult to define and apply (like those of J.M. Clark's 'workable competition'). Instead, structural standards prevailed until the 1980s.

In 1959 (writing with Melvin G. de Chazeau), Kahn showed that vertical integration in the oil industry could reduce competition, but he did not recommend major policy actions. He spent much of the 1960s absorbing the field of utility regulation, while working with AT&T and other firms as an expert.

This led to his comprehensive two-volume magnum opus on regulation (1970, 1971), which used economic analysis extensively to cut through the surface patterns and details. It was extremely well-timed for two large purposes, which helped to make it a landmark for its impact as well as its brilliance and comprehensiveness. First, it summed up the lessons of utility regulation after the 1920s–1960s golden era of regulatory activity. Second, it crystallized and explored the intensifying economic critiques of regulation in a wide range of industries. But Kahn avoided the trap of saying that deregulation was easy. He showed in exhaustive detail that to deregulate – to replace regulation with fully effective competition – had its own array of difficulties. His prescient analysis helped frame the stubborn competitive troubles that deregulation has faced in a swath of sectors (such as airlines, railroads, telecommunications, electricity and water).

Kahn was both bold and clear about main points, and also subtle and very detailed about the more nuanced issues. He used core microeconomic theory, but with a deft touch for real conditions and for policies' genuine effects. On the important topic of marginal-cost pricing, he stressed that the powerful efficiency gains could be large, in theory. But he also discussed thoroughly its practical difficulties, both in this treatise and in many later writings and testimony about deregulation.

Kahn also pioneered in performing actual regulation and deregulation in important real-world sectors. Previously, few economists had been appointed to regulatory commissions; usually only lawyers and politicians were appointed. But Kahn was made chair of the New York regulatory commission during 1976–77, and he pushed it to make extensive use of sound economics and to remove unnecessary controls.

Then he was made chairman of the Civil Aeronautics Commission in 1977, with support for decisive actions to deregulate. By 1978 he had taken a complicated series of formal and behind-the-scenes actions that succeeded in achieving the commission's outright abolition. That brought an immediate explosion of competitive influx and price-cutting. Later, he inveighed against backsliding (by permitting rigid pricing and competition-suppressing mergers) that reduced the competition.

On the key related topics of price discrimination and predatory actions, Kahn further enriched the debate. He clarified discrimination's efficiency role for static conditions, but he was also alert to its anti-competitive impact, when dominant airlines used it to eliminate small rivals by deep price cuts. He showed repeatedly in testimony and writings that 'pin-point' price cuts were eliminating small firms and newcomers.

After 1978, Kahn was influential in pressing for the deregulation of trucking and the railroads in 1980. After 1980, he wrote and testified about telecommunications and other sectors.

His 1971 treatise raised the standards for economic coherence and clarity in subsequent debates about regulation and deregulation. He stressed valid economic analysis and detailed practical judgments of policies. Many of his judgments in specific industries and policies were eventually controversial, in the nature of these complex issues. But Kahn's major work enhanced and enriched the debates.

Most relevant publications

(1953), 'Standards for antitrust policy', *Harvard Law Review*, **67**, November, pp. 26–54.

(1954), *Fair Competition: The Law and Economics of Antitrust Policy* (with Joel B. Dirlam), Ithaca, NY: Cornell University Press.

(1959), with Melvin de Chazeau, *Integration and Competition in the Petroleum Industry*, New Haven, CT: Yale University Press.

(1970, 1971), *The Economics of Regulation*, 2 vols, New York: Wiley; republishd Cambridge, MA: MIT Press, 1988.

(1984), 'Kahn and the economist's hour', in Thomas McGraw (ed.), *Prophets of Regulation*, Cambridge, MA: Harvard University Press, ch. 7, pp. 222–99.

(1987), 'Current issues in telecommunications regulation: pricing' (with W.B. Shew), *Yale Journal on Regulation*, **4**, pp. 191–256.

(1998), *Letting Go: Deregulating the Process of Deregulation*, E. Lansing, MI: Michigan State University.

E. WALTER ADAMS

James A. Brock

Innovations

Empirical study of the structural foundations of economic and market power, their adverse consequences in a free society, and the public policies required to combat them.

Personal history

Born 1922, Vienna, Austria; died 1998.

Degrees BA Brooklyn College, 1942; PhD, Yale University, 1947.

Principal positions Professor, Distinguished Professor, and President, Michigan State University, 1947–1992.

Other Consultant and counsel, US House and Senate Small Business Committees, 1950–56; member, US Attorney General's National Committee to Study the Antitrust Laws, 1953–55; Consultant, US Senate Judiciary Committee, 1959–62; presidential appointee, US Advisory Commission on International Education and Cultural Affairs, 1961–69; Visiting Professor, Falkenstein Seminar, Frankfurt, Germany, University of Paris, and University of Ancona; R.J. Reynolds Professor of Economics, Wake Forest University; Vernon Taylor Professor of Economics, Trinity University (TX); Expert testimony before congressional committees, 1949–90; President, American Association of University Professors, 1972–74.

The unifying innovation and contribution of Walter Adams's work is his extensively documented contention that the competitively structured market plays a vital role in a free society, not only by promoting good economic performance narrowly construed (efficiency, innovativeness) but, more importantly, as a system of checks and balances for regulating economic decision-making and guarding against the abuse of economic decision making power in a democratic society.

To perform these vital tasks, Adams showed that the private market must be competitively structured, comprising no undue concentration, no excessive corporate size, and no artificial barriers to new competitors. He contended that these structural prerequisites were neither 'automatic' nor immutable but, instead, require deliberate antitrust enforcement to achieve and sustain. The paramount challenge, as he saw it, was to 'make competition work'. This emphasis also shaped his analysis of American antitrust policy and his criticisms of its failure to be structurally focused on the goal of rooting out existing concentrations of private power (through monopoly and oligopoly policy), as well as preventing such concentrations from arising in the first place (through a preventive policy against mergers and acquisitions). Adams also showed how private concentrations of economic power are both the cause, and the effect, of government policies, rather than determined by any dictates of modern technology and, further, that the economic problems they engender require structural remedies aimed at fostering competitive market structures. As a corollary, his publications and addresses forcefully reminded the economics profession of the importance of taking seriously the manifold problems caused by concentrations of private market power.

This emphasis emerged early in Adams's career, when he served as staff member and economic consultant to Senate and House committees investigating concentration in major American industries. In this capacity he produced congressional reports exposing the monopolistic and cartelistic relationships between private firms and government regulatory agencies in the airline and trucking fields, and called for paring back such counterproductive, anti-competitive regulation long before this position became a mainstream view in the economics profession. These and other studies culminated in a 1955 book, *Monopoly in America: The Government as Promoter*, published with Horace Gray.

Another notable report he produced during this period was a painstakingly detailed exposé of the evolution and operation of the international oil cartel over the first half of the twentieth century (a Senate Small Business Committee report considered so explosive that its public availability was generally suppressed for two decades). He returned to the oil industry during the energy crises of the 1970s, advocating that the vertical market power of the major oil companies was the linchpin for their industry-wide control; that the integration of the oil giants into alternative energies institionalized a profound conflict of economic interest regarding the optimal development of each energy source; and recommending that both types of integration should be structurally dissolved.

On the legislative policy front, in 1951 he drafted a new antitrust statute for the House Judiciary Committee which called for the study and dissolution of dominant firms unable to defend their market dominance on the basis of proven superior economic performance – a proposal later taken up by the White House Task Force on Antitrust Policy (Neal Report) in 1968; Senator Phillip Hart's proposed Industrial Reorganization Act of 1972; and 'no-fault' monopoly policies propounded during the late 1970s. He also long advocated a 'cap and spin' policy toward large mergers: Fortune 500 firms making large acquisitions should be required to spin off viable commercial operations equal in financial size to those they desired to acquire, in order to prevent mergers from continuing to serve as the primary means for concentrating control of American industry.

Another Adams innovation was editing a collection of case studies of major industries, *The Structure of American Industry*, which was first published in 1950, subsequently went through nine editions (plus two recent editions by a co-author), and became a mainstay for industrial organization economists and university courses in industrial economics. Adams's objective was to provide a diverse, continually updated collection of industry studies, contributed by leading economists in each field, as a way of offering a real-world laboratory in which to assess the consequences of varying market structures for market conduct and, ultimately, for economic performance and public policy. An ancillary purpose, he wrote in the preface to numerous editions of the book, was to provide an antidote to the economist's proclivity for abstract, mathematical model building.

During the 1960s Adams contested the claim, most notably asserted by John Kenneth Galbraith, that the giant firm inhabiting a highly-concentrated industry was foreordained by the economics of modern technology. Through a number of publications and in a remarkable Senate hearing organized around a debate between these two intellectual combatants, Adams provided factual evidence refuting this faith in the virtues of economic bigness. Perhaps most famously, he and Joel Dirlam demonstrated in a landmark study that organizational giantism and oligopoly concentration in the American steel industry had failed to promote either invention or innovation and, instead, had rendered the largest US steel produers inefficient, technologically backward, and vulnerable to competition from abroad. Adams also published a major paper in the *Quarterly Journal of Economics* (1953) disputing Galbraith's thesis that countervailing power between buyer and seller (and between employer and employee) would automatically emerge to protect society from abuses of market power; in later publications, he demonstrated how vertically opposing power blocs coalesce with, rather than countervail, each other, including the case of management and organized labor in the regulated industries, as well as via management–labor coalitions joining together to successfully lobby for government restraints on foreign competition in automobiles and steel. In a related vein, Adams disputed the Schumpeterian claim that monopoly and oligopoly were economically desirable and inevitable, showing through a number of industry studies how monopolists and oligopolists were able to construct storm shelters to shield themselves from Joseph Schumpeter's 'gales of creative destruction'.

Throughout the remainder of his career, during the 1980s and 1990s, Adams continued to refine, expand and further document these positions, particularly in refuting the growing *laissez-faire* orientation of the economics profession and the rise of the 'Chicago school' (ironically, the university where Adams first enrolled in graduate school before his studies were interrupted by combat service in the Second World War). He continued to document how the existence of market power contradicted abstract claims concerning the beneficent operation of markets – how poorly performing oligopolies could lobby government for protection from the consequences of their deficient performance, including the capacity of collapsing corporate giants like Chrysler to obtain government bailouts rather than submit to the discipline of the private marketplace as *laissez-faire* advocates assume they do. He was equally critical of 'industrial policy' proposals emanating from liberal quarters: these too, he maintained, were fatally flawed by virtue of their failure to explicitly recognize the deleterious consequences of the concentrations of economic power they would sanction and encourage. Adams continued to analyze these and related issues and challenges in his uniquely far-reaching historic and philosophical way, ranging from medieval statecraft and the 'gilded age' in America, to the European Theater of the Absurd.

His lifetime of work, analysis and contemplation of these issues culminated in a book, *The Bigness Complex: Industry, Labor, and Government in the American Economy*, published in 1987 with James Brock (a second edition of which was issued in 2004). Two of Adams's dissertation students also co-edited a collection of his seminal publications in 1991, *Antitrust, the Market, and the State: The Contributions of Walter Adams*. One of these, Kenneth Elzinga, perhaps best captured the innovations of Walter Adams in observing that he uniquely combined the economics of Henry Simon, the politics of Paul Douglas, the philosophy of John Dewey and the jurisprudence of Louis Brandeis. Throughout his professional life, Adams prodded industrial organization economists to expand their horizons, and to deepen their empirical analyses, in order to appreciate that the field of industrial economics encompasses the transcending challenges of maintaining an economically efficient and free society.

Most relevant publications

(1950–95), *The Structure of American Industry*, 9 edns, London: Macmillan and Englewood Cliffs, NJ: Prentice Hall.
(1953), 'Competition, monopoly, and countervailing power', *Quarterly Journal of Economics*, November, pp. 464–92.
(1955), *Monopoly in America: The Government as Promoter*, London: Macmillan.
(1958), 'The role of competition in the regulated industries', *American Economic Review*, May, pp. 427–43.
(1966), 'Big steel, invention, and innovation', *Quarterly Journal of Economics*, May, pp. 167–89.
(1971), *The Test*, London: Macmillan.
(1977), 'Vertical divestiture of the petroleum majors: an affirmative case', *Vanderbilt Law Review*, November, pp. 1115–47.
(1986), 'The "new learning" and the euthanasia of antitrust', *California Law Review*, October, pp. 1515–66.
(1987), *The Bigness Complex: Industry, Labor and Government in the American Economy*, New York: Pantheon (2nd edn, 2004, Stanford, CA: Stanford University Press).
(1989), *Dangerous Pursuits: Mergers and Acquisitions in the Age of Wall Street*, New York: Pantheon.
(1990), 'The Sherman Act and the economic power problem', *Antitrust Bulletin*, Spring, pp. 1–34.
(1991), *Antitrust Economics on Trial: A Dialogue on the New Laissez-Faire*, Princeton, NJ: Princeton University Press.
(1991), 'Pareto optimality and antitrust policy: the old Chicago and the new learning', *Southern Economic Journal*, July, pp. 1–14.
(1991), *Antitrust, the Market, and the State: The Contributions of Walter Adams*, Armonk, NY: M.E. Sharpe.
(1993), *Adam Smith Goes to Moscow: A Dialogue on Radical Reform*, Princeton, NJ: Princeton University Press.
(1996), 'Predation, "rationality", and judicial somnambulance', *University of Cincinnati Law Review*, Spring, pp. 811–78.

F. JOE S. BAIN

Richard E. Caves

Innovations

Concept and measurement of entry barriers; structure–conduct (behavior)–performance paradigm; testing hypotheses in cross-section.

Personal history

Born 1912, Spokane, WA, USA; died 1993.

Degrees BA, UCLA, 1935; MA, PhD Harvard University, 1939, 1940.

Principal positions Assistant Professor, Associate Professor, and Professor of Economics, University of California, Berkeley, 1939–75.

Joe S. Bain made major contributions to the substance of industrial organization (IO) and to its empirical research methods. His work shaped the research frontier of empirical IO for several decades, and its mark remains readily evident in undergraduate textbooks. His single most prominent substantive contribution was the concept of barriers to entry (Bain, 1956). A review of its theoretical and empirical content conveniently leads to Bain's other contributions.[1]

Barriers to entry: concept and market equilibrium

The competitiveness of a market, Bain proposed, depends not just on the number of sellers (and buyers) actually present but also the stock of potential entrants (the 'general condition of entry'). This stock was regarded as a queue fronted by the potential competitor needing the smallest departure of market price and quantity from pure competition to induce it to enter. The potential entrants might be homogeneous, or they might control heterogeneous assets that would favor them in varying ways and degrees as potentially profitable entrants and thereby place them in the queue. The structural bases for entry barriers clearly suggest the types of assets that could push their owners toward the head of the queue of entrants, but the factors that determine the queue's ordering empirically were pursued only much later. Bain presumed that the condition of entry into an industry is structural and stable over time, implying that its state today would rest on the same factors that governed entry in the past. The current condition would then be correlated with the market's number of incumbents. An industry with numerous actual competitors would likely face easy entry (many candidates subject to little or no disadvantage). More important, highly concentrated incumbents would likely face an entry queue limited in numbers and with successive members subject to increasing net disadvantages. The door was opened for strategic interdependence between incumbents and entrants (discussed subsequently).

How might incumbents' actions be affected by the supply of potential entrants? If incumbents are numerous, they make independent price or output decisions, and something approaching pure competition should prevail in the short run. Entry may or may not be induced, but that expected consequence does not affect individual incumbents' actions. If incumbents are few and recognize their interdependence, the short-run policies they select should take account of whether or not entry is induced. (Cooperating oligopolists need consensus on the condition of entry as well as the usual requisites for coordinating their own actions.)

Looking back after the game-theory revolution, one is pulled up short by the assumption that entry is fully determined by the incumbents' current price (plus structural variables). Bain (1956, p. 97) recognized that entrants' conjectures need not depend in any simple way on incumbents' actions currently observed by potential entrants. In a quest for plausible patterns of interdependence between incumbents and entrants, however, he proposed that an entrant might focus on two: that incumbents keep their prices constant following entry (and reduce their outputs); and that incumbents sustain their outputs (and reduce prices) when entry occurs. In the absence of other salient conditions, Bain proposed, these cases should bracket entrants' conjectures and thus define the opportunities for incumbents to affect the likelihood of entry.[2] Whatever the potential entrant's conjecture, its decision to enter embraces adjusting the variables in its control (such as plant scale and level of sales-promotion outlays) so as to maximize its expected post-entry profits (Bain, 1956, pp. 55, 133).

That brings us to the alternative short-run market outcomes that determine whether entry will be induced. It is effectively impeded when incumbents can profitably forgo some short-run profits in order to maintain a price/output choice that will deter entry, obtaining their reward in higher profits in subsequent periods. This is the 'limit price' policy choice. The limiting case of effectively impeded entry occurs when the short-run monopoly price/output fails to attract entrants ('blockaded entry'). Entry is ineffectively impeded when short-run monopoly profits more than offset the incumbents loss of expected future profits due to entry. Effectively impeded entry is more likely, the higher is the structural disadvantage of the least disfavored potential entrant, since short-run monopoly profits then cannot much exceed the profits that flow from impeding entry. Impeding entry also is encouraged by an inelastic supply of potential entrants – those a few places back in the queue are substantially more disfavored. Conversely, entry tends to be ineffectively impeded when entry barriers are low and the supply of entrants elastic, so that short-run monopoly profits ('grab the bundle and run') much exceed short-run entry-deterring profits.[3] There remains, though, the possibility that entry is effectively impeded despite low barriers because competition among incumbents keeps price close to incumbents' marginal costs. Bain recognized but did not stress that ineffectively impeded entry is a transient state of the market (ibid., p. 24). Entry will occur, likely to raise industry output and lower price, deterring further entry and leading to a long-run equilibrium.[4]

The model carries the implication that price can exceed marginal cost, a distortion that Bain evaluated using the marginal-cost level attained by the most efficient incumbent. This seems puzzling, since the standard equilibrium in a competitive industry calls for market price to be equal to the marginal cost of each active producers. The explanation is that Bain assumed away diseconomies of scale, so that any producer capable of attaining a low variable cost in a competitive market would expand output, displacing rivals with higher variable costs. This assumption is worth noting for its relevance to subsequent controversies with the Chicago school, which argued that monopoly profits (due to impeded entry) were being confused with rents to efficient producers who (because of diseconomies of scale) could not profitably take over the whole market. Clear identification of this source of difference could have spared a good deal of debate.

Barriers to entry: empirical measurement

The second major contribution of Bain's work on entry barriers lies in his painstaking empirical measurement of their height in a sample of 20 US manufacturing industries. While data from the US Census of Manufactures were used, the project relied heavily on information supplied by company executives via interviews and questionnaire responses. Pinning down each source of entry barriers required conceptual development as well as empirical digging. Of the three types of barriers that Bain identified, only scale economies had been widely recognized previously, and Bain (ibid., p. 61) noted tartly that previous positions on the extent of scale economies rested mainly on opinion rather than information. He did identify and accept a previous consensus on the typical form of the manufacturing firm's long-run average cost curve: increasing returns at small scales up to a minimum optimal scale, then constant costs over a substantial range of output levels. He took no firm position on the existence of diseconomies of large scale, but reported no evidence that actual manufacturing firms encounter them. In order to facilitate empirical measurement he characterized scale economies in an industry's long-run average costs by two parameters – minimum optimal scale expressed as a fraction of the size of the relevant market, and the proportional elevation of unit costs at operating scales smaller than minimum optimal scale. His direct estimates of scale economies from industry sources indicated varying heights of scale-economy entry barriers, but they did suggest that most US industries can achieve minimum optimal scales in production with a moderately large number of competitors present in the market.[5]

Bain (ibid., p. 142) called the sources of entry barriers associated with product differentiation 'varied and complex', and his work indeed left behind a number of active controversies. That is understandable, since there was little preceding research on which to build, other than the model of monopolistic competition associated with the concept of product differentiation. Potential buyers of differentiated products have diverse tastes, and they incur costs of informing themselves about the match between their tastes and the product varieties available to serve them. These information costs can be high, because some differentiated goods are complex and/or purchased infrequently. For goods consumed in a social setting ('conspicuous consumption'), sources of hard information might hold little relevance for the buyer. Either way, Bain (ibid., pp. 66, 116, 143) argued, the incumbent firm enjoys the advantage that at least some potential consumers already know that its brand 'works', putting the entrant in an asymmetrical position of prompting consumers to try its untested brand. Schmalensee (1982) later formalized this effect. The entrant's best response to such a barrier is either to quote consumers a lower price than incumbents offering comparable quality or to undertake more extensive sales promotion. The product-differentiation barrier, Bain held, also had supply-side aspects. Scale economies might exist in advertising and other sales-promotion outlays; Bain (1956, pp. 65–6, 133) lamented his lack of empirical evidence on this point. Besides, the control of distribution via vertical integration or long-term contracts could augment entrants' costs or limit their options. Overall, Bain judged product differentiation to be the most important source of entry barriers in his sample of industries, and the source of the highest barriers.

Absolute-cost disadvantages comprise a group of factors that can elevate the average costs of an entrant above those of incumbents. Bain associated these with failures in input markets that forced entrants to pay more than incumbents. The clearest case involves an incumbent's monopolization of the input, such as control of limited sources of natural resources, or ownership of process patents. Bain mentioned other distortions, such as long-term contracts and trade secrets, but the foundations needed for evaluating long-term contracts were laid only two decades later (see von Weizsäcker, 1980). Bain also flagged access to capital as a source of absolute-cost barriers, and he identified it empirically with the size of the investment needed to install a plant of minimum optimal scale. Present-day models of capital-market imperfection might pin the disadvantage on other factors, such as the greater risk associated with the success of an entrant (relative to the continuation of an incumbent). In general the normative significance of absolute-cost barriers received only a light treatment from Bain and indeed is difficult to resolve today. For example, some absolute-cost disadvantages of entrants represent shake-down costs that the incumbents themselves previously incurred. The transient disadvantage then is presumptively not a distortion, but one might emerge in the tactical advantages that the incumbent can exploit while the entrant's shake-down is under way.

Indeed, this problem with absolute-cost barriers leads into the question of entry barriers' overall welfare significance. Neither Bain nor his principal critics took a comprehensive view of the welfare issues, causing the subsequent discussion to generate more heat than light (for an overview, see Geroski et al., 1990). Bain focused on entry barriers' effect on the industry's price–cost margin and the associated deadweight loss. This was generally predicted to grow with the height of the barriers, with exceptions for ineffectively impeded entry (which implied larger immediate and smaller subsequent losses) and for competition among incumbents too severe to lift the market price to entry-attracting levels. He recognized the welfare trade-off between allocative and productive efficiency invoked by large minimum optimal scales, but did not develop it formally. Stigler (1968) focused instead on the efficiency of the input transaction allegedly underlying the absolute-cost barrier. He defined an entry barrier as imposing some cost on an entrant that was not borne by the incumbent when it entered. This is clearly part of the net welfare outcome, but the effect of the absolute-cost barrier on the market equilibrium at the time of entry still matters. Entrant and incumbent could face identical entry costs, but the incumbent's *current* lower costs could still place the entrant at a competitive disadvantage. Or the entrant's elevated cost could stem from some (costly) investment by the incumbent in devising and installing an entry barrier.[6] The overall normative evaluation of entry barriers in an industry requires that differential or distorted entry costs, short- and long-run deadweight losses, and long-run effects on productive efficiency all be weighed in the balance.

The structure–conduct (behavior)–performance paradigm

Barriers to New Competition added entry barriers to the generally recognized market-structure elements – the number of sellers and the presence or absence of product differentiation. Bain went further, however, by developing the generalization that numerous exogenous or structural features of the market could influence the behavior of parties competing in it and thereby the normative properties of the resource allocation that resulted. The aspects of behavior importantly affected by structure are those believed to affect the normative outcome. The paradigm is implicitly defined backward: the relevant aspects of resource allocation in a market are those believed to affect economic welfare; the relevant aspects of conduct are those that affect the equilibrium values of these dimensions of resource allocation; and the salient aspects of structure are those that influence these patterns of conduct. Bain (1942) began assembling this structure under the influence of E.H. Chamberlin's *Theory of Monopolistic Competition* (1933), which focused on the key structural elements of the number of sellers and differentiation of the product. He continued with a short paper (Bain, 1950) that recognized the presence of several salient and independent dimensions of market performance and suggested hypotheses linking these dimensions of performance to elements of market structure that could theoretically influence them. Furthermore, his massive study of the Pacific Coast petroleum industry (Bain, 1944–47) was clearly organized around the framework.[7]

Thus, the idea was in place that theoretical models of imperfect competition could yield empirical predictions open to serious statistical testing.[8] This idea challenged the positions of nay-sayers who had previously blocked this rapprochement of theory and systematic empiricism. Price theorists observing the diversity of theoretical models of oligopoly had pronounced its market outcome to be indeterminate for lack of a one-size-fits-all model such as pure competition or pure monopoly. Empirical students of IO had nursed their own negativism in the view that performance outcomes in oligopoly could or did depend on managerial whim and random event rather than systematic and observable aspects of market behavior. Bain's paradigm invited us to line up market models with their competing assumptions clearly identified and stated as operational properties of market structure or performance. It also invited an emphasis on structural determinants of performance. J.M. Clark's (1940) approach to 'workable competition' in oligopoly had pressed for an independent role of conduct patterns, which Bain considered to be both endogenous (to market structure) and difficult to classify and distinguish empirically. In a later contribution Bain (1960) argued against the proposition that empirical patterns of price leadership (conduct) could be sorted into those based on the leader's information advantages (improving performance) and those implementing collusion (impairing performance).

The paradigm has been criticized for lacking the formal structure of a coherent theoretical model. That was never its purpose; rather, it supplied a framework in which models could be arrayed for comparison and their empirical predictions extracted for testing.

Statistical testing of hypotheses

Bain (1951) also pioneered the statistical testing in cross-section of hypotheses about the determinants of market performance. His approach (in hindsight) was the simplest and most obvious – to relate the (excess) profit rates of firms classified to a sample of manufacturing industries to a measure of the industries' oligopolistic structure: the share of industry shipments held by the eight largest firms ('concentration ratio'). His main empirical finding was that industries with eight-firm concentration less than 70 percent registered profit rates only 57 percent as high as their more concentrated brethren. The paper remains worth reading for the care taken with the data and formulation of the hypothesis. The maximum set of industries for which concentration (1935) and leading-firm profit (1936–1940) data were available numbered 149. These were screened to eliminate several classes of industries: those for which profit data were available from too few firms; those with regional submarkets (for which national concentration ratios would be inappropriate); and those with heterogeneous product lines and the leading firms diverse in the spread of their activities across those product lines. The surviving sample contained 42 industries. In the event, the key relationship confirmed for the 42 industries would have been rejected for the whole 149, if the screening had been omitted.

Exactly how should the hypothesis be formulated, and what controls should be employed? In evaluating Bain's decisions, we must recognize that in the 1940s multivariate ordinary least squares regression was a venture into the unknown. He chose to employ a simple test for significant mean differences between highly concentrated and less concentrated industries. He based this specification on a pattern evident in his data. However, in other writings Bain clearly accepted the idea that the likelihood of successful cooperation among oligopolists, declining with the number of rivals in the market, at some point drops to zero. The existence of a threshold hence no doubt struck him as theoretically plausible, although he did not push the point. He also checked the correlations between his profit and concentration measures (on the one hand) and other structural or quasi-structural variables: the industry's average firm size, capital intensity, durability of goods, type of buyers. The effects of averaging profit rates over time and across firms were considered.

In *Barriers to New Competition* (1956, ch. 7) he faced the problem of testing the joint effects on performance of entry barriers and seller concentration in a dataset with only 20 observations (industries). With characteristic caution he eschewed statistical tests and confined himself to cross-tabulations (pp. 197–8). Consistent with Bain (1951), these showed sharp breaks between 12 industries with 'high' and eight with 'low to moderate' concentration, and between five industries with 'very high' and 15 with 'moderate' or 'substantial' barriers. Mann (1966) subsequently performed the statistical test on an expanded version of Bain's dataset and rejected the null hypothesis. While one senses that cross-industry tests descended from Bain (1951) have now yielded up much of their value, they have provided a large and invaluable residue of findings about the associations among market structure, conduct and performance. They have taken us some distance toward dealing with another problem that Bain uncovered – the dependence of some aspects of structure (notably concentration) on other, more fundamental ones.

International differences

Bain (1966) made another contribution to empirical research strategies in IO by analyzing international differences in a given industry's national branches. Being able to observe (say) the cement industry as it is organized and performs in each of a number of countries opens the possibility of testing the effect of fundamental structural factors (for example, market size) and policies while holding constant fundamental features of technology and buyers' behavior. Bain chose to focus on the effect of market size on seller concentration and its components – the concentration of plants and the extent of multi-plant operation by the largest firms. He sampled 34 manufacturing industries in eight countries, the United States and seven others varying in national market size down to Sweden and in level of development to India. Missing observations and data problems abound, but the data roughly suggest an intriguing pattern. Mean plant size in the typical industry is a good deal smaller in other countries than in the United States. Plant concentration is not proportionally much higher in these other (smaller) countries than in the United States because of the large differences in plant sizes. And seller concentration is only modestly higher in other countries than in the United States, because multi-plant development of leading firms is greater in America.

In hindsight, some of Bain's procedures suffer from the lack of a theoretical framework that would indicate appropriate strategies of measurement and testing. However, the implements for which one would nowadays reach to undertake this study (the Cournot model, for example) were then not in everybody's tool kit. The international comparative approach later launched other major research efforts. The investigation of multi-plant economies of scale by Scherer et al. (1975) followed directly on Bain's work, and Sutton (1991) showed how such an approach can draw upon an elegant theoretical framework.

Notes

1. For an earlier survey emphasizing the context of IO's development, see Shepherd (1976).
2. This analysis appears in Bain (1956, ch. 3), at which point only scale economies have been introduced as a source of entry barriers. Bain did not attempt to address the conjectural interdependence between incumbents and potential entrants for the other empirical sources of disadvantage to entrants.
3. As with several other theoretical issues concerning entry barriers, Bain set out the essence of the argument, but (in quest of safe empirical generalizations) did not try to pin down the theoretical fine points. In this instance, Masson and Shaanan (1982) provided clarification.
4. Bain only mentioned that entrants might occasionally turn up endowed with attributes enabling them to displace incumbents; entry as an aspect of turnover gained attention much later.
5. Bain (1956, p. 61) discussed and criticized another technique for inferring scale economies that later became popular – the survivor technique.
6. The whole subsequent discussion of contrived entry barriers unfortunately leads to few clear normative conclusions, because the barrier-raising outlays also serve non-strategic and normatively innocent functions.
7. An unresolved question is the degree to which the formulation of the framework is due to Edward S. Mason, who taught IO at Harvard to Bain and other IO notables in that generation. Mason published little, but his pedagogy was apparently built around some version of the paradigm.
8. The approach was implemented at the undergraduate textbook level in Bain (1968).

References

Bain, Joe S. (1942), 'Market classifications in modern price theory', *Quarterly Journal of Economics*, **56** (August): 560–74.

Bain, Joe S. (1944–47), *The Economics of the Pacific Coast Petroleum Industry*, 3 vols, Berkeley, CA: University of California Press.

Bain, Joe S. (1950), 'Workable competition in oligopoly: theoretical considerations and some empirical evidence', *American Economic Review*, **40** (May): 35–47.

Bain, Joe S. (1951), 'Relation of profit rate to industry concentration: American manufacturing, 1936–1940', *Quarterly Journal of Economics*, **65** (August): 293–324.

Bain, Joe S. (1956), *Barriers to New Competition: Their Character and Consequences in Manufacturing Industries*, Cambridge, MA: Harvard University Press.

Bain, Joe S. (1960), 'Price leaders, barometers, and kinks', *Journal of Business*, **33** (July): 193–203.

Bain, Joe S. (1966), *International Differences in Industrial Structure: Eight Nations in the 1950s*, New Haven, CT: Yale University Press.

Bain, Joe S. (1968), *Industrial Organization*, 2nd edn, New York: John Wiley.

Clark, J.M. (1940), 'Toward a concept of workable competition', *American Economic Review*, **40** (June): 241–56.

Geroski, Paul, Richard J. Gilbert and Alexis Jacquemin (1990), *Barriers to Entry and Strategic Competition*, Chur, Switzerland: Harwood Academic.

Mann, H. Michael (1966), 'Seller concentration, barriers to entry, and rates of return in thirty industries, 1950–1960', *Review of Economics and Statistics*, **48** (August): 296–307.

Masson, Robert T. and J. Shaanan (1982), 'Stochastic dynamic limit pricing: an empirical test', *Review of Economics and Statistics*, **64** (November): 413–22.

Scherer, F.M., Alan Beckenstein, Erich Kaufer and R. Dennis Murphy (1975), *The Economics of Multi-Plant Operation: An International Comparisons Study*, Cambridge, MA: Harvard University Press.

Schmalensee, Richard (1982), 'Product differentiation advantages of pioneering brands', *American Economic Review*, **72** (June): 349–65.
Shepherd, William G. (1976), 'Bain's influence on research into industrial organization', *Essays on Industrial Organization in Honor of Joe S. Bain*, ed. Robert T. Masson and P. David Qualls, Cambridge, MA: Ballinger, pp. 1–17.
Stigler, George J. (1968), *The Organization of Industry*, Homewood, IL: Richard D. Irwin.
Sutton, John (1991), *Sunk Costs and Market Structure: Price Competition, Advertising, and the Evolution of Concentration*, Cambridge, MA: MIT Press.
von Weizsäcker, C.C. (1980), *Barriers to Entry: A Theoretical Treatment*, Berlin: Springer Verlag.

G. WILLARD FRITZ MUELLER

Bruce Marion

Innovations

Served dual role of Chief Economist and Director of Bureau of Economics of the Federal Trade Commission (FTC) which allowed him to advise commissioners on policy issues and provided access to other policy makers in Washington during 1961–69; rebuilt the Bureau of Economics into one of the leading economics groups in Washington, enabling him to become one of the most influential economists in Washington during the 1960s; the prime mover behind the FTC Line-of-Business (LOB) Reporting Program and Pre-merger Notification Programs; served as executive director of the President's Cabinet Committee on Price Stability in 1968; was advisor and active participant in antitrust policy over nearly four decades; organized and nurtured large-scale multi-university studies of competition in the US food system from 1972 to 1996.

Personal history

Born 1925, Ortonville, MN, USA.

Degrees BS and MS University of Wisconsin-Madison, 1950, 1951; PhD Vanderbilt University, 1955.

Principal position William F. Vilas Research Professor, Department of Agricultural and Applied Economics, Department of Economics and Law School, University of Wisconsin-Madison, 1969–98.

Other Executive Director, President's Cabinet Committee on Price Stability, 1968–69; Chief Economist and Director, Bureau of Economics, Federal Trade Commission, 1961–69; Assistant Professor to Professor, University of Wisconsin-Madison, 1957–61; Lecturer to Assistant Professor, University of California-Davis, 1954–57; United States Navy, 1942–46.

Like his mentor, George W. Stocking, Willard 'Fritz' Mueller's career blended the fields of applied economics and antitrust law to analyze and design policy prescriptions for limiting market power. Convinced of the central role that market structure plays in affecting competition, Mueller devoted much of his career to studying empirically the forces influencing market structure and the competitive impact of market structure on market behavior.

Perhaps Mueller's greatest 'innovation' was to demonstrate that an extremely capable and energetic economist, backed by a capable staff and access to key policy makers, could play a central role in formulating economic-based legal rules for antitrust enforcement. Mueller rebuilt the Bureau of Economics from obscurity in 1961 to one of the most influential groups of economists in Washington by 1969. The output of the Bureau was prodigious, with 48 economic studies published during 1966–70. Mueller's dual role as chief economist to the Commission and Director of Bureau of Economics of the FTC gave him access to the commissioners and congressional policy makers. This enhanced greatly his effectiveness inside and outside the Commission. He was a powerful economist in Washington, often an ally of Walter Heller, the Chair of the Council of Economic Advisors. He had entrée to White House staff as well as many members of Congress and their staffs. The 1960s is known as one of the most aggressive decades of antitrust enforcement in no small measure due to Mueller's initiatives.

Several innovative programs and actions came out of this period. The LOB Reporting Program had its genesis with Mueller's efforts throughout the 1960s to obtain better data from large corporations. He continued to pursue these efforts while serving ten months in the Executive Office of the President in 1968 and later while working with congressional committees. These efforts were consummated with the approval of the LOB program in 1974.

Mueller's long interest in mergers led to innovative policy approaches: 'merger guidelines' for specific industries in 1967 and the FTC pre-merger notification program, approved in 1969. The latter program required corporations with assets of $250 million or more to notify the Commission at least 30 days prior to acquiring any company with assets of $10 million or more. These programs allowed antitrust agencies to challenge mergers before they were consummated and assets co-mingled. Mueller subsequently consulted with and testified before the House and Senate committees that enacted the Hart–Scott–Rodino Act of 1976. Peter W. Rodino, Jr, Chairman of the Senate Judiciary Committee, praised Mueller for the studies he prepared for the committee and for his 'helpful counsel to the Committee during the deliberations on the pre-merger notification program under the Hart–Scott–Rodino Act of 1976, probably the most significant advance in antitrust enforcement over the past three decades'. Senator Philip S. Hart, Chairman of the Senate Antitrust Committee, before whom Mueller testified frequently, characterized Mueller as one of the most 'articulate' voices in developing 'a vigorous and imaginative national antitrust enforcement policy'.

After returning to the University of Wisconsin-Madison in 1969, Mueller continued his active involvement in the nation's antitrust policy and enforcement. Over four decades he was an economic advisor to congressional committees, individual members of Congress, and the executive branch. From 1960 to 1996, he testified 28 times before congressional committees.

Drawing on his experience working with the FTC Bureau of Economics and the National Commission of Food Marketing, which he assisted during 1967–68, Mueller recognized that teams of economists often were better able to conduct research and influence antitrust policy than isolated scholars. During the 1970s and 1980s, he led an 18-university research consortium that produced several landmark studies of competition in the food manufacturing and food retailing industries. Once again he demonstrated the impact that economists may have if they have access to good data (often obtained through congressional committees), conduct careful analyses and have access to key policy makers. The research group received awards from the American Agricultural Economics Association for scholarly excellence in 'Public Policy', 'Quality of Communications' and 'Quality of Research Discovery'. Appropriately for a Wisconsin economist, Mueller's last major study was an innovative analysis of price manipulation of the National Cheese Exchange, a classic thin market. The four-year study led to congressional hearings, a

Governor's Task Force, replacement of the National Cheese Exchange with a spot cheese market on the Chicago Mercantile Exchange, and a change in the US Department of Agriculture's milk-pricing regulations.

Mueller most prized his role as a teacher and researcher, and enjoyed working with his undergraduate and graduate students, as well as his academic colleagues. These efforts resulted in numerous published works, his first in 1952 and his last in 2004.

Most relevant publications

(1955), 'The *Cellophane* Case and the new competition' (with G.W. Stocking), *American Economic Review*, **29**, pp. 27–63.

(1957), 'Business reciprocity and the size of firms' (with G.W. Stocking), *University of Chicago Journal of Business*, April, pp. 73–95.

(1969), *Economic Report on Corporate Mergers*, Staff Report of the Federal Trade Commission, Washington, DC, pp. 754.

(1975), 'Antitrust in a planned economy: an anachronism or an essential complement?', *Journal of Economic Issues*, June, pp. 159–77.

(1978), *The Celler–Kefauver Act: The First 27 Years of Enforcement*, Report to Subcommittee on Monopolies and Commerce of Judiciary Committee, House of Representatives, Washington, DC.

(1979), *The Food Retailing Industry: Market Structure, Profits and Prices* (co-author), New York: Praeger Press.

(1984), *The Food Manufacturing Industries: Structure, Strategies, Performance and Policies* (co-author), Lexington, MA: Lexington Press.

(1987), *The Sunkist Case: A Study in Legal–Economic Analysis* (co-author), Lexington, MA: Lexington Books.

(1991), 'An empirical test of the free rider hypothesis' (with F. Geithman), *Review of Economics and Statistics*, May, pp. 301–308.

(1996), *Cheese Pricing: A Study of the National Cheese Exchange* (co-author), Madison, WI: University of Wisconsin-Madison Press, p. 210.

(2004), 'The revival of economics at the FTC in the 1960s', *Review of Industrial Organization*, **25**, pp. 91–105.

H. CARL KAYSEN

William G. Shepherd

Innovations

He applied oligopoly theory creatively in 1951–52, published in 1956 a major case study of the *United Shoe Machinery* antitrust case, broadened in 1957 the analysis of large corporations, and co-wrote the landmark 1959 study of the harms of tight oligopoly.

Personal history

Born 1920, Philadelphia, PA, USA.

Degrees BA University of Pennsylvania, 1940; MA, PhD, Harvard University, 1947, 1953.

Principal positions Professor of Economics, 1950–66, Harvard University; Professor of Political Economy, Massachusetts Institute of Technology, 1976–90.

Other Director, Institute for Advanced Studies, Princeton, 1965–76.

Beginning in 1945 as something of a boy wonder in economics broadly, Kaysen reached star quality in the field in the 1950s, ranging from issues in theory to applied work to legal–economic issues. During 1946–52 he published a variety of creative papers on the dynamic theory both of monopoly and of oligopoly situations.

Then he pioneered in a unique experimental position as an economic adviser to Judge Charles Wyzanski for the major antitrust case involving the *United Shoe Machinery Corporation*. Such a neutral judge's economic adviser had never been arranged before. Kaysen can be credited with much of the economic soundness of the final opinion in the case. But the experiment has not been repeated. As expert-witness work mushroomed in the 1970s, with the mammoth AT&T and IBM cases and hundreds of others, adversaries would have attacked and rejected any 'neutral' judge's economist for supposed bias.

The debate on large firms opened in 1932 by A.A. Berle and G.C. Means had developed much theory and also practical research about the managers' array of motivations. Kaysen broke with that trend in 1957, arguing forcefully that large firms should be held to high standards of social contributions as well as narrow commercial ones.

Perhaps his deepest impact came with the Kaysen–Turner book of 1959, *Antitrust Policy*, which addressed the long-pending policy question of oligopoly. The book defined the distinct case of 'tight oligopoly', where concentration was high and the leading firms often behaved like a 'shared monopoly'. They thoroughly assessed the extent of tight oligopoly in the US economy, finding that it was a major section of the economy. They urged making it presumptively illegal because of its economic harms, though they did not clearly set a firm policy step to cure the problem.

Kaysen then left this field after 1960, when he was just 40, joining the Kennedy administration as its chief activist for arms control and the avoidance of nuclear danger.

During 1965–76 he headed the renowned Institute for Advanced Studies at Princeton University.

Most relevant publications

(1946), 'A dynamic aspect of the monopoly problem', *Review of Economic Studies*, pp. 1–15.
(1952), 'Dynamic aspects of oligopoly price theory', *American Economic Review*, **42**, May, pp. 198–210.
(1956), *United States* v. *United Shoe Machinery Corporation: An Economic Analysis of an Anti-trust Case*, Cambridge, MA: Harvard University Press.
(1957), 'The social significance of the modern corporation', *American Economic Review*, **47**, May pp. 311–19.
(1959), *Antitrust Policy: An Economic and Legal Analysis* (with Donald F. Turner, Jr), Cambridge, MA: Harvard University Press.

I. DONALD F. TURNER

William G. Shepherd

Innovations
He articulated the 'tight-oligopoly' concept; shifted US antitrust to a fuller reliance on economic content; created a major antitrust case to remove AT&T's large vertical monopoly; conceived and issued the first antitrust guidelines for mergers; co-authored the now-standard price–cost definition of 'predatory pricing'; and urged that conglomerate mergers had no anti-competitive role.

Personal history

Born 1921, USA; died 1994.

Degrees BA Northwestern University, 1941; PhD (Economics), Harvard University, 1947; LLB Yale, 1950.

Principal position Professor of Law, Harvard University, 1954–79.

Other Assistant Attorney General for Antitrust, US Department of Justice, 1965–68.

Turner was a unique figure. He was both a prolific and renowned legal scholar at Harvard Law School and also an economics PhD who created some of the first highly sophisticated 'law–economics' thought, even before that field took form in the 1970s. He wedded deep and sophisticated research with the direct personal experience of making and changing America's antitrust policies.

In 1959 he wrote (with Carl Kaysen) a pathbreaking proposal for strict antitrust policy toward tight oligopoly (1959). Their book combined thorough legal analysis with comprehensive economic data about the scope and effects of actual oligopoly concentration in US industry.

Then in 1965, after publishing other research on antitrust issues, he was appointed by Lyndon Johnson as head of the Antitrust Division in the Department of Justice, the senior US antitrust agency. He held this post for three tumultuous years. From the start, he raised the rigor and depth of economics in making antitrust choices.

As part of that, he created an economic adviser position (Special Economic Assistant to the Assistant Attorney General), which became a fixture. (Among the 43 pioneers profiled here, those who were special economic assistants include William S. Comanor, Oliver E. Williamson, William G. Shepherd and Leonard W. Weiss.)

Turner prepared a major legal case in 1966 to remove AT&T's long-standing vertical monopoly. Though the case was stymied by higher officials, the same result was reached when a similar 1974 case led to AT&T's break-up in 1984.

He rejected claims that the spectacular 1966–69 wave of conglomerate mergers posed any threat to true economic competition. Those mergers did not change the structures inside any markets, and so Turner denied that they would affect market power.

He originated the idea of creating and publishing official 'merger guidelines' to show and explain America's current merger policies; in 1968 he prepared and issued the first actual guidelines, based on economic criteria. In their more recent revised forms, the guidelines remain the anchor of merger policies.

In perhaps his most striking innovation, in 1975 he published (with Philip Areeda) a new, lucid economic definition of 'predatory pricing'. Based on comparing price with marginal cost – if price is not lower than marginal cost, there is no anti-competitive effect (or 'predation') – the Areeda–Turner rule quickly became standard antitrust policy, and it remains so.

Then in 1978, Turner published (also with Areeda) an immense, encyclopedic, economics-based and virtually definitive seven-volume coverage of antitrust policies. It completed the conversion of antitrust law to a thorough economic basis. It was an instant landmark and, in successive editions, it has remained so.

Most relevant publications

(1959), *Antitrust Policy: An Economic and Legal Analysis* (with Carl Kaysen), Cambridge, MA: Harvard University Press.

(1975), 'Predatory pricing and related practices under Section 2 of the Sherman Act' (with Philip Areeda), *Harvard Law Review*, February 697–733.

(1978), *Antitrust Law* (with Philip Areeda), 7 vols, Boston, MA: Little, Brown.

J. GEORGE JOSEPH STIGLER

Sam Peltzman

Innovations
Economic analysis of regulation, politics and law; economics of information and oligopoly.

Personal history

Born 1911, Renton, WA, USA; died 1991.

Degrees BBA University of Washington, 1931, PhD University of Chicago, 1938.

Principal position Charles R. Walgreen Professor of American Institutions, University of Chicago, Chicago, USA 1958–91.

Other Professor Columbia University, New York, 1947–58. Nobel Laureate in Economics, 1982.

Industrial organization emerged as a recognizable field within US economics some time in the 1930s. Edward Chamberlin's *Theory of Monopolistic Competition* (1933) probably deserves much of the credit for this development, perhaps along with A.A. Berle and G.C. Means's *The Modern Corporation and Private Property* (1932). At its inception the field was centrally concerned with the operation of markets and firms, especially those aspects which seemed to deviate from the textbook model of perfect competition. The main policy concern of early industrial organization was antitrust enforcement.

The field has broadened considerably since those early days. An important example occurred in the 1960s when industrial organization subsumed the economic analysis of much public regulation beyond antitrust. Indeed, the field is commonly called 'IO/regulation' today. George Stigler had much to do with that development, and I have chronicled that elsewhere (Peltzman, 1993).

In this profile I shall concentrate on Stigler's contribution to industrial organization in its original conception. Stigler did not have many kind words for either Chamberlin or Berle and Means, but he shared their interest in the operation of firms and markets and in the related antitrust policy issues. In a career that began just after industrial organization was born, he made landmark contributions to the field.

His contributions to the traditional industrial organization of competition, monopoly and antitrust (hereafter 'IO') were many and varied. His own distillation of the published work (Stigler, 1968) contains 22 articles and notes. They cover issues such as how concentration and economies of scale ought to be measured, what constitutes a 'barrier to entry', the methodological flaws in Chamberlin's magnum opus and the statistical flaws in the analysis of price rigidity. Some of these issues will seem quaint or obscure to the current generation of IO economists. But two items in the collection probably will define his legacy to the field, and here I shall focus exclusively on these. They are his articles on the economics of information and the theory of oligopoly.

The articles are related intellectually and appeared within three years of each other in the early 1960s, when Stigler was at the peak of his intellectual power and influence. The first was 'The economics of information' (Stigler, 1961). It grappled with the mundane, but theretofore largely neglected truth that information about the market was costly to produce. Much of the analysis is couched in terms of information about prices, perhaps because price theory is, after all, centrally concerned with prices. However, the theory Stigler developed was applicable to almost any variable aspect of a transaction, such as the quality of the good, delivery times and so forth.

To understand Stigler's contribution in 'The economics of information' it is well to look back to where price theory was at the time he wrote. A central result of the theory was the 'law of one price', whereby the same good had to sell at the same price in the same location (or could differ across locations only within bounds set by transport costs). Simple arbitrage reasoning seemed to compel the result. But, of course, a stroll through the neighborhood would reveal that the 'law' was being routinely violated.

The reaction of economists of the time to the massive empirical failure of one of their central tenets was varied. There was the Talmudic reaction: what is a 'location'? What is a 'transport' cost? There was the retreat to methodology: the law holds in long-run equilibrium, a condition we are not privileged to observe in the world. Among IO economists, there was the search for the monopolist under every bed: the law holds under perfect competition, so price dispersion signals some market imperfection; ubiquitous price dispersion was just one more example of the infirmities of perfect competition models in the post-Chamberlin era.[1] The overall view that competition was nice to teach to undergraduates but not otherwise to be taken seriously by adults was then perhaps even more common than it is today.

Stigler viewed all this huffing and puffing as beside the point. All of the explanations and evasions emanated from a fictitious world in which information about prices was costless.[2] Only if all the market participants knew the full distribution of bid and ask prices could competitive arbitrage surely eliminate price dispersion. But this surfeit of information would not automatically materialize if the information were costly to produce and disseminate. With costly information, the law of one price has to be wrong. It posits an equilibrium where the marginal value of information is zero (you cannot gain by getting another price quote because every price is the same) in a world where the marginal cost of the information is positive. But the larger logic of competition implies equality between marginal values and costs.

Stigler's article is nothing more or less than an adumbration of what that standard equalization of marginal benefits and costs means in the context of price information. For one thing, the marginal value of search has to be positive in the full long-run perfectly competitive equilibrium. That is, there is price dispersion. The buyer (seller) could in principle find a lower (higher) price somewhere, but it does not pay to look for it. Our task then is to analyze this dispersion.

Stigler does some of this in the article. He shows, for example, why large buyers will pay lower prices than small buyers (under perfect competition), why price dispersions are greater where there is much buyer/seller turnover and so on. However, as with much of his work, the main impact of the article was in the way it framed a question. Here the question was 'what are the implications of costly information?' There would follow a new subfield that pursued those implications in a variety of contexts. The most obvious were explorations of the supply and demand for information. These led to results like the reservation-price search rule[3] on the demand side and signaling models of advertising on the supply side.[4] The more subtle applications extended well beyond IO. For example, the notion that unemployment is an equilibrium phenomenon arising out of employer/employee search for information became integral to labor economics and macroeconomics. Both fields were thus relieved of the same kind of discomfort with persistent non-zero unemployment as had been occasioned elsewhere by persistent price dispersions.

Stigler's (1964) article 'A theory of oligopoly' is also an application of his economics of information. Here the central problem was how oligopolists acquired information about rival behavior. The general problem had been lurking since Augustin Cournot and became more explicit after Joseph Bertrand. Cournot's famous equilibrium – significant departures from competition with few rivals – implicitly assumed free information about rival outputs. Bertrand's equilibrium – marginal cost pricing under duopoly – made the information problem explicit. If a rival could conceal a price reduction long enough, Cournot's equilibrium would degenerate to marginal-cost pricing with only two rivals. The corollary to Bertrand is that significant departures from competition require sufficient timely information among rivals about each other's actions. Stigler's theory pursues that corollary in a world where, in addition to the usual costs of acquiring, communicating and verifying information, there are legal costs as well. That is, direct communication of prices between competitors and various mechanisms for internalizing information such as joint sales agencies, mergers and so on are all subject to antitrust penalties.

Accordingly, the question Stigler grapples with is whether a non-competitive equilibrium is stable when each seller must independently discover what rivals are doing. The specific information mechanism that Stigler emphasizes is the seller's own sales. That is, if a rival undercuts your price, you will find that your sales dry up. Your private information (sales declined) allows inferences about rival actions (some rival-reduced price). However, sales can decline – or rise – for a variety of (unobservable) reasons unrelated to rivals' pricing. Buyers enter and leave the market from time to time, their demands move around randomly and so on.

The heart of the oligopolist's information problem, according to Stigler, is to filter this random 'noise' from the 'signal' of rival behavior. This filtering takes time, and the stability of a non-competitive equilibrium hinges on how long it takes for the signal to emerge. If it takes long enough, Bertrand-style competition will prevail, because the rival who initiates a price reduction will reap the fruits (higher sales) for a long enough time to make that strategy irresistible. Stigler's great insight was then to connect this time required for learning to the structure of the market within which the rivalry occurred.

A simple example will illustrate the connection: imagine that ten sellers collude on the price of widgets to 100 buyers who buy one widget each week. Buyers are indifferent to whom they buy from, given price. So, since the price is initially the same across the sellers, each buyer picks a seller by throwing darts at a ten-section board every week. This random selection process is the only source of noise in the example. But it is sufficient to create a temptation to cheat. Without cheating, each seller will average ten units sold per week, but the standard deviation of each seller's sales will be three per week. Thus good or bad luck could produce considerable deviation from the average in any one week without any deviation from the collusive agreement.

Now suppose a cheater can gain an extra five sales per week by discounting the collusive price by, say, 10 percent. The mean of the honest rivals' sales generating process has shifted down by 5/9 per week (five customers lost to nine rivals), but with a standard deviation of 3 the loss cannot be detected right away. Eventually the nine rivals will awake: the standard deviation of the mean will decline with the square root of the number of weekly 'draws' from the new process. For example, after 100 weeks the standard error of the mean sales per firm will be only 0.3. They will at that point look back on sales that have averaged something like 0.6 less than the 10 they expected, compare that loss to the 0.3 standard error and conclude that bad luck cannot account for the shortfall. With no other source of variation in the story, rivals will be able to infer that someone has cheated.

The difficulty, of course, is that even if prices fell to marginal cost in week 101 two years' worth of cheating profits may be much more profitable than adhering to the collusive price. In that case, the collusion will unravel at the beginning, because it will pay no one to remain honest.

Now imagine that there are two rivals instead of ten. All else the same, expected weekly sales per firm are now 50, with a standard deviation of 5. A cheating strategy with the same short-run payoff as in the previous case (five extra sales for a 10 percent discount) will now be detectable after a month or so,[5] compared with two years in the previous case. If a month's worth of cheating profits are not great enough to offset the long-run costs the collusive equilibrium can be sustained indefinitely. The intuition behind this connection between market structure (two firms versus ten) and the likelihood of a stable collusive equilibrium is simple: with only two firms, much of the previous noise becomes internalized. Imagine that the old firms 1–5 and 6–10 had merged to form the two-firm industry. Now darts that land on section 1 instead of 2 or 3 or 4 or 5, and so on do not create noise when once they did. This reduction in noise[6] speeds detection of the signal.

Stigler's article goes on to use the logic underlying the above example to connect the likelihood of a stable non-competitive equilibrium to aspects of market structure beyond the number of sellers, such as the number of buyers, their loyalty and, importantly, the concentration of output. Indeed the connection between expected price and concentration in Stigler's theory probably remains the major theoretical underpinning of the literature on the empirical relation between profits and concentration that was blossoming at the time. That literature began well before Stigler's article, but the connection between concentration and profitability (viewed then as a proxy for super-competitive prices) did not rigorously follow from any oligopoly model until Stigler's.[7]

Stigler's oligopoly theory also had a considerable influence on antitrust policy. It provided a rigorous basis for regulation of mergers, something that was hard to find in the preceding literature.[8] Stigler's theory suggested that the relevant measure of concentration was the Herfindahl–Hirschmann index (the sum of squared market shares), and this measure later became the standard for judging mergers in the Department of Justice's merger guidelines. It also contributed a new way of understanding a host of practices that had previously seemed either benign or hard to understand. For example, sharing of information among rivals, such as had occurred in open price trade associations could no longer be excused on grounds that the sharing stopped short of an agreement. If the practice speeded dissemination of private price information, this could help stabilize an agreement. On the other side of the market, a preference among substantial buyers for negotiating prices with sellers rather than accepting the lowest published price could be understood as a defensive strategy that helped keep rival sellers in the dark about each other's price offers[9] and thereby encouraged rivals to deviate from an agreement. Stigler, father of the economics of information, understood that more information did not always mean more competition.

No account of Stigler's influence on IO would be complete without some mention of his intellectual influence at Chicago. He was on the faculty of the Graduate School of Business and Economics Department from 1958 until his death in 1991. In that time he was, literally, a towering figure among Chicago economists. He was the recognized leader among a large group of IO economists who resided in economics, business and law. This tripartite collaboration was unusual in its time and contributed greatly to a distinct approach to IO that was to have long-lasting consequences for academic and policy discourse.

Stigler was, for example, a great friend of Aaron Director, the second economist hired by the Law School.[10] Director was skeptical about much of the then prevailing wisdom in antitrust, especially in areas like vertical restraints (such as exclusive dealing and resale price maintenance) and predatory pricing. However, Director published little, so Stigler took on himself a facilitating role: He convinced Director to establish a new *Journal of Law and Economics* and Stigler urged colleagues to write articles inspired by Director's teachings. Two prominent examples of this mid-wifery were Lester Telser's (1960) article on resale price maintenance and John McGee's (1958) article on predatory pricing. Works like this ultimately became the basis for what is sometimes called the Chicago view in antitrust policy. This includes more tolerance for vertical restraints and more skepticism about allegations of predation than had theretofore been common. Ultimately the courts adopted much of this view.

George Stigler rarely wrote an article which was the last word in its subject. Unlike his other great friend at Chicago, Milton Friedman, Stigler had few students to carry on a more or less well-defined research program. He stayed largely aloof from public policy. His influence rests largely in the kind of questions he asked and the kind of colleagues he brought together at Chicago. While he was skeptical that there was a recognizable Chicago school in economics generally or IO in particular, he was probably wrong about that. And his work is probably the main reason for that.

Notes

1. But so too does the opposite. Evidence in the cement antitrust case of 1948 revealed 11 identical bids of $3.286854 per barrel of cement for a highway contract. The court rejected the defendants' exculpatory invocation of the law of one price under competition.
2. Or, more precisely, arbitrarily cheap.
3. Whereby the buyer sets a lower-bound price and then searches until he or she finds that price or a lower one.
4. Stigler briefly discussed advertising as a supply response to the demand for information in his article. In the ensuing decade or so much was made of distinctions between 'informative' advertising – the type Stigler seemed to be talking about when he discussed price search – and the 'persuasive' advertising that Chamberlin seemed to have in mind. The signaling model, due to Nelson (1974), shows how apparently persuasive ads with little hard information content can nevertheless be informative by signaling a product's quality.
5. Here one rival would lose five sales per week. Suppose the mean loss has to be 2.0 times the standard error to be considered 'significant'. With a weekly standard deviation of 5, this condition will occur after 4 weeks on average, when the standard error of the mean will be around 2.5.
6. It can be measured by the coefficient of variation of a firm's sales – that is, the standard deviation divided by the mean. This is 30 percent in the first case (3/10) and only 10 percent in the second (5/50).

7. Of course, Cournot and his descendants have such a relation implicit. They focus on the number of firms rather than concentration. But the negative correlation between numbers and concentration suggests a positive correlation between prices and concentration. Stigler's theory is able to separate the information advantages of high concentration from those stemming from fewness of rivals.
8. For example, consider a triopoly operating under Cournot rivalry that becomes a duopoly via merger. In the simplest case, industry profits rise but the merged firm's profits fall (because it only has half the total versus 2/3 for the merging firms). Thus, a naive reading of Cournot suggests no incentive to anti-competitive mergers.
9. If the large buyer's policy is to buy at some published price, then the rival sellers can learn each other's prices to that buyer simply by obtaining each other's catalogues.
10. Henry Simons was the first.

References

McGee, John S. (1958), 'Predatory price cutting: *The Standard Oil* (N.J.) case', *Journal of Law and Economics*, **1**, October, pp. 137–69.
Nelson, Phillip (1974), 'Advertising as information', *Journal of Political Economy*, **82**, July/August, pp. 729–54.
Peltzman, Sam (1993), 'George Stigler's contribution to the economic analysis of regulation', *Journal of Political Economy*, **101**, October, pp. 818–32.
Stigler, George J. (1961), 'The economics of information', *Journal of Political Economy*, **69**, pp. 213–25.
Stigler, George J. (1964), 'A theory of oligopoly', *Journal of Political Economy*, **72**, February, pp. 44–61.
Stigler, George J. (1968), *The Organization of Industry*, Homewood, IL: Richard D. Irwin.
Telser, Lester G. (1960), 'Why should manufacturers want fair trade?', *Journal of Law and Economics*, **3**, October, pp. 86–105.

K. WILLIAM JACK BAUMOL

Stephen Martin

Innovations

Analysis of alternative firm objective functions in imperfectly competitive markets; theory of contestable markets; application of economics to antitrust and regulatory policy; economic analysis of the arts.

Personal history

Born 1922, New York City, USA.

Degrees BSS City College, New York, 1942; PhD University of London, 1949; various honorary degrees.

Principle positions Professor of Economics, Princeton University, 1949–92, since then, Emeritus Professor; Professor of Economics, New York University, since 1971; Director, C.V. Starr Center for Applied Economics, NYU, 1983–2000.

Other Assistant Lecturer, London School of Economics, 1947–49; Junior Economist, US Department of Agriculture, 1942–43, 1946.

William J. Baumol is a polymath whose contributions to the field of industrial economics are a portion of his professional opus.

While acknowledging that there is an unavoidable arbitrary element to any classification scheme, I discuss Baumol's contributions to industrial economics under four headings: theory generally, the theory of contestable markets, the economics of antitrust and regulation, and studies of particular industries.

Baumol (1958, 1959 [1967]) explores the implications of sales maximization as an objective function, alternative to that which is usually assumed (profit or value maximization, depending on whether one works with a static or a dynamic model) for firms in imperfectly competitive markets. Analysis of the strategic implications of such alternative objective functions, sales maximization in particular, has become a standard element in the analysis of imperfect competition.

Over and above the substantive contribution, two methodological points come out of this work. Baumol traces his study of revenue maximization to his experience consulting with US corporations (1958, p. 187; 1967, pp. 45–9). That is, and this is explicit in the title of Baumol (1959 [1967]), the study of revenue maximization is based on observation of firms' behavior. The assumptions of the model are justified on the ground of realism. Baumol's discussion (1967, pp. 2–9) of the relation between his methodological approach and that of Friedman (1953) should be noted.

Baumol also takes the view (1958, p. 188, footnote 1) that economics, as such, is agnostic as far as indicating what a firm's objective function *ought* to be. Rather, economic analysis serves to analyze the implications of alternative objective functions for firm and/or market performance.[1]

Baumol and Bradford (1970, p. 265) defend what they describe as a 'mislaid maxim', a result that has been lost sight of although it has 'appeared many times in the literature', having 'been reported by most eminent economists in very prominent journals'. This result is that (ibid., p. 265): 'generally, prices which deviate in a systematic manner from marginal costs will be required for an optimal allocation of resources, even in the absence of externalities'. In related work, Baumol (1979a) makes a point about the best market performance that can be obtained using a price system, and by implication about feasible goals for antitrust or regulatory policy. The point is that (ibid., p. 579): 'Generally, the best that any fixed set of prices can achieve is the Ramsey (1927) solution, whose welfare yield is constrained by Walras' law' and that the implied welfare level will in general fall short of the first-best level. Hence (ibid., p. 580): 'the welfare loss required by the acceptance of the Ramsey solution is generally unavoidable under any standard price system in which the individual decision maker treats prices as fixed parameters whose values are beyond his control, and where prices are not discriminatory'.

The importance of potential competition for market performance has been another mislaid maxim of economics.[2] After Baumol et al.'s (1982) *Contestable Markets and the Theory of Industry Structure* and the follow-on literature, it seems unlikely that this particular maxim will ever be mislaid again. The book emphasizes the implications of free and easy entry and exit for market performance and market structure, including the case of multi-product firms. Empirical tests of the applicability of the theory to specific industries (in particular but not limited to the passenger airline industry) contributed much insight into the subtle ways in which strategic behavior on the part of incumbent firms may raise entry costs.

Baumol (1979b, 1996) has applied rigorous economic analysis to the question of antitrust policy toward predatory behavior.

On his own and with co-authors,[3] Baumol early on produced industry studies characterized by an attention to institutional detail that is characteristic of current practice.

Scholars who maintain their research productivity typically expand their contributions to a field moving forward in time, by a continuing stream of publications. Baumol has done this. Exceptionally, the list of his contributions to industrial economics has expanded going backward in time as well. As theoretical industrial economics has reintegrated itself with mainstream economic theory and as the distinction between antitrust economics and the economics of regulation has faded, publications of his which at their appearance would have been thought to enrich other branches of economics are now seen as part of the literature of industrial economics. In a real sense, his contributions to industrial economics have anticipated the broad lines of development of the field.

Notes

1. Baumol (1982) takes a similar position as regards the social welfare function.
2. The importance of potential competition for equilibrium market performance was emphasized by Chadwick (1859), Gunton (1888), Liefmann (1915) and Machlup (1942). Entry conditions were, as Baumol et al. (1983) note, central to the structure–conduct–performance paradigm.
3. For example, Baumol (1971), Baumol and Bowen (1966).

References

Baumol, William J. (1958), 'On the theory of oligopoly', *Economica*, **25**, August, 187–98.
Baumol, William J. (1959 [1967]), *Business Behavior, Value and Growth*, New York: Harcourt, Brace & World; rev. edn, 1967.

Baumol, William J. (1971), 'Economics of Athenian drama: its relevance for the Arts in a small city today', *Quarterly Journal of Economics*, **85**(3), August, 365–76.
Baumol, William J. (1979a), 'Quasi-optimality: the price we must pay for a price system', *Journal of Political Economy*, **87**(3), June, 578–99.
Baumol, William J. (1979b), 'Quasi-permanence of price reductions: a policy for prevention of predatory pricing', *Yale Law Journal*, **89**(1), November, 1–26.
Baumol, William J. (1982), 'Book review' (of Steven Kelman, *What Price Incentives*, Boston, MA: Auburn House, 1981), *Journal of Economic Literature*, **20**(3), September, 1105–6.
Baumol, William J. (1996), 'Predation and the logic of the average variable cost test', *Journal of Law and Economics*, **39**(1), April, 49–72.
Baumol, William J. and William G. Bowen (1996), *Performing Arts, the Economic Dilemma: A Study of Problems Common to Theater, Opera, Music, and Dance*, New York: Twentieth Century Fund.
Baumol, William J. and David F. Bradford (1970), 'Optimal departures from marginal cost pricing', *American Economic Review*, **60**(3), June, 265–83.
Baumol, William J., John C. Panzar and Robert D. Willig (1982), *Contestable Markets and the Theory of Industry Structure*, New York: Harcourt Brace Jovanovich.
Baumol, William J., John C. Panzar and Robert D. Willig (1983), 'Contestable markets: an uprising in the theory of industry structure: reply', *American Economic Review*, **73**(3), June, 491–6.
Chadwick, Edwin (1859), 'Results of different principles of legislation and administration in Europe of competition for the field, as compared with competition within the field, of service', *Journal of the Royal Statistical Society*, **22**, September, 381–420.
Friedman, Milton (1953), 'The methodology of positive economics', in Milton Friedman, *Essays in Positive Economics*, Chicago and London: University of Chicago Press, 3–43.
Gunton, George (1888), 'The economic and social aspect of trusts', *Political Science Quarterly*, **3**(3), September, 385–408.
Liefmann, R.L. (1915), 'Monopoly or competition as the basis of a government trust policy', *Quarterly Journal of Economics*, **29**, February, 308–25.
Machlup, Fritz (1942), 'Competition, pliopoly, and profits', *Economica*, **9**, February, 1–23; May, 153–73.

L. JOHN ROBERT MEYER

John C. Spychalski

Innovations
Pioneering applications of statistical methods and neoclassical price theory in critiques of industry performance and other economic phenomena.

Personal history

Born 1927, Pasco, WA, USA.

Degrees BA University of Washington, 1950; PhD Harvard University, 1955; Hon. Dr (Sc), Lowell Technological Institute, 1973.

Principal position James W. Harpel Professor of Capital Formation and Economic Growth, Emeritus, Harvard University, Cambridge, MA, USA, 1997– .

Other Harpel Professor, Professor of Transportation, Logistics and Distribution, and Professor of Economics, Harvard University, 1983–96; 1973–83; 1959–68. President, National Bureau of Economic Research, 1967–77; Professor of Economics, Yale University, 1968–73; Vice-Chairman of the Board, Union Pacific Corporation, 1981–83.

As an innovative and seminal work, Meyer's co-authored (with M.J. Peck, J. Stenason and C. Zwick) book, *The Economics of Competition in the Transportation Industries* (Cambridge, MA: Harvard University Press, 1959), stands pre-eminent among his industry performance-focused works. It provided a pathbreaking blend of statistical, economic and institutional analysis supportive of the proposition that many of the then-extant critical problems in intercity freight and passenger transport stemmed from excessive government regulation. Its findings inspired an upsurge in research on the effects of transport regulation. The result was a widely accepted intellectual rationale supportive of the post1975 dismantling of most of the comprehensive system for economic regulation of transport that had been enacted incrementally between 1887 and 1940.

In the wake of deregulation, Meyer led co-authored investigations of its impacts on airline fares, service and profitability (*Airline Deregulation: The Early Experience*, 1981; *Deregulation and the New Airline Entrepreneurs*, 1984; and *Deregulation and the Future of Intercity Passenger Travel*, 1987). The findings in each were largely favorable, and hence supportive of prescriptions for deregulation proffered earlier by Meyer and others.

In the early 1960s, rising road congestion coupled with central city decline, prolific suburban development, and impoverishment in the urban transit industry sparked calls for government-funded rehabilitation and expansion of public transit service. Meyer responded with co-authored book-length studies of the comparative costs of automobile, bus, and rail transit and demographic and land-use data (*The Urban Transportation Problem*, 1965, and *Autos, Transit and Cities*, 1981). A central conclusion was that elimination of all subsidy for both automobile and public transit use would be preferable to transit subsidization.

Unlike his prescription for deregulation, however, this option has not yet, four decades after its initial publication, gained acceptance among policy makers.

Meyer's work on transport industry policy has extended beyond the USA. Following service as an advisor on shifts from government to market-provided transport services in developing countries and former communist nations, Meyer co-authored publication of *Going Private: The International Experience with Transport Privatization* (1993), and *Moving to Market: Restructuring Transport in the Former Soviet Union* (1996).

The financial crisis that enveloped operators of most of the rail mileage in the northeastern US and portions of the Midwest and West in the early 1970s moved the Council of Economic Advisers to appoint Meyer as chair of a task force charged with assessment of the railroad industry's condition and prospects. The ensuing report (*Improving Railroad Productivity: Final Report of the Task Force on Railroad Productivity*, 1973) influenced rail deregulation legislation enacted in 1974 and 1980. It also opened the way to Meyer's service on the boards of several major railroads.

Meyer's scholarship has spanned diverse phenomena beyond the ambit of industrial organization, as revealed by titles of his other co-authored and co-edited books, including *The Investment Decision: An Empirical Study* (with Edwin Kuh, Cambridge, MA: Harvard University Press, 1957); *The Economics of Slavery and Other Essays on the Quantitative Study of Economic History* (with Alfred H. Conrad, Chicago, IL: Aldine Press, 1964); and by articles such as 'Economic theory, statistical inference, and economic history' (with Alfred H. Conrad, *The Journal of Economic History*, Vol. 17, December, 1957); 'The New England states and their economic future: some implications of a changing industrial environment' (with Robert A. Leone, *The American Economic Review*, Vol. 68, May, 1978); and 'Measurement and analysis of productivity in transportation industries' (with Jose Gómez-Ibáñez in *New Developments in Productivity Measurement and Analysis*, Chicago, IL: University of Chicago Press, 1980). The titles of the last two articles reflect interests aligned with his service as President of the National Bureau of Economic Research (1967–77).

Meyer's personal bibliography is replete with co-authored entries. It thus is impossible for an outside observer to measure Meyer's contributions *vis-à-vis* those of others. In the words of one 'who was there':

> He [Meyer] would gather around him a team of faculty and doctoral students to work on each book, but he inevitably did more than his share, generating the intellectual framework and key insights and drafting and redrafting the manuscript. By example and direction, he taught dozens of young scholars how to do research and set a standard of generosity in giving credit and coauthorship to his collaborators. (Gómez-Ibáñez et al., 1999, p. 2)

In summing up, it can be said with certainty that the results of Meyer's collaborative research contributions have exerted significant impact on the work of other scholars, and on the formation and execution of policy in the public and private sectors.

Reference

Gómez-Ibáñez, José A., William B. Tye and Clifford Winston (eds) (1999), *Essays in Transportation Economics and Policy: A Handbook in Honor of John R. Meyer*, Washington, DC: Brookings Institution Press.

13. The 1960s to the mid-1980s

A. RICHARD E. CAVES

William S. Comanor

Innovations
The intersection between international trade and industrial organization. Most work in industrial organization (IO) rests on the foundation of a closed economy, or one that is influenced minimally by external factors. Much of Caves's work rejects that simplifying assumption and explores the consequences for industrial behavior and performance of international considerations. Caves was also a major figure in the approach to industrial organization that emphasized the structure–conduct (behavior)–performance paradigm, although he moved away from that in his later years. He spent the great bulk of his career as a distinguished member and sometimes chair of the Department of Economics at Harvard University.

Born 1931, Akron, OH, USA.

Degrees BA Oberlin College, 1953; MA Harvard University, 1956, PhD Harvard University, 1958.

Principal position Professor of Economics, Harvard University, Cambridge, MA, 1962–2003.

Caves was a giant in the field of industrial organization. Although his graduate studies were completed at Harvard, he spent five formative years at the University of California at Berkeley, where Joe Bain was a important colleague. When he returned to Harvard in the summer of 1962, he had not yet reached his 31st birthday but still had completed three important books while in California. These volumes, all published by the Harvard University Press and part of the Harvard Economic Studies, set the stage for much of his future work. These books are: *The Canadian Economy: Prospect and Retrospect* (with Richard H. Holton, 1959); *Trade and Economic Structure: Models and Methods*, 1960; and *Air Transport and Its Regulators: An Industry Study*, 1962.

IO had developed in the context of a large and generally closed economy such as the United States in the early postwar years. Caves saw the need to extend that analysis to other settings, and in particular to small and more open economies. In that environment, competition and market results depend as much on international as on domestic factors so one could not accurately appraise the behavior of firms and industries without dealing with both sets of forces. He led the way towards a broader analysis that encompassed both sets of considerations.

While at Berkeley, Caves encountered Joe Bain, who was one of the originators of the structure–conduct–performance paradigm that had become a leading tool for IO research. Caves pursued this approach in one of his first efforts following his return to Harvard: a small but influential text on industrial organization. The volume was entitled: *American Industry: Structure, Conduct, Performance.* It was published in 1964 and went through seven editions, with the last one published in 1992.

Although written originally as a module for an introductory economics text, it had a larger life than that. The earlier approach was to emphasize industry studies with the hope of finding commonalities from the considerable factual detail amassed in each study. The structure–conduct–performance paradigm, described lucidly in Caves's brief volume, followed directly from that effort for it emphasized these commonalities, and in particular, how the structure of a market along with expected patterns of firm conduct could influence performance in the industry. Although largely rejected by the 1980s and 1990s, this approach served to motivate an impressive body of IO research in earlier years, and for which Caves was an important pioneer. Its more recent rejection on the grounds that it could not incorporate the major feedback effects on various dimensions of market structure does not lessen the important contributions that Caves made.

Caves's 1962 study of the airline industry represented his early contribution to this body of research. He employed that paradigm extensively in this volume. In that era, the airline industry was tightly regulated by the Civil Aeronautics Board. Caves's purpose was not simply to examine this industry but also to evaluate the effects of direct regulation. As he expressed it then, his effort was 'after bigger game than [merely] a scholarly evaluation of the air-transport industry' (p. 3). He sought to determine the effects of public regulation and concluded that this industry was 'more workably competitive than some unregulated industries in the economy' (pp. 448–9).

A later important study in this vein is his paper with Michael Porter entitled 'From entry barriers to mobility barriers: conjectural decisions and contrived deterrents to new competition', which was published in the *Quarterly Journal of Economics* in 1977. As with the airline study, this paper rested on the structure–conduct–performance paradigm. Its goal was to establish the impact of an incumbent's actions on the height of entry barriers.

In addition, this paper extended the concept of entry barriers to a broader and more empirically relevant setting where there are limits on the growth of existing firms as well as on new firms seeking to enter a market. The writers emphasized that such restrictions may also retard competitive pressures and be as important as entry barriers for market results. In adopting this approach, Caves and Porter set the stage for the more recent analysis that emphasizes the role of firms rather than industries. In this sense, this paper represents an important component of the structure–conduct–performance literature as well as an early step beyond it.

His later work on individual industries shifted away from that paradigm but remained directed at the ways firms behaved and performed. His concerns were the same but his approaches and methods had shifted to the new methodologies in use. Both his constancy and shift are evident in two important papers written on different facets of the pharmaceutical industry: one published with Mark Hurwitz in 1988, and the other with Michael

Whinston and Mark Hurwitz in 1991. These papers remain important contributions to the economic literature on the pharmaceutical industry.

Caves's concerns with international factors and the competitive effects of international trade led him to study and write about economies where international considerations were more important. This work included important volumes on the British, Canadian and Japanese economies.

His 1968 volume, *Britain's Economic Prospects*, was a significant contribution. In that era, there was much concern about the performance of the British economy. The Brookings Institution commissioned a broad overview of British economic policies in the hope that a collection of external observers might provide a useful report and offer helpful recommendations. Caves was selected to direct this study. He in turn selected his collaborators but reserved the review of British industrial policies for himself.

Caves saw the need for increased competitive vigor throughout the British economy but cautioned that the problems of 'excessive product differentiation, inappropriate degrees of integration, sub-optimal use of research and development, [and] an inefficient marketing and investment planning are deficiencies which might melt slowly and incompletely before the heat of increased market rivalry' (p. 322). More specific types of interventions might be called for, but he cautioned that their effectiveness was still untested: 'policy toward industry can serve as a useful stick, but not as a magic wand' (p. 323).

Caves's work on the Canadian economy is more extensive and represents one of his most longstanding interests. His very first paper, published nearly 50 years ago, in 1957, was entitled 'The inter-industry structure of the Canadian Economy', and his first book on that subject appeared two years later. What followed was a virtual torrent of books and articles about the Canadian economy: from 'Policies for economic growth in Canada' in 1965 and 'Canadian economic policy and impact of international capital flows' (with Grant Reuber) in 1969 to 'Trade liberalization and structural adjustment in Canada: the genesis of intra-industry trade' in 1991. Through these works and others, Caves had become one of the leading commentators on the Canadian economy. He pioneered the study of competitive conditions in small open economies and applied that analysis to the Canadian experience.

During the 1970s, Caves directed his attention towards Japan. In that era, the Japanese economy was the most prominent engine for growth in the world, and Caves became interested in how industry was organized in a non-Western context. Along with Masu Uekusa, he contributed a chapter entitled 'Industrial organization' to *Asia's New Giant: How the Japanese Economy Works*, and then extended that article into a book: *Industrial Organization in Japan*. Both were published in 1976. Again, Caves's work explored the interactions between domestic and international factors that were so important for the Japanese experience. He was directing his talents at a new subject area but with equal clarity and insightfulness.

In addition to his work on individual economies, Caves focused on firms that were not linked to any economy. He studied the substantial roles played by multinational firms and their impact on economic performance. He produced a major volume on this subject, *Multinational Enterprise and Economic Analysis*, which was originally published in 1982. His purpose was to offer a synthesis of the considerable business and economic literature that dealt with these entities.

Caves suggested that a principal reason for these firms is their possession of the critical intangible asset resulting from their knowledge of how to produce a cheaper or better product at current input prices. Such assets yield additional returns to these firms, which are not often available to smaller, single-nation enterprises. He examined these issues and reported that the presence of these enterprises resulted largely from a complicated form of transactional economies.

Public policy issues towards these enterprises are equally complex. In addition to the obvious questions of how national taxes should be levied on multinational enterprises, there are issues of 'natural-resource rents, competition policy for industrial markets, and the creation and transfer of industrial knowledge' (Caves, 1982, p. 298). In all of these areas, Caves continued his exploration into the consequences of business regulation.

The striking feature about Caves's contribution to industrial organization is the breadth and scope of his work. Rather than set a narrow agenda, he established a broad path to follow, and has done so consistently for nearly 50 years. The organization and performance of firms and industries in an open economy has served as his underlying theme, and he contributed much to our understanding of how these factors interact.

It is sometimes suggested that modern scholars are in effect working on the shoulders of all those who went before. They can only reach their current positions and see the landscape before them because of those who had worked earlier. Otherwise, their vista would be much lower than it is. There is little doubt but that scholars in the future will rest heavily on the pioneering work of Richard Caves. He is clearly a major pioneer in the construction of the edifice of industrial organization.

Most relevant publications

(1957), 'The inter-industry structure of the Canadian economy', *Canadian Journal of Economics and Political Science*, **23**, August, pp. 313–30.
(1959), *The Canadian Economy: Prospect and Retrospect* (with Richard E. Holton), Cambridge, MA: Harvard University Press.
(1960), *Trade and Economic Structure: Models and Methods*, Cambridge, MA: Harvard University Press.
(1962), *Air Transport and Its Regulators: An Industry Study*, Cambridge, MA: Harvard University Press.
(1964–92), *American Industry: Structure, Conduct, Performance*, 7 edns, Englewood Cliffs, NJ: Prentice-Hall.
(1968), et al, *Britain's Economic Prospects*, Washington, Brookings Institution.
(1976), *Industrial Organization in Japan* (with Masu Uekusa), Cambridge, MA: Harvard University Press.
(1977), 'From entry barriers to mobility barriers: conjectural decisions and contrived deterrents to new competition' (with Michael E. Porter), *Quarterly Journal of Economics*, May, 241–61.
(1979), Monopolistic export industries, trade taxes, and optimal competition policy' (with A.A. Auquier), *Economic Journal*, September, pp. 559–81.
(1980), *Competition in the Open Economy* (with Michael E. Porter and A. Michael Spence), Cambridge, MA: Harvard University Press.
(1982), *Multinational Enterprise and Economic Analysis*, Cambridge: Cambridge University Press.
(1988), 'Persuasion or information? Promotion and the sales of brand-name and genetic pharmaceuticals' (with Mark A. Hurwitz), *Journal of Law and Economics*, **31**, October, pp. 299–320.
(1990), *Efficiency in U.S. Manufacturing Industries* (with D. Barton), Cambridge, MA: MIT Press.
(1991), 'Patent expiration, entry and competition in the U.S. Pharmaceutical Industry' (with Michael D. Whinston and Mark A. Hurwitz), Brookings Paper on Economics Activity: Microeconomics, Washington, pp. 1–65.

B. LELAND L. JOHNSON

William G. Shepherd

Innovations

He explained how regulation could have three harmful effects: it would encourage excess costs and too much investment, while also inducing the monopoly firm to capture dominance in adjacent markets in anti-competitive ways.

Personal history

Born 1930, USA.

Degrees BA Univesity of Oregon, 1952; MA 1953, PhD 1956, Yale University.

Principal position Senior economist, RAND Corporation, Santa Monica, CA, 1963–?

The Averch-Johnson paper burst on the regulatory scene in 1962, giving a major push to economic doubts and debates about regulation that had already begun growing. Johnson provided the article's economic content and explanation in clear prose, while Averch provided a mathematical proof.

Their critique of regulation had three points. The most original point was that regulation applied incentives for the firm to increase its levels of investment beyond what efficiency alone would prescribe. That 'gold-plating' effect became known as the Averch–Johnson (or 'AJ') effect, and it rattled the proponents of regulation. True, it had been hinted at in many earlier regulatory cases, which required that the utility invest only in equipment that would be 'used and useful'. Yet Averch–Johnson provided the first solid economic rationale.

The second effect was the tendency of the firm to prefer a bloating of all its costs under regulation. It could enhance its profits, but it could also cushion the management against risks by providing abundant quality and depth of resources. This danger had long been more familiar in the literature.

Averch–Johnson's third harmful effect was that the firm would be induced to capture monopoly positions in adjacent markets. For this, the firm would be using funds that would otherwise be taken away by regulation. So the firm's true cost of subsidizing its own actions to capture monopoly power was zero.

The paper inflamed a series of severe claims against the public regulation of all sectors, from railroads and airlines to electricity, telecommunications, postal and other industries. Averch and Johnson had only indicated that inducements and tendencies existed, with no specific predictions or measures of the degree of impacts. Their economic originality was striking, since the literature on regulation had given only scattered hints of these possible cost-raising, 'gold-plating' and 'market-capturing' effects.

The issues were extensively debated in the 1960s and 1970s, and they quickly became a fixture in complaints about regulation's economic faults. But there was little applied research into the actual effects, and even then it focused only on the electricity industry. It found only moderately reliable indications of mild tendencies, not strong proof of large distortions. By comparison, the capturing of adjacent markets has been a leading count against regulated monopolies like AT&T, other more recent telecommunications firms, electric firms and others. AT&T had done it repeatedly before the 1980s, when it was the massively powerful monopoly telephone system of virtually the entire United States. Since then the problem persists in the 'unregulated affiliate' problem for electric and other partly regulated firms.

Johnson also pursued and developed the analysis of policies on telecommunications over several decades, but those did not involve such distinctive contributions.

Most relevant publication

Averch, Harvey, and Leland L. Johnson (1962), 'Behavior of the firm under regulatory constraint' *American Economic Review*, December, pp. 1052–69.

C. LEONARD W. WEISS

F.M. Scherer

Innovations

First collection of industry case studies that blended theory, historical evidence and policy; improvements in the measurement of industry concentration; extension of the structure–conduct (behavior)–performance paradigm to the analysis of such variables as wages, discriminatory hiring, and selling costs; and shifting the emphasis of SCP studies from profits to prices.

Personal history

Born 1925, Eugene, OR, USA; died 1994.

Degrees BS Northwestern University, 1945; PhD Columbia University, 1954.

Principal position Professor of Economics, University of Wisconsin, 1962–90.

Other Wayne State University, San Jose State College, and University of Minnesota; Special Assistant to the Assistant Attorney General, US Department of Justice, 1969–70. Served in US Navy, 1943–47.

After a career intially emphasizing international trade and urban economics, Leonard Weiss moved into the field of industrial organization with a blockbuster burst. His 1961 book, *Economics and American Industry*, provided a systematic introduction to industrial organization through a series of case studies blending exposition, mostly geometric, of the relevant theory, with a detailed analysis of seven industries' historical experience and the policy measures that either contributed to or attempted to remedy deficiencies in their performance. There had been excellent industry case-study collections before, but no one before Weiss provided a systematic theoretical framework. And most such studies had been written by an assemblage of industry specialists, not by a single author mastering the details of numerous industries. The industries were selected by Weiss to illustrate a broad range of structural and performance conditions, including purely competitive agriculture (with more intense focus on dairying), textile manufacturing (pure competition with less government intervention), monopolized aluminum, electric power (regulated monopoly), oligopolistic steel, automobiles (a differentiated oligopoly), and monopolistically competitive retailing (with detailed studies of gasoline stations, pharmacies and liquor stores). An additional chapter explored the bilaterally monopolistic bargaining between steel companies and the steelworkers' union. Updated but truncated versions of the book (deleting the textiles, aluminum and automobile chapters) were published under a different paperback title in 1967 and 1980.

The last chapter of Weiss's 1961 book set out upon a quite different methodological path. Following the structure–conduct–performance (SCP) paradigm pioneered by Joe S. Bain and George Stigler, Weiss examined cross-sectional relationships between indices of seller concentration in 23 manufacturing industry groups and several performance measures:

profit returns, changes in profit returns, changes in wholesale price indices, advertising outlays, long-term output growth, long-term productivity growth and wage changes. The analyses consisted mainly of two-variable cross-sectional scatter diagrams, but with them, Weiss staked out an agenda that would occupy much of his remaining research career.

One of his first published articles (1963a) tracked what was becoming the standard regression analysis of how seller concentration affected industry profitability, but taking into account other variables such as industry growth and the stage of the business cycle. Weiss recognized early on, however, that industry structure itself depended endogenously upon the pricing policies that firms pursued. His 1976a article with Allyn Strickland was one of the first, following Comanor and Wilson in 1967, to use a simultaneous equations approach to estimate the relationships among profits, market structure and advertising. In 1983 (with two others) he was the first to analyze the magnitude and determinants of manufacturers' selling costs other than advertising.

That structural effects might be endogenous and that elevated price–cost margins might reflect efficiencies as well as monopoly (or oligopoly) power was recognized by Weiss to be a fundamental issue. In a classic debate with Harold Demsetz, Weiss (1974) surveyed the existing empirical literature and articulated an approach to resolving the question utilizing individual firms' market share data. As others followed through on his suggestion, he chose to push his research in another direction. The standard theories of oligopoly, he insisted, emphasized price setting *per se* and not so much the profitability variables upon which most SCP analyses focused. Teaming up with his own students (during his tenure at Wisconsin he directed 47 PhD dissertations) and other economists, he organized a compendium of studies (1989) in which price, not profits, was the variable to be explained using a variety of controls, including market structural variables. His conclusion from analyzing 12 industry clusters with 121 datasets was that in the preponderance of cases, prices rose with seller concentration, although seldom by large increments.

As an economist interested in the effect of market structure on performance, Weiss directed a substantial portion of his research to understanding the determinants of structure and ensuring that it was correctly measured. In his first formal SCP analysis (1963a), he subjectively adjusted concentration ratios so that they appropriately reflected competitive conditions in the relevant markets. Seeking more objective measures, he tapped *Census of Transportation* data to develop a systematic method (1972a) for distinguishing between regional and national markets. Coupling this method with his vast knowledge of real-world industries, he compiled a compendium of adjusted manufacturing industry concentration ratios circulated in unpublished form and used by many economists in their quantitative analyses.

Unwilling to take existing structural measures for granted, Weiss sought to identify the determinants of market structure more precisely. An early (1964) paper evaluated the reliability of the 'survivor' method in identifying efficient plant-operating scales. Another paper (1965) worked out a methodology for disentangling the structural influences of mergers, new entry, exit, and existing firms' internal growth and decline. In still another effort (1976b), he surveyed company officials and leveraged his insights to estimate for 33 industries the extent to which economies of scale required relatively large plant sizes. He found that a considerable fraction of industries' capacity was embodied in plants of inefficiently small scale and that the higher seller concentration was, the smaller the fringe of inefficient capacity was likely to be. Recognizing that market structures might become more concentrated as a consequence of random growth variations under some version of Gibrat's law, Weiss found support for the hypothesis that growth was more erratic in industries with highly differentiated products (1963b).

In this and in other facets of research, Weiss was sensitive to the dynamics of price, cost and market structure relationships. In a series of papers exploring the 'administered price' hypotheses originated by Gardiner Means, Weiss showed that changes in cost were the most important drivers of price changes. But he went beyond that not unsurprising insight to reveal (1966b) that there were differences over the business cycle in the price-setting behavior of concentrated as compared to atomistic industries. The former were slower to advance their prices in periods of open inflation, but then 'caught up' (or set a pattern for further changes) when capacity was less fully utilized.

The focus on cost changes led naturally to the question of whether labor wages were related to market structure. Pioneering the use of Census of Population statistics covering individuals to test market structural hypotheses, Weiss ascertained (1966a) that wages indeed rose with seller concentration, but by paying higher wages, the more concentrated industries attracted workers with better education and other identifiable 'quality' characteristics. Among other things, the analysis suggested discrimination against black workers by concentrated industries. From this it was a logical step to study with his University of Wisconsin colleague Jeffrey Williamson (1972b, 1975) how improved education could advance the progress of minorities out of poverty.

To summarize, Leonard Weiss's research program covered most of the issues raised by the Bain–Stigler SCP paradigm, and in many of those areas, he made pioneering methodological as well as substantive contributions. It would be fair to say that his work set the stage for the next wave of empirical research in industrial organization, in which, but for a debilitating illness, he most likely would have played an active role.

Most relevant publications

(1961), *Economics and American Industry*, New York: Wiley; paperback abridgements issued as *Case Studies in American Industry*, Wiley: 1967 and 1980.

(1963a), 'Average concentration ratios and industrial performance', *Journal of Industrial Economics*, August, 237–54.

(1963b), 'Factors in changing concentration', *Review of Economics and Statistics*, February, 70–77.

(1964), 'The survival technique and the extent of sub-optimal capacity', *Journal of Political Economy*, June, 246–61.

(1965), 'An evaluation of mergers in six industries', *Review of Economics and Statistics*, May, 172–81.

(1966a), 'Concentration and labor earnings', *American Economic Review*, March, 96–117.

(1966b), 'Business pricing policy and inflation reconsidered', *Journal of Political Economy*, April, 177–97.

(1972a), 'The geographical size of markets in manufacturing', *Review of Economics and Statistics*, August, 245–57.

(1972b), 'Black education, earnings, and interregional migration: some new evidence' (with Jeffrey Williamson), *American Economic Review*, June, 372–83.

(1974), 'The concentration–profits relationship and antitrust', in Harvey J. Goldschmid, H. Michael Mann and J. Fred Weston (eds), *Industrial Concentration: The New Learning*, New York: Little-Brown, pp. 184–232.

(1975), 'Black education and earnings: even newer evidence' (with Jeffrey Williamson), *American Economic Review*, March, 241–4.

(1976a), 'Advertising, concentration, and price cost margins' (with Allyn Strickland), *Journal of Political Economy*, October, 1109–22.

(1976b), 'The economies of scale and the extent of suboptimal capacity', in Robert T. Masson and P. David Qualls (eds), *Essays in Industrial Organization in Honor of Joe S. Bain*, Cambridge: Ballinger, pp. 123–42.

(1983), 'The size of selling costs' (with George Pascoe and Stephen Martin), *Review of Economics and Statistics*, November, 668–72.

(1989), *Concentration and Price*, Cambridge, MA: MIT Press.

D. JACOB SCHMOOKLER

F.M. Scherer

Innovations

Demand-induced technological innovation, the logic of inter-industry technology flows.

Personal history

Born 1917, Woodstown, NJ, USA; died 1967.

Degrees AB Temple University, 1940; PhD University of Pennsylvania, 1951.

Principal position Professor of Economics, University of Minnesota, 1957–67.

Other Instructor, University of Pennsylvania, 1946–51; Assistant Professor, Michigan State University, 1951–57.

Jacob (Jack) Schmookler was the first economist successfully to explore statistically the economics of technological innovation at a detailed industry level. He crystallized the notion of endogenous technological change and its influence on economic growth two decades before the concept was reinvented by macro economists. Most of his key findings are brought together in his 1966 book. The underlying data and an extension of work in progress at the time of his death are in a 1972 book.

Before Schmookler made his contributions, the conventional wisdom in economics was that technological innovations were supply-side driven, for example, as advances in knowledge opened up new opportunities for profitable invention and innovation. Through the extensive analysis of time-series and cross-sectional patent data and historical case studies, Schmookler demonstrated that demand–pull influences were also important: the more intense the demand, the more creative groups and individuals were drawn to work on an unsolved problem and the more patentable inventions they generated.

Struggling during the early 1960s to reconcile the conflicting knowledge–push and demand–pull hypotheses, Schmookler argued that both could be important, just as (following Alfred Marshall) it takes the two blades of a scissors to cut paper. He hypothesized that superior command over relevant areas of knowledge, for example, specialization in chemistry, electronics, or machine construction determined the industry locus of work to satisfy unmet demands; the demand itself might be found in a quite different industry. To operationalize this view, he conceived the notion of a technology flows matrix of the form:

$$
\begin{array}{lc}
 & \text{Industry expected to use the technology} \\
 & 1 \ldots\ldots\ldots\ldots i \ldots\ldots\ldots\ldots n \\
\text{Industry developing the technology}
\begin{array}{c} 1 \\ \vdots \\ i \\ \vdots \\ m \end{array}
&
\begin{bmatrix}
t_{11} \ldots\ldots\ldots t_{1i} \ldots\ldots\ldots t_{1n} \\
\\
t_{i1} \ldots\ldots\ldots t_{ii} \ldots\ldots\ldots t_{in} \\
\\
t_{m1} \ldots\ldots\ldots t_{mi} \ldots\ldots\ldots t_{mn}
\end{bmatrix}
\end{array}
$$

where the row industries originate technological innovations and the column industries use them, and industry *n* encompasses final consumption. Technology flows on the diagonal of the matrix, for example, t_{11} and t_{ii}, represent process technology – that is, inventions, usually of a cost-saving nature, that improve production activities within one's own sphere of activity. Much of Schmookler's empirical work focused on capital goods inventions. He died prematurely before he was able to implement his technology flow concept. A large-scale effort by the author of this biography to construct a technology flows matrix and test his demand–pull hypotheses (*Journal of Industrial Economics*, March 1982) yielded strong support for capital goods inventions and weaker support for intermediate materials inventions. The influence of demand proved to be at least as strong for inventions that crossed industry boundaries as for intra-industry (process) inventions.

Among Schmookler's other contributions was a 1952 article that anticipated the productivity growth decomposition for which Robert Solow won the Nobel Prize in 1987. In a 1959 article he weighed into the growing controversy over the technological innovativeness of large as compared to small firms by showing that for every eight patented inventions resulting from full-time research and development employees, five came from employees engaged only part-time in inventive activity, often in smaller companies. Schmookler also collaborated with Richard R. Nelson in organizing a 1960 conference that brought economists together for the first time to struggle with the economics of innovation and their relationship to productivity growth. The results were published in 1962 under the title, *The Rate and Direction of Inventive Activity* (Princeton, NJ: Princeton University Press).

Most relevant publications

(1952), 'The changing efficiency of the American economy, 1869–1938', *Review of Economics and Statistics*, **34** (August), 214–31.

(1959), 'Bigness, fewness, and research', *Journal of Political Economy*, **67** (December), 630.

(1966), *Innovation and Economic Growth*, Cambridge, MA: Harvard University Press.

(1972), *Patents, Invention, and Economic Change* (Leonid Hurwicz and Zvi Griliches, eds), Cambridge, MA: Harvard University Press.

E. FREDERIC M. SCHERER

John E. Kwoka

Innovations
Empirical testing of Schumpeterian hypotheses about the determinants of patenting and technological innovation. Key analyses of inter-industry technology flows, research and development (R&D) and productivity growth, innovation and international trade. His industrial organization textbook was a landmark integration of all aspects of the field, including theory, empirical evidence, and antitrust policy. Scherer's studies of the defense industry, of scale economies in manufacturing, and of mergers are modern classics.

Personal history

Born 1932, Ottawa, IL, USA.

Degrees BA University of Michigan, 1954; MBA, PhD Harvard, 1963, 1968.

Principal positions Faculties of Princeton University, University of Michigan, Northwestern University, Swarthmore College and Kennedy School of Government (Harvard). Research position at the International Institute of Management, Berlin. Also Director of Bureau of Economics, Federal Trade Commission.

Scherer has been a towering figure in industrial organization. It is not excessive to say that he has helped to define the modern field, to set its agenda, and to bring it to the attention of many economists and non-economists who were previously unaware of its importance and relevance to their own work. His primary research interests have involved empirical testing of Schumpeterian and neo-Schumpeterian hypotheses, but his contributions have been numerous and range widely over the field.

Scherer got into economics in a somewhat roundabout manner. Early on, he was intrigued by the career of Thomas Edison, but the sciences did not spark his interest in college. While at Michigan, however, his exposure to Kenneth Boulding, Z. Clark Dickenson and Shorey Peterson prompted him to consider economics. Then, after stints in the army and at the family-owned trucking company, Scherer entered Harvard Business School. There coursework and research into manufacturing processes, patents and innovation, and the defense industry identified issues of enduring interest to him. The research into the defense industry under Joe Peck and David Novick in particular convinced him that his real interest lay in economics. This resulted in two books, one of which – *The Weapons Acquisition Process: Economic Incentives* (1964) – ultimately served as his doctoral dissertation. Scherer switched to Harvard's economics department, where he studied with Jesse Markham, Richard Hefleblower and Thomas Schelling, and from which he got his PhD in 1963.

Over the next 40 years, Scherer would author or co-author 21 books and more than 150 articles. One persistent theme has been Scherer's conviction that 'technological change has had, and will continue to have, much more of an impact on material well-being than the niceties of static resource allocation to which microeconomists devote most of their attention' (*Innovation and Growth: Schumpeterian Perspectives*, 1984, p. vii). This conviction originated with his reading of Joseph Schumpeter's *Capitalism, Socialism, and Democracy* while at the University of Michigan, and resulted in a lifetime of research that has at various times proven and disproven Schumpeter's central hypotheses. Collectively, this undertaking has rewritten much of what we know about technological change and technology policy.

Scherer's initial foray into this area was prompted by the then-common prediction that the 1956 antitrust decrees opening up AT&T's and IBM's patents would hinder technological progressiveness. The following year, together with some of his fellow students at Harvard Business School, Scherer surveyed 69 companies concerning the role of patents in their R&D decisions. In contrast to the prediction, they found that patents in fact played little role in actual R&D decision making, implying that the compulsory licensing provisions of the decrees would not have adverse effects. Later research by a number of economists confirmed this result.

This exercise illustrated several enduring characteristics of Scherer's research and methodological bent. It foreshadowed a career of questioning commonplace assertions and of subjecting hypotheses to empirical test, rather than simply accepting those assertions or relying on theoretical demonstrations in support of them. It also illustrated Scherer's willingness to go out into the real world and develop new data whenever existing data were inadequate for the issue at hand. In this latter respect, Scherer distinguished himself from many of his fellow industrial organization economists, who increasingly attempted to correct for poor data with higher-powered econometric techniques – if they did empirical analysis at all.

Scherer's 1965 article on market structure and patenting in the *American Economic Review* ('Firm size, market structure, opportunity, and the output of patented inventions') demonstrated the power of this approach. Having compiled new data on more than 350 firms, Scherer probed key Schumpeterian hypotheses about the structural determinants of inventive output, measured by a count of patents and checked against R&D employment. He examined firm size, market concentration and diversification as possible causal factors. He tested for nonlinear scale effects in the relationship and for differences among industry groups. And despite his appreciation for Schumpeter's work, Scherer's tests rejected most of his hypotheses. In particular, neither large firm size nor high market concentration was found to be uniquely supportive of more patenting.

The importance of this paper was considerable. It represented the first large-scale test of widely held views about technological change. It illustrated the power of empirical research as well as the importance of compiling necessary data. Its approach would be widely followed by later research into technological change. And it demonstrated another enduring characteristic of Scherer's work – a deep respect for facts. Whatever might have been his prior beliefs or expectations, Scherer accepted the results of good empirical research – his own and that of others.

Scherer's contributions to the literature on technological change continued apace. Perhaps most notable among many articles is his 1967 paper on R&D under rivalry, which analyzed the role of market structure on the timing and certainty of R&D projects ('Research and development resource allocation under rivalry'). He introduced the notion of a development possibility function, which related development costs and timing. Mathematical and graphical analysis then established that for reasonably high-profit innovations, an atomistic industry would innovate and do so quickly. For low-value innovations, however, an atomistic industry might not produce sufficient returns to any single firm to induce it to undertake the innovative effort, so that at least some degree of concentration would ensure the innovation, even if a bit more slowly. These insights were enormously helpful in disentangling the relationship between innovation and market concentration, a topic about which there was much confusion.

Another notable advance in this area occurred some 15 years later with Scherer's study of inter-industry technology flows ('Interindustry technology flows in the United States', 1982). This exercise sought to identify the actual industry of origin of new technologies that benefit a particular industry. These industries might not be the same insofar as process and even product advances might arise from firms in an 'upstream' industry supplying the industry in question. In such cases the count of the using industry's patents would understate its technological advance (since its advances originate elsewhere), and for the industry of origin, R&D expenditures and patent count bear no relationship to its own technological progressiveness.

To examine these questions, the Scherer team examined more than 15,000 patents obtained by 443 large US corporations for which R&D and other data were reported in the Federal Trade Commission's (FTC's) 1974 Line of Business survey. Using sectors for each patent were exhaustively recorded. The result was a vast matrix of technology flows among US industries, which documented the considerable inter-relatedness of industries' technology experience. In addition, industry labor productivity was shown statistically to depend upon both own and using industries' R&D expenditures. This demonstrated the importance of looking beyond the industry's own efforts in assessing the reasons for productivity growth.

But earlier, and barely three years into his professional career, Scherer found himself where so many instructors do – dissatisfied with available textbooks. That, together with an interest in speaking to a wider audience of industrial economists than his work on R&D captured, led him in 1966 to begin work on what would be the first modern comprehensive textbook in industrial organization. *Industrial Market Structure and Economic Performance* would be three years in the making. Its appearance was a watershed event in the field. It evaluated huge amounts of literature, both theoretical and empirical. It synthesized findings into a coherent framework for understanding what the literature did and did not say. Its critiques of the literature constituted a research agenda for the next generation, or two, of students and faculty alike.

The book contained the first comprehensive statement of the economics of antitrust policy – from mergers to vertical restraints, from monopolies to cartels. Because of that and because of its scholarship and readability, *Industrial Market Structure and Economic Performance* had influence far beyond the narrow field of industrial organization economics. Lawyers, both academic and practicing, policy makers inside and outside government, business leaders, faculty and students in business schools and schools of public policy, as well as economists in all fields, picked it up and found that it spoke to issues they were dealing with. It became the standard source of understanding about a wide range of policy questions. It is said that at least one clerk in every Supreme Court Justice's office at the time had a copy of Scherer's book on his or her shelf.

There were, of course, predecessors to this book, Joe Bain's *Industrial Organization* perhaps the most important. Scherer's perspective differed, however, in that it did not lie in Bain's famous 'structure–conduct (behavior)–predominance' tradition. Rather,

Scherer emphasized feedback effects, the complex role of firm strategies, and of course the importance of technological change, none of which occupied as important a place in the discipline prior to this treatise. As a result of its sheer scholarship, its encyclopedic nature, and its readability, the three editions of *Industrial Market Structure and Economic Performance* (1970, 1980, 1990) would dominate the field for 25 years.

This account of the book's impact would be incomplete without reference to its role in the debates initiated by the Chicago school of economics. That school's often vehement attacks questioned the modeling, the empirical work, the interpretation and the credibility of the received body of knowledge about industrial markets. Scherer and others challenged the Chicago school for its simplistic theorizing, for its dismissal of (indeed, sometimes contempt for) empirical testing, and for its ideological policy prescriptions. During this time, Scherer's book provided careful guidance to those who believed, as did his mentor Schumpeter, that 'history, statistics, and theory' all mattered in the study of industrial economics and policy.

Some 26 of Scherer's contributions to economic policy are collected in *Competition Policy, Domestic and International* (2001). Written over a period of 30 years, these address a wide range of policy issues, including the goals of antitrust policy; the policy implications of such business practices as vertical restraints, focal point pricing, and petroleum exchanges; efficiencies and remedies in merger and monopoly cases; the use and misuse of patents; and the role of competition policy in an increasingly global economy. Taken as a whole, these essays blend theory, statistics and history into compelling analyses that speak to key issues of competition policy.

While most of Scherer's contributions to policy have taken the form of such essays, on one occasion he took a non-academic, policy position in government. For two years beginning in 1974, he was Director of the Bureau of Economics – essentially the chief economist – at the Federal Trade Commission. Scherer has termed this a 'memorable and gratifying experience' ('An accidental Schumpeterian', 1996, p. 12) with much of his time devoted to fostering the FTC's Line of Business program's pioneering data collection exercise, as well as to overseeing such antitrust cases as cereals and the petroleum industry investigation. He later expressed frustration with the Reagan administration's subsequent reversal of many of his efforts at the FTC.

Three other areas at the frontiers of industrial organization have also been scrutinized by Scherer. Previously mentioned was his early analysis of the defense industry. Until that time, the defense industry was seen essentially as a government program with its own rationale and budget determined by politics, both domestic and foreign. As he did with many other topics, Scherer applied industrial organization economics to this industry. His focus was on incentives in the system – optimal incentives, reputation effects, the effects of small numbers, alternative cost-sharing mechanisms, multi-dimensional objectives, administrative controls and post-contract performance. This approach was pathbreaking not only because it was a novel way of viewing the defense industry, but also because it anticipated a movement in the profession a generation later that viewed transactions generally as matters of incentives and contracts.

The Weapons Acquisition Process: Economic Incentives (1964) was notable also because it contained a passage that reflected Scherer's concerns about the uses of economics in policy. His Preface began with the following passage: 'The publication of this volume terminates a long struggle with my conscience. It is difficult to write a book of this sort without suppressing doubts about the morality of modem weapons development and production efforts' (p. ix). He went on to set out his reservations about the uses of weapons systems, their opportunity cost, and the merits of improving the efficiency of the acquisition process. One rarely encounters such open reflection on the purposes served by economic analysis.

Another landmark study probed economies of scale. Scherer's research with Alan Beckenstein, Erich Kaufer and Dennis Murphy was prompted in part by two observations: (i) most large firms were large because of multiplant operation rather than by virtue of their scaling up a single plant, and (ii) in other countries individual plants were generally much smaller than in the US but firms had similar numbers of plants. All this suggested the importance of multiplant operation, importance that might exceed the gains from the traditional 'scaling up' view of economies. In this research, Scherer et al. first identified a number of economies that arose from multiplant structures, as well as some limits to firm growth from that strategy. They then applied these insights into 12 major industries in the US and five other developed industrial economies, developing information through interviews with company officials and painstaking data compilation.

The resulting treatise, *The Economics of Multi-Plant Operation: An International Comparisons Study* (1975), significantly generalized previous empirical inquiries into scale economies. It highlighted the importance of multiplant economies, including such forces as advertising, investment planning, R&D and transport costs. Its conclusions became the foundation for the elucidation of economies of scale that appeared in *Industrial Market Structure and Economic Performance* which represented the state of our understanding about actual economies for a very long time – some might say, from a practical perspective, even to this day.

The third notable area of inquiry by Scherer concerned mergers. Again, the research was prompted by important questions for which the evidence was anecdotal or based at most on modest data: what effects do mergers have on economic performance? Are mergers generally successful? Why are so many mergers deliberately undone by subsequent divestiture? And once again Scherer's effort to amass evidence was on a huge scale. He and co-worker David Ravenscraft linked nearly 6000 mergers to the companies and time period of the FTC's Line of Business data source. This permitted the performance of individual lines of business to be tracked statistically through merger, sell-off, or divestiture. Together with case-study evidence and survey work, this represented one of the most comprehensive efforts at assessing mergers in the US.

The results, published in *Mergers Sell-Offs, and Economic Efficiency* (1987), refuted many commonly held views about mergers. Scherer and Ravenscraft reported, for example, that target firms were considerably more profitable than nontarget firms, belying the view that mergers were intended to improve weak firms' performance. Further, they found that nearly half of all acquired units were subsequently divested, and the rate was particularly high for conglomerate acquisitions. Units that were acquired and retained on average experienced severe postmerger profit declines. Mergers among units of similar size fared somewhat better, those taken over via tender offers significantly worse. All in all, the picture of mergers that emerged was one described as 'widespread failure, considerable mediocrity, and occasional success' (*Industrial Market Structure and Economic Performance*, 1990, p. 173).

Scherer's research into mergers illustrates the characteristics that have made his work so important. Time and again, he has asked the big questions. Then he has painstakingly compiled vast amounts of the data required to address the questions. Finally, he has uncovered novel, often startling and provocative, answers to those questions. His studies of particular issues, his monumental textbook, his lifelong attention to technological change – all justifiably ensure his pre-eminent place in the history of industrial organization and policy.

Most relevant publications

(1964), *The Weapons Acquisition Process: Economic Incentives*, Cambridge, MA: Harvard Business School Division of Research.

(1965), 'Firm size, market structure, opportunity, and the output of patented inventions', *American Economic Review*, December, 1097–125.

(1967), 'Research and development resource allocation under rivalry', *Quarterly Journal of Economics*, August, 359–94.

(1970), *Industrial Market Structure and Economic Performance*, 2nd edn, 1980, 3rd ed with David Ross (ed.), 1990, Boston, MA: Houghton Mifflin.

(1975), *The Economics of Multi-Plant Operation: An International Comparisons Study* (with Alan Beckenstein, Erich Kaufer and R.D. Murphy), Cambridge, MA: Harvard University Press.

(1982), 'Industrial technology flows in the United States', Cambridge, MA: *Research Policy*, **11**, 227–45.

(1984), *Innovation and Growth: Schumpeterian Perspectives*, Cambridge, MA: MIT Press.

(1987), *Mergers, Sell-offs, and Economic Efficiency* (with David J. Ravenscraft), Washington, DC: Brookings Institution.

(1996), 'An accidental Schumpeterian', *The American Economist*, Spring, 5–13.

(2001), *Competition Policy, Domestic and International*, Cheltenham, UK and Northampton, MA, USA: Edward Elgar.

F. WILLIAM G. SHEPHERD

John Howard Brown

Innovations

Highlighting the role of individual firm market share in the exercise of monopoly power; critiques of the empirical weaknesses of received techniques.

Personal history

Born Ames, IA, USA, 1936.

Principal position Professor, University of Massachusetts.

Other University of Michigan; Special Assistant to the Assistant Attorney General for Antitrust.

Degrees BA (Economics, with honors), Amherst College, 1957; MA, PhD (Economics), Yale University, 1958, 1963.

William G. (Geoff) Shepherd's contributions to industrial organization have been manifold, particularly including his role as long-serving editor of the *Review of Industrial Organization,* where he nurtured many younger scholars. A major scholarly contribution has been recognizing and documenting the role of individual firms' market shares in the exercise of market power. .

In his 1972 paper, 'The elements of market structure' (1972a) he demonstrated that in a sample of 231 'large' firms from 1960–69, individual firm market share was the most important, and almost invariably, statistically significant determinant of firm rate of return. The effect held over a large variety of specifications and overshadowed the effect of market share jointly held by the largest firms in an industry. This result explains the puzzling (to the neo-classical economic theorist) fixation that corporate executives have on their firm's market shares. These equations also highlighted the important role of advertising and firm growth in explaining rate of return. Coupling firm market share in estimating equations with high barriers to entry likewise demonstrated the powerful effects of firm market share, high barriers and firm revenue growth.

Like this paper, the rest of Shepherd's work has been noteworthy for its careful empiricism and willingness to tack against the currents of received professional opinion. Exemplars of this care and tough-mindedness can be found throughout his *oeuvre*, notably in his 1970 book, *Market Power and Economic Welfare.* This book, as the title suggests, lays out the relationships between market power and economic performance.

In the first part, Shepherd lays the theoretical groundwork for economic understanding of market power. In the second part, he describes the identifiable extent of market power in the American economy circa 1970. This represents, to a degree underemphasized in the book, a substantial amount of original research. For instance, in evaluating claims about the level of industrial concentration in this book, Shepherd recognizes that many SIC industries do not correspond to economically meaningful markets (pp. 106–7). He adjusts the census published figures to reflect actual markets and finds that concentration was substantially higher than reported. The third part appraises the performance of industries where market power is present across a wide array of measures.

Reflecting the same tough-mindedness, he notes that the structure–conduct (behavior) –performance model while used by 'most systematic research … has become something of a cookbook formula for dissertations on specific industries' (p. 18). One result of this, as he notes a few pages later is that: 'The rush to 'test' concepts empirically has degenerated frequently into a sort of scientism, in which lack of findings in a faulty test using slender evidence was asserted to disprove the existence of otherwise likely phenomena' (p. 23).

Yet another example of Shepherd's myth-busting style is his 1982 article, 'Causes of increased competition in the U.S. economy, 1939–1980'. Since at least the 1930s economists in the nascent field of industrial organization had been concerned with declining competition across a broad spectrum of American industries, particularly manufacturing. (See Burns, Arthur R., *The Decline of Competition: A Study of the Evolution of American Industry*, McGraw-Hill, New York, 1936 for example.) In this article, Shepherd leads this sacred cow to the slaughterhouse, demonstrating that the extent of competition in the American economy had actually increased over the period in question.

As he notes, '*the degree of competitiveness appears in more than one dimension*' (p. 615, emphasis in original). Which makes the very measurement of 'competition' a process fraught with difficulty. As always, Shepherd is cautious about reductionism in measuring competition, observing that: 'Concentration ratios measure only one element of market structure' (p. 615). At the time, concentration ratios were the standard yardstick in empirical industrial organization, held to almost solely define market structure. Beyond this, he remarks that: 'market structure itself does not fully determine the degree of competitiveness. For each specific structure (apart from perfect competition) a range of behavioral competitiveness is possible' (p. 615).

With this foundation, Shepherd divides the markets in the economy into four categories: monopoly, dominant firm, tight oligopoly and effectively competitive. The last category represents all those markets where the exercise of market power is unlikely to rise to the level of a public policy issue. Compiling and evaluating data from a broad range of sources, Shepherd concludes that approximately 75 percent of national income in 1980 originated in sector markets that were effectively competitive. This represented a dramatic change from 1939 where scarcely one half of all output stemmed from markets which might be classified as competitive. Both pure monopoly and dominant firm market structures which are most likely to see the troublesome exercise of monopoly power fell to one half of their 1939 values.

Examining the causes of these dramatic developments, Shepherd concludes that four forces were responsible for this transformation. The first was increasing competition from imports where 13 industries generating 3.8 percent of national income were subjected to effective competition from imports. More controversially, Shepherd attributes a substantial role to antitrust enforcement. In fact, he finds that 20 industries representing over 8 percent of national income became more competitive due to antitrust actions. A third factor that Shepherd examines is the trend towards deregulation of substantial portions of the economy. A final source, which Shepherd was unable to quantify adequately was the role of declining economies of scale (relative to market size) in many industries.

Further application of Shepherd's careful empiricism led him to conclude that the survivor test proposed by Stigler is an empty vessel, providing little practical guidance about the degree and evolution of economies of scale in manufacturing industries (1967). As he notes, 'The primary limitation is that the technique gives *descriptive*, not *normative,* estimates of "optimality": it tells what *is*, not necessarily what is *optimum* or *efficient* in terms of net social costs' (p. 115, emphasis in original). This limitation has several implications for the use of survivorship as an analytical technique. First, that survival may be influenced by market power more than technical efficiency. Second, that no analysis of why efficient sizes have changed is possible. Finally, survivorship does not indicate the degree of efficiency of surviving plant sizes or the relative inefficiency of shrinking sizes.

Beyond these conceptual objections, Shepherd is also critical of the practical empirical difficulties of correctly implementing the technique. His most important objection is that the results of applying survivor analysis to industries is, even when an appropriate standard of measurement can be developed, and adequate and, most importantly, comparable data are available, the results are most often ambiguous regarding the nature of the changes an industry has experienced. His conclusion is that: 'these results fall short of the early promise of the survivor technique: the failures are many, the proven successes are few' (p. 122). The effectiveness of his critique can be judged by the absence of virtually any applications of the technique subsequent to his article.

A final thread in Shepherd's work is his continuing struggle against Panglossian appraisals of the benefits of competition. There is literally no reason to doubt the benefits conferred through the operation of competition in a market economy. However, Shepherd has been at pains to make clear that extent of competition, as opposed to the exercise of monopoly power, is an empirical question. His criticisms of the Chicago school's optimistic views of market power are one instance of this. His work on the extent of and trends in competition in the US economy as an example of this empiricism counterpoised to theoretical argumentation has already been discussed.

Another consequence of this is that he was one of the most effective opponents of the notion of contestability as proposed by W.J. Baumol et al. in the later 1970s and early 1980s (1984). Shepherd's critique of contestability begins by identifying the core idea of contestability as the notion of 'ultrafree entry'. This implies that entry occurs without costs or lags, is met passively by incumbent firms, and is costlessly reversible. Like his critique of the survivor technique, Shepherd begins on the conceptual level, discussing the internal inconsistencies and empirical irrelevancy of 'contestability.' Turning to empirical issues, he notes that a substantial body of empirical research points to competition among existing firms, and the barriers to entry in markets as explanations for firm pricing behavior. Further, Shepherd points out a paucity of cases that might be plausibly identified with contestable markets. Even the cases that Baumol et al. specifically suggested such as airlines, appear on further examination to provide little support for the concept.

Most relevant publications

(1966), 'Residence expansion in the British telephone system', *Journal of Industrial Economics*, **14**(3), June, 263–74.

(1967), 'What does the survivor technique show about economies of scale?', *Southern Economic Journal*, **34**, July, 113–22.

(1970), *Market Power and Economic Welfare: An Introduction*, New York: Random House.

(1972a), 'The elements of market structure', *Review of Economics and Statistics*, **54**(1), February, 25–37.

(1972b), 'Structure and behavior in British industries, with U.S. comparisons', *Journal of Industrial Economics*, **21**(1), November, 35–54.
(1973a), 'Entry as a substitute for regulation', *American Economic Review*, **63**(2), Papers and Proceedings of the Eighty-fifth Annual Meeting of the American Economic Association, May, 98–105.
(1973b), 'Managerial discrimination in large firms' (with Sharon G. Levin), *Review of Economics and Statistics*, **55**(4), November, 412–22.
(1982), 'Causes of increased competition in the U.S. economy, 1939–1980', *Review of Economics and Statistics*, **64**(4), November, 613–26.
(1984), '"Contestability" vs. competition', *American Economic Review*, **74**(4), September, 572–87.
(1986), 'Tobin's *q* and the structure–performance relationship: comment', *American Economic Review*, **76**(5), December, 1205–10.

G. HARVEY J. LEIBENSTEIN

William G. Shepherd

Innovations
He created the concept of X-efficiency in 1966, and he analyzed and applied it in extensive detail.

Personal history

Born 1922, USA; died 1992.

Degrees BS, MA Northwestern University, 1945, 1946; PhD Princeton University, 1951.

Principal position Professor of Economics, Harvard University, Cambridge, MA, 1966–92.

Others Department of Economics, University of California, Berkeley, 1951–67.

The 'X-efficiency' term (and its reverse version, X-inefficiency) was created by Leibenstein in 1966, to denote all forms of inefficiency *other* than allocative efficiency as it is defined in neo-classical microeconomic theory. That theory assumed that rational choices would prevent any X-inefficiency from ever existing, because all firms would maximize profits by squeezing costs to the minimum. Leibenstein's X-inefficiency idea deviated from theoretical traditions, but it agreed both with business knowledge and with the growing study of large-firm behavior and its departures from theoretically strict business efficiency.

Leibenstein pressed the idea creatively and forcefully, noting that X-inefficiency could grow to large dimensions, much larger than the slivers of misallocative losses that theorists had focused on. Against A.C. Harberger's 1954 estimate that allocative inefficiency was tiny, at 0.1 percent or less, Leibenstein noted that X-inefficiency can often be large – on the order of 10 to 20 percent of total costs – and he argued that it is often widespread and deeply rooted. He noted such important examples as weapons firms selling to the Pentagon, monopolies, and other firms not facing market pressures.

Liebenstein urged that X-inefficiency had two main elements: the firm's absorption of excessive amounts of inputs, and the low levels of workers' efforts that may occur during their time at work. Low effort levels was a particularly novel concept in scholarly circles, and it helped lead to extensive new research in the field of labor economics. Low effort could be the larger part of X-inefficiency in many actual instances.

Leibenstein elaborated his full statement of X-inefficiency's importance in a 1976 book, *Beyond Economic Man*.

Most relevant publications
(1966), 'Allocative efficiency vs. "X-efficiency"', *American Economic Review*, June, pp. 392–415.
(1976), *Beyond Economic Man*, Cambridge, MA: Harvard University Press.

H. WILLIAM S. COMANOR

William G. Shepherd

Innovations

He studied the determinants of innovation in the drug industry; he showed (with Thomas Wilson, 1967 and 1974) how advertising might create and raise monopoly power; he noted the importance of X-inefficiency in judging mergers; he estimated the effect of monopoly profits in making the distribution of wealth in the US more unequal; and he explored important aspects of vertical restrictions that could reduce competition.

Personal history

Born 1937, Philadelphia, PA, USA.

Degrees BA Haverford College, 1959; PhD Harvard University, 1963.

Principal positions Professor of Economics, University of California at Santa Barbara, 1975–; also Professor of Health Services, UCLA, 1993–.

Other Harvard University, 1961–68; Special Economic Assistant to the Assistant Attorney General for Antitrust, 1965–66; Graduate School of Business, Stanford University, 1968–73; Director, Bureau of Economics, Federal Trade Commission, 1978–80.

Comanor used theory and detailed evidence in the early 1960s to find whether drug-industry patents and advertising might tend to reduce research and development (R&D) activity and the resulting flow of new pharmaceutical drugs. He generally noted that innovation would be reduced.

He then (with Thomas Wilson) pioneered in 1967 and 1974 in studying how intensive advertising could raise entry barriers and increase market power. They developed the concept of 'advertising intensity' (total spending on advertising, as a percentage of total sales revenue). They prepared a range of firm- and industry-based data on profitability, market structure, scale economies and advertising. They used the data to estimate advertising's effects in a wide range of US industries. Comanor and Wilson concluded that the significant correlation of advertising intensity with profit rates reflect causation; hence, they said, advertising causes market power.

Comanor also pointed out (1969, with Harvey J. Leibenstein) that X-inefficiency can be a large harm caused by rises in monopoly power – large enough to exceed any beneficial economies of scale that a merger might yield. The point countered Oliver E. Williamson's stress on mergers' economic benefits, even if they hurt competition.

Next Comanor prepared (1975, with Robert H. Smiley) a strikingly original test of monopoly's effect in increasing the inequality of the distribution of wealth in the US after the 1870s. The model assumed a range of values for monopoly's strength, the rate of retention of family fortunes, and other parameters. The model and data indicated a substantial effect on the wealth distribution in the century before the 1970s, ranging roughly from 10 to 25 percent of the total distribution. The paper stands as an unchallenged classic.

In the early 1980s, Comanor developed the theory of vertical restrictions, exploring whether vertical restrictions would reduce competition; he found that they could, in certain situations.

Throughout, Comanor has applied high standards of rigor and technique, and his writing is invariably lucid and concise.

Comanor also pioneered as the first Special Economic Assistant in 1965–66, appointed by Donald F. Turner, who was then the head of the senior US antitrust agency (the Antitrust Division in the US Department of Justice). This position gave innermost economic access to and involvement with all important Antitrust Division decisions. It also embodied Turner's resolve to raise the economic quality of US antitrust. This important situation continued with a series of later Special Assistants, including Oliver E. Williamson, William G. Shepherd, H. Michael Mann, Leonard W. Weiss, Kenneth G. Elzinga and George Hay.

In 1978–80 Comanor doubled this achievement when he also became the Chief Economist of the Federal Trade Commission (Director of the Bureau of Competition). No other economist has served this leadership role in both of the US antitrust agencies.

Most relevant publications

(1965), 'Research and technical change in the pharmaceutical industry', *Review of Economics and Statistics*, May.
(1967), 'Advertising, market structure and performance', *Review of Economics and Statistics* (with Thomas Wilson), November, 423–40.
(1969), 'Allocative efficiency, X-efficiency, and the measurement of welfare losses', *Economics* (with Harvey J. Leibenstein), August, 304–9.
(1974), *Advertising and Market Power* (with T.A. Wilson), Cambridge, MA: Harvard University Press.
(1975), 'Monopoly and the distribution of wealth' (with R.H. Smiley), *Quarterly Journal of Economics*, May, **89**, pp. 177–94.
(1985), 'Vertical price fixing, vertical market restraints, and the new antitrust policy', *Harvard Law Review*, March.

I. OLIVER E. WILLIAMSON

William G. Shepherd

Innovations

In the early 1960s, Williamson did research on large firms, eventually developing in the 1970s the idea of 'transactions costs' as part of 'new institutional economics'. In 1968 he explored the possible 'trade-off' between the price-raising harms that a merger might cause, vs. the possible benefits from greater economies of scale.

Personal history

Born 1932, Superior, WI, USA.

Degrees BS MIT, 1955; MBA Stanford University, 1960; PhD Carnegie-Mellon University, 1963.

Principle positions Professor of Business Administration, Economics and Law, University of California, Berkeley, CA; at Berkeley, 1963–68, 1988–; Professor of Economics, University of Pennsylvania, Philadelphia, PA, 1968–83.

Other Fellow, Econometric Society, 1977; President, American Law & Economic Association, 1998. Special Economic Adviser to the head of the Antitrust Division, 1966–67. Professor of Economics, Law and Organization, Yale University, 1983–88.

In the early 1960s, Williamson was (with Richard Cyert and James G. March) among those involved in the growing study of real motivations and effects in large corporations. Work by Williamson and others continued the research line that had been opened by A.A. Berle and G.C. Means in 1932 and was enlarged by A.D.H. Kaplan, Joel B. Dirlam and Robert F. Lanzillotti in 1958. Williamson drew on various ideas of Ronald H. Coase, Herbert Simon, Kenneth Arrow and Alfred Chandler to explore several of the possible effects when corporate executives strayed from strict profit-maximizing behavior.

Williamson often coined unusual terms – such as 'expense preferences' and 'bounded rationality' and 'credible threats' – for ideas that had arisen in the literature. He also discussed possible research methods for measuring these effects.

He later developed this into the 'transactions costs' approach, which further explored the inner patterns within large firms. He showed how 'bounded rationality' (reflecting managers' limited data and abilities) might lead to predictable deviations from the conventional predictions of profit-maximizing actions within firms. By 1980 he presented this as a fundamental new system of thought, a 'new institutional economics'.

His research approach primarily used theory and judgments about business experience, rather than large-scale econometric testing. Transactions costs have attracted discussion as a subfield that studies the inner workings of enterprises. It has not led to substantial changes in antitrust policies.

In 1968, Williamson argued that merger policies should be changed to allow for possible economies of scale. He showed with a diagram that such economies (a horizontal rectangle) might be larger than the monopoly effects of a merger (shown by the long-recognized 'welfare triangle'). This 'trade-off' should, he said, lead officials to permit such mergers, when the mergers would give net gains in efficiency.

Since he was then the economic adviser to Donald F. Turner, who was in charge of the Antitrust Division during 1965–68, Williamson's point gained added attention. Previously, the policy had been skeptical of self-interested and unverifiable claims of economies; decisions would focus on the harm to competition and consumers.

Others soon showed that Williamson's analysis tended to understate the monopoly harms of mergers and to accept the claims of economies. Moreover, he omitted X-inefficiency as a possible cost of rising monopoly power, as well as the precedential effects of each merger-policy decision on later mergers. The decision on today's merger may influence hundreds of other future merger plans. But he did give merger economies more role in antitrust debates for some years.

Most relevant publications

(1964), *The Economics of Discretionary Behavior*, Englewood Cliffs, NJ: Prentice-Hall.
(1968), 'Economies as an antitrust defense', *American Economic Review*, March, pp. 18–36.
(1975), *Markets and Hierarchies*, New York: Free Press.
(1985), *The Economic Institutions of Capitalism*, New York: Free Press.

J. HAROLD DEMSETZ

William G. Shepherd

Innovations

He articulated the hard-line Chicago school position; he proposed replacing the regulation of utilities by the threat of losing the franchise; and he stressed the 'efficient structure hypothesis'.

Personal history

Born 1930, Chicago, IL, USA.

Degrees BS University of Illinois, 1953; MBA, MA, PhD Northwestern University, 1954, 1959, 1959.

Principal position Professor of Economics, UCLA, Los Angeles, CA, 1971–.

Other University of Michigan, 1958–60; University of Chicago, 1963–71.

Harold Demsetz joined with George J. Stigler in advocating the hard-line Chicago school free-market position. Demsetz also extended that approach in two ways, which urged the removal of constraints on business freedom.

First, he argued in 1968 that traditional regulation was unnecessary and should be abolished. Instead, the monopolist would face only a periodic need to renew its monopoly franchise. Under threat of losing its franchise, the firm would, Demsetz said, behave as if it were under absolutely complete competitive pressure. Critics pointed to problems of adequate information and predictions that could plague the franchise auctions, and they doubted that this pressure would be thorough and reliable. It would, for example, intensify the firm's incentives to exploit some or many consumers. But Demsetz's basic logic did have some merit; periodic reviews of regulated firms' performance can apply beneficial pressure toward efficiency and innovation.

Demsetz was equally severe against antitrust policies. He argued in 1973 that the standard causation of the structure–behavior (conduct)–performance triad should be reversed, under the logic of an 'efficient-structure hypothesis'. Assuming that markets contained no imperfections at all, he argued that when any firm holds dominance over the market and reaps high profits, that could occur only if the firm had won them by its superior efficiency and innovations. Market power would not exist; only exceptional performance which yields illusory 'monopolies' which must behave like efficient and innovative competitors. Demsetz also said that perfect-market conditions would guarantee that no anti-competitive actions could occur.

The view requires that all markets, including capital markets, fit perfect assumptions. For empirical support, Demsetz offered a table of summary data about company size classes and profit rates.

Most relevant publications

(1968), 'Why regulate utilities?', *Journal of Law & Economics*, April, **10**, pp. 55–65.
(1973), 'Industry, structure, market rivalry, and public policy', *Journal of Law and Economics*, April, pp. 1–90.

K. PAUL W. MACAVOY

William G. Shepherd

Innovations

He showed that much of the historical basis of US railroad regulation involved the creation of monopoly power; analyzed the case for deregulating natural gas; criticized eletricity regulation in 1974 and helped to lay the basis for its later deregulation; and clarified the role of OPEC's (Organization of the Petroleum-Exporting Countries) market power in the rise of oil prices after 1973.

Personal history

Born 1934, Haverhill, MA, USA.

Degrees BA Bates College, 1955; MA, PhD Yale University, 1956, 1960.

Principal positions Professor of Management Studies, Yale University School of Management, Yale University, 1977–83, 1990– and Dean, 1992–94.

Other Professor, Sloan School of Management, MIT, 1963–75; President's Council of Economic Advisers, 1975–76; Dean and Professor, Graduate School of Business Administration, University of Rochester, NY, 1983–91.

Starting in the 1960s, MacAvoy marked out innovative positions and did creative applied research on a range of issues especially related to regulated sectors (energy, transportation and telecommunications).

First, he re-examined early US railroad regulation, at the time when the Interstate Commerce Commission (ICC) was formed in 1888. He found that there was intense competition – not natural monopoly – on many routes in most of the US. Therefore, the creation of ICC regulation involved blocking out that competition artifically, replacing effective competition with weak and ineffective regulation.

He then turned to natural gas and urged that the conditions for effective competition were widespread in that industry.

In 1974 he joined with Stephen Breyer (later a Justice on the US Supreme Court) in a detailed analysis of the regulation of electricity by the US Federal Power Commission (FPC; soon renamed as FERC, the Federal Energy Regulatory Commission). Though the FPC had been unusually effective in the 1960s, MacAvoy and Breyer urged that it be replaced with a reliance on competition in nearly all of the industry. This contributed importantly to the growth of the effort to deregulate the industry. MacAvoy pushed further for marginal-cost pricing and other market-based changes in electricity while he was on the Council of Economic Advisers in the mid-1970s. He also pressed for abolishing the regulation of US airlines. In fact airline deregulation occurred in just a year, while the electricity deregulation campaign finally flowered in the 1990s, though with mixed results.

MacAvoy turned to the oil industry, where OPEC actions had helped to force up oil prices sharply in 1973–74 and 1979. He showed that the oil industry was affected by a powerful long-run trend toward increased scarcity. The resulting rise in long-run scarcity prices could explain much (though not all) of the rise in oil prices. Much of OPEC's seeming monopoly impact instead merely reflected short-term variations around the longer upward trend.

MacAvoy also made innovative studies of AT&T, its break-up, and the subsequent struggles among its parts.

Most relevant publications

(1974), *Energy Regulation by the Federal Power Commission*, with Stephen Breyer, Washington, DC: Brookings Institution.

(1982), *Crude Oil Prices: As Determined by OPEC and Market Fundamentals*, Cambridge, MA: Ballinger.

(1983), 'Winning by losing: the AT&T settlement and its impact on telecommunications' (with Kenneth Robinson), *Yale Journal on Regulation*, November, **1**(1), 1ff.

L. HARRY M. TREBING

William G. Shepherd

Innovations
He developed sophisticated analyses of utility regulation, and later urged the dangers of simple deregulation; he also improved telecommunications and postal regulation; and during 1966–92 he arranged a vast series of conferences that improved the understanding of regulation economics among virtually all its participants.

Personal history

Born 1927, Baltimore, MD, USA.

Degrees BS, MA University of Maryland, 1950, 1952; PhD University of Wisconsin, 1958.

Principle positions Professor of Economics and Director of the Institute of Public Utilities, Michigan State University, 1966–92, then Emeritus; Associate Professor, Indiana University, 1962–66, and Assistant Professor, University of Nebraska, 1957–62.

Other Chief, Economic Studies Division and Chief Economist, 1965–66, and Industry Economist, 1963–65, at the Federal Communications Commission (FCC). Chief Economist, US Postal Rate Commission, 1971–72. Numerous task forces, advisory panels, and expert commissions, of states and the US government agencies.

Trebing drew on and improved the regulatory ideas of his mentor, Martin G. Glaeser, and he clarified the modern lessons of the whole regulatory literature. He presented a wide range of analyses that noted the strengths of regulation, toward such classic sectors as telecommunications, electricity, gas and the postal system, and transportation industries such as railroads and airlines. His work also involved a massive series of conferences that he designed and mounted during 1966–92.

In his research papers, policy debates and the conferences, Trebing advanced several main themes. One is that the classic allocational efficiency goals need to be supplemented by innovation, and also broadened to include other public interests and impacts. A second theme is that regulation is a complex and evolving process, which has needed to change as the industries have changed. Trebing stressed that static price and cost criteria were only a small part of regulation's goals; innovation, product quality and variety, fairness and social effects should also be promoted.

In his third theme, Trebing analyzed the major troubles when deregulation yields weak competition. Frequently, the deregulation process stops when the former regulated monopoly firms capture a dominant or tight-oligopoly position. Trebing was an early critic, stressing this neglected problem from the 1960s on.

He was closely involved in the economics and regulation of the telephone industry in the 1960s, rising to be the FCC's Chief Economist in 1965–66. The industry was then changing into the more complicated 'telecommunications' sector. From the 1960s on – as the older copper-wire and local-exchange telephone systems were altered successively by computers, data transmission, optical fiber, wireless technology, and most recently the internet and VOIP – Trebing gave skeptical and incisive analysis of how regulation should change.

He built the Institute of Public Utilities, as its first director during 1966–92; he mounted scores of large conferences (two-week, one-week and shorter) on all facets of utilities, regulation and deregulation, both at the Institute and at the National Association of Regulatory Utility Commissioners. Altogether, over 10,000 people attended these conferences, once or repeatedly, including virtually all important participants in all regulated industries.

He was highly skeptical of deregulation, repeatedly stressing the limits of pure theory as a guide for complex policies. He showed that many theoretical attacks on regulation were overstated and misleading. His educational efforts substantially enhanced the understanding of regulatory commissioners, their staff, officials of utility firms, experts on all sides, and also the public. Moreover, he continued all these efforts at full speed after 1985 and was still publishing papers in 2006.

Most relevant publications

(1976), 'Market structure and regulatory reform in the electric and gas utility industries', in Werner Sichel (ed.), *Salvaging Public Utility Regulation*, Lexington, MA: Lexington Books pp. 79–116.
(1977), 'Broadening the objectives of public utility regulation', *Land Economics*, February, **53**, pp. 106–22.
(1984a), 'Public utility regulation: a case study in the debates over effectiveness of economic regulation', *Journal of Economic Issues*, March, **18**, pp. 223–50.
(1984b), 'Public control of enterprises: neoclassical assault and neoinstitutional reform', *Journal of Economic Issues*, June, **18**, pp. 353–68.

M. DENNIS CARY MUELLER

Stephen Martin

Innovations
Life cycle of the firm, industry; analysis of mergers; persistence of profits; welfare costs of market power.

Personal history

Born 1940, Milwaukee, WI, USA.

Degrees BS (Maths) Colorado College, 1962; PhD Princeton University, 1966.

Principle positions Professor, University of Vienna; 1994–; Professor, University of Maryland, College Park, 1977–94; Assistant and Associate Professor, Cornell University, 1968–76; Assistant Professor, Simon Fraser University, 1965–66; Director, International Institute of Management/Industrial Policy, Berlin, 1982–83; Federal Trade Commission, Research Contract, 1978–81; Postdoctoral Fellow, Center for Study of Public Choice, Virginia Polytechnic Institute and State University, 1972–73.

Mueller (1992, p. 163) writes: 'Alas the real world does refuse to conform to our models'. Faced with a choice between studying the real world and elaborating models of markets that may or may not have their counterpart in the real world, Mueller has consistently opted for the former.

Firm and industry life cycle
Mueller (1967) estimates a model of firm decisions about capital investment, spending on research and development (R&D), spending on advertising, and dividend payments. It is marked by careful attention to issues of simultaneity, and includes a discussion of the merits of structural versus reduced-form estimation. This work appeared at least five years before these same issues were tackled in the empirical literature that worked with industry- rather than firm-level data.

Grabowski and Mueller (1972) continue this line of research, studying capital investment, R&D spending, and dividends at the firm level in a comparison of the predictive power of the managerial and neoclassical (value-maximization) models of the firm. The results favor the managerial model.

Mueller and Tilton (1969) rely heavily on case-study evidence to assess the impact of R&D costs over an industry technology cycle that is defined as having four stages: innovation, imitation, technological competition and standardization. With respect to the first stage, they find that: 'Neither large absolute size nor market power appears to be a necessary condition for successful development of most major innovations' (p. 573). It is at the third stage, technological competition, that the nature of the R&D process tends to favor the large firm and raise the cost of entry.

These various strands of research are brought together in Mueller (1972), 'A life cycle theory of the firm'. This paper contrasts the implications of the models of the value-maximizing firm and the managerial, growth-maximizing firm for a firm's life cycle. Successful early innovation and sufficient subsequent growth may place management in a position to pursue its own interests at the expense of those of stockholders. A review of the evidence suggests support for managerial growth maximization.

Marris and Mueller (1980) compare and contrast neo-classical, internal organization, managerial (static and dynamic), and life-cycle models of the corporate firm. They discuss rent seeking, under the heading 'competition for monopoly', and incentives to invest in innovation in imperfectly competitive markets. Their conclusion advocates the study of the corporation as it is, not as it is modeled (a similar approach to empirical research in industrial organization is put forward by Coase, 2006).

Mergers

Mueller (1985) examines the impact of mergers on market share for a sample of firms ranked by the US Federal Trade Commission as being among the 1000 largest US firms in 1950 and in 1972. Conglomerate and horizontal mergers are studied separately. In both cases, merger appeared to reduce the acquired firm's market share, compared with otherwise identical firms not involved in a merger. This is evidence against the argument that the threat of takeover disciplines managers who do not maximize stockholder value: to a significant extent, firms in this sample did less well for their shareholders after takeover than they did before.

Working with an international sample, Mueller and three co-authors (Gugler et al., 2003) find that mergers increase profit and reduce market share, on average. Mergers that increase profitability by increasing market power are more likely to involve large firms; mergers that increase profitability by increasing efficiency are more likely to involve smaller firms.

Mueller (1969) analyzes conglomerate mergers in a growth-maximization framework. Mueller (1977b) surveys the literature on the effects of conglomerate mergers; Mueller (1980) discusses US mergers in the decade before the first oil shock; Mueller (1989) surveys mergers generally.

Distilling the evidence on mergers, managerial discretion is seen as permitting managers to engage in mergers that reduce efficiency and stockholder value. One policy response would be to increase the amount of information available to stockholders. Competition authorities might also block mergers that seem likely to reduce efficiency.

Persistence of profit

Mueller (1977a) founded a literature that explores the extent to which market forces do (or more precisely, in terms of the results obtained, do not) result in the convergence of extremely high or extremely low profits to normal levels.

The results obtained reject convergence. Confirming results for a number of countries are reported in Mueller (1990). Megna and Mueller (1991) present evidence that the persistence of profitability at the firm level is not due to a systematic failure to capitalize the intangible assets of firms operating in high R&D or high-advertising industries.

Mueller (1997) elaborates on Mueller (1972) and on Mueller (1977a). Here the focus is on the kinds of factors (learning by doing and other supply-side forces, demand inertia that may be reinforced by advertising) that allow, in many industries, one of the early leading firms to maintain a dominant position, and that allow the high profitability of early leaders to persist.

Welfare cost of market power

Cowling and Mueller (1978) critique and extend the literature flowing from Harberger's (1954) estimates of the deadweight welfare loss due to the exercise of market power. Working with firm rather than industry data and taking account of welfare losses arising from efforts to obtain or maintain positions of market power, they obtain a range of deadweight welfare loss estimates which, even at the low end, are substantially larger than those of Harberger.

Resumé

There is a remarkable coherency to the research agenda that has resulted in the works discussed above. A recurring theme is that economic theory teaches that price competition leads to a Pareto optimum in general equilibrium if all markets are perfectly competitive, but it offers no such presumption if competition is in dimensions other than price or if some markets are imperfectly competitive. It offers no presumption that the fact of persistence demonstrates that organizational forms that persist are efficient. To understand the performance of firms as they are in the kinds of markets in which they are found, and to understand the performance of those markets, economists should analyze what firms actually do, and how markets actually work.

References

Coase, Ronald (2006), 'The conduct of economics: the example of Fisher Body and General Motors', *Journal of Economics & Management Strategy*, **15**(2), 255–78.

Cowling, Keith and Dennis C. Mueller (1978), 'The social costs of monopoly power', *Economic Journal*, **88**, December, 727–48.

Grabowski, Henry G. and Dennis C. Mueller (1972), 'Managerial and stockholder welfare models of firm expenditures', *Review of Economics and Statistics*, **54**(1), February, 9–24.

Gugler, Klaus, Dennis C. Mueller, B. Burcin Yurtoglu and Christine Zulehner (2003), 'The effects of mergers: an international comparison', *International Journal of Industrial Organization*, **21**(5), May, 625–53.

Harberger, Arnold C. (1954), 'Monopoly and resource allocation', *American Economic Review*, **44**(2), May, 77–87.

Marris, Robin and Dennis C. Mueller (1980), 'The corporation, competition, and the invisible hand,' *Journal of Economic Literature*, **18**(1), March, 32–63.

Megna, Pamela and Dennis C. Mueller (1991), 'Profit rates and intangible capital', *Review of Economics and Statistics*, **73**(4), November, 632–42.

Mueller, Dennis C. (1967), 'The firm decision process: an econometric investigation', *Quarterly Journal of Economics*, **81**(1), February, 58–87.

Mueller, Dennis C. (1969), 'A theory of conglomerate mergers', *Quarterly Journal of Economics*, **83**(4), November, 643–59.

Mueller, Dennis C. (1972), 'A life cycle theory of the firm', *Journal of Industrial Economics*, **20**(3), July, 199–219.

Mueller, Dennis C. (1977a), 'The persistence of profits above the norm', *Economica*, **44**(176), November, 369–80.

Mueller, Dennis C. (1977b), 'The effects of conglomerate mergers: a survey of the empirical evidence', *Journal of Banking and Finance*, **1**, December, 315–47.

Mueller, Dennis C. (1980), 'The United States, 1962–1972', ch. 9 in Dennis C. Mueller (ed.), *The Determinants and Effects of Mergers: An International Comparison*, Cambridge, MA: Oelgeschlager, Gunn & Hain, and Königstein/Ts: Verlag Anton Hain, 1980.

Mueller, Dennis C. (1985), 'Mergers and market share', *Review of Economics and Statistics*, **67**(2), May, 259–67.

Mueller, Dennis C. (1986), *Profits in the Long Run*, Cambridge: Cambridge University Press.

Mueller, Dennis C. (1989), 'Mergers: causes, effects and policies', *International Journal of Industrial Organization*, **7**(1), March, 1–10.
Mueller, Dennis C. (ed.) (1990), *The Dynamics of Company Profits: An International Comparison*, Cambridge and New York: Cambridge University Press.
Mueller, Dennis C. (1992), 'The corporation and the economist', *International Journal of Industrial Organization*, **10**(2), June, 147–70.
Mueller, Dennis C. (1997), 'First-mover advantages and path dependence', *International Journal of Industrial Organization*, **15**(6), October, 827–50.
Mueller, Dennis C. (2003), *The Corporation: Investment, Mergers, and Growth*, London and New York: Routledge.
Mueller, Dennis C. and John E. Tilton (1969), 'Research and development costs as a barrier to entry', *Canadian Journal of Economics*, **2**(4), November, 570–79.

N. ROGER G. NOLL

William G. Shepherd

Innovations
He was involved by 1971 in the early efforts toward the deregulation of utilities; he also analyzed the emerging forms of television and cable TV patterns; and in 1975 he pioneered with thorough research into the economics of the sports industry.

Personal history

Born 1940, Monterrey Park, CA, USA.

Degrees BS California Institute of Technology, 1962; MA, PhD Harvard University, 1965–67.

Principal position Professor of Economics, Stanford University, 1984–.

Other California Institute of Technology, 1965–84; Chair, Division of Humanities and Social Sciences, Cal Tech, 1978–82.

Noll made a series of important innovations about regulation and such sectors as telecommunications, transportation and sports. His analysis has always been independent-minded and unusually sophisticated about complex causes and situations.

He explored many features of regulation and deregulation. By 1971 he published an innovative treatise on reforming regulation that looked toward applying competitive market processes to a variety of sectors. Much later, in 1983 he wrote (with Bruce Owen) an incisive and sophisticated analysis of the political forces that tend to distort both regulation and any simple efforts at reforming regulation.

On the sports industry, Noll published early, extensive research (1974) on the economic determinants and policy choices for league sports, particularly baseball. He estimated demand equations that explained the determinants of team profits, and he analyzed the effects of salary caps and revenue sharing. Later he analyzed promotion and relegation systems, the contraction of baseball, and lessons of organization theory about sports leagues. He soon became a leading authority on the economics and policy choices of sports leagues.

As a major co-author of *Economic Aspects of Television Regulation* (with Merton J. Peck and John J. McGowan, 1973), he analyzed television's future trends and regulation's likely effects. He predicted a variety of developments, including the tendency of cable TV to enlarge mass entertainment choices, rather than high culture, social services and education.

Later, Noll's interests evolved toward a broader study of the processes of politics and the formation of policies, and of other topics like public goods and air pollution permits. Noll also became prominent in academic administration at Cal Tech and Stanford University.

Most relevant publications

(1971), *Reforming Regulation*, Washington, DC: Brookings Institution.
(1973), *Economic Aspects of Television Regulation* (with Merton J. Peck and John J. McGowan), Washington, DC: Brookings Institution.
(1974), *Government and the Sports Business*, Washington, DC: Brookings Institution.
(1983), *The Political Economy of Deregulation* (with Bruce Owen), Washington, DC: American Enterprise Institute.
(1985), *Regulatory Policy and the Social Sciences*, Berkeley, CA: University of California Press.

O. SAM PELTZMAN

William G. Shepherd

Innovations
He extended the theory of regulation (1976); and he offered evidence for the 'efficient-structure' hypothesis.

Personal history

Born 1940, New York City, NY, USA.

Degrees BBA City College NY, 1960; PhD University of Chicago, 1965.

Principal position Professor of Economics and Financial Services, Graduate School of Business, University of Chicago, Chicago, IL, 1978–.

Other Assistant and Associate Professor, UCLA, 1967–73; Sr Member, US President's Council of Economic Advisers, 1990–91; Editor, *Journal of Political Economy*, 1974–89; Editor, *Journal of Law and Economics*.

Peltzman was a protégé of George J. Stigler, who from 1957 led the optimistic free-market 'new' Chicago school. Peltzman wrote on regulation's effects on banking, drugs, automobile safety and advertising. But much of his main research has been on broader policy topics (for example, voting, the formation of policies, education), which are outside the industrial organization field. Peltzman participated in forming the 'efficient-structure hypothesis', and in 1977 he presented the most extensive evidence for that hypothesis that members of the new Chicago school have provided.

He also extended the theory of public regulation to study the interests that regulators really follow; this was along rational-choice lines earlier discussed by Stigler.

Most relevant publications
(1976), 'Toward a more general theory of regulation', *Journal of Law and Economics*, August, 211–40.
(1977), 'The gains and losses from industrial concentration', *Journal of Law and Economics*, October, 229–63.

P. RICHARD SCHMALENSEE

William G. Shepherd

Innovations
He enlarged the use of pure theory in the 1970s, especially on advertising; he restated regulation's economic effects; he clarified demand inelasticity as an estimator of market power (1982); he showed prospects for competition in the electricity industry; and he extended the study of firm and industry effects in causing higher profitability.

Personal history

Born 1944, Belleville, IL, USA.

Degrees BS, PhD MIT, 1965, 1970.

Principal positions Professor of Economics and Management, 1970–, and Dean, 1988–, Sloan School, MIT, Cambridge, MA.

Other Economics faculty, University of California, San Diego, 1970–77; Member, US President's Council of Economic Advisers, 1989–91.

Schmalensee made several significant advances, mainly in raising the level of technical rigor in analyzing competition. He also developed factual methods for testing theoretical lessons in this field.

Joining the new wave of research on advertising, he extended the Comanor–Wilson approach by using more explicit theoretical analysis, relying especially on Hotelling-type models of spatial analogies for differentiated products. He then studied the ready-to-eat cereals industry in depth, as part of a major Federal Trade Commission case against the leading cereals producers. His 1978 paper became a standard in the advertising literature.

He also expanded the analysis of pricing by firms with market power, using moderate technical advances to draw conclusions about the effects on competition.

In 1979, he enlarged the growing skeptical literature on regulation with a comprehensive book that recast the economic issues with more technical rigor. He kept a neutral position on the need for deregulation.

In a 1982 paper directed to legal scholars, Schmalensee actually clarified the economic criteria for monopoly by focusing on the simple role of demand elasticity. Schmalensee argued that clear tests of demand elasticity could bypass the need to define markets clearly.

He (and Paul M. Joskow) showed in detail in 1983 the emerging possibilities for shifting the US electricity industry from regulation to competition. The book anticipated much of the difficult efforts in the 1990s to deregulate the industry, though it did not envisage the scandals and market abuses that erupted after 2000, especially in California and adjacent states.

Finally, Schmalensee tried to sort out the firm- and industry-based causes of high profitability, in an empirical 1985 paper. Although his ideas and findings met sharp criticism, he did substantially open and energize the topic.

Schmalensee later co-edited with Robert D. Willig in 1988 a broad review of 'new IO theory' in the field.

Most relevant publications

(1972), *The Economics of Advertising*, Amsterdam: North-Holland.
(1978), 'Entry deterrence in the ready-to-eat cereal industry', *Bell Journal of Economics*, Autumn, 305–27.
(1979), *The Control of Natural Monopolies*, Lexington, MA: DC Heath.
(1982), 'Another look at market power', *Harvard Law Review*, June, 1789–816.
(1983), *Markets for Power: An Analysis of Electric Utility Deregulation* (with Paul L. Joskow), Cambridge, MA: MIT Press.
(1988), *Handbook of Industrial Organization* (with Robert D. Willig, eds), Cambridge, MA: MIT Press.

Q. A. MICHAEL SPENCE

F.M. Scherer

Innovations
Theory of market signaling; contributions to theory of optimal product variety, market entry through investment and the theory of entry deterrence, and learning curve economics.

Personal history

Born 1943, Montclair, NJ, USA.

Degrees AB Princeton University, 1966; AB, MA Oxford University (Rhodes Scholar), 1968; PhD, Harvard University, 1972.

Principal positions Professor, Harvard University, 1975–90; Dean, Faculty of Arts and Sciences, Harvard University, 1984–90; Dean, Stanford University Graduate School of Business, 1990–99; Venture Capitalist, 2000–; Associate Professor, Stanford University, 1973–75.

Few economists, and very few indeed toiling in the vineyards of industrial organization, have managed to win a Nobel Memorial Prize in economics for the work presented in their PhD dissertation. The only known case is A.M. (Mike) Spence, who shared the Nobel Prize in 2001 with Joseph Stiglitz and George Akerlof. The award to Spence, however, was not for work in industrial organization, but for his pioneering exploration into the rationale of market signaling, with emphasis on such labor market implications as acquiring educational credentials to seek employment, academic admissions and job promotions within organizations. Possible applications to advertising and image differentiation are mentioned briefly in the final chapter of Spence's 1974 book, where Spence refers to parallel research on advertising by Philip Nelson and cites a paper that Nelson presented at a University of Chicago conference in 1972 and published in 1974.

Following a brief assistant professorship at Harvard, Spence was an associate professor between 1973 and 1975 at Stanford, where he wrote what may be his most important contribution to the industrial organization literature. The context demands scrutiny. At Stanford during that time, the principal theme for research in industrial organization was the host of problems left unsolved by Edward Chamberlin's *Theory of Monopolistic Competition* (1933). An oral tradition for graduate students and others working in industrial organization at Stanford at the time was set by James N. Rosse, with one of the highest ratios of research stimulated to own publications in the history of economic thought. Curiously, Spence does not mention Rosse in his paper (June 1976a) nor does he cite the parallel work of Kelvin Lancaster. Spence's approach, quite unlike Lancaster's, was to analyze the optimal product variety problem in terms of monopoly demand and cost functions in a multi-product context. Spence's approach is much more amenable to empirical verification than alternative models, although Spence attempted no test. He observed that the incentive for multiplication of product varieties, each of which entails a front-end fixed launch cost, is the incremental producer's surplus that can be gained from adding a new product. From a welfare perspective, however, the key, especially in the absence of first-degree price discrimination, is how much unappropriated surplus the producer leaves for consumers. This in turn depends upon the shape of demand curves. Concave downward demand curves leave relatively less surplus for consumers than convex functions, with corresponding tendencies toward product over- and underproliferation, respectively. Spence's contribution helped fill the most important theoretical void left by Chamberlin.

From Stanford, Spence returned to Harvard, where the prevailing research tradition emphasized entry, entry deterrence by dominant firms, and their consequences for market performance – that is, following the paradigm established much earlier by Joe S. Bain. In his Autumn 1977 paper, Spence showed how, by building excess capacity, a dominant firm could reduce its marginal costs for high levels of output, and thus it could expand and react more aggressively to entry, leaving less residual demand for entrants than was implied under the output maintenance assumptions of Bain and Paolo Sylos-Labini. Given the added entry deterrence capability permitted with excess capacity, pre-entry prices could be higher than those implied by standard limit-pricing models. Spence had apparently prepared a preliminary version of his paper at the time controversy escalated over the Areeda–Turner 'price less than average variable cost' approach to proving predation in antitrust cases alleging monopolization. As a result, he and Richard Caves were strategically positioned to provide an appendix to the Areeda–Turner rejoinder (1976b) showing that an average cost floor below which predation was inferred allowed stronger deterrence than a marginal cost floor, permitting less-efficient small-scale would-be entrants to be deterred. These discussions in turn elicited the important 'Q rule' alternative from Oliver Williamson in a 1977 *Yale Law Journal* article which, however, failed to capture the hearts and minds of judges setting US antitrust precedents.

Subsequent work by Spence carried the analysis of entry along new and more dynamic lines. His Spring 1979 article analyzed investment trajectories through which early entrants into new markets could preempt rival entry opportunities and create structural asymmetries permitting the exercise of Stackelberg leadership strategies. His Spring 1981 article analyzed the evolution of market structures when firms' costs fall with accumulated production experience, that is, with learning by doing. Among the contributions in that article to a burgeoning literature was a demonstration that, with zero discount rates, true marginal cost equals marginal cost at the foot of the learning curve (but is higher with positive discount rates). Spence also went beyond naive Cournot approaches to the problem of rivalry with learning by doing, exploring how closed-loop approaches altered the results, as they would be expected to do when there are initial asymmetries and firms attempt *à la* Stackelberg to influence rival responses.

In 1984, Spence turned from an emphasis on scholarship to administration, becoming Dean of Harvard's Faculty of Arts and Sciences, second only to the president at Harvard in influence, and then in 1990 assuming the decanal position at Stanford's Graduate School of Business. He retired from Stanford in 2000 and pursued what is said to have been a successful career in venture capital.

Most relevant publications

(1974), *Market Signaling: Informational Transfer in Hiring and Related Processes*, Cambridge, MA: Harvard University Press.

(1976a), 'Product selection, fixed costs, and monopolistic competition', *Review of Economic Studies*, **43** (June), 217–35.

(1976b), Appendix to Philip Areeda and Donald F. Turner, 'Scherer on predatory pricing: a reply', *Harvard Law Review*, **89** (March), 897–900.
(1977), 'Entry, capacity, investment and oligopolistic pricing', *Bell Journal of Economics*, **8** (Autumn), 534–44.
(1979), 'Investment, strategy and growth in a new market', *Bell Journal of Economics*, **10** (Spring), 1–19.
(1981), 'The learning curve and competition', *Bell Journal of Economics*, **12** (Spring), 49–70.

R. ROBERT D. WILLIG

William G. Shepherd

Innovations

He was a co-author of analytical concepts about regulatory economics and competition, especially including sustainability and contestability.

Personal history

Born 1947, New York, NY, USA.

Degrees BA (mathematics) Harvard University, 1967; MS (operations research), PhD Stanford University, 1968, 1973.

Principal position Professor, Princeton University, 1978–.

A gifted theorist, Willig wrote with William J. Baumol and others in the 1970s and 1980s on issues related to the AT&T company, which had been since 1900 the near-complete telephone monopoly of the US. First they analyzed the regulation of public utilities, clarifying reasons for letting AT&T retain its monopoly. Then when deregulation of AT&T became likely, Baumol and Willig focused on reasons for freeing AT&T from restraints in competing with new entrants.

Two main ideas from this effort were 'sustainability' and 'contestability'. Sustainability refers to a set of discriminatory prices which would allow a natural monopoly to stay in business by gaining enough revenues. The Baumol group labeled these inverse-elasticity prices as 'Ramsey' prices, which would fit static efficient conditions. They did not focus on the transition to competition, when Ramsey prices would lose their allocative relevance and would be anti-competitive.

Willig, Baumol and John Panzar in 1982 offered 'contestable markets' theory, saying it was a complete replacement for the entire theory of competition itself. The contestability theory rested on two pure assumptions: that both entry and exit were perfectly free (for example, sunk costs must be zero), and that entry and exit would both be instantaneous and unlimited. The resulting threat of instant, total entry would nullify any market power, even if the incumbent were a total monopolist. Contestability would discourage the monopolist's efforts to raise price, even by just a penny.

Baumol and Willig often acknowledged that the theory was an exercise, useful for its seminar insight, and they conceded that no real market closely fits the theory. Yet the tone changed in their frequent testimony on real cases of mergers, pricing and regulation. There they said that the contestability idea gave definitive 'proof' that any actual anti-competitive effects would not occur.

As a leader of the 'new IO theory' wing of the field, Willig later co-edited the two-volume analytical review *Handbook of Industrial Organization* (1989).

Most relevant publications

(1982), *Contestable Markets and the Theory of Industry Structure* (with William J. Baumol and John C. Panzer), New York: Harcourt Brace Jovanovich.
(1989), Editor (with Richard Schmalensee), *Handbook of Industrial Organization*, Amsterdam: North-Holland.

S. JOSEPH E. STIGLITZ

F.M. Scherer

Innovations
Impact of information asymmetries on market equilibrium; monopoly exploitation of a depletable resource; commodity pricing cartels; economics of research and development (R&D) rivalry; product differentiation.

Personal history

Born 1943, Gary, IN, USA.

Degrees AB Amherst College, 1964; PhD, Massachusetts Institute of Technology, 1966.

Principal positions Professor, Yale University, 1970–74; Professor, Stanford University, 1974–76 and 1988–2001; Professor, Oxford University, 1976–79; Professor, Princeton University, 1979–88; Member and then Chairman, US Council of Economic Advisers, 1993–97; Vice President and Chief Economist, World Bank, 1997–2000; Professor, Columbia University, 2000–.

The extraordinary productivity of 'Joe' Stiglitz led in 2001 to a Nobel Memorial Prize in Economics, shared with A. Michael Spence (see Profile Q, above) and George Akerlof. His contributions span a broad array of topics in mathematical economics, including (mostly later in his career) industrial organization. His MIT dissertation, supervised by Robert Solow and a fellow Gary, Indiana, native, Paul Samuelson, modeled several aspects of economic growth and income distribution. Even before he began the work on the consequences of informational asymmetries that won a Nobel Prize, he published extensively on such diverse topics as factor proportions, investment behavior, portfolio risk, public finance, labor economics, economic development and much else.

The research that led to his shared Nobel Prize stemmed from a resurgence of interest in the economics of information, manifested *inter alia* in well-attended conferences on the topic at Princeton in 1973 and Stanford in 1975. The work given special emphasis by the Nobel Prize committee (Rothschild and Stiglitz, 1976a) explored why insurance companies offer a variety of contracts, specifying both price and quantity (that is, amount of insurance provided) and inducing consumers to self-select into risk classes. The sorting behavior with nonlinear outlay schedules emphasized by their analysis is applicable in many other situations, with an older and wider tradition in tax policy and public utility pricing. Possible extensions to educational screening and sorting in labor and financial markets were mentioned in passing.

The OPEC (Organization of the Petroleum-Exporting Countries) oil price shock of 1973–74 apparently triggered Stiglitz's first work in the mainstream of industrial organization economics. His 1976b article extended insights by Harold Hotelling and Robert Solow, among others, on how monopolized resource providers differed from their competitive counterparts in the rate at which they depleted their resource. Stiglitz showed that, depending upon demand elasticities and costs, monopolists were sometimes indeed, but not always, our grandchildren's best friend, conserving resources for the long run by setting initially high demand-limiting prices. A later paper with Dasgupta (1982) investigated how the eventual switch to a backstop technology, available initially only at higher cost, depended upon market structure.

Another plunge into the mainstream of industrial organization topics appears to have begun in the intellectual ferment existing at Stanford University during the 1970s (see Profile Q, above of A. Michael Spence). Dixit and Stiglitz (1977a) worked out with unusual virtuosity the mathematics underlying Edward Chamberlin's qualitative conjectures on monopolistic competition and optimal product diversity. The insights in that paper are less novel than those in a predecessor (1976a) article by Spence, acknowledged by Dixit and Stiglitz.

From monopolistic competition, Stiglitz moved on to the endogenous relationships between market structure and the speed and intensity of R&D investments. Two papers with Dasgupta (1980a, b) extended a particularly rich mathematical treatment to insights advanced earlier by Arrow (1962), (less elegantly) Scherer (1967), and several others. They concluded, as others had, that 'the question ... of whether restricted competition leads to more research than free competition is truly complex', requiring the stance of Harry S. Truman's apocryphal two-armed economist.

OPEC's success in raising crude oil prices led other less-developed nations to consider cartelization as a remedy for the volatile and frequently low prices they received for the primary commodities in which they specialized. The World Bank and the US Agency for International Development commissioned Stiglitz and David Newbery to undertake a major book (1981) on commodity cartels, with particular focus on buffer stock cartels. Their approach was mostly theoretical, but there were also empirical analyses – the only ones among the works cited here. They found *inter alia* that the emphasis on linear supply and demand functions in the substantial earlier literature yielded biased results. Exploring diverse causes of commodity price variability, introducing risk aversion into buffer stock schemes, and stressing the impact on primary commodity producers' income, they concluded that the benefits from price stabilization schemes were likely to be smaller than previous studies had suggested.

A more broad-based contribution by Stiglitz to the field of industrial organization was his leadership in organizing, with Frank Mathewson, a star-studded May 1982 conference on 'New Developments in the Analysis of Market Structures', out of which a conference volume (1986) emerged. In his introduction to the published volume, Stiglitz highlighted five significant areas of advance in the theory of non-socialist market structures during the 1970s:

- While much of the earlier literature took market structure as given, the new theory of market structure begins by asking what determines the number of firms? What are the barriers to entry? By what mechanisms can existing firms deter entry?
- In the new view ... it is not only the number of firms in the market which matters, but also their relationship with one another.
- Recent work has questioned whether all participants work to maximize the value of the firm and whether there is unanimity of goals between managers and shareholders.

- Recent advances in the economics of uncertainty and information have reexamined the economics of vertical integration and where the boundaries of the firm emerge.
- The standard welfare analysis has little to say about modern industrial economies, where technological change and information problems are of central importance.

None of these insights was really new, as perusal of the profiles in this volume for Jeremiah Jenks, Edward Chamberlin, Joe S. Bain, Herbert Simon, E.A.G. Robinson, Ronald Coase, Edwin Mansfield and many others will reveal. A more balanced interpretation might be that advances in theory during the 1970s, to which Joe Stiglitz made notable contributions, carried earlier insights to unprecedented heights of rococo mathematical splendor.

In 1993 Stiglitz migrated to Washington, first as a Member and then Chairman of President Bill Clinton's Council of Economic Advisers and then as Chief Economist and Vice President of the World Bank. In the latter function he publicly challenged many traditional but discredited shibboleths of the economic development community and spurred the consideration of important new initiatives. Returning to academia in 2000, he has continued to publish, but with a new emphasis on books and articles addressing more popular audiences.

Most relevant publications

(1976a), 'Equilibrium in competitive insurance markets: an essay on the economics of imperfect information' (with Michael Rothschild), *Quarterly Journal of Economics*, **90** (November), 629–49.

(1976b), 'Monopoly and the rate of extraction of exhaustible resources', *American Economic Review*, **66** (September), 655–61.

(1977a), 'Monopolistic competition and optimum product diversity' (with Avinash Dixit), *American Economic Review*, **67** (June), 297–308.

(1976b), 'Monopoly, non-linear pricing and imperfect information: the insurance market', *Review of Economic Studies*, **44** (October), 407–30.

(1980a), 'Industrial structure and the nature of innovative activity' (with Partha Dasgupta), *Economic Journal*, **90** (June), 266–93.

(1980b), 'Uncertainty, industrial structure, and the speed of R&D' (with Partha Dasgupta), *Bell Journal of Economics*, **11** (Spring), 1–28.

(1981), *The Theory of Commodity Price Stabilization* (with David Newbery), Oxford: Oxford University Press.

(1982), 'Market structure and resource depletion' (with Partha Dasgupta), *Journal of Economic Theory*, **28** (October), 128–57.

(1986), *New Developments in the Analysis of Market Structure* (edited with G. Frank Mathewson), Cambridge, MA: MIT Press.

Index